"*An informed, impressive, and pers*   *l for the* *layperson and amateur skeptic alike.*   *research,* *and it shows.*"

—Benjamin Radford, M.Ed., author of *Scientific Paranormal Investigation* and Research Fellow for the Committee for Skeptical Inquiry

"*David G. McAfee's newest book should be on every skeptic's bookshelf, and on every believer's, too. It is a thorough treatment of a number of topics that inspire undue credulity—some much more harmful than others—but all requiring skepticism. Having interviewed hundreds of authors on these sorts of subjects over the years, and having read all of their books, I enthusiastically recommend* No Sacred Cows. *It is an important work of skepticism steeped in solid research, open-minded inquiry, and a humane interest in helping believers better understand and accept the world as it really is.*"

—D. J. Grothe, editor, *On The Beauty of Science*, and director, Institute for Science and Human Values

"*McAfee's new book is important and deserves to be read widely. It is based on years of research and tackles all sorts of false but common and often dangerous beliefs, superstitions, and fallacies. It teaches us to challenge assumptions, look for evidence and think critically. To be able to do that seems today more important than ever. I recommend this well-written, fascinating book to anyone who feels that sacred cows should have no place in our lives.*"

—Prof. Edzard Ernst, Emeritus Professor of Complementary Medicine at the Peninsula School of Medicine, University of Exeter, and author of *A Scientist in Wonderland: A Memoir of Searching for Truth and Finding Trouble*

"No Sacred Cows *is a fascinating, insightful and most enjoyable read. McAfee's evaluation of his thorough academic research is interwoven with anecdotes of personal experiences and an intriguing variety of interviews. This book should be read widely and discussed often.*"

—Dr. Lynne Kelly, author of *The Skeptic's Guide to the Paranormal* and *The Memory Code*

"*With* No Sacred Cows, *which provides a bold and fresh look bringing solid research and consistently entertaining prose to the problem of irrational belief, McAfee has entered the strange worlds of true believers and come out alive. This remarkable book is a grand tour of fraud and delusion that everyone should read. Both irrational believers and seasoned skeptics will find much of value here.*"

—Guy P. Harrison, author of *Good Thinking* and *50 Simple Questions for Every Christian*

"*If you've been waiting for a book that promotes atheism, skepticism and humanism without the chauvinistic snickering and intellectual snobbery that is all too common in this genre, then* No Sacred Cows *is your book. McAfee has successfully melded an array of academic research, anecdotes, and exhaustive interviews to present a thoroughly enjoyable, timely, and important read.*"

—C. J. Werleman, author of *The New Atheist Threat* and *Crucifying America: The Unholy Alliance Between the Christian Right and Wall Street*

"*This is a must read book. It goes beyond religious delusion, exploring a wide range of aspects that so many of us unwittingly get drawn into, unaware that we are equally deluded about them. McAfee has put several years of painstaking research, investigation, enquiry and interviews into this comprehensive work. The upshot is that we must learn to question everything and not be satisfied with anything less than verifiable evidence regarding all things in life. McAfee points out the uncomfortable truth that whatever we think may be the case, we all 'believe' in some things that are completely untrue—and he proves his point. He makes you want to be more vigilant in every area of life.*"

—Jim Whitefield, author of *The Bible Delusion* and *The Mormon Delusion* series

NO
SACRED
COWS

Investigating Myths, Cults, and the Supernatural

DAVID G. MCAFEE

Foreword by Yvette d'Entremont

PITCHSTONE PUBLISHING
DURHAM, NORTH CAROLINA

Pitchstone Publishing
Durham, North Carolina
www.pitchstonepublishing.com

10 9 8 7 6 5 4 3 2 1

Library of Congress Cataloging-in-Publication Data

Names: McAfee, David G., author.
Title: No sacred cows : investigating myths, cults, and the supernatural /
    David G. McAfee ; foreword by Yvette d'Entremont.
Description: Durham, North Carolina : Pitchstone Publishing, 2017. | Includes
    bibliographical references and index.
Identifiers: LCCN 2016052922| ISBN 9781634311182 (pbk. : alk. paper) |
ISBN
    9781634311205 (epdf) | ISBN 9781634311212 (mobi)
Subjects: LCSH: Supernatural. | Religion. | Parapsychology. | Occultism.
Classification: LCC BL100 .M27 2017 | DDC 130—dc23
LC record available at https://lccn.loc.gov/2016052922

This book is dedicated to my wife and my parents for supporting me throughout all my endeavors, and to Mister Spock, Carl Sagan, and the Amazing James Randi, for leading the way in logical, evidence-based thinking.

CONTENTS

FOREWORD

In this burgeoning community percolating with critical thought, there exists a rationale of Internet bravado that the best way to get one's point across is to be a caustic prick about every opinion that one can spew at top volume into the twitterverse.

And in that moment, instead of lurching forward, desperate to make his attack into the ether, David sits back. He thinks, and takes a moment to laugh and enjoy. He lets his cat curl up in his lap, invites people who agree with him and disagree with him to join him for a conversation, and he nudges.

Okay, maybe it's more than a nudge. Sometimes it's a jab. But the jabs are never angry, and they're not at the people he disagrees with; they're at the ideas. And at the core of what David does, there's always a love of discourse. It's apparent that he's aiming to make his readers better-informed critical thinkers.

And it's really hard to do that by being a hardened dick.

Wait, that's not quite what I meant. But it's what I meant.

(I'm the scientist who writes dick jokes; I can't help myself).

Applying scientific thought to the world around you is not always easy to do without losing your sense of humor or balance. In *No Sacred Cows*, David manages to ask hard questions both of himself as a researcher and of an audience that, as rational as they may be, always comes in with personal biases, anecdotes, and experiences that have colored their worldview. He does this without being off-putting or backing down. David tackles some of my favorite subjects that are just outside the realm of religion but that are nonetheless superstitions—no matter how hard their proponents try to claim scientific credibility. Psychics, ghosts, and faith healing, oh my!

In this regard, some of our work overlaps. Every time, someone swears

9

a loved one was really helped by the magical potion that a wizard sold them, they're convinced that we're delivering a cruelty for pointing out they might have been swindled.

Or, they're convinced that every critique David makes in this book is right except the one thing that they're sure worked for them . . . and David and I and all other skeptics are wrong about that one thing. All the scientific data is right on everything *except that one thing that they—or perhaps even you—love*. Funny that.

Indeed, a lot of people reading this will have anecdotes of their own about one thing or another in here. That's okay.

But David's not doing this to pick on you. He's doing this because, in the light of day, he's giving your ideas a nudge. Maybe a jab.

And as Californians, the only sacred cows to us are served at In-N-Out, pending double-blind peer-reviewed study.

—Yvette d'Entremont, SciBabe.com

INTRODUCTION

"For the great enemy of the truth is very often not the lie—deliberate, contrived, and dishonest—but the myth—persistent, persuasive, and unrealistic. Too often we hold fast to the clichés of our forebears. We subject all facts to a prefabricated set of interpretations. We enjoy the comfort of opinion without the discomfort of thought."

—John F. Kennedy

In the same way that a belief in **magic** isn't necessary for a person to enjoy a good **illusion**, belief in supernatural forces or entities isn't needed for one to be interested in the systems that propagate them. In fact, for as long as I can remember, religious traditions and rituals—specifically, what people believe and why—have been among my favorite topics to study, despite the fact that I was never actually a believer in deities and I didn't associate with any **faith**. I, like noted magician Harry Houdini, am a skeptic who has always been *"a great admirer of mystery and magic."*[1] After attending a (mostly nondenominational) Christian church as a child with my family, I quickly realized Christianity wasn't for me . . . but I still found myself fascinated by the tradition and the phenomenon of religion in general. Curious about what other groups believed, I began visiting houses of worship of various Christian denominations, as a silent observer, as early as 13 years old. Not long after that, I began studying other religions and the philosophies that inspired them.

My interest in religion grew over the years and, by the time I graduated high school, nobody was surprised that I decided to major in religious studies at the University of California, Santa Barbara (UCSB). There I began to really delve into all religions from a phenomenological and historical approach with an academic lens, as opposed to learning about a particular faith from the point of view of an observer in a house of worship. The anthropological mentality that was encouraged in the context of my secular religious studies education, which is not to be confused with theology,[2] was of the utmost importance. It taught me to treat myths as myths across all cultures, so that I rightfully learned about the Genesis creation narrative alongside the creation stories of Native American traditions and the ancient Greeks.[3] After all, learning about ideas or belief systems solely from the perspective of a believer isn't the way healthy, inquiring minds analyze what's potentially true.

I continued to read about the origins and interactions of the major and minor belief systems, as well as to attend various religious ceremonies, throughout college. I concluded not only that the anthropological approach to the phenomenon of religion in my studies was fulfilling, but also that it could help put religion as a cultural construct into context for someone who may not understand that fact—for whatever reason. When one is raised in a particular faith, for instance, he or she is often **ignorant** of the realities that can be uncovered through an objective study of the many faiths around the world. I feel it is important to show people that religions come and go all the time, all without a trace of evidence supporting their supernatural claims, and that modern religions around today are no different from those that have gone extinct. The best way to do that is to educate them about all religions and show them that no faith is special or unique—that they are all creations of the human mind. By taking on this task, there's no telling how many previously unaware people we could help. It is for this reason that I have a vision of a future in which the study of religion is a purely academic endeavor, with mega-churches converted into hospitals or perhaps even centers for secular education about various belief systems.

If a believer seeks out this education by reading an allegedly holy text and examining the history of the corresponding tradition from a modern and intellectual perspective, it's not probable that he or she will have the powerful **spiritual** experience that's often associated with hearing well-rehearsed sermons. Instead, the person is more likely to find the archaic principles put forth in the text to be devoid of much modern relevance and its supernatural claims to be without scientific support. This is part of why I actively encourage teaching religious studies from an objective approach in public schools, something that isn't properly practiced in many countries and isn't implemented almost at all in the United States.[4] In such classes about religion, children can learn about the origins of myths and the histories (and indeed the importance) of various religious institutions, allowing them to see all religions as part of the same phenomenon. This prevents kids from falling into the trap of seeing one as inherently superior to all others, and is something I discuss in my children's books on critical thinking, religion, and the origin of beliefs.[5] It's not just about religion, though. In all areas of life, good parents and teachers should educate the younger generations about how to analyze the evidence and reach conclusions, and not provide answers as absolute Truths, with a capital "T."

SKEPTICAL ACTIVISM

It was at UCSB that my growing interest in religions sparked an entrance into the world of secular activism. I saw the harms that had been justified using religious ideologies and I sought to keep people in modern times from repeating one of humanity's greatest mistakes: treating religion as something separate and divine—as opposed to using it as a tool to better understand ourselves. I wanted people to be able to learn lessons from religious tales without using the dogma itself as a basis for discrimination. After graduating from UCSB with a double major in English and Religious Studies, with an emphasis on Christianity and Mediterranean religions, I published two books: *Disproving Christianity and Other Secular Writings* and *Mom, Dad, I'm an Atheist: The Guide to Coming Out as a Non-Believer.*[67] I continued to write and learn about religion, but my propensity toward skepticism of unfounded claims in general, along with my interest in the unknown and unknowable, led me to study other supernatural beliefs, too. I soon realized that, while it may not always be apparent, I have something in common with preachers, people who claim to be **psychics**, **ghost** hunters, etc. We're all interested in the supernatural; I just don't think it's real.

I researched things like witchcraft, ghosts, and psychics, using the same anthropological and historical methods I was used to in my religious studies courses, and saw many similarities between these ideas and their cousins— the beliefs grounded in religious faith. I found that supernatural beliefs, including religions, were often passed from generation to generation— and that they all rely on the unknown. I also documented a number of psychological similarities between those who believe in all sorts of other-worldly claims. Through my studies, for instance, it quickly became clear to me that some people who substitute or complement their religious beliefs with other beliefs in the supernatural or paranormal are equally defensive of those nonreligious concepts. This tells me a lot of things, including that emotional reasoning is likely an important component of all these ideas. There are key differences, too. Organized religions are often more popular and receive more deference than nonreligious supernatural ideas, for example. But millions of people are still duped by nonreligious supernatural claims each year and, despite the cultural perceptions, I found more similarities than differences between them and their more organized counterparts.

How believers deal with events that they tie to their unfounded yet firmly held beliefs, whether they're paranormal or religious or neither, is one nearly universal parallel in thinking between people with differing beliefs. Here's a story that simply explains how preexisting biases make skepticism and objectivity almost impossible for many believers, and why one should always be wary of comfortable and convenient answers to the universe's most complicated questions:

A BRIGHT LIGHT SHOWS UP IN THE SKY OUT OF NOWHERE, AND FOUR PEOPLE WITNESS THE EXTRAORDINARY EVENT, WHICH NONE OF THEM CAN EXPLAIN.

THE PARANORMAL INVESTIGATOR SAYS SPIRITS FROM THE AFTERLIFE ARE TRYING TO GET THEIR ATTENTION, THE PREACHER CLAIMS THE LIGHTS ARE JESUS SIGNALING THE END TIMES AS THE BIBLE FORETOLD, AND THE ALIEN VISITATION BELIEVER CALLS THE LIGHT PROOF THAT EXTRA-TERRESTRIALS ARE COMMUNICATING WITH THEIR HOME PLANET FROM EARTH.

BUT THE CURIOUS SKEPTIC RESERVES JUDGMENT, CONSIDERS ALL POSSIBLE SCENARIOS, AND LOOKS FOR THE MOST REASONABLE, LOGICAL, AND NATURAL EXPLANATION—WILLING TO FOLLOW THE EVIDENCE, NO MATTER THE RESULT.

BRANCHING OUT

After *The Belief Book* series, I knew I couldn't just write another book debunking a different religion, because it'd be a step back in thinking.[8] I decided to shift the topics of my writing so that it could be more easily applied to all sorts of false beliefs, and the processes by which we rid ourselves of those flawed ideas. I wanted to take the same anthropological approach that helped me to understand world religions and use it as a lens to view all unfounded and faith-based claims, as well as to investigate the origins and histories associated with all myths—popular and rare—and use that research as the basis for my writing.[9] I wanted to experience and test as many of the claims as possible for myself and find out firsthand what they had to offer. When it comes to the supernatural, some people say, "Simply believe," and others say, "Reject it all as nonsense," but I say, "Let's explore." As philosopher Dr. Wayne W. Dyer cautioned, "*The ultimate ignorance is the rejection of something you know nothing about yet refuse to investigate.*"

Although I think this investigative approach to the paranormal is a good one, I'm not under the delusion that my work is inherently *special* or that my ideas have never before been seen. Critical thinking has been around forever and I simply want to help popularize it for everyone. I can't count the number of times I've dreamed up of what I thought was a revolutionary idea, only to then realize James Randi or Carl Sagan or another great thinker had the same idea years earlier. As Dr. Michael F. Shaughnessy of Eastern New Mexico University and Jeanine Pinkney have noted, the quest for critical thinking is "*nothing new.*"

"*In ancient legend, Eve craved the fruit of the Tree of Knowledge, and Socrates goaded the young men of Athens to question assumptions and discern subtleties,*" Shaughnessy and Pinkney wrote in *Teaching Critical Thinking Skills: A Modern Mandate.*[10] "*However, such earlier efforts were not accompanied by legal or social mandate that all children must develop proficiency. Indeed, Eve and Socrates were punished for their quests.*"

After some time engaging in discussions involving the implausible and paranormal, I was surprised at the large number of atheists, some (but not all) of whom actively opposed religion and/or belief in deities, who were sucked into other equally ridiculous notions and belief systems. I concluded that, whether it's supernatural claims, **superstitions**, or unfounded and far-fetched **conspiracy theories**, unsubstantiated beliefs serve as sanctuaries for the nonreligious yet faithful. Some people might even give up belief in gods and religion only to find new beliefs about which to be irrational and apologetic; they simply *want* to believe (see chapter 4). I also found out that, by consistently treating religion the same as any other superstitious belief, some religious believers would unintentionally make that same connection and recognize that they are indeed related. They could see that I don't *hate their god* and that I'm not picking on their particular religion, I'm just doing what I do—pointing out the flaws in faith-based thinking and promoting **scientific skepticism** and logical reasoning. Similarly, some people who advocate for **astrology** or any other pseudoscientific practice recognized that my objections were about evidence, and not disdain for **spirituality** or magic. Some believers do more with this realization than others, including giving up supernatural beliefs entirely, but it's an important point to note regardless of the long-term outcome of the individuals at issue.

THE SUPERNATURAL SURGE

Although secular supernatural beliefs and theistic religious beliefs are similar and often connected, they are different in one key aspect: adherence to unaffiliated paranormal ideas is continuing to grow in areas where organized religion is slowly being disregarded in light of modernity and the age of information. For instance, in America, polls suggest that somewhere between 31 and 48 percent of adults believe in ghosts.[11][12][13] The situation in Britain is even more astounding. In October 2013, a "Belief in Post-Religious Britain" survey for the Christian think tank Theos found that 77 percent of participants believed that, "*there are things in life that we simply cannot explain through science or any other means,*" while 59 percent believed in "*some kind of spiritual being or essence.*"[14] Although the numerous polling agencies vary in their estimates, each of them reports a growth in belief in nonreligious supernatural concepts over previous years.

Popular media is at least partly responsible for the renewed popularization of some nonreligious but faith-based beliefs, including psychics, ghosts, **Bigfoot**, and the ancient astronaut theory. At the center of this pop culture resurgence are "reality" television shows and "documentaries" that promote the beliefs, including shows like *Crossing Over with John Edward, Ghost Hunters, Finding Bigfoot,* and *Ancient Aliens.* One popular series that purports to show evidence of the paranormal, *Most Haunted,* makes me wonder what, specifically, *most haunted* actually means. Is it the building that has been scientifically shown to have the most ghosts per square foot? It must be difficult to measure "hauntedness" levels without a single scientifically proven haunting.

TV shows built on supernatural foundations are based on unproven (and in many cases unprovable) ideas, yet they are often taken as true accounts by uninformed viewers. This acceptance ushers in a new generation of believers who buy into the false hope and outright lies the shows often peddle, and is basically a paranormal version of the CSI effect, which attributes jurors' unrealistic expectations when it comes to evidence partly to TV crime dramas like *CSI: Crime Scene Investigation*.[15] Because of the credulity of the public at large when it comes to these faulty claims, it's important to point out that otherworldly TV shows and faux documentaries are not accurate representations of reality and they certainly don't prove any outlandish theories or paranormal claims. In fact, for the most part, they are heavily edited programs mostly meant for entertainment purposes. Unfortunately, however, that doesn't mean some people aren't convinced by them.[16] For the most part, I fault dishonest filmmakers. As English journalist Nick Cohen has noted, however, there is enough blame to go around.

"Compulsive liars shouldn't frighten you. They can harm no one, if no one listens to them. Compulsive believers, on the other hand: they should terrify you. Believers are the liars' enablers. Their votes give the demagogue his power. Their trust turns the charlatan into the president."

While these misinformation videos may seem to answer questions at times, the "answers" provided aren't valuable and they are not to be confused with real scientific understandings or typical results. Much like the search for gods throughout history, these shows and movies have provided zero solid evidence for any supernatural or otherworldly claim. The pursuit of deities is so much like these other claims, in fact, that I expect there will one day be a show that follows so-called *God Hunters*—people who travel to sites of alleged religious **miracles** with **electromagnetic field (EMF) meters** and **audio recorders** to search for signs of divine intervention.[17] After all, there are already numerous profitable TV shows spawned from this same flawed premise: a group of people searching fruitlessly for that which has never been shown to exist. It's both sad and true that some people, including many producers of these shows, convince audiences they are making sense out of nonsense just by being intellectually dishonest in their presentation of the facts and ignoring answers rooted in real scientific research. That is not to say, however, that I can't enjoy TV shows and other media related to the paranormal. In fact, I particularly enjoy when documentaries purport to show the "best evidence" for ghosts, psychics, and **aliens** who visit earth, because they expose how little evidence exists for those claims.[18]

In *Long Island Medium*, an American reality series on Discovery's TLC (formerly and ironically dubbed *The Learning Channel*) network, viewers follow the life of alleged medium Theresa Caputo. Like most so-called psychics, Caputo pretends to speak to her customers' dead relatives, providing false hope—and faulty information—in exchange for a paycheck. Using classic **cold-reading** tactics, dramatized emotional interactions, and skillful editing, *Long Island Medium* has convinced thousands of people that Caputo can talk to the dead. But that doesn't change the fact that no psychic has ever scientifically proven his or her talent—and this case is no different. In fact, stage magician and well-known skeptic James Randi called the show "*utter nonsense and dangerous*," and his James Randi Educational Foundation (JREF) awarded Caputo a Pigasus Award for Performance in 2012 for being the "psychic" performer who fooled the greatest number of people with the least effort in the preceding year.[19] This example, while not inherently unique, draws attention to how easy it can be to fool others into believing the impossible, using nothing more than basic deception tactics and video editing (see chapter 11).

For nearly two decades, the JREF, a nonprofit organization founded by Randi in 1996, offered a million-dollar prize to anyone who could show, under proper observing conditions, scientific evidence of any paranormal, supernatural, or occult power or event. A number of other skeptical organizations have tested paranormal claims, as well. The Independent Investigations Group at the Center for Inquiry–Los Angeles, for example, an international network of trained investigators who look into paranormal claims, administers a substantially similar $100,000 challenge.[20] Between 1997 and 2015, when the JREF announced it would terminate the challenge in favor of becoming a grant-making organization, the group received hundreds of official, notarized applications for its Million Dollar Paranormal Challenge. Randi's own words, however, highlight how unlikely it is that any supernatural claim will ever be empirically verified: "*I don't expect that the million will ever be won, simply because there is no confirming evidence for any paranormal claims to date,*" he said.

Despite the fact that no supernatural or paranormal forces have ever been shown to exist, belief in them remains rampant—even among the nonreligious and otherwise intelligent.

"The hard but just rule is that if the ideas don't work, you must throw them away. Don't waste any neurons on what doesn't work. Devote those neurons to new ideas that better explain the data. Valid criticism is doing you a favor."

—Carl Sagan

NOTES

1.   *"I am a great admirer of mystery and magic. Look at this life—all mystery and magic."* —Harry Houdini

2.   I majored in Religious Studies at a public university and learned about all religions, their histories, and how they interacted with one another over time. Theology classes, usually offered by private religious institutions, are often overtly religious in nature and involve studying scriptures from the perspective that they are divinely inspired.

3.   It was obvious to me throughout my religious studies education and earlier that, if one was interested in learning about the "*mythologies*" of humanity's future, he or she would only need to examine the religions of today.

4.   David G. McAfee, "Why We Should Teach Religion to Children," Richard Dawkins Foundation for Reason and Science, September 28, 2013, richarddawkins.net/2013/09/why-we-should-teach-religion-to-children.

5.   David G. McAfee and Chuck Harrison, *The Belief Book* (Great Britain: Dangerous Little Books, 2015) and David G. McAfee and Chuck Harrison, *The Book of Gods* (Atheist Republic, 2016).

6.   David G. McAfee, *Disproving Christianity and Other Secular Writings* (Great Britain: Dangerous Little Books, 2011).

7.   David G. McAfee, *Mom, Dad, I'm an Atheist: The Guide to Coming Out as a Non-Believer* (Great Britain: Dangerous Little Books, 2012).

8.   While writing a book titled *Disproving Islam* or *Disproving Judaism* would be more of a lateral move than a step back, I think it's important to note that many of the ideas in *Disproving Christianity* can be logically applied to other faiths, especially the Abrahamic traditions.

9.   For this book, I took the skills I used studying religion as a natural phenomenon and applied them to researching all sorts of false and paranormal beliefs. I call this discipline *supernatural studies*.

10. Jeanine Pinkney and Michael F. Shaughnessy, "Teaching Critical Thinking Skills: A Modern Mandate." *International Journal of Academic Research* 5, no. 3 (2013).

11. "31% Believe in Ghosts," Rasmussen Reports, October 30, 2011, www.rasmussenreports.com/public_content/lifestyle/holidays/october_2011/31_believe_in_ghosts.

12. Lee Speigel, "Spooky Number Of Americans Believe In Ghosts," *Huffington Post*, February 2, 2013, www.huffingtonpost.com/2013/02/02/real-ghosts-americans-poll_n_2049485.html.

13. Sean Alfano, "Poll: Majority Believe in Ghosts." *CBS News*, October 29, 2015, www.cbsnews.com/2100-500160_162-994766.html.

14. *The Spirit of Things Unseen* (London: Theos, 2013), www.theosthinktank.co.uk/publications/2013/10/17/the-spirit-of-things-unseen-belief-in-postreligious-britain.

15. Nicholas J. Schweitzer and Michael J. Saks, "The CSI Effect: Popular Fiction about Forensic Science Affects the Public's Expectations about Real Forensic Science," *Jurimetrics* (2007): 357–364.

16. Sometimes I wonder what the world would be like if everyone believed what they saw on these supernatural mockumentaries and TV shows, but then I realize it wouldn't make much of a difference since so many people already do.

17. These methods and devices are commonly used by paranormalists looking for evidence of ghosts. They will be more thoroughly described in chapter 10.

18. I'll talk more about entertainment surrounding the supernatural and fictional in chapter 8.

19. Karen Stollznow, "Long Island Medium: A Tall Story," James Randi Educational Foundation, March 6, 2016.

20. "*The IIG $100,000 Challenge*," Independent Investigations Group, March 6, 2016, iighq.org/index.php/challenge.

1

NO SACRED COWS

"We live, after all, in a world where illusions are sacred and truth profane."
—Tariq Ali

You know what they say: "never talk about religion or politics." That is, of course, unless you want to engage in discussion about some of the most important topics of this or any generation. Keeping certain beliefs out of discussions might keep them protected from further examination, but I don't think that's a good thing. Every idea should receive criticism and challenges to determine its worth—without exception. There is no special treatment; there are no sacred cows. As Winston Churchill said, "*Criticism may not be agreeable, but it is necessary. It fulfils the same function as pain in the human body. It calls attention to an unhealthy state of things.*"

WHAT IS A "SACRED COW"?

In Hinduism and some other religions, cattle are especially revered and considered a *sacred* symbol of wealth or the earth, or of a giver of nourishment.[1] There is a lot of academic debate[2] over how the sanctity of cows became a part of Hinduism (Was it a result of the economic or ecological[3] benefits, a purely spiritual belief, or something else altogether?), but one thing is for sure: despite drastic changes in the way we live, that reverence didn't cease in the modern era. In fact, the veneration of the cow and its elevated status within certain cultures has continued and even thrived over time. While this phenomenon might sound odd or extreme to some outsiders, the fact is that cultures and people very often have their own locally familiar yet outlandish beliefs that they accept without much scrutiny, largely due to tradition alone.

As an idiom, a sacred cow has come to mean any idea that is thought to be immune from question or criticism. Many believers (of all sorts) insist that their particular sacred cows be avoided at all costs, often arguing that their beliefs are too old, widely held, or otherwise unworldly to be criticized or—in some extreme cases—even discussed in any way. For example, a religious person might feel comfortable disregarding the notion of **telepathy** as nothing more than nonsense, while clinging to petitionary prayer as a sacred and spiritual connection above critique or material examination. Likewise, a believer in psychics might scoff at a religious **fundamentalist**'s strict adherence to a completely unsupported dogma, while excusing or ignoring the fact that no so-called mediums have ever proven their abilities and refusing to address the topic entirely.

In each of the two scenarios described above, the believer rejects criticisms of their sacred ideology while actively mocking another person's—all without realizing what is really going on. This type of dissociative reasoning is possible with any topic, but is exacerbated by the very nature of all things supernatural or otherwise unfalsifiable because these subjects are often considered to be inherently (and conveniently) beyond practical investigation. This approach may seem like a safe one for believers who don't want their ideas to be tested, but it creates a problem for anyone asserting that the supernatural world affects our own. Many religious believers, for instance, claim their god is "outside space and time" and can't be shown to be real, but then in the next breath say their god came to earth as a man or inspired holy books. This "argument" is put forth by all kinds of believers who insist they know a significant amount about a supernatural presence that interacts with people on earth, and it always fails. The reasoning is flawed because claiming that your particular god, ghost, or other *unknowable* force or entity is beyond proof is rigging the game—and often nothing more than an attempt to distract from the real issue: a lack of substance. The bottom line is that you can claim that your sacred cow can't be tested by scientific inquiry, but then you can't say it intervenes in the world—because, if it does, we can investigate it. This *beyond reproach* mentality, over time, has contributed to the social taboos on investigations (and sometimes even discussions) involving religion, the supernatural, and other cherished beliefs. Fortunately, not all researchers conform to these taboos. Can you imagine what the world would look like if every scientist—or even the vast majority of them—thought a particular hypothesis was too *sacred* to test or replace? It would undermine the very nature of scientific inquiry itself. American astronomer and cosmologist Carl Sagan, it seems, would agree. He said, "*There are no forbidden questions in science, no matters too sensitive or delicate to be probed, no sacred truths.*"

DON'T MARRY YOUR BELIEFS

Some people, especially those with firmly held yet unproven beliefs, think my writing is necessarily argumentative—that skeptical inquiry cannot be encouraged without confrontation. But what they call arguments should actually be regarded as discussions . . . and possibly some of the most important in human history.

I'm aware that the topics I discuss are controversial, but, despite what some people believe, I don't mean to offend anyone with what I do. I'm very clear about my intentions: I want to help people think critically, analyze their beliefs, and follow the evidence wherever it leads. That means I don't have the time or desire for bigotry and discrimination. Contrary to how many see my work, I don't want to make fun of anyone or the forces they think are real. I want to make people think about questions that would otherwise just be background noise—easily ignored because of errors in information processing or as a result of cultural or familial **indoctrination.**

I love exposing false beliefs in myself and others but, unfortunately, as a result of **cognitive dissonance**—the uncomfortable feeling resulting from holding conflicting notions—facts and reasonable discussion can seem like ridicule when they work against firmly held beliefs. We love to be right and, as a result, our brains often try to protect our firmly held beliefs ... even when they've been proven to be wrong repeatedly. This is especially true when it comes to so-called **core beliefs**, ideas that are fundamental, inflexible, absolute, and generalized. While core beliefs can be altered, it is often a difficult task involving therapy.[4] Carl Sagan calls this subservience to cognitive dissonance "*one of the saddest lessons of history.*"

"*If we've been bamboozled long enough, we tend to reject any evidence of the bamboozle. We're no longer interested in finding out the truth,*" Sagan wrote in his book, *The Demon-Haunted World: Science as a Candle in the*

Dark.[5] *"The bamboozle has captured us. It's simply too painful to acknowledge, even to ourselves, that we've been taken. Once you give a charlatan power over you, you almost never get it back."*

When I talk about human biases or about the importance of empirical evidence, I'm not attacking anyone's particular ideas—but that doesn't stop many people from feeling that way. It would seem strange to me that so many people are outwardly offended by reasonable, evidence-based thinking when it comes to their sacred cows, if I didn't understand the process behind the feelings of offense. While I personally don't consider asking for evidence of otherwise unsubstantiated claims a negative action, I can see how—from the perspective of someone clinging tightly to them and perhaps experiencing cognitive dissonance—it might seem that way. It's actually quite easy to understand. If you try to rescue an abused dog, he might lash out at you. If you corner the dog in an attempt to bring him to a safer place, he will probably growl and bite and defend his dirty basement corner where he has been chained for years. It's all he knows and he will do anything to protect it from uncertainty. The point is we shouldn't be so firmly tied to our beliefs that objectivity and critical analysis of those ideas is made impossible, because all good ideas should be open to change with new data (see chapter 2). If we hold tightly to notions that might be false, attacking those who present an alternative, we could end up like the abused dog biting his rescuer.

The ability to change one's opinions with new information is a good indicator of a rational mindset, which is exactly why we should all avoid becoming too entrenched in our beliefs. Once we become married to our ideas, criticism feels like oppression and we can subconsciously force ourselves to reject that which makes the most sense in favor of preserving existing notions. Too often people let their beliefs and opinions become a part of their identity and, for those individuals, challenges to those ideas can become personal "attacks" in their minds.[6] To combat this tendency, I recommend reserving your judgment on subjects for which there isn't yet sufficient data; reevaluating ideas later is much easier if you aren't already attached to a specific belief. If you aren't careful when it comes to evaluating ideas and forming beliefs, you could end up like those James Randi classifies as *"the Believers."*

"These are folks who have chosen to accept a certain religion, philosophy, theory, idea or notion and cling to that belief regardless of any evidence that

might, for anyone else, bring it into doubt," Randi wrote.[7] *"They are the ones who encourage and support the fanatics and the frauds of any given age. No amount of evidence, no matter how strong, will bring them any enlightenment."*

It's important to remember that, if you get upset merely because someone else criticizes your idea, that emotion is likely not because of them—but because your most cherished belief, with which you have come to identify, was challenged. I do my best to avoid tying myself to any unproven beliefs partly because those who do are often subconsciously forced to respond to criticisms of their faith-based ideas with a defensive demeanor, and because I don't want my feelings to negatively affect how I analyze the world. So, when you do experience cognitive dissonance, it is both difficult and necessary to recognize and act on your own thinking bias. It's not a bad thing . . . it's just a reminder that more research is in order.

SPECIAL PROTECTIONS FOR RELIGIOUS BELIEFS

In religion, **blasphemy** is the term created to protect the allegedly sacred belief systems from any seemingly negative response. The problem with this idea, of course, is that the religion in question serves as a sacred cow that cannot be constructively criticized and therefore might not be improved. Sir Salman Rushdie, a British Indian writer who faced death threats and an Iranian government–backed **fatwa** calling for his assassination in 1989,[8] explained how blasphemy laws and sacredness in general suppress thinking.

"The moment you say that any idea system is sacred, whether it's a religious belief system or a secular ideology, the moment you declare a set of ideas to be immune from criticism, satire, derision, or contempt, freedom of thought becomes impossible," he said.[9]

There are currently thirteen countries around the world where apostasy or blasphemy is actually punishable by death, according to the 2013 Freethought Report, published by the International Humanist and Ethical Union.[10] In these countries, a person can be legally sentenced to death, often by hanging, for nothing more than not believing in a particular god or for criticizing a specific religious belief. This number only includes governments with the death penalty for misconduct toward a religion, but more than 22 percent of countries and territories in the world have antiblasphemy laws or policies, with punishments ranging from monetary fines to jail. While some countries might treat such laws as the antiquated relics they are, in other countries they are actively enforced. For example, in 2012 alone, there were at least twenty-seven blasphemy cases filed in Pakistan.[11]

Even outside of legal systems, people are regularly punished or killed by **extremists** for something as simple as a declaration of atheism, or for drawing a cartoon that is said to depict the prophet of Islam, Muhammad.[12] Criticizing or even simply portraying Muhammad is arguably one of the biggest taboos—one of the most widely held sacred cows—in the world. This approach toward representations of Muhammad, which is championed by some but not all Muslims and may or may not be related directly to blasphemy, has been compared to the views of many Americans toward flag burning.[13] It's important to note that, while many of the sanctions against blasphemy are related to Islam—all thirteen of the countries with the death penalty for apostasy or blasphemy are Muslim nations—in the Dark Ages of Christianity things were even worse for those who didn't believe. Blasphemy laws in general have led to real-world problems in a number of different religions and cultures. For example, in 2015, A Myanmar court sentenced three people to a prison term of more than two years for "*insulting Buddhism.*"[14]

Aside from the unfortunate fact that many nations still have laws against blasphemy, the word itself doesn't mean anything to those who don't believe. A Christian saying I'll go to **Hell** because I blaspheme against their god is similar to me insisting they are blaspheming against [insert mythological character here], and exactly the same as a Muslim telling a Christian that they're blaspheming against Allah every day and that they'll burn in Jahannam for eternity as a result. Why doesn't the Christian feel guilty for *these* blasphemies? After all, there are more than 1.6 billion Muslims in the world.[15] The answer is that these groups don't believe the same things are sacred, and don't give equal credence to other (competing) faiths. That leads us to our next question: why is blasphemy such an important component to so many religions? Well, as nineteenth-century lawyer and author Robert G. Ingersoll once said, "*This crime called blasphemy was invented by priests for the purpose of defending doctrines not able to take care of themselves.*"

It's important to note that I and other skeptics are not participating in forced deconversions—and I personally would never support banning religion or phrases that conflict with my beliefs as we have seen with blasphemy laws. These dogma-inspired rules limit mere speech based on a presupposed divine significance of a particular religious belief, as well as the assumed desires of a mythological character. I don't personally think the promotion of skepticism and clear, evidence-based thinking should ever be seen as a necessarily negative action, but that doesn't stop these ordinances combatting criticism from being created and enforced. Are these laws protecting religious beliefs logical? If a person's criticisms of your ideas are a real threat to your belief system, then can you really say it's the criticisms that are the problem? If firmly held beliefs can't withstand routine intellectual challenges and critiques, then the believers should ask themselves why they are so certain about them—instead of imposing punishments on doubters. As novelist George R. R. Martin wrote in *A Clash of Kings*, "*When you tear out a man's tongue, you are not proving him a liar, you're only telling the world that you fear what he might say.*"

ELIMINATE SACRED COWS

Sacred cows are ideas that some believe are best unexamined, but the mindset that any idea should be exempt from rigorous challenges is directly opposed to the scientific method. It's safe to keep firmly held beliefs from public observance, where they can remain unchallenged and often separate from reality, but truly strong and worthy ideas thrive where they can be verified by qualified people. To cling to beliefs that can't be verified by others, and instead are based on personal experience or anecdotal testimonies or tradition, is to reject **peer review** and the very basis of scientific inquiry (see chapter 7).

I want to rid myself of all the sacred cows in my own life, whether I recognize them as such or not, because I don't see the value in having beliefs that aren't true—and because beliefs that *are* true aren't harmed by healthy criticism. The process of discovering and escaping false beliefs is simple, but it can also be extremely difficult if you consider those beliefs to be beyond question. You must critically examine all available information (including and especially when it validates your existing opinion), follow the evidence objectively, and then invite others to try to disprove you. In essence, a scientific mindset is in direct conflict with—and can help us eliminate—our faulty ideas. Applying scientific scrutiny to your and others' firmly held beliefs can make you, as author and columnist Cassandra Duffy has said, *"the slaughterhouse for sacred cows."*

I think we should always strive to challenge our own beliefs, regardless of whether we deem them sacred. Even though it may not be the most popular position, I want my beliefs to reflect reality as closely as possible—and that's what makes me a skeptic and a rationalist. Rational skepticism means not simply assuming your beliefs are true, but actually questioning whether or not the claims put forth are supported by empirical research—and then believing (or disbelieving) accordingly. I'm constantly asking myself, "What if I'm wrong?"[16] If I'm wrong and proven to be so, I try to change my position and accept the correct one without hesitation or aggression. That's because I don't want my ideas to be based solely on those of my family, friends, or society—and I don't want any prior beliefs to keep me from learning new information. If one is truly searching for what's real in life, and not just for convenient false promises, then critical analysis and an open market of ideas are of the utmost importance. That is why, when attempting to separate fact from fiction, one should never simply accept preconceived notions and assume. Instead, form a hypothesis, test, and conclude.

Unsubstantiated beliefs are often those to which people cling the tightest, as well as those they *say* are the strongest, but this façade falls apart when skeptical inquiry is involved. Believers in all sorts of unverifiable things claim their view is the transcendent truth and superior to all others—faithful and nonfaithful alike—yet still maintain that it be protected from the same challenges to which all other ideas are subjected. This mentality shows that people are regularly scared to analyze themselves or to have their beliefs called into question—but why? Why should important concepts be beyond discussion? Talking about and looking into our sacred cows can only foster a more rational outlook if done well and often enough, and I think we can all agree that's a good thing. Even if you are the most faithful person in the world, looking more deeply into the subject(s) of that faith should be a good thing because you'll become more familiar with your beliefs. Perhaps it will even make your faith stronger! However, open dialogue isn't always seen as productive by defensive believers due to false confidence in faith-based notions and an unwillingness to critically examine preconceived notions. These are not positive qualities, as many seem to believe. My view is the opposite. I don't claim to have any absolute knowledge; instead, I point to what the evidence suggests while maintaining a mindset open to change with new data.

DESTROY FALSE BELIEFS WITH INFORMATION

I think healthy criticism, inquiry, and knowledge about all sides of an argument are necessary parts of a discussion for any person legitimately looking to determine what's real. And that's why I encourage people to expose themselves to as many ideas as possible, especially those that don't confirm their own beliefs, in the never-ending search for the facts. The great thing about learning is that we can find out something important from researching every side of any issue at hand, including information from biased and unreliable sources, as long as we do so with a critical eye. If nothing else, reading material you disagree with helps you learn about the *other side* of any particular debate. Not everyone agrees with my all-inclusive approach of exposing people to all sides of an argument. Anyone who has ever advocated for the burning or banning of a book, for instance, thinks certain information should be destroyed or made inaccessible. With that I could not disagree more.

One particular example of attempted idea destruction in my own life took place on October 20, 2013, when Christian apologist and philosophical theologian William Lane Craig published a piece called "Garbage In, Garbage Out" on his Reasonable Faith website.[17] In the post, Craig was responding to one of his anonymous fans who read my book, *Disproving Christianity*, and was subsequently finding it "*hard to believe in God.*" The questioner was seeking advice from Craig, a well-known advocate of "reasonable" Christianity, but what they received was anything but reasonable. Craig's response, published alongside the question on the website, was simply to "*Quit reading the infidel material.*" Craig offered a total of four "suggestions" to help resolve his reader's crisis of faith:

1. *Make first and foremost a recommitment of your heart to Christ . . .*
2. ***Quit reading and watching the infidel material you've been absorbing . . .***
3. *Begin a program of equipping yourself in Christian doctrine and apologetics . . .*
4. *Attend some apologetics conferences . . .* [my emphasis]

If Christianity is the transcendent truth and superior to all other faithful and nonfaithful worldviews, as Craig believes, then why does it need to be protected from criticism? Why do Christians, in Craig's view, need to "equip" themselves before being exposed to any opposing material?

Where Craig says, "*Just believe*," I say investigate. I would never warn a fellow atheist to avoid reading the Bible or another holy book out of **fear** that the strong arguments contained within them might compel that person to become religious. I champion the opposite approach by encouraging believers and nonbelievers alike to educate themselves about all of the world's religions, including a basic understanding of the traditions' core tenets and holy books. The fact is that, if you study comparative religion, it's more difficult to be fundamentally religious because the great faiths are all very similar at their most elementary levels. Each organization has similar **cult** beginnings and "prophets," they each began as local and cultural myths before being applied to a global context, and they are almost always spread through a combination of violence and proselytization. Educational research and academic group analysis only reinforce these facts, so there's no need to avoid them in an effort to preserve my beliefs.

My approach regarding exposure to opposing views isn't limited to religion. The same goes for all other superstitions and unsubstantiated claims, because knowledge about these beliefs is what ultimately destroys them. If you learn when and where a specific philosophy or concept was introduced, and you understand its pitfalls and abuses from a historical perspective, you can much more easily reject it despite any emotional ties that may be present. The best fix for any false belief or flawed perspective is more knowledge. As Pakistani secular activist Alishba Zarmeen once said, "*The best cure for patriotism is carefully studying history and the best cure for religion is studying the scriptures.*"[18]

DON'T SUPPRESS CRITICISM

I would never attempt to (nor would I want to) take away a person's right to believe anything, whether it's true or false, because to me it's important that people be able to believe in anything that doesn't interfere with others' rights. On this topic I agree with comedian Ricky Gervais, who once told CNN, "*If someone said, 'We're banning religion,' I'd march to not have it banned. Because it's your right to believe what you want. And it's your right to be wrong. And I'll fight for that right."*[19]

I might critique false beliefs, whether they are based on religion or the supernatural or something else entirely, but I would never force my way of thinking on anyone. People can choose to read my writing or simply ignore it. If they do hope to retain their special beliefs—and if those beliefs would be destroyed by looking into my work—then I recommend they avoid my books. Beliefs need to allow criticism, and I would never limit the topics of my writing to protect my beliefs or out of reverence to the beliefs of others. I have the right to point out the simple fact that faith-based beliefs are by their very nature unsubstantiated, just as believers have the right to persist in them regardless. I respect people's right to believe, as long as I have the right to point out flaws in those beliefs, but I don't have to respect the ideas themselves. People should respect other people (until they've been shown underserving of it), but not all ideas deserve that leniency. Beliefs aren't protected just because they are firmly held; they need discussion and analysis to determine their worth.

Ideas considered to be great deserve the same amount of scrutiny as the dubious claims, if not more. There are certain steps we should all take prior to forming an opinion on any topic, from the existence of gods to the costs and benefits of gun control and everything else in between. The inquiring person should ideally begin from an objective and unbiased mindset, weigh evidence on all sides of the discussion accordingly, and follow the logical arguments and **empirical data** to make a sound conclusion. If you have a sacred cow, which you refuse to analyze with a critical eye, then those steps can't really be followed properly. Even when they are, however, the process can't end there because ideas have to be self-correcting. After we have reached a conclusion, if we truly want the facts, we should still be able to hear the arguments from other sides and possibly incorporate that new information into our lives. In this way, criticism of all ideas is not just an action that should be tolerated—it's an essential part of seeking the truth.

"A thing is not proved just because no one has ever questioned it. What has never been gone into impartially has never been properly gone into. Hence scepticism is the first step toward truth. It must be applied generally, because it is the touchstone."

—Denis Diderot

NOTES

1. W. Norman Brown, "*The Sanctity of the Cow in Hinduism*," *Madras University Journal* 28, no. 29 (1957).

2. Gauri Pitale and Andrew Balkansky. "Holy Cow! India's Sacred Cow Revisited," *Popular Anthropology Magazine* 2, no. 2 (2011): 11–17.

3. V. M. Dandekar, "India's Sacred Cattle and Cultural Ecology," *Economic and Political Weekly* (1969): 1559–1566.

4. Amy Wenzel, "Modification of Core Beliefs in Cognitive Therapy," *Standard and Innovative Strategies in Cognitive Behavior Therapy* (2012): 17–34.

5. Carl Sagan, *Demon-Haunted World: Science as a Candle in the Dark* (New York: Ballantine Books, 1997).

6. "*Let me never fall into the vulgar mistake of dreaming that I am persecuted whenever I am contradicted.*" —Ralph Waldo Emerson

7. James Randi, *The Mask of Nostradamus: The Prophecies of the World's Most Famous Seer* (Amherst NY: Prometheus Books, 1993).

8. "BBC on This Day | 14 | 1989: Ayatollah Sentences Author to Death," *BBC News*, February 14, 1989, news.bbc.co.uk/onthisday/hi/dates/stories/february/14/newsid_2541000/2541149.stm.

9. Rushdie is also quoted as saying that "*respect for religion*" has become a code phrase for "*fear of religion.*" "*Religions, like all other ideas, deserve criticism, satire, and, yes, our fearless disrespect,*" he added.

10. Matt Cherry, "Freedom of Thought 2013: A Global Report on the Rights, Legal Status, and Discrimination Against Humanists, Atheists, and the Non-religious," in *Freedom of Thought Report*, ed. Bob Churchill (International Humanist and Ethical Union, July 2013), freethoughtreport.com/wp-content/uploads/2013/07/FOTReport2013.pdf.

11. Jackie Northam, "Blasphemy Charges on the Rise In Pakistan," *NPR*, November 20, 2012, www.npr.org/2012/11/20/165485239/blasphemy-charges-on-the-rise-in-pakistan.

12. Adam Withnall and John Lichfield, "Charlie Hebdo Shooting: At Least 12 Killed as Shots Fired at Satirical Magazine's Paris Office," *Independent*, January 7, 2015, www.independent.co.uk/news/world/europe/charlie-hebdo-shooting-10-killed-as-shots-fired-at-satirical-magazine-headquarters-according-to-9962337.html.

13. Dalia Mogahed, the Director of Research at the Institute for Social Policy and Understanding in Washington, DC, has drawn this comparison, saying, "*It is a human impulse to want to protect what's sacred to you.*"

14. "Myanmar Court Jails Three for Insulting Buddhism," *Al Jazeera English*, March 17, 2015, www.aljazeera.com/news/2015/03/myanmar-court-jails-insulting-buddhism-150317063346508.html.

15. "The Global Religious Landscape," Pew Research Center, December 17, 2012, www.pewforum.org/2012/12/18/global-religious-landscape-exec/.

16. "*A question that sometimes drives me hazy: am I or are the others crazy?*" — Albert Einstein

17. William Lane Craig, "Garbage In, Garbage Out," ReasonableFaith.org, October 20, 2013, www.reasonablefaith.org/garbage-in-garbage-out.

18. I might say that "*nationalism*" or "*jingoism*" would be more appropriate than "patriotism" here, but I suppose it depends on your definition of patriotism.

19. "Interview with Ricky Gervais," *CNN*, March 2, 2012, edition.cnn.com/TRANSCRIPTS/1203/04/pmt.01.html.

2

HOW TO EFFECTIVELY DISCUSS SACRED COWS

"The single biggest problem with communication is the illusion that it has taken place."
—**George Bernard Shaw**

Important topics, those that inform our decisions and shape how we interpret our experiences, should never be taken off the table when it comes to legitimate discourse. Preventing or otherwise avoiding real discussions involving firmly held beliefs, much like burning books, will never get a person closer to the truth. When the free flow of ideas is interrupted, including when it comes to things like religion, other supernatural claims, and pseudoscientific practices, nobody wins.

So, we know dialogue is important. But do we have to hurt people's feelings in talks involving sacred cows? It was philosopher Daniel C. Dennett, often referred to as one of the "Four Horsemen of the Non-Apocalypse," who said, *"There is no polite way of asking somebody: have you considered the possibility that your entire life has been devoted to a delusion?"* While I agree with Dennett on a number of issues, including that the question is a good one to ask, I do think it's possible to minimize the negative feelings resulting from any interaction . . . including those involving religion, myths, and superstitions. Dennett took on this task himself in his book *Intuition Pumps and Other Tools for Thinking*,[1] when he promoted rules of conduct put forth years earlier by noted social psychologist Anatol Rapoport:

How to compose a successful critical commentary:

1. *You should attempt to re-express your target's position so clearly, vividly, and fairly that your target says, "Thanks, I wish I'd thought of putting it that way."*

2. *You should list any points of agreement (especially if they are not matters of general or widespread agreement).*

3. *You should mention anything you have learned from your target.*

4. *Only then are you permitted to say so much as a word of rebuttal or criticism.*

Dennett called Rapoport's Rules the "*best antidote*" for the "*tendency to caricature one's opponent*," but admitted that following them was always "*something of a struggle*" for him.

"*Some targets, quite frankly, don't deserve such respectful attention, and—I admit—it can be sheer joy to skewer and roast them*," Dennett wrote. "*But when it is called for, and it works, the results are gratifying.*"

Ray Hyman, professor emeritus of psychology at the University of Oregon, has also published a brief guide to "*proper criticism.*" Hyman, a member of the Committee for the Scientific Investigation of Claims of the Paranormal Executive Council, suggests eight simple steps to "*upgrade the quality of their criticism.*"[2]

1. *Be prepared.*

2. *Clarify your objectives.*

3. *Do your homework.*

4. *Do not go beyond your level of competence.*

5. *Let the facts speak for themselves.*

6. *Be precise.*

7. *Use the principle of charity.*

8. *Avoid loaded words and sensationalism.*

MY DISCUSSIONS

People's beliefs, whether they realize it or not, very often affect their actions—and that's why it is and will always be incredibly important that we challenge, doubt, and work to correct any and all misguided notions. But in my culture and many others, to discuss these issues in any substantive way has long been considered taboo. Despite this fact, as a religious studies graduate and the author of secular-themed works, I've had to get used to dealing with religious and other supernatural debates nearly every day— and I've had to do so in a calm, rational, and friendly manner. As a result, I've learned that, contrary to popular opinion, you *can* reach some believers through rational dialogue; indoctrination is difficult to undo, but not impossible. In fact, in some rare cases, years of false beliefs fall away after the believer is exposed to certain sources of information, even those found on Twitter or Facebook, for the first time.[3]

Over the years, through a number of interactions with believers in all sorts of woo and other nonsensical or unproven ideas, I've learned the importance of clear and effective discussions—especially when it comes to someone's sacred cow(s). I discovered that talking about inherently controversial subjects, including religion and skepticism in general, can actually be a rewarding experience if carried out correctly. Millions of people all over the world devote their lives to worshiping one deity or another—or otherwise base their decisions on supernatural (or nonexistent) forces. And if I can help even a few of these people by engaging in rational discussion about the topic(s), then I consider that a positive contribution. But I find I'm most successful in these talks when I don't endeavor to change anyone's mind to my way of thinking. Instead, I think it's easier to recommend steps that will get them to the truth regardless.[4]

It's not all about the other person, either; I love what I do because I learn from every exchange in which I take the time to participate. Even if the opposition's argument isn't novel, I still challenge myself to think differently and gain new knowledge through that process. Sometimes I get to teach someone something,[5] and I love that experience, but the only thing I enjoy more is learning, and that happens every day. But whether or not these interactions are positive depends on how you handle them. If your goal in a discussion is not to simply beat your interlocutor, but instead to acquire and share new information, then it's easy to come out a winner in the end (see chapter 7). Epicurus, an ancient Greek philosopher, demonstrated his understanding of this concept when he said, "*In a philosophical dispute, he gains most who is defeated, since he learns the most.*"

YOU CAN REACH SOME PEOPLE, SOMETIMES

I often hear people say, "They're never going to change their minds!" But the fact is that, from Christians and Scientologists denouncing their faiths to so-called **Truthers** admitting they were misled, I've seen some great examples of evidence-based thinking from people who once believed. Even if you aren't trying to necessarily change minds, it's important to recognize that it does happen all the time—we've all held irrational beliefs at some point and we eventually gave them up. For instance, some people may have never believed in good **luck** charms or gods, but were still fooled by other popular misconceptions—perhaps they bought into the myth that the Great Wall of China is visible from space,[6] or that shaving hair causes it to grow back faster, darker, or thicker.[7] People are sometimes able to shed their false beliefs, including at times ideologies with which they were indoctrinated, and to suggest otherwise is disingenuous. It's not an easy task and doesn't typically happen overnight, but I never assume logical discourse is a lost cause without first attempting it. If some people can give up their faith-based beliefs through skeptical analysis, then others can, too. At very least, discussions like this can plant a new seed of skepticism or critical thought and provide something for them to think about in the future.

I understand that tempers flare in debates about religion and the supernatural, as well as all kinds of other contentious subjects, but I think it's important to remember that believers aren't necessarily stupid or overly dogmatic. In fact, many people who believe in religions or other paranormal claims are extremely intelligent; they just **compartmentalize** their beliefs. They demand evidence for almost every other extraordinary claim in life except those to which they cling most tightly—their sacred cows (see chapter 7). But that doesn't make them dumb or evil. The average believer is guilty of nothing more than gullibility, wishful thinking, and being indoctrinated, keeping him or her from critically examining beliefs. These are tough obstacles to overcome, but, in my experience, it is mild, calm, rational discussion that is responsible for the majority of breakthroughs in this area—not emotional rhetoric and ridicule.

UNDERSTAND AND ADJUST FOR COGNITIVE DISSONANCE

Confrontation most often results from religious and other sacred cow conversations for one simple reason: you're telling a person that some of his or her most fundamental beliefs are probably false. This can be a scary thought, but the fact that you are telling believers they're likely to be wrong isn't necessarily a bad thing, especially if you recognize and demonstrate that the error isn't unique to them and that it can be corrected. They might believe strongly because their family or culture does—or because that's the only position they've entertained—and looking at these possible reasons and considering them in your replies can help guide a discussion.

Popular ideas are often taken for granted as the truth without much thought, so, when they are false, cognitive dissonance is almost always a factor. It's hard to accept the fact that your entire society might be wrong about something, but it happens all the time, so being able to voice your opinions and challenge those of the majority is critical. Unfortunately, as discussed earlier, cognitive dissonance can keep people from listening to ideas or arguments that contradict their own firmly held beliefs on a topic. This process was perhaps best described by psychiatrist and philosopher Frantz Fanon, who was born in the 1920s.

"Sometimes people hold a core belief that is very strong. When they are presented with evidence that works against that belief, the new evidence cannot be accepted," Fanon wrote in *Black Skin, White Masks*.[8] *"It would create a feeling that is extremely uncomfortable, called cognitive dissonance. And because it is so important to protect the core belief, they will rationalize, ignore and even deny anything that doesn't fit in with the core belief."*

If someone gets upset about a particular argument or statement of fact, then that emotional reaction isn't your fault, but you can still anticipate and adjust for it. The best way to handle this is not to treat the situation with kid gloves or to simply give up, but instead to go out of your way to show exactly why your words aren't meant to insult—they are meant to share ideas and communicate. Sticking to the facts and avoiding any appeals to emotion helps others see your good intentions, which may ultimately help you diffuse a potentially hostile situation.

FIND COMMON GROUND

Discussions surrounding hot-button issues are difficult because of the *Us vs.*

Them mentality that is present in our very nature, but controversy itself can also be a powerful learning tool.[9] So how do we overcome the former and take advantage of the latter? We establish similarities and work from there. Finding common ground can apply to anything—any point on which you can agree with your interlocutor—and it almost always improves the quality of a discussion. For me, studying religions and the supernatural has always been a passion. From a very young age, I remember being intrigued by what my friends and family believed—and, perhaps more importantly, why they believed it. I'm very passionate about the same stories to which some believers cling so fervently, and keeping this in mind and pointing it out can make a *debate* into more of a *discussion*.

Many people who are opposed to supernatural beliefs in general tend to forget how interesting the concepts themselves can be, but it's important to note that most of these nonbelievers probably agree that ancient mythology and magic are incredibly interesting topics. If you can apply that same intrigue to modern belief systems and myths, you may be able to find more common ground with believers than either party previously thought possible (see chapter 4). This is not to say, however, that an interest in the supernatural must be your common ground. This can and likely will be different for everybody. I recommend talking with your debate partner(s) and asking friendly questions to find out where you might already agree and starting from that point.

ASK QUESTIONS

Sometimes you can say more with a simple question than you possibly could with any definitive statement, and that's because questions make us think. Statements of fact, even when they are true, don't always encourage a person to think more deeply about an issue. Questions are better at spawning fruitful dialogue and, in turn, additional queries. The authors of *Critical Thinking Handbook: Basic Theory and Instructional* explain how questions "*define tasks, express problems and delineate issues,*" while answers "*often signal a full stop in thought.*"[10]

> *Deep questions drive our thought underneath the surface of things, force us to deal with complexity. Questions of purpose force us to define our task. Questions of information force us to look at our sources of*

information as well as at the quality of our information. Questions of interpretation force us to examine how we are organizing or giving meaning to information. Questions of assumption force us to examine what we are taking for granted. Questions of implication force us to follow out where our thinking is going. Questions of point of view force us to examine our point of view and to consider other relevant points of view.

Questions are powerful drivers of growth. Without needing to provide any information themselves, they stimulate further thought, provoke entirely new discussions, and are responsible for major advancements in science and technology. In fact, inquiry itself is the cornerstone of the scientific method, as well as of my own personal philosophy, "Question everything, and worship nothing." Comedian George Carlin pointed out the importance of asking questions (as opposed to simply taking in information) when he said, "*Kids who want to learn to read are going to learn to read. It's much more important to teach children to question what they read. Children should be taught to question everything. To question everything they read, everything they hear.*"

Questioning information you're provided, as Carlin suggested, is critically important. But deeper questions, those that make you rethink your preconceived notions and reconsider why you believe something, can be even more powerful. And if you ask reasonable questions in a friendly manner, other participants in the conversation may be forced to think through their positions logically, instead of simply reacting based on emotional impulses. The best way to do this, in my opinion, is to model your line of questioning after the **Socratic Method**, which has been proven to work over thousands of years.

If you've ever taken a university-level philosophy class, you've probably heard of the Socratic Method. This process, named after the classical Greek philosopher Socrates, is a question-based system for promoting critical thinking and reaching conclusions in a debate. While it has been interpreted and modified in many ways, the method itself is simple: you ask a number of questions and follow-ups in an attempt to expose a potential contradiction in another participant's thinking, and then you work together to come up with a tenable solution. This is often used in teaching as a means to help students think for themselves,[11] but it works incredibly well in general discussions, as well.

My advice is to use this method in the least abrasive way possible, allowing questions to guide the discussion and stimulate learning on all sides. At times, it may even be acceptable to answer a question with another (hopefully thought-provoking) question when responding to someone else. Like Socrates and others before me, I think good questions can lead to internal answers, which are often the most rewarding ones.

STAY ON POINT

This recommendation is fairly simple and it applies to every debate, regardless of the subjects being discussed: stick to the topic at hand. If you're talking about whether or not petitionary prayer yields legitimate, measurable, observable results, then don't allow the dialogue to be shifted toward **evolution**, Young Earth creationism, morality, or jihad. And if you're debating the existence of peer-reviewed scientific evidence for some ancient mystical force, don't let the other party base their argument solely on anecdotal accounts. When people feel like they are losing a particular debate, it is not uncommon for them to attempt to shift the conversation in progress in search of a more comfortable topic where they feel they will have more footing. They may even change the standards of deciding the argument currently in progress, instead of switching topics entirely, which is called *moving the goalposts*.[12] However, by simply ignoring that behavior and sticking to the original discussion, the other party is forced to participate in the predetermined issue (or abandon the debate altogether). I also recommended familiarizing yourself with other **logical fallacies**, both formal and informal, to avoid distractions resulting from all sorts of faulty argument patterns.

Just as it is important to ignore any attempts to change the topic or move the goalposts, it's equally crucial to not be distracted by *argumentum ad hominem* fallacies, personal attacks through which a person attempts to discredit another person's argument,[13] or general name-calling. Of course, before engaging in discussion, you probably want to ensure the other party is willing to have a friendly debate and accept new evidence. But if during the course of the talk, a participant resorts to insults, whether they are ad hominem character attacks in an attempt to undermine your argument or not, it is usually a sign that he or she has become flustered and is seeking a quick way out. By ignoring the insults completely, repeating unanswered questions or calls for evidence if necessary, and sticking to the actual issue, the name-caller will have no choice but to give up the immature behavior and/or surrender entirely.

TREAT THOSE YOU DEBATE LIKE THEY'RE ON AN HONEST SEARCH FOR REALITY

While it may not always be the case, friendly and effective debates are easier if you assume your counterpart is legitimately searching for the truth—and not simply seeking convenient lies. This ensures that the discussion remains informative and real, and that you don't seem condescending or rude. It's possible that, through this process, a party's tendency to immediately dismiss any opposing view out of hand could be softened or destroyed entirely. By treating the individual with respect and ignoring behavior to the contrary, defenses are weakened, and new information is more easily shared.

Even if you don't think your debate partner is looking for truth, you should note that it's not all about the person with whom you're engaging— outsiders are often on their own journey toward the truth and it's important to remember that. Whether you're discussing sacred cows with your family, in an online forum, or in a professional debate hall, observers should be kept in mind. It's possible that onlookers of your debates are on the fence about the topic at hand, and that they are seeking answers. Understanding this very basic concept ensures the discussion flows smoothly because it helps to eliminate feelings the participants may have for one another and forces the discussion to be centered on the facts.

> *"A good leader can engage in a debate frankly and thoroughly, knowing that at the end he and the other side must be closer, and thus emerge stronger. You don't have that idea when you are arrogant, superficial, and uninformed."*
>
> **—Nelson Mandela**

NOTES

1. Daniel C. Dennett, *Intuition Pumps and Other Tools for Thinking* (New York: W. W. Norton & Company, 2013).

2. Ray Hyman, "Proper Criticism," *Skeptical Inquirer* 25, no. 4 (2001): 5–55.

3. Adrian Chen, "Conversion via Twitter," *New Yorker,* November 23, 2015, www.newyorker.com/magazine/2015/11/23/conversion-via-twitter-westboro-baptist-church-megan-phelps-roper.

4. The only thing I enjoy more than reasonable, logical thinking is writing about that process and how to do it properly—sharing it with others. You can never go wrong when encouraging people to be rational and follow the evidence.

5. *"I never teach my pupils, I only attempt to provide the conditions in which they can learn."* —Albert Einstein

6. Arthur Waldron, *The Great Wall of China: From History to Myth* (Cambridge: Cambridge University Press, 1990).

7. Rachel C. Vreeman and Aaron E. Carroll, "Medical Myths," *British Medical Journal* 335, no. 7633 (2007): 1288–1289.

8. Frantz Fanon, *Black Skin, White Masks* (New York: Grove Press, 2008).

9. Lee Warren and Derek Bok Center, "Managing Hot Moments in the Classroom," Derek Bok Center for Teaching and Learning, 2006, isites.harvard.edu/fs/html/icb.topic58474/hotmoments.html.

10. Richard Paul and Linda Elder, *Critical Thinking Handbook: Basic Theory and Instructional Structures*, 2nd ed. (Dillion Beach, CA: Foundation for Critical Thinking, 2000).

11. Bob Brownhill, "The Socractic Method," in *The Theory and Practice of Teaching*, ed. Peter Jarvis (London: Kogan Page, 2002), 70–78.

12. Theo Clark and Jef Clark, *Humbug! The Skeptic's Field Guide to Spotting Fallacies in Thinking* (Nifty Books, 2005), 101

13. Michael C. LaBossiere, *42 Fallacies for Free* (2002).

3

RELIGION IS ORGANIZED SUPERSTITION

*"The problem is that one man's superstition is another man's religion,
and vice versa. Many Protestants today still see Catholicism as being rife
with superstition ... while atheists and agnostics would see bien-pensant
Protestants as worshiping an equally absurd form of the supernatural."*
—**David Gibson**

Superstitions have historically helped people and groups feel more in control
when they were actually powerless and, despite our many advancements,
the modern era is no different. We still can't control or know everything,
but we will always want to, so we continue to create false answers—religious
and nonreligious alike—to fill that void.

Until now, most of my writings have been focused on exploring the
fallacies, contradictions, and irrationality associated with one particular
associate of superstition: religion.[1] My first book, *Disproving Christianity*,
was a critique of biblical literalism and an analysis of the world's most
followed religion from a secular perspective. My second, *Mom, Dad, I'm an
Atheist*, sought to help freethinkers of all backgrounds tread the dangerous
landscape of public disbelief in a society largely dominated by religious
and theistic assumptions, as well as to help debunk common myths about
atheism itself. I also co-wrote *The Belief Series*, a trilogy of interactive study
guides that seek to teach kids of all ages about the origins of beliefs, gods,
and religions. But religion isn't the only false belief system, and theism isn't
the only false belief. I want to do my best to encourage critical thinking

and evidence-based worldviews for all, and criticism of the world's religions is just one part of that goal.

In the past, I emphasized my activism in favor of secularism and against the major religions because it is those traditions and their accompanying stagnant moral guides that breed much of the intolerance in the world, and are responsible for so many hindrances to humanity's scientific advancement. While it is well established that religion itself is a cultural universal,[2] and that it likely has or had evolutionary benefits,[3] it is also becoming less and less necessary every day and is now (slowly) losing relevance in the age of information, at least in the West. In fact, one recent study showed that the Christian share of the population in the United States, by far the largest religious group in the country, fell from 78.4 percent to 70.6 percent between 2007 and 2014.[4] And in another survey, researchers found that 38 percent of Harvard freshmen identified as atheist or agnostic while only 34 percent described themselves as Christian.[5]

I think this notable decline in religious identification, sometimes referred to as the "*rise of the nones*,"[6] is occurring partly because credible information is more widely available and—if given the chance—most people prefer to have facts over faith. However, it is also due to the fact that everyone with an Internet connection can see the damages religion causes or, at very least, justifies. These religions and their followers affect believers and nonbelievers alike all across the world and, when religion excuses violence, impedes scientific progress, and gives motivation to strip people of human rights, I understand why so many would distance themselves from it or even feel that excessive criticism is warranted and necessary. Let me be clear: I have no problem with people following a religion, but I also think it's possible to take many life lessons from various religious philosophies without having to literally believe in the religions themselves. I further recognize that religions are most harmful when imposed on others, as opposed to when practiced at a personal and philosophical level, and I adjust my assessments accordingly.

I DON'T HATE RELIGION

My critiques of various world religions shouldn't be confused with disdain for the belief systems themselves or for those who adhere to them. Pointing out the negative aspects of religious influences and inconsistencies within specific belief systems does not equate to persecution or hatred of those systems' followers, and I maintain my lifelong passion for studying religions and their rich histories. That's why I, for one, don't hate believers or religion. It's not that black and white for me—I don't have to either endorse all actions done in the name of religion or condemn its practice entirely. I hate religious extremism, but I don't hate meditation or meditative prayer; I hate that religious ideals have consistently impeded science and invaded secular governments, but I don't hate church-run food drives and soup kitchens; I hate the *God-is-on-our-side* mentality and that millions of people think that religion is necessary to live a happy and moral life, but I don't hate peaceful religious practices or people who happen to believe differently. So, no, I don't hate religion. In fact, I love religion. I love learning about it. I love finding out how it came to be, and about the specific components of various religious traditions. I just hate how it is abused. I hate how it is taken out of its own original context and used to discriminate against people. I hate how it has infiltrated the governments of certain states and countries. The answer to that isn't to end religion. It's to end those abuses.

I love the study of religion so much that I often find myself opposing fellow nonbelievers who say they dislike all religions, or that they want to ban it entirely, usually in reference to the more popular Abrahamic faiths. In my opinion, if you don't *hate* ancient Greek myths, you shouldn't *hate* modern religions.[7] You might oppose that they are taken as reality in today's times or that they are incorporated into legislation, but that doesn't equate to a blanket *hatred* of the stories themselves. The myths wouldn't have power without people who take them as literal truths. The fact is that religion is a human universal, and it isn't something we could simply erase, even if we wanted to. It's an integral part of our history and, for better or worse, it will likely help shape much of our future. Religion was one of our initial attempts to explain the unknown, long before the scientific process was developed, taught, and refined, so it's not surprising that it is still important to so many people. As Christopher Hitchens once explained, religion was humanity's "*first—and is in some ways therefore the worst—chance to explain human nature and the natural order.*"

"*It was our first attempt at philosophy, just as it was our first attempt at astronomy and biology. We embarked on it in a time of fearful infancy, when we didn't know that we lived on a rounded planet in a tiny solar system which had a center around which we revolved,"* Hitchens said.[8] *"We didn't know that there were microorganisms that we couldn't see, but that explained a lot about both our health and our ill-health. We were told we were given dominion over all animals and we were wrong, because there were no dinosaurs in that list, no marsupials, because the people who wrote this didn't know they existed, and we were certainly never given dominion over microorganisms and we'll never get that, because they rule!"*

Religion was our first attempt at a lot of things, and it continues to be an inspiration for major (charitable and horrific) acts around the world every day, so it's reasonable to conclude it will likely exist for the foreseeable future. But does it have to exist in an essentially stagnant state as it has for thousands of years? Many people, whether they identify with a tradition or not, think we can change religion for the better. I tend to agree.

I SUPPORT SECULARIZATION

Unfortunately for me and many others, being a nonbeliever doesn't exempt me from the damaging effects of institutionalized religion. And I advocate for secularism to push back against the encroachment of religion into the U.S. government, which is supposed to have a wall of separation between Church and State that would prevent these occurrences and place religion back into its proper position as a personal endeavor. The result of this much-needed separation—when properly enforced—is a nation in which those who wish to worship are allowed to do so freely of their own accord, and those of us who do not have or want religion in our lives can avoid being governed or limited by it.

Religions are unique in that they are the only known superstition-based belief systems that have, historically and in modern times, retained a stranglehold on so many societies and governments. In the United States, for instance, there are some (of course not all) Christians who regularly attempt to force their religion into the legislation and public policy of a secular nation—and with some success. Whether it's something as simple as "IN GOD WE TRUST" being printed on our currency or as damaging as teaching Young Earth creationism and other false sciences to our children in public schools, we are constantly being affected by religious influences. It has halted studies in life-saving fields of medicine like stem-cell research and has been used as the primary justification for stripping numerous groups of their civil rights, first for African Americans and women, and then for homosexuals. In other regions, especially in the war-torn Middle East, Islam has been at the root of similar but more violent and intrusive injustices when combined with government.

Many people, believers and nonbelievers alike, are quick to point out that it's just the extremists and fundamentalists of each religion who are at the root of the major issues, and that's largely true, but it's also important to note that to give the doctrines themselves leniency in criticism is to allow the fringe groups to use their faith to hold back the progress of others. Further, while fundamentalists themselves are undoubtedly problematic, there may be something wrong with a religion itself if those who strictly adhere to its most fundamental principles are violent bigots and sexists.

I didn't start out writing about secular issues because I give deities or religious claims any particular credence in relation to other supernatural beliefs, but because the depth to which theism and religiosity have permeated society has made them the most harmful, which is demonstrated by the fact that so many people are discriminated against (and much worse in some regions) for simply not believing in that which lacks proof. That standard doesn't exist for any other superstition or paranormal assertion. For perspective: in modern America, believing in an invisible person-like creature would likely be considered unhealthy, but believing it hears your thoughts and takes human form is actually the norm. And while most Americans today find comfort in the fact that their elected officials pray and get guidance from clergymen, they might be appalled if those same politicians used a crystal ball and consulted psychics. In fact, even as far back as the 1980s, there was public controversy over the fact that President Ronald Reagan and his wife were "*deeply interested in astrology.*" There was a media frenzy when people discovered that Nancy Reagan not only had an astrologer on call, but also used astrology to time her husband's events in an attempt to keep him safe. She even credited her astrologer with predicting an assassination attempt on the president in 1981, though the seer only said "*there was going to be an incident on that day,*" according to news reports at the time.[9] In this way, through a double standard and only in the minds of those who give them such reverence, religions are separate from other superstitions.

WHAT DOES "RELIGIOUS FAITH" MEAN?

With enough study of religious history, one becomes acutely aware that confidence in the unknowable and unprovable is not a virtue—and that it isn't unique to any particular culture or group. In fact, every supernatural religion seems to utilize the same type of *spiritual* faith, which in many cases is nothing more than a justification for believing in (and often worshiping) that which is unverifiable based only on tradition or emotion. Some believers might argue that faith just means trust (*with evidence*), in the way we might have faith in engineering or in physics. While this may be one of many valid definitions, this isn't the only type of faith religions rely on. Biology professor Jerry Coyne has also called attention to the varying definitions of faith, and how many people (mostly religious believers) insist that scientists rely on the same wishful thinking as those who promote religions. He says the "*faith*" he has in science is "*completely different from the faith believers have in God and the dogmas of their creed.*"[10] He illustrates this by putting forth four separate statements:

1. "*I have faith that, because I accept Jesus as my personal savior, I will join my friends and family in Heaven.*"

2. "*My faith tells me that the Messiah has not yet come, but will someday.*"

3. "*I have strep throat, but I have faith that this penicillin will clear it up.*"

4. "*I have faith that when I martyr myself for Allah, I will receive 72 virgins in Paradise.*"

Coyne, currently a professor emeritus at the University of Chicago in the Department of Ecology and Evolution, notes that, while each sentence uses the word "faith," number three used it differently. The remaining religious claims, he said, used faith as defined by philosopher Walter Kaufmann: "*intense, usually confident, belief that is not based on evidence sufficient to command assent from every reasonable person.*"

"*Indeed, there is no evidence beyond revelation, authority, and scripture to support the religious claims above, and most of the world's believers would reject at least one of them. To state it bluntly, such faith involves pretending to know things you don't,*" Coyne wrote for *Slate.* "*In contrast, the third statement relies*" *on evidence: penicillin almost invariably kills streptococcus bacteria. In such cases the word faith doesn't mean 'belief without good evidence,' but 'confidence derived from scientific tests and repeated, documented experience.'*"

Paul Bloom, the Brooks and Suzanne Ragen Professor of Psychology at Yale University, explains why some people see faith and science as though they are on the same footing. He says that, while science and religion are "*as different as can be*," for most people their scientific and religious views often *feel* the same. That's because these beliefs are "*learned, understood, and mentally encoded in similar ways.*"

"*Scientific practices—observation and experiment; the development of falsifiable hypotheses; the relentless questioning of established views—have proven uniquely powerful in revealing the surprising, underlying structure of the world we live in, including subatomic particles, the role of germs in the spread of disease, and the neural basis of mental life,*" Bloom wrote for *The Atlantic.*[11] "*Religion has no equivalent record of discovering hidden truths.*"

The word "faith" can be used in a number of different ways, and I think it's important to differentiate them because one usage—religious or spiritual faith—acts as an excuse to believe despite a lack of evidence. In researching this distinct type of faith, I was able to draw a clear line between *blind faith* and what might be considered *supported faith*. I began by analyzing the first two definitions of faith provided by the *American Heritage Dictionary of the English Language*:

1) *Confident belief in the truth, value, or trustworthiness of a person, idea, or thing.*

2) *Belief that does not rest on logical proof or material evidence.*[12]

My argument is that everyone, including scientists, use the first version of faith. We're all confident, for instance, that the sun will set tonight and rise again tomorrow. We believe this because it has been shown to be reliable over time. We have scientific backing for that notion. The second description of faith, while perhaps equally widespread, can be dangerous when used to justify worldly actions. I saw this second meaning, which is often tied to religions and other supernatural concepts, again when I looked at Dictionary.com's second definition of faith: "*Belief that is not based on proof.*"[13] I then moved on to *Merriam-Webster's* second definition, which is *"belief and trust in and loyalty to God,"* and looked at its subsection just below. *Webster's* 2b(1) defines faith as *"firm belief in something for which there is no proof."*[14] I already saw a pattern emerging, but Oxford Dictionaries had perhaps the clearest definition of religious faith. In the number two spot, Oxford defines faith as *"Strong belief in God or in the doctrines of a religion, based on spiritual apprehension rather than proof."*[15] There are also definitions of this type of blind religious faith that come straight from religious leaders and holy texts themselves. Hebrews 11:1, for example, defines faith as *"being sure of what we hope for and certain of what we do not see."*[16] Martin Luther, founder of the Protestant Reformation, said, *"Reason is the greatest enemy that faith has; it never comes to the aid of spiritual things, but—more frequently than not—struggles against the divine Word, treating with contempt all that emanates from God."*[17]

The definition of religious faith seems pretty undisputed in these contexts, but even if you define faith as *spiritual hope*, or something similar, it stands in opposition to methodological scrutiny. On the opposite side of the faith spectrum, we have scientific skepticism, or the search for whether claims are supported by empirical research and have reproducibility. There are only two options when you properly apply this mentality to faith-based claims: the process will either eradicate the belief through a systematic uncovering of evidence against it or (in theory) it will render faith useless by verifying the underlying facts that support the initial claim. This is why, while not every atheist is a scientific skeptic, scientific skepticism will always lead a person to reject god-claims; they can't be established scientifically. It's worth mentioning that a number of faithful scientists do believe in god(s) (and other unsubstantiated forces), but they aren't applying scientific skepticism to claims made by religions. Not many scientists are truly scientific skeptics, and even fewer apply the rigorous methodology to everything in their lives (see chapter 7).

The bottom line is that the vast majority of religions, historically and in modern times, are based on blind trust in unverifiable texts—and not expectations held based on lifetimes of testing and observation. In this way, *religious faith* is inherently unscientific: it is based on ancient and unsupported reports. Having faith in humanity or in an idea—like honesty or **love**—is great, but if a concept needs your faith to exist, then that should make you think twice about holding onto it so tightly.

"IT TAKES FAITH TO BE AN ATHEIST!"

Some religious believers insist that atheism takes faith, or that nonbelief itself is a religion, but these attempts to use religion and faith as derogatory terms are often nothing more than deflections from the real issue: faith alone isn't evidence of anything. I think these assertions sometimes stem from defensiveness, and other times they come from a fundamental misunderstanding of what atheism means. When I say I'm an atheist, I'm not necessarily making a positive claim . . . I do not *believe in* atheism and there's no religion or doctrine associated with the label. I am merely rejecting faith-based claims put forth by others—claims that lack solid evidence and therefore rely on the same spiritual apprehension as do all religions. My rejection of a belief in all deities is no different from a Christian, Muslim, or Jew who rejects Thor, Zeus, or any other man-made deity. Does it take faith for modern religious believers to *not* believe in these gods? No. Their existence is asserted without evidence, and therefore it can be rejected in the same fashion.[18] When it comes to supernatural religious claims, the so-called evidence put forth by the Bible is equal to that put forth by the Qur'an, which is equal to that put forth by the Bhagavad Gita. In practical terms, what separates a Christian's faith from the faith of a Muslim, a Scientologist, a Mormon, or a member of some obscure cult? If the criterion for faith is believing what you can't see, there are many organizations and groups who fit the bill. So, why is this considered a good thing?

I reject all religions and all superstitions. I don't pray to any idols, I don't believe in supernatural forces, I don't congregate with other atheists to worship atheism, and I don't tithe to an atheist church. The only requirement for one to be an atheist is to simply not believe in gods. I do think it's possible for my atheistic and naturalistic worldview to be altered, but not by something as trivial and arbitrary as blind faith. If there were evidence for one or more deities that was substantial enough to warrant peer review and strong enough to withstand rigorous testing, I'd become a *believer*—but I still wouldn't be a worshiper. So far , deities have only been shown to exist in the imaginations of humans, and no independent act or force has ever been proven to involve divine intervention.

RELIGION ISN'T SPECIAL

If a superstition is *a belief or way of behaving that is based on fear of the unknown and faith in magic*,[19] then I think it's fair to describe religions as (mostly archaic) organized superstitions. Superstition isn't an insult; it's just the broader umbrella term, under which some religious practices and beliefs most certainly fit. When asked which church I attend or which religion I follow, for instance, I often say, "I'm not superstitious," just to cover all the potential bases. It might be difficult for some believers—and even former believers—to accept it, but, whether you carry a four-leafed clover for good luck or worship Jesus for salvation, the faith-based belief stems from the same place and follows the same format:

SUPERSTITION: "IF I CARRY THIS CHARM, I'LL HAVE GOOD LUCK IN ALL MY ENDEAVORS!"

RELIGION: "IF I ACCEPT JESUS, I'LL LIVE FOREVER IN HEAVEN AFTER DEATH!"

There are important connections that link all superstitions, along with other flawed but potentially comforting beliefs, and that's why personal religious or mystical experiences can and should be treated the same way as the alleged experiences of those who believe they saw ghosts or were abducted by aliens. Religion does enjoy some special cultural protections, but that's where the differences between it and other supernatural belief systems end, because religion is itself a form of organized and encultured woo that has been making adults believe in magic for all of recorded history. In that sense, letting the Bible or the Qur'an dictate how our governments manage things like stem-cell research and human rights is like letting a **Ouija board** govern the creation and enforcement of our most important laws.

While the title of this chapter is "Religion Is Organized Superstition," religions can more accurately be described as collections of superstitions and other beliefs—often accompanied by moral teachings and creation myths. To make this connection clear, it's important to note that **superstition** itself—the tendency to falsely link a cause to an effect[20]—is a natural impulse that is well understood within an evolutionary context.[21] Humans are pattern-seeking creatures by nature, which means we search for what's familiar about our surroundings to help us make sense of them. For instance, our ancient ancestors may have (falsely) associated all rustling grass with a predator's approach. In most instances, the wind was likely the cause, but that doesn't take away from the lives that were saved because of that assumption of danger. Petitionary prayer—defined as an act in which one person (who is by definition unworthy) asks that the laws of the universe be altered to achieve an earthly result—a common practice in the Christian religion and a number of other faiths,[22] is just one example of a superstitious principle that many religions share. The individual saying the prayer (no matter to which deity or supernatural force it is directed) sees the positive *results* (or hits) as divine intervention, and ignores those prayers that remain unanswered (misses), much like a gambler would. While it may make the believer feel better psychologically, this form of intercessory prayer, much like witchcraft, **prophecies**, **homeopathy**, mediums, and astrology, has been debunked time and time again as a solution to real-world problems.[23] And it—just like the other supernatural and result-seeking spiritual activities and practices—relies on the false connections between cause and effect that are at the core of superstitious behavior. In other words, prayer is just another superstition—and it affects the future in the same way fortune cookies accurately predict it.

Prayer isn't the only superstition found within Christianity, Islam, and other religions, and depending on the specific denomination or sect, there may be a whole slew of archaic traditions and idols that are supposed to invoke divine (supernatural) acts yet have never been shown to do so in a scientific setting. I decided to emphasize prayer because belief in it is common across a number of belief systems and because, by understanding the nature of one superstitious experience or belief, we can give ourselves greater insight into why people may believe in the others. All of these claims can and should be independently analyzed and tested, as well as traced back to their roots during the religion's early formation and sometimes much earlier, in an attempt to discern a possible value. But so far, no supernatural practice or religious rite has been shown to have any predictable effect on the outside world.

WHERE RELIGION MEETS SUPERSTITION

Many religious scriptures, including the Christian Bible,[24][25] actually condemn other supernatural practices—such as sorcery, communication with the dead, and witchcraft. The problem for religious believers here is that none of those things have actually been shown to exist, so the fact that their holy books call for their dismissal and cast them as evil and sinful doesn't work very well to convince a thinking person that the religions are really rooted in reality.[26] Another issue is that dogmatic condemnations of *other* supernatural forces don't actually keep all religious believers from embracing those mysterious (and unfounded) powers. Clinical psychologist and professor Jonathan C. Smith wrote about this in his book, *Pseudoscience and Extraordinary Claims of the Paranormal*:

> *Jesus rejected temptations from Satan to turn stones into bread and fly off mountains to impress the masses. Buddha warned against meditation distractions of psychic powers. Mohammad condemned magic as deceptive evil contrary to God's will. Yet virtually every major world religion has devotees that are passionate advocates of the paranormal.*[27]

Religious texts often say mediums are real and even caution believers to kill those who practice witchcraft (see chapter 6). That says a lot about those who hold those scriptures to be divine in modern times, but it might tell us even more about those who wrote the books in the first place. For example, it's possible that the Bible condemns these other supernatural practices for the same reason that many religions consider all competing faiths evil: *competition*. I've often argued, for instance, that petitionary prayer is in many ways the same as summoning, witchcraft, and other practices that allegedly bring manifestations of earthly desires through supernatural intervention. So, by condemning competing imaginary forces (and even ordering the deaths of those who practice them), such as request-based magic, a religion can more easily ensure the progression of belief in another—like prayer. This conflict between religion and witchcraft was in the media spotlight in July 2015 when Pope Francis visited Bolivia, a nation that "*cherishes animal sacrifices and pagan worship.*"[28]

SUPERSTITION IN PRACTICE

Superstitious behavior is an evolutionary adaptation that, much like religion, probably served an important role in our ancestors' early development. But if superstition is rooted in our desire to survive in a dangerous world—our assumption of danger in the rustling grass—then what does that mean for the curious doubters? Skepticism may be a valuable trait in modern times, but that wasn't always the case, necessarily. Perhaps my desire to know the unknown would have led me to investigate the noise in the bush, which could have ended my bloodline. Superstition might have saved my life, and it may have been responsible for our ancestors' survival in general. Even evolutionary biologist Richard Dawkins, known for his strict adherence to science over faith, once joked about how "*being too scientific is a bad thing.*"

"*I had a cousin who as a little boy put his finger in the mains and got a shock,*" Dawkins said. "*So, he did it again just to make sure. He's a real scientist, but not very good for survival.*"

The fact is that, today, superstitions aren't about survival as much as they are about comfort. Some researchers even suggest the physical movements associated with certain superstitions, like knocking on wood or throwing salt, have an effect on us that is inherently reassuring. The authors of that study say those rituals "*reduce the perceived likelihood of anticipated negative outcomes because they involve avoidant actions that exert force away from one's representation of self, which simulates the experience of pushing away bad luck.*"[29] In other words, those who don't even believe in superstitious rituals could benefit (psychologically) from acting on them.

Knowing why humans behave this way is crucial. In order to better promote rational thinking and nonreliance on false sciences and paranormal explanations, it helps to better understand the phenomenon of superstition as it presents itself in various people and cultures. But superstition isn't unique to people—it's present in other animals, too. In fact, American psychologist and behaviorist B. F. Skinner showed that even lab pigeons exhibited similar behavior.[30] Skinner placed a number of hungry pigeons in a cage attached to an automatic food delivery system that sent food at various times regardless of the bird's actions. He found that the pigeons associated the coming of the food with whatever activities they were performing at the time, in much the same way humans might associate a prayer with a promotion at work. The test subjects invented their own rituals and repeated them based on the misconception that they were bringing the food. This is not unlike what we see in people, for instance, when a baseball player decides to wear his "lucky socks" every time he plays just because of that one home run he hit while wearing them.[31] Comedian and TV host Steve Allen succinctly described how, once belief in a superstition like prayer is established, it is further perpetuated rather easily. *"If you pray for rain long enough, it eventually does fall,"* he said. *"If you pray for floodwaters to abate, they eventually do. The same happens in the absence of prayers."*

Luck—the ultimate superstition—has been described by American illusionist Penn Jillette and others as *"statistics [or probability] taken personally."* In other words, luck—good or bad—is how we interpret events in our life. Statistically, some people (and even objects) are guaranteed to have more positive interactions than others because that is the nature of coincidence—and it works the other way, too, with negative experiences. In addition to that, our pattern-seeking minds have the ability and inclination to count *hits* and discount *misses*.[32] In some ways, the human brain is actually primed to reach and reinforce false conclusions (usually as some sort of mental shortcut), and many people take advantage of that fact when it comes to the perception of luck and to pseudoscience in general.[33]

Once our minds are made up that particular people, items, or actions bring beneficial results or are inherently "lucky," we tend to become more positive[34] and notice more events perceived as good luck (see chapter 7). The same thing happens with bad luck. A good example of this is the Friday the 13th superstition.[35] Friday the 13th (and the number 13 in general) is considered a bad **omen** in many cultures—so much so that it has spawned a series of horror films, resulted in increased rates of **triskaidekaphobia** (defined as a fear of the number 13), and even caused building owners to exclude the 13th floor from their construction plans[36]—but it's also considered by some to be good luck. Is there any truth to the bad-luck myth? Probably not. There is conflicting data,[37] but a 2008 study by the Dutch Centre for Insurance Statistics (CVS) actually showed that fewer reports of traffic accidents, fires, and theft occurred on Friday the 13th dates than on other Fridays.[38] Could it be because people are more careful those days, or that they just stay at home? No matter the reason, as Alex Hoen, a CVS statistician, notes, *"Statistically speaking, driving is a little bit safer on Friday 13th."*

The Friday the 13th superstition is thought to have Christian origins, with some experts suggesting the myth is based on religious beliefs surrounding the 13th guest at the last supper—Judas.[39] This is particularly relevant considering the fact that religious believers often exhibit similar behavior as those who believe in good and bad luck, especially as it relates to symbolic trinkets, markings, blessings, curses, and even statues.

WHY DO SO MANY PEOPLE BELIEVE?

The supernatural in general is appealing to many people for a lot of different reasons, but one of the keys is the *unknown* factor. We humans fear the unknown, which causes us to create **heavens,** hells**,** ghosts, **reincarnation** schemes, and more to save us from the greatest mystery of all: death. As Bertrand Russell wrote in his 1957 work entitled *Why I Am Not a Christian,* "*It is not rational arguments, but emotions, that cause belief in a future life. The most important of these emotions is fear of death.*" So, that fear is there and it contributes to belief in certain supernatural concepts, but we are also creative thrill-seekers who crave the unknown because the potential itself is interesting and exciting.[40] This leads us to invent aliens, psychics, and paranormal monsters of all kinds. For me, the key—the happy medium—is to be able to indulge our interest in these inherently mind-stimulating topics without having to actually *believe* they are real.

A great number of urban legends, bad-luck charms, and other superstitions are at least partially the result of various societies' attempts to control their populations' behavior through fear-based myths—and religions are no different. Today, most nations have comprehensive law enforcement and a judicial system, but that wasn't true in ancient times. Faith-based institutions were responsible for some of the first written legal codes, justice systems, and more, and for those to be successful the believers needed to be fearful of something much larger and more powerful than themselves. Whether it's fear of the unknown or fear of losing something valuable, fright is a powerful force that compels a lot of superstitious behavior. Jiddu Krishnamurti, who was an Indian philosopher and writer, described its role in the process quite well. He is quoted as saying, "*Fear is the destructive energy in man. It withers the mind, it distorts thought, it leads to all kinds of extraordinarily clever and subtle theories, absurd superstitions, dogmas, and beliefs.*"

While some argue there is an *upside* to fear,[41] that positive spin isn't often present when fear is mixed with important decision-making. For example, in the United States, scared travelers chose to fly less and drive more after the attacks of September 11, 2001, which killed almost 3,000 people. As a result of this shift to the more statistically dangerous method of transportation, Professor Gerd Gigerenzer, a German psychologist specializing in risk, estimates that an extra 1,595 Americans died in car accidents in the year following the tragedy.[42]

Fear and hope are just two emotions that can make some people believe in all sorts of unsupported ideas from a variety of sources, including holy books, conspiracy theory websites, and everything in between. But the good news is that an education in rationality, critical analysis, and evidence-based thinking is the cure for all of these faulty beliefs and the lapses in proper logic that cause them. Whether it's out of a deep-seated need to believe in something great and unknown or indoctrination akin to strict childhood religious instruction, people flock to all sorts of unsubstantiated claims as realities. Most of the time, this results in people convincing themselves (and others) that there's something supernatural when a natural explanation has *always* sufficed. It's true that, in some cases, we simply don't have a definitive answer and must be content with saying, "*I don't know.*" Other times, however, things are already explained sufficiently and believers continue to assume the presence of mysterious forces due to their own misunderstandings of the subject or the underlying facts. The bottom line is that, whether you believe in end-of-the-world prophecies, an all-powerful **Illuminati,** or the inerrancy of the Bible, you exhibit the same lack of critical thinking and blatant disregard for evidence. Religion, pseudoscientific claims, and all faith-based ideas thrive on the same weaknesses in normal human thinking, making critical thought the most important tool.

Over many thousands of generations, humans have invented witches, **demons**, and all sorts of nonnatural entities—usually in an attempt to explain what was at the time considered to be unexplainable. But what was unexplainable in those times may not be so now; something that is unknown isn't always *unknowable*. Many concepts that were once mysteries are now well understood as a result of rigorous testing, scientific inquiry, and observation over time. As our scientific understanding has evolved, we have learned, for instance, that it isn't demonic possession that causes illness, nor is it a god, angel, or **spirit** that prompts recoveries. Similarly, each of the billions of asserted supernatural claims throughout our long history—in every recorded case—has been shown to have a possible (and therefore more probable) natural explanation. This evolution of thought is exactly why most humans no longer pray to a Sun God, a God of the Sea, or a God of Love. The gaps in our knowledge that all gods and superstitions occupy are being filled up with every new discovery and with every new scientific breakthrough. It might be easier to pretend to know that gods, aliens, or ghosts are the cause of a particular action or event, but by understanding history we can see it's more honest to continue searching for the real answer.

"My practice as a scientist is atheistic. That is to say, when I set up an experiment I assume that no god, angel, or devil is going to interfere with its course; and this assumption has been justified by such success as I have achieved in my professional career. I should therefore be intellectually dishonest if I were not also atheistic in the affairs of the world."

—J. B. S. Haldane

NOTES

1. To be more precise, I'd say religions are belief systems that often incorporate hundreds or even thousands of different superstitions.

2. Kevin Schilbrack, "The Social Construction of 'Religion' and Its Limits: A Critical Reading of Timothy Fitzgerald," *Method & Theory in the Study of Religion* 24 (2012): 97–117.

3. Steven Pinker, "The Evolutionary Psychology of Religion," presented at the 2004 Annual Meeting of the Freedom From Religion Foundation.

4. "2014 Religious Landscape Study," Pew Research Center, conducted June 4–September 30, 2014.

5. David Freed and Idrees Kahloon, "Religion," *Harvard Crimson*, March 12, 2016, features.thecrimson.com/2015/freshman-survey/lifestyle/.

6. "'Nones' on the Rise," Pew Research Center, October 8, 2012, www.pewforum.org/2012/10/09/nones-on-the-rise/.

7. When asked to give a one-sentence definition of mythology, comparative mythologist and writer Joseph Campbell said, *"Mythology is what we call someone else's religion."*

8. Christopher Hitchens, "God Is Not Great," acceptance speech for 2007 Emperor Has No Clothes Award presented by the Freedom From Religion Foundation.

9. Steven V. Roberts, "White House Confirms Reagans Follow Astrology, Up to a Point," *New York Times*, May 3, 1988, www.nytimes.com/1988/05/04/us/white-house-confirms-reagans-follow-astrology-up-to-a-point.html.

10. Jerry A. Coyne, "Why Scientists Have No Faith in Science," *Slate*, November 14, 2013, www.slate.com/articles/health_and_science/science/2013/11/faith_in_science_and_religion_truth_authority_and_the_orderliness_of_nature.html.

11. Paul Bloom, "Scientific Faith Is Different from Religious Faith," *Atlantic*, November 24, 2015,http://www.theatlantic.com/science/archive/2015/11/why-scientific-faith-isnt-the-same-as-religious-faith/417357/.

12. "Faith," *The American Heritage Dictionary of the English Language* (New York: Houghton Mifflin Harcourt, 2000).

13. "Faith," Dictionary.com, www.dictionary.com/browse/faith.

14. "Faith," *Merriam-Webster*, www.merriam-webster.com/dictionary/faith.

15. "Faith," Oxford Dictionaries, www.oxforddictionaries.com/us/definition/american_english/faith.

16. Other descriptions of Christian faith in the Bible can be found in 2 Corinthians 5:7, 1 Corinthians 2:5, and more.

17. Blaise Pascal, a Christian philosopher, is also quoted as saying, "*Faith embraces many truths which seem to contradict each other.*"

18. This maxim is akin to *Hitchens's Razor*, "*What can be asserted without evidence can be dismissed without evidence.*" Christopher Hitchens, *God Is Not Great: How Religion Poisons Everything* (New York: Twelve Books, 2007), 150..

19. "*Superstition*," *Merriam-Webster*, www.merriam-webster.com/dictionary/superstitions.

20. Kevin R. Foster and Hanna Kokko, "The Evolution of Superstitious and Superstition-like Behaviour," Proceedings of the Royal Society of London B: Biological Sciences 276, no. 1654 (2009): 31–37.

21. Ewen Callaway, "Superstitions Evolved to Help Us Survive," *New Scientist*, September 10, 2008, www.newscientist.com/article/dn14694-superstitions-evolved-to-help-us-survive.html#.Ud16TfnVBsk.

22. Matthew 21:20–22: "*When the disciples saw this, they were amazed. 'How did the fig tree wither so quickly?' they asked. Jesus replied, 'Truly I tell you, if you have*

faith and do not doubt, not only can you do what was done to the fig tree, but also you can say to this mountain, 'Go, throw yourself into the sea,' and it will be done. If you believe, you will receive whatever you ask for in prayer.'"

23. Kevin S. Masters, Glen I. Spielmans, and Jason T. Goodson, "Are There Demonstrable Effects of Distant Intercessory Prayer? A Meta-analytic Review," *Annals of Behavioral Medicine* 32, no. 1 (2006): 21–26.

24. Leviticus 19:31: *"Do not defile yourselves by turning to mediums or to those who consult the spirits of the dead. I am the LORD your God."*

25. 1 Samuel 15:23: *"Rebellion is as sinful as witchcraft, and stubbornness as bad as worshiping idols. So because you have rejected the command of the LORD, he has rejected you as king."*

26. Exodus 22:18: *"Do not allow a sorceress to live."*

27. Jonathan C. Smith, *Pseudoscience and Extraordinary Claims of the Paranormal: A Critical Thinker's Toolkit* (New York: John Wiley & Sons, 2011).

28. Sarah Marsh, "In Land of Pachamama, Bolivians Hope for Pope of 'Good Intentions,'" Reuters, July 5, 2015, www.reuters.com/article/us-pope-latam-bolivia-idUSKCN0PE0E920150705>.

29. Reversing one's fortune by pushing away bad luck. Yan Zhang, Jane L. Risen, and Christine Hosey, *Journal of Experimental Psychology: General* 143, no 3 (June 2014): 1171–1184.

30. B. F. Skinner, "'Superstition' in the Pigeon," *Journal of Experimental Psychology* 38, no. 2 (April 1948): 168–172.

31. This is not to say, however, that all baseball players exhibit superstitious behavior. Babe Ruth famously said, *"I have only one superstition. I touch all the bases when I hit a home run."*

32. *"The root of all superstition is that men observe when a thing hits, but not when it misses."* —Francis Bacon

33. Helena Matute, Ion Yarritu, and Miguel A. Vadillo, "Illusions of Causality at the Heart of Pseudoscience," *British Journal of Psychology* 102, no. 3 (2011): 392–405.

34. Darke, Peter R., and Jonathan L. Freedman. "Lucky events and beliefs in luck: Paradoxical effects on confidence and risk-taking." Personality and Social Psychology Bulletin 23, no. 4 (1997): 378-388.

35. The fear of Friday the 13th is known as *"paraskevidekatriaphobia."*

36. *"My hotel doesn't have a 13th Floor because of superstition, but c'mon man …*

people on the 14th floor, you know what floor you're really on. 'What room are you in?' '1401.' 'No, you're not. Jump out of window, you'll die earlier!'" —Mitch Hedberg

37. C. D. O'Brien, "Friday the 13th: Doubly Unlucky," *British Medical Journal* 308, no. 6926 (1994): 473.

38. Tineke Van Der Struik, "Friday 13th Not More Unlucky, Dutch Study Shows," Reuters, June 13, 2008, uk.reuters.com/article/us-luck-idUKL1268660720080613>.

39. John Roach, "Friday the 13th Phobia Rooted in Ancient History," *National Geographic News*, August 12, 2004.

40. Eduardo B. Andrade and Joel B. Cohen, "On the Consumption of Negative Feelings," *Journal of Consumer Research* 34, no. 3 (2007): 283–300.

41. Maggie Penman, "Things That Go Bump in The Lab: Halloween And The Science Of Fear," *NPR*, October 27, 2015. www.npr.org/2015/10/27/450911424/things-that-go-bump-in-the-lab-halloween-and-the-science-of-fear.

42. James Ball, "September 11's Indirect Toll: Road Deaths Linked to Fearful Flyers," *Guardian*, September 5, 2011, www.theguardian.com/world/2011/sep/05/september-11-road-deaths.

4

BLURRED LINES
BETWEEN ATHEISM AND SKEPTICISM

"I believe in evidence. I believe in observation, measurement, and reasoning, confirmed by independent observers. I'll believe anything, no matter how wild and ridiculous, if there is evidence for it. The wilder and more ridiculous something is, however, the firmer and more solid the evidence will have to be."

—Isaac Asimov

You can believe in any claim in the whole entire world, except for the existence of gods, and still be an atheist. But if you are an atheist who hangs on to other irrational beliefs that don't hold water when met with serious inquiry, you aren't likely to be a skeptic, a naturalist, or a science-minded person in general.

Atheists have one thing in common: disbelief in deities (for any reason). This means that an atheist can believe in ghosts, psychics, witchcraft, homeopathy, unsubstantiated global conspiracy theories, and other superstitious, paranormal, and nonsensical claims, and still, in fact, be an atheist. You can be an atheist who believes in any number of nondivine supernatural things, but you can't be a scientific skeptic—someone who bases belief on empirical research—or a naturalist—someone who disbelieves in supernatural or spiritual forces in general.

Being an atheist doesn't make anyone a clearheaded and rational thinker, but, fortunately for us, there is hope. By promoting skepticism of all things unfounded and contrary to the scientific method, we can encourage the search for reality while helping to establish freedom from all magical thinking. And by advocating for rationality and logical reasoning, we can directly combat things like religion in government, prejudice and discrimination, and anything else that doesn't withstand scrutiny. Jennifer Hancock, a writer and speaker specializing in humanistic leadership, points out that critical thinking is *"not just for debunking religion."* Applied skepticism can benefit every aspect of your life, including medicine, marketing, politics, pseudoscience, theological nonscience, and interpersonal relationships, she says.

That's what's best about critical thought: when properly applied, it can positively affect every part of life—and every global issue. By helping people be more logical and reasonable, we can resolve all sorts of problems. Reasonable people are less likely to be religious fundamentalists, to perform racist acts, or to murder innocent people. In other words, we don't have to fight against religion directly to make the world a better place; we can simply spread critical thinking far and wide.[1]

WHAT IS RELIABLE EVIDENCE?

A person's stance on the existence of one or more deities is irrelevant to his or her belief in any other unsubstantiated forces or ideas, but gods and other religious claims are among the most popular unproven beliefs, so they can be connected in that sense. If you don't fall for the religion-based scams, that's great—but you should be able to apply the same logic to other claims that rely on blind faith. If you believe in ghosts but not gods, for instance, you might supply personal experience involving cold spots or EMF readings as evidence. But if your standard for evidence is that low, then holy books, reported visions and miracles, and so-called **intelligent design** should also count as "evidence" for god(s). An objective analysis tells us that those things aren't hard evidence, so instead of choosing the belief with which you're more comfortable or adopting both ideas, you should rethink your standard.

For scientific skeptics, the test to determine if belief is warranted comes down to one thing: empirical data. If you don't believe in something until it's been proven, you save yourself a lot of time and energy. If someone writes off the existence of Bigfoot, but entertains a belief in alien intervention because of eyewitness testimonies, then there is a clear contradiction that they must face and address. By maintaining a consistent and high standard for evidence, you can dismiss a huge number of lies and myth-based assertions using limited tests and a little scientific research.

By being consistent in our search for the truth, we can see that, whether it's a question of aliens on earth, ghosts, or gods, the evidence presented falls short of establishing any sort of otherworldly beings. Seeing this connection and demanding hard evidence for all extraordinary claims helps us not only shed false beliefs from our past but also avoid being tricked in the future. To exempt any idea from scrutiny leaves open the possibility of being deceived and, for that reason, all important claims should be subject to verification and evaluation based on available information from reliable sources (see chapter 15).

INHERITING BELIEF SYSTEMS

While people are certainly capable of reaching the right answer through incorrect or illogical methods, for me, the reasoning is what's important. Sometimes what we believe in isn't as important as why we believe in it, and whether or not we are able to reach conclusions based on rational thought processes. A good example of this would be an atheist who was born into a family of atheists and inherited that belief without giving it any consideration, in essence reaching the right answer through a bad process. If you were raised to believe a certain thing, it's important to analyze whether that belief is founded in reality or whether it's nothing more than a byproduct of obedience or convenience.

For me, being an atheist doesn't mean I hate god or even religion, or that I haven't looked into claims made by theists. It means that none of the extraordinary god-claims ever presented have met the burden of proof. As is the case with myself and many other nonbelievers, *atheism* can simply be the conclusion reached after looking for empirical evidence for the existence of deities and finding none. But that doesn't mean that every nonbeliever has applied that same standard of evidence to all other claims, and it is entirely possible for some people who are raised without gods and religion to be raised with (or raised to be susceptible to) other irrational beliefs.

A person born into a family that doesn't value religion, but does profess a strong belief in ghosts or psychics or other supernatural phenomena, might cling to those beliefs out of familiarity instead while disregarding religion and deities as unworthy of consideration. Just as many believers are indoctrinated with a particular religion, it is possible for families and cultures to teach the validity of other false beliefs in the same manner. In the case of an atheist who wasn't taught a religion, he might never have even considered or evaluated religious claims—and nonbelief may be the assumed default. While I do see childhood indoctrination of any unproven claim as inherently bad, I would still recommend that people who were raised secularly educate themselves about the world's religions as much as possible.

WHAT DOES "ATHEISM" REALLY MEAN?

Contrary to popular belief, atheism is not synonymous with *antitheism* and not all atheists actively fight against religion—or even against its influence in government. There are many nonbelievers who aren't activists, who don't oppose religion at all, or who are simply not interested in discussing any person's beliefs or lack thereof. In fact, there are a number of self-proclaimed atheists (some Buddhist, Taoist, Pagan, and even some LaVeyan Satanist atheists, for example) who are themselves religious. It's also important to note that there is no *group* necessarily associated with all atheists. If you don't actively believe deities exist, you're an atheist.

I am an atheist who also happens to be an advocate, but it's not all about religion or theism for me. I write about and investigate all sorts of unsubstantiated assertions because they are all the result of the same failure in the thinking process. Many of these ideas are also incredibly common, making them influential throughout the world. No matter where you live or who your family is, you are likely surrounded by myths that slowly attempt to creep into reality. I find that extremely interesting, but I also think we should do our best to combat their spread by avoiding faith-based beliefs in favor of an evidence-based worldview (at least on matters of great importance). In the past, I have emphasized much of my activism against the influence of religious beliefs because of their prevalence in society, but the fact is that, if belief in Santa Claus as a cosmic gift-giver were common among a large number of adults, and that belief was in turn used to shape legislation or justify the impediment of scientific research and of other people's rights, I would definitely spend more of my time refuting that myth.

For my part, unless I'm specifically addressing a belief's influence in culture, I try not to treat gods any differently from other unproven myths. They are the same to me at their very core: without hard evidence, there's nothing that justifies belief for me. I don't believe in the Abrahamic god for the same reason that I don't believe in Xenu, Thor, Zeus or, for that matter, in angels, **demons**, ghosts, wizards, or Santa. What I reject foremost is the assertion that a belief in any supernatural being or entity should be accepted, especially when mere faith—and not scientific evidence—is the justification.

ATHEIST VS. AGNOSTIC

To clarify, the terms *atheist,* a person who *disbelieves or lacks belief in the existence of God or gods,*[2] and *agnostic,* someone who *believes that nothing is known or can be known of the existence or nature of God,*[3] are not mutually exclusive. In fact, nobody *knows* (or *can* know) for sure whether or not gods exist, just as we don't know for sure any unfalsifiable forces don't exist. Whether we admit it or not, we are all functionally agnostic on many topics, including on the idea of a detached, deistic creator. Regardless of belief, you simply don't *know*. Throughout my discussions and debates on the topics of god(s) and religion, however, I've noticed a fairly consistent pattern: many people, religious and nonreligious alike, are under the false impression that anyone who is an atheist claims to *know* that deities couldn't possibly exist. I think this stems from the fact that those people are confusing *belief* with *absolute knowledge*. An atheist doesn't believe in gods, an agnostic doesn't know for sure, and both definitions can apply to me and many others. Agnostic doesn't mean *on the fence*; it means *without knowledge*. So, given those definitions, consider this: being an agnostic atheist means I accept what's known about the world, I don't believe in what's not known, and I don't pretend to know the rest.

I am an *agnostic atheist,* but I don't always include the *agnostic* moniker because I'm equally agnostic about every religion's proposed god(s) as I am about werewolves and vampires.[4] When it comes to man-made myths—stories that we can trace back to their origins through history—disbelief isn't *just* about a lack of evidence; there are other factors as well. In those cases, it's important to understand the belief, where it came from, and what purpose it may have served before confidently categorizing it as a human construct. But not all "divine" assertions are religious in nature—deists, polytheists, and other less-rigid adherents, for example, often believe in one or more general "forces" responsible for things like creation. While there is no scientific evidence supporting the existence of these detached deities, there is also no way for us to fully and adequately dispute the claims. I acknowledge that I can't know with certainty whether or not some generic, nonintervening god-figure exists somewhere in or outside of the cosmos, which is precisely why it doesn't make sense for me to believe in one. I address the possible existence for a deistic god, and why I don't worship one, in my second book, *Mom, Dad, I'm an Atheist.* Here is a relevant passage: *"If there is a Creator-God, it has used methods of creation that are indistinguishable from nature, it has declined to make itself known for all of recorded history, it doesn't intervene in affairs on earth, and has made itself impossible to observe. Even if you believe in that God … why would you think it would want to be worshiped?"*

So, if we are all agnostic, the next step is to find out if you're an agnostic *theist* or an agnostic *atheist.*[5] To find out, you just answer one simple question: "Do you actively believe in the existence of a god or gods?" Any person who declares themselves an *agnostic* to avoid answering this question should be able to analyze claims put forth by various people and religions about their respective deities, look at the evidence available, and form an opinion. They will still be agnostic, as we all are, but that doesn't stop them from either rejecting or accepting belief. For anyone interested in trying to define their own ideas in this way, I recommend looking at the facts and definitions themselves, as opposed to relying on what you've heard about them in the past. There is a lot of misinformation out there.

I also think it's important to mention that, while definitions are crucial to conveying ideas, sometimes it's more important to avoid getting hung up on terms like *agnostic* and *atheist.* Emotional objections to definitions are common when people don't want to associate themselves with a particular group or descriptor, which is seen most often when the relevant terms are cast as emotionally charged labels by others. So it may be best to deal with the ideas directly rather than be distracted by identification.

RIGOROUS SKEPTICISM IS MORE IMPORTANT THAN "ATHEISM"

Not all atheists are skeptics or naturalists, and some don't arrive at their position after analyzing evidence at all. Many people reject gods and religion not because they are unconvinced by all faith-based claims, but because they have issues with its organized nature or with their family's faith and its specific tenets. For instance, many people say they left their religion and became atheists because of other religious people and their behavior. While it's good that they got out of a situation they likely didn't choose in the first place, a distaste for the actions of fellow believers is not a very good reason to disbelieve in any claim. It can be a good excuse to start looking closer at the evidence, or a catalyst that causes you to disassociate yourself from a particular group, but it doesn't have any bearing on the deity question.

For nonbelievers who identify as such for non-evidence-based reasons, the move to nonreligiosity can be a much more emotional decision than for those of us who gave consideration to the arguments and data. Their step away from religion could be the result of anything—from a simple familial rebellion to a reaction against a negative or traumatizing experience within the faith—and it is not uncommon to see a return to religion later in life. But recognizing a lack of evidence through skeptical analysis is the only *good* reason to be an atheist (or to disbelieve in anything else, for that matter). Religious hypocrisy, separation of church and state, and human rights issues, for example, are unrelated to the existence of gods and should be treated as completely separate. I'm not an atheist because I don't like religion or its effects—that's an entirely different (yet arguably more important) question that has nothing to do with *belief* itself. I'm an atheist because of a distinct lack of real evidence for the existence of deities, which leaves me without reason to believe in any. I do care deeply about the negative effects religion has had on people and society as a whole, but that is not a component of my atheism. In fact, there are many religious people who also advocate for secularism and denounce violence in the name of faith.

If you're an atheist, it means you haven't fallen for the god gambit, but the existence of deities isn't the only commonly held yet likely false notion. Skepticism and critical thought protect from all forms of faith-based ideas. Although the god question is often one of the most controversial ideas for which we can utilize skepticism, it's not always the most relevant one. That's why it's important to stress critical thinking and reason in all areas of life above all else. I want to encourage those who reject the world's many god claims to apply the same skeptical scrutiny to ghosts, psychics, unsubstantiated conspiracy theories, and just about any topic—supernatural or not. By promoting evidence-based processes in a variety of situations, it's not only possible to help those who were indoctrinated into religion when they were too young to know better escape those confines, but also to keep people from being fooled by other false beliefs. In other words, saying you are an atheist only answers one question: "Do you believe in god(s)?" It is not a guiding force or dogma. Critical thinking and rationality, however, are much more. They are all-encompassing methods that can actually help you achieve, learn, and grow. As such, I don't care a lot about *atheism* per se. It just doesn't mean very much. Atheism, to me, is less important than secularism, skepticism, and logical thought (although it can be the result of all three of these things). In fact, atheism is actually most useful when it is a *byproduct* of skepticism. After all, skepticism is one of the primary reasons atheism is so crucial. If religion went extinct, atheism would be largely irrelevant, but skepticism and logical thinking processes will always be needed.

Being an atheist doesn't necessarily make you smart, skeptical, or even nonreligious. While there may be a correlation between the mentalities of those who blindly accept scriptural inerrancy and those who fall for other cons and schemes, some supernatural beliefs, far-fetched conspiracy theories, and faith-based notions have actually become a refuge for the faithful yet nonreligious. Consider how, according to some studies,[6] atheists and agnostics are up to 76 percent more likely than Christians to *believe in* the existence of **extraterrestrial** life,[7] despite the lack of unambiguous empirical evidence for their existence. It's not really about religion because, when you learn how to critically examine your preconceived notions, all sorts of unfounded beliefs are likely to fall away. If you base your disbelief in gods (or in anything else) on emotional reactions and rhetoric, and not on a lack of evidence, the conclusion isn't necessarily going to be helpful in other areas. If you learn to think critically, be skeptical, and demand evidence of all claims, however, you will probably end up *not believing* in all sorts of unproven ideas.

An evidence-based worldview doesn't just help you get to the right answer on one issue; it can also lead to additional logical conclusions and improve the way you form and analyze ideas over time. If you spend your time thinking about the *process* of thinking, and how to do it better, those changes will manifest. As is true with most positive behaviors, practice in this area does wonders. This isn't something you have to wait to do either. Learning how to look at the evidence and critique ideas should begin as early as possible. I think it's important to teach everyone, including young children, how to separate facts from falsehoods because indoctrination is such a powerful force and kids will often trust their parents or guardians implicitly.

SPIRITUALITY AND WONDER

I'm often asked whether or not an atheist must necessarily give up all forms of spirituality, and the simple answer is "No." If someone doesn't actively believe deities exist, he or she is an atheist and any other beliefs are irrelevant to that fact. That being said, spirituality—like religion—in its more popular forms generally presumes the presence of a **soul**, something that is indefinable, unprovable, and separate from the material, physical, and natural world. I must therefore refrain from believing in spiritual assertions that include a soul for the same reason I don't believe in all other supernatural claims: because they are by their nature unfalsifiable. As a scientific skeptic, I'm concerned with whether claims are supported by empirical research and can be repeated in a controlled setting.

To show believers the vagueness of the *soul* concept, on which spirituality is most often considered to be reliant, I've often asked them to attempt to explain this mystical spiritual life force to someone who has never been told about it. They obviously don't have any evidence to present—only words and feelings—so it is difficult to make a compelling case.[8] If you can define a soul and then show using the scientific method that it exists, I'll accept that information and move on, but until then it should be treated just like any other unsupported idea created by humans out of fear of what's "after" this life. That's not to mention the fact that, as Canadian experimental psychologist Steven Pinker points out, if we do have a soul, it is not so far out of reach after all. We have been able to change just about everything that makes us who we are, so that must mean we have power over the soul, too.

"*The supposedly immaterial soul, we now know, can be bisected with a knife, altered by chemicals, started or stopped by electricity, and extinguished by a sharp blow or by insufficient oxygen,*" Pinker says.

While most people seem to use *spirituality* as a byproduct of belief in the soul or in other supernatural forces, others define it a little bit differently. Instead of basing spirituality on a separation from the worldly, others do the opposite and associate it with a feeling of connection to the natural universe itself, or to other people or animals in general. Carl Sagan was one of those people. He said that he "*will feel free to use the word*" spirituality.

"*In its encounter with Nature, science invariably elicits a sense of reverence and awe. The very act of understanding is a celebration of joining, merging, even if on a very modest scale, with the magnificence of the Cosmos,*" Sagan wrote. "*Science is not only compatible with spirituality; it is a profound source of spirituality. When we recognize our place in an immensity of light years and in the passage of ages, when we grasp the intricacy, beauty and subtlety of life, then that soaring feeling, that sense of elation and humility combined, is surely spiritual.*"

Sagan's description of spirituality may not be accepted by everyone, but there is no doubt that he and others have overwhelming feelings often associated with it. This fact is in direct opposition to a claim made by Oprah Winfrey, who, in a 2013 interview with athlete, author, and motivational speaker Diana Nyad,[9] said atheists aren't atheists if they believe in "*awe*" and "*wonder*" and "*mystery.*" Regardless of what Winfrey and others may suggest, naturalists, including myself, are not devoid of the appreciation, awe, and wonderment that many consider to be other forms of so-called spirituality. In fact, I am genuinely amazed and intrigued by the many wonders and mysteries of the natural world, so much so that I see no need to invent the supernatural realm. I have found that being a scientific-minded person and looking for consistent results and data—only believing in exchange for solid evidence—has helped me ensure that my awe and wonder aren't wasted on fallacies.

I think realizing and being appreciative of the natural beauty of the world around us—and the interconnectedness of every living and nonliving particle in the universe—is something that a scientific and naturalistic worldview fosters. We are all made up of the same materials. The carbon, nitrogen, and oxygen atoms that make up our bodies and all other organic matter were forged when ancient stars died. In fact, recent studies suggest stardust itself contains complex organic matter.[10] We are a tiny part of the universe living this one life for which we make our own meaning and our own purpose. That is both beautiful *and* supported by the scientific consensus. As Neil deGrasse Tyson has said, "*So you're made of detritus [from exploded stars]. Get over it. Or better yet, celebrate it. After all, what nobler thought can one cherish than that the universe lives within us all?*"

So, am I spiritual? If belief in spirits or the supernatural is a prerequisite for spirituality, then no I am not a spiritual person. However, if you define spirituality as having a sense of inspiration or connection when it comes to the natural world, then I am. I have all the same positive emotions as "spiritual" people have, and I, too, am filled with hope—another trait nonbelievers are often accused of lacking. I just do my best to separate those feelings and wishes from the facts. Theoretical physicist Richard P. Feynman explains how a scientific view of certain things doesn't detract from their inherent beauty.

> *Poets say science takes away from the beauty of the stars—mere globs of gas atoms. Nothing is "mere." I too can see the stars on a desert night, and feel them. But do I see less or more? The vastness of the heavens stretches my imagination—stuck on this carousel my little eye can catch one-million-year-old light. A vast pattern—of which I am a part ... What is the pattern, or the meaning, or the why? It does not do harm to the mystery to know a little about it. For far more marvelous is the truth than any artists of the past imagined! Why do the poets of the present not speak of it? What men are poets who can speak of Jupiter if he were a man, but if he is an immense spinning sphere of methane and ammonia must be silent?*[11]

This form of complex wonder and spirituality, which can be derived from the natural world and even the scientific method itself, is powerful enough to give some people a deep sense of purpose. It's often said that naturalists don't have a *meaning of life*, but why does meaning have to come from a god or **afterlife** or even spirituality?[12] Can't it be anything? The pursuit of love? Or, perhaps, the progression of one's own bloodline? Shouldn't it be a person's individual responsibility to give life meaning, instead of having to rely on heavily flawed religious traditions and paranormal beliefs to provide the framework? Everyone's meaning in life is different. For me, it's accomplishing what I can in this short time we have on earth,[13] caring for my loved ones, and making a difference in the lives of those around me. I just don't see how supernatural beliefs are necessary for that. Australian writer, researcher, and science educator Lynne Kelly has addressed the common misconception that nonbelievers' lives are somehow without meaning or devoid of happiness:

"Some believers accuse skeptics of having nothing left but a dull, cold, scientific world. I am only left with art, music, literature, theatre, the magnificence of nature, mathematics, the human spirit, sex, the cosmos, friendship, history, science, imagination, dreams, oceans, mountains, love and the wonder of birth," she wrote.[14] *"That'll do me."*

That'll do for me, too.

THE CONSEQUENCES OF SKEPTICAL HYPOCRISY

While an atheist who bases his or her conclusion on evidence should logically apply that standard to other claims, that's not always the case. And if an atheist *does* fall prey to some other supernatural or otherwise unfounded claims, he or she is not a "bad atheist" —that person is just failing to practice scientific skepticism. And that's perfectly fine. But I'll continue to write about those flawed beliefs and how they are based on faith and trickery and little else, as well as about the fact that there's no scientific evidence that points to their validity, in the hopes that even one reader is able to apply some much-needed skeptical inquiry to beliefs that were previously unquestioned. It's important to note that, just as some atheists have told me to "stick to religion!" to preserve their other faith-based pseudoscientific beliefs, some self-proclaimed skeptics have told me to avoid religious topics entirely as though they're beyond reproach, usually out of blind reverence or childhood indoctrination. Those "skeptics" scoff at pseudoscience and nonreligious supernatural concepts, but often still believe Jesus walked on water or that Muhammad ascended to Heaven on a winged horse.[15]

By applying skepticism publically, and by drawing attention to commonly believed myths and superstitions of all kinds, we can demonstrate exactly why skepticism is a virtue—and why blind spiritual faith is a crutch. But let me be clear: religion and superstitions have their own evolutionary purposes and I don't *hate* them. In fact, I treat faith-based religions and other similar supernatural claims the same way I treat all unfounded beliefs and ineffective cultural rituals: with curiosity and detachment. I do think, however, that eventually we could reach a major milestone in the evolution of the human race—a time in which we no longer rely on superstitions and dogma to explain the unknown.

Some people believe *skepticism* is merely about doubting certain claims, which is understandable as it is another common usage, but it can actually be much more than that. Doubt is not scary; we should embrace it. But doubt also isn't enough . . . we need testing and problem solving to reach the right answers. Scientific skepticism, which utilizes all of these methods, can be an invaluable tool to help determine what is real and what is supported by data, without regard to prior beliefs. It is about not allowing personal biases, ideals, or faulty logic to persuade our beliefs. As Carl Sagan once said, *"Skeptical scrutiny is the means, in both science and religion, by which deep thoughts can be winnowed from deep nonsense."*

"We live in a world where unfortunately the distinction between true and false appears to become increasingly blurred by manipulation of facts, by exploitation of uncritical minds, and by the pollution of the language."

—Arne Tiselius

NOTES

1.   An evidence-based mentality can be extremely rewarding, and it is for this reason that some of my favorite messages I get are from people who say they were already atheists but that my work helped with skepticism in other areas.

2.   "Atheist," Oxford Dictionaries, www.oxforddictionaries.com/us/ definition/american_english/atheist.

3.   *"Agnostic,"* Oxford Dictionaries, www.oxforddictionaries.com/us/ definition/american_english/agnostic.

4.   Because every single person is agnostic about a vague deity figure, despite what they believe, the label isn't usually necessary.

5.   There are of course certain people who may not fit fully into either category, but this point is relevant to the vast majority of people across the world.

6. David A. Weintraub, *Religions and Extraterrestrial Life: How Will We Deal with It?* (New York: Springer, 2014).

7. Troy Mathew, "Science or Sacrilege? Atheists and Agnostics Are 76% More Likely than Christians to Believe in the Existence of Extraterrestrial Life," Survata Blog, September 19, 2013, www.survata.com/blog/science-or-sacrilege-atheists-and-agnostics-are-76-more-likely-than-christians-to-believe-in-the-existence-of-extraterrestrial-life/.

8. *"One can't write directly about the soul. Looked at, it vanishes."* —Virginia Woolf

9. "Soul to Soul with Diana Nyad: 'I'm an Atheist Who's in Awe,'" Oprah.com, www.oprah.com/own-super-soul-sunday/Soul-to-Soul-with-Diana-Nyad-Im-an-Atheist-Whos-In-Awe-Video.

10. Sun Kwok and Yong Zhang, "Mixed Aromatic-Aliphatic Organic Nanoparticles as Carriers of Unidentified Infrared Emission Features," *Nature* 479, no. 7371 (2011): 80–83.

11. Richard P. Feynman, Robert B. Leighton, and Matthew L. Sands. *Feynman Lectures on Physics* (Reading, MA: Addison-Wesley, 1964).

12. In *Mom, Dad, I'm an Atheist,* I address the claim that those who don't believe in god(s) have no meaning in their lives: "*I don't claim to know an over-arching 'Meaning of Life,' but I do operate under the understanding that life should not be lived under the pretense that it is simply a 'test' propagated by an invisible, intangible, Creator-God. And it should not be spent identifying with religious traditions and organized groups that, historically, have been at the root of a tremendous amount of oppression and violence.*"

13. "*The meaning of life is not to be discovered only after death in some hidden, mysterious realm; on the contrary, it can be found by eating the succulent fruit of the Tree of Life and by living in the here and now as fully and creatively as we can.*" — Paul Kurtz

14. Lynne Kelly, *The Skeptic's Guide to the Paranormal* (London: Allen & Unwin, 2004).

15. Qur'an, sura 17 (Al-Isra), ayah 1

5

WHAT'S THE HARM?

"I truly believe that claims of astrologers, psychics, spiritualists, mind-readers, spoon-benders, practitioners of complementary and alternative medicine, acupuncturists, faith healers, and creationists should be taken very seriously. Not because these claims may be true or false. Instead, I believe that extraordinary claims can have extraordinary consequences."
—Jonathan C. Smith

It's not gods, religion, psychics, alternative theories, or ghosts that bother me; it's any lapse in critical thinking with the potential to harm. People sometimes have difficulty identifying the negative effects of superstitions and false beliefs, particularly if they are holding the beliefs, but the harm is almost always there. That's because, while they may not always be used to directly justify slavery or war,[1] any idea that unwittingly disconnects someone from reality can be bad in the long run. I'm a skeptic because I demand evidence and I'm an activist because I demand a world free from the harms of faulty and misleading information.

FAKE NEWS

The harmful effects of misinformation stole national attention during the 2016 U.S. presidential election, when people questioned whether faulty reports—sometimes referred to as **"fake news"** — influenced the results in favor of President Donald J. Trump.[2] After the election, people finally started to see how propaganda and false beliefs could cause real damage,[3] but the term fake news quickly backfired and began to mean something entirely different.

In what seemed like no time at all, "fake news" was nothing more than a buzzword used by all sides to write off anything they disagreed with. Defending his popularity, Trump himself even stated that "*Any negative polls are fake news.*"[4] Alex Jones, a radio show host known for purveying false information and conspiracy theories through his Infowars.com website,[5] also jumped on the fake news bandwagon, claiming former Secretary of State Hillary Clinton is "*notorious for #fakenews.*"[6] This is despite the fact that InfoWars itself has been added to lists of fake news sites to avoid.[7] Now, I don't know if they're "FAKE NEWS," but I do know sites like InfoWars and Breitbart News, formerly run by Trump's chief strategist Stephen Bannon, have incredibly biased and poorly sourced content and opinions (see chapter 15).

ACTUAL MISINFORMATION (AND DISINFORMATION)

Identifying "real" fake news, and not that which has been written off as such, is of the utmost importance. Misinformation is necessarily bad because it isn't real *knowledge*, and people's faith-based notions impede scientific inquiry, provide false data upon which to base decisions, and discourage evidence-based thinking in general. So-called psychics, for instance, perpetuate false hopes and beliefs and provide inaccurate information on which some clients base their lives. This causes harm in the same way as homeopaths and other alleged **faith healers**, who encourage what are essentially placebos over real medicine, which can cause (and has caused) serious medical problems for many people. But proponents of psychics, ghosts, homeopathy, etc., don't just offer nontruths, provide false hope, and substitute placebo for reality. These modern snake oil-peddlers harm others in numerous ways, including by conning them out of their hard-earned money.

I'm an activist against fundamentalist religion because of the harm it causes to society, and an activist against all unsubstantiated beliefs in general because of the harm they cause to the mind and the individual. I advocate for rational skepticism and evidence-based thinking because I think having verifiably true ideas, in general, is more useful than having false beliefs. For starters, what people believe directly influences how they behave and how they vote, which means those beliefs often end up affecting others.[8] For example, a person who believes the Bible is divinely inspired might look at antigay passages contained within it and decide to fight against equal rights for same-sex couples. While this is not always the case and it's just one example, it shows how false beliefs can cause real harm to other people.

When seeking out specific information on the harm caused by faulty thinking, there is no better resource than *What's the Harm?*,[9] a website created by Tim Farley that has catalogued stories of more than 670,000 people who have been injured or killed as a result of someone not thinking critically. From **acupuncture** and **astral projection** to **vaccine** denial and witchcraft, *What's the Harm?* provides credible links to news articles showing how millions of people have lost billions of dollars—and sometimes their lives—in the pursuit or purveyance of false information.

WITCH HYSTERIA

One catalyst of great harm to humans throughout history has been the Bible's antiwitchcraft writings, which give us important information about how many Christians, Muslims, and Jews believe they are supposed to treat people thought to be witches. These passages most notably contributed to the infamous Salem witch trials—a series of hangings of people accused of witchcraft in Massachusetts in the late 1600s. There were 20 people killed in Proctor's Ledge in Salem as a result of these hearings,[10] which were often initiated by minor transgressions such as unusual behavior, and dozens of others were jailed for months.[11] Those killed during the trials included George Jacobs Sr., who was hanged on August 19, 1682. Jacobs was reportedly killed after failing to perfectly recite the Lord's Prayer, according to the Salem Witch Museum[12] and local historian David Goss.[13] Today, in the United States, there are no more wide-scale witch hunts. The practice of witchcraft itself, however, has been revived there by the contemporary Wicca movement—and Salem remains a hotbed for those who practice Pagan Witchcraft.[14]

You may think this issue has been resolved, but the antiwitch sentiment inspired by the Hebrew Scriptures *and* the New Testament still causes enormous issues today throughout the world. In Saudi Arabia, for instance, religious police continue to pursue so-called magical crimes and alleged witches are often put to death.[15] Accusations of witchcraft are also especially prominent in parts of Africa, where increasing allegations against kids actually *"pushes children towards traffickers"* in the region. Researchers at United Kingdom–based charity Stepping Stones Nigeria and the Child Rights and Rehabilitation Network (CRARN), which was formed in 2003 to shelter children who had been accused as part of a literal witch hunt that killed 120 people in six weeks, say the belief in child "witches" in Akwa Ibom State, Nigeria, affects people of all different backgrounds. That includes *"the literate and illiterate, the wealthy and poor, the law enforcement agents, social welfare workers law makers and most specifically the leaders of revivalist Pentecostal churches,"* according to a paper presented by Stepping Stones.[16]

"Such people believe that a mysterious, spiritual spell is given to a child through food and/or drink. The child who eats this spell, is then called out in the night where his soul will leave the body to be initiated in a gathering of witches and wizards," Gary Foxcroft, the group's program director, wrote in the report. He further noted that the initiated child *"will then have the spiritual power to cause widespread destruction, such as murdering innocent people and causing diseases like HIV/AIDS, malaria, hepatitis, typhoid and cancer."*

"This belief is supported and propagated by many pastors in the local churches," Foxcroft added. *"Stepping Stones Nigeria and CRARN strongly feel that the pastors who promote the belief in child 'witches' often do so to extract fees for 'delivering' the child(ren)."*

Foxcroft and others who protest the witch hunts in Africa say approximately 15,000 children have been labeled witches in the states of Akwa Ibom and Cross River, and the problem is spreading to other areas such as Nepal. Additionally, researchers report that around 50,000 kids have been accused of witchcraft in the Democratic Republic of Congo.[17] The majority of the adolescents accused have been completely abandoned and left to their own devices on the streets, according to child advocates in the region.[18] In a study conducted by the United Nations Children's Fund (UNICEF),[19] which provides long-term humanitarian services to children, researchers found that young people accused of witchcraft in parts of Africa *"may be killed, although more often they are abandoned by their parents and live on the street."*

*These children are more vulnerable to physical and sexual violence
and to abuse by the authorities. In order to survive and to escape
appalling living conditions, they use drugs and alcohol. Often victims
of sexual exploitation, they are at increased risk of exposure to sexually
transmitted diseases and HIV infection.*

The report from UNICEF's Regional Office for West and Central Africa
further states that the frequency of witchcraft accusations against children
is growing and that the issue *"deserves greater attention from governments."*
The persecution of witches has become a *"lucrative business"* for revivalist,
charismatic, or Pentecostal churches in many countries, according to the
authors of the report.

*Their pastor-prophets fight against witchcraft in the name of God,
identifying witches through visions and dreams, and then offering
treatment—divine healing and exorcism—to the supposed witches.
This "spiritual" work, often of a violent nature, reinforces beliefs in
witchcraft and increases accusations.*

Witchcraft causes harm to more than just those who stand accused.
In some regions, for instance, people with albinism have been hunted
and killed due to the mistaken belief that their body parts are good luck.
Approximately 56 albinos have been killed for their body parts in Tanzania
and the eastern Burundian provinces on or near Tanzania's border, according
to a Red Cross advocacy report.[20] Benjamin Radford, a research fellow and
investigator with the Committee for Skeptical Inquiry, has pointed out
numerous other examples of harm to albinos resulting from false beliefs in
witchcraft.

"*Throughout Africa witch doctors are consulted not only for healing
diseases, but also for placing (or removing) magic curses or bringing luck in love
or business,*" Radford wrote for *Discovery News*.[21] "*The belief and practice of
using body parts for magical ritual or benefit is called muti. Muti murders are
particularly brutal, with knives and machetes used to cut and hack off limbs,
breasts, and other body parts from their living victims.*"

A STORY OF PSYCHIC DECEPTION

Harm from false beliefs comes in many forms and there are a seemingly infinite number of examples. But when I think about the billions of dollars people have spent on false hope and faux remedies—and the wasted time and emotional energy spent pursuing these fruitless endeavors—one story sticks out as especially destructive to those who were duped. That is the tale of self-proclaimed psychic and medium Sylvia Browne, who died in November 2013 at age 77.[22]

Prior to her death, Browne made headlines when she falsely predicted the death of Amanda Berry, who was kidnapped in 2003 and escaped from her captors early in May 2013,[23] and reminded the world of the damages that can be caused by high-profile psychics who pretend to have a supernatural "gift."

Browne made the **prediction** in November 2004 on Montel Williams' syndicated television show, where she was a weekly guest for many years. Browne reportedly told Louwana Miller, Berry's late mother, that she could "*see*" Berry's jacket in a dumpster with "*DNA on it.*"[24]

"*She's not alive, honey,*" Browne told Miller on *The Montel Williams Show*. "*Your daughter's not the kind who wouldn't call.*"

Miller, who died in March 2006, said she believed Browne "*98 percent.*" Miller never saw her daughter again, and would never know that she was still alive. In 2013, Berry escaped the home where she had been held captive for nearly nine years and called the police, who rescued her and two other victims.

But that wasn't the first time one of Browne's lies caught up to her. In fact, in 2003, also on Montel Williams' show, Browne similarly told Pam and Craig Akers that their son Shawn Hornbeck, who had been missing since October 2002, was not alive.

Browne told the Akers that their son was dead, near two jagged rocks, within a 20-mile radius of where he was taken. Hornbeck, by then 15 years old, was found alive in January 2007.[25]

In 1999, in yet another instance of harmful psychic reporting, Browne told the grandmother of an abducted girl that she had been taken into slavery in Japan. The grandmother of Opal Jo Jennings was tortured with the idea that the girl could be suffering in that way, but it was eventually discovered that the girl had already been dead for a long period of time—

and all of Browne's so-called predictions about her were entirely made up.

Browne hasn't been the only alleged psychic peddling faulty information. Even today, tens of thousands of people claim they can predict the future, read others' minds, or know otherwise inaccessible information, and charge money to tell people their ideas. The problem, of course, is that no psychic has ever scientifically proven his or her ability (see chapter 11).

Many people have lost hundreds of thousands of dollars in schemes perpetrated by psychic con artists, with a great number even losing their homes and families. Some, as in the cases referenced here, were tormented with faulty information about their missing loved ones. It's indisputable that some so-called seers have caused immeasurable harm to their victims.

HARM IN ALL ITS FLAVORS

I advocate for rational skepticism toward all types of claims because every superstition, as well as every supernatural and irrational belief and lapse in critical thinking, has the potential to harm the believer or society in one way or another. By being consistent in our application of skepticism across the board, and encouraging others to do the same, we can make sure there are fewer false beliefs in the world. In turn, we will make the world a better place.

While there are a lot of *big* problems to which religion and superstition contribute, harm can even come from something as benign as a symbol or omen that causes a person to behave differently than they would under normal circumstances, thereby altering events and outcomes. When I see people going out of their way and potentially causing harm to themselves to avoid things that they believe cause bad luck, for instance, I can't help but see a self-fulfilling **prophecy**. Instances like this remind me of a quote by Chrysler Corp. founder Walter Chrysler, who said, "*The reason so many people never get anywhere in life is because when opportunity knocks, they are out in the backyard looking for four-leaf clovers.*" A believer might be inconvenienced in any number of ways in his or her attempts to avoid negative repercussions that only exist in the mind, and this is true with many faulty beliefs. We see this phenomenon any time a person makes bad decisions in the world based on a piece of flawed information. Unsubstantiated beliefs can also be harmful because they inherently lead to other similarly incorrect ideas—once you've accepted one notion on dubious sources or blind faith, others come easier, too. That said, as long as you are careful not to impose your beliefs on other people—and you're intellectually honest in your approach—you can limit the harm you cause to others through your delusions.

Even an idea as simple as **water dowsing (divining)** can cause real harm and false hope. In early 2014, with California facing one of the most severe water shortfalls in the state's history, Gov. Jerry Brown declared a drought state of emergency, calling on Californians to conserve water in every way possible. In such desperate times, many dowsers for hire— who practice a pseudoscientific craft that has never been established scientifically—reported that requests for their services were more popular than ever.[26] However, according to the U.S. Geological Survey (and scientific consensus), so-called "successful" water dowsing ventures are reported because "*in many areas underground water is so prevalent close to the land surface that it would be hard to drill a well and not find water.*"[27] Other forms of dowsing, including those used in the search for oil, buried metals, and explosives, have also been adopted by governments and law enforcement agencies, forcing taxpayers to foot the bill despite the fact that their success rate is "*no better than random chance.*"[28]

It isn't just dowsers taking advantage of droughts who exploit the public's fear—it's a common tactic for charlatans who knowingly try to promote their brand of superstition. In March 2014, for instance, when Malaysia Airlines Flight 370 disappeared mid-flight, people who claimed to be psychics came out of the woodwork. A number of purported seers said they *knew* what happened to the plane, but their answers were extremely diverse and often contradictory. The responses ranged from "*The plane was hijacked by several onboard*"[29] to "*The plane went down somewhere with its passengers still alive,*"[30] and everywhere in between. As expected, however, none of these prophecies yielded any useful information that proved to be helpful for investigators involved.

HARM TO ANIMALS

Humans aren't the only beings negatively influenced or affected by our superstitious tendencies. One example of interspecies harm stems from demand for rhino horns—often used in traditional Chinese medicine (TCM) and as a status symbol to portray success—based on unfounded ideas that they can treat fever, rheumatism, gout, snakebites, **hallucinations**, typhoid, headaches, and even "devil possession." Rhino poaching hasn't been curtailed by the prevalence of data in the information age, which makes scientific evidence showing the inefficacy of rhino horn readily available. In fact, in 2012, a record number of 668 rhinos were killed across South Africa.[31] There is a thriving illegal market for rhino horn despite the fact that claims made about it—including all "medicinal" uses and the assertion that the horn is an aphrodisiac—are completely and demonstrably false. This is primarily because not enough people value the scientific findings involved. The information is there, but it's not being absorbed.

Tigers in India and China are also killed due to the fictitious belief that their bones can treat rheumatism, arthritis, and impotence, despite the fact that these alleged cures have never been shown scientifically.[32] Rhinos and tigers are just two of the many nonhuman animals harmed by our false beliefs, and we see incredibly similar situations when it comes to use of antelope and buffalo horns, deer antlers, and other items in TCM.[33] Another example of our tendency to harm animals through our own false beliefs is the endangered bird trade in Hyderabad, India, where many people believe releasing certain types of birds will bring luck and ward off evil. Traders at the Murgi Chowk (literally "chicken corner") market openly sell endangered owls, kestrels, parrots, and more.[34] These aren't isolated incidents, either. In November 2014, about 5,000 buffaloes were slaughtered in one day to appease the Hindu goddess Gadhimai in a barbaric ritual that takes place every five years.[35]

Even black cats, which in some areas represent the coming of bad luck, can suffer and die as a result of human superstitions. In fact, black cats *and* dogs are often less likely to be adopted from shelters than differently colored felines for a variety of reasons, including cultural perceptions. This is often referred to as "black dog syndrome."[36] A study published in the *Open Veterinary Science Journal* in 2013 further revealed that black cats require the longest time to adopt in part because they "*continue to be plagued by a negative association with superstition, specifically—magic and witches.*"[37]

This connection with magic and witches may lead some people to select cats of other colors. To help mitigate the negative ramifications of poor photogenic properties and an association with superstition, it is suggested that shelter staff pay more attention to the naming of black cats, refraining from "classic" black animal names (e.g., Blackie, Gypsy, Midnight, etc.). It is possible that "cute" or "human" names might help black cats.

These are just a few examples of the many times humans have killed or tortured other animals based on our own false beliefs, and we will likely never stop this behavior, but that's no reason to give up. It's a reason to fight harder to promote an evidence-based worldview. If even one healthy, loving animal is passed over for adoption (and likely euthanized as a result) because of superstitious thinking, that's a life that could have been saved through nothing more than the application of skeptical scrutiny.

WHERE IS THE LINE?

The potential for superstitions to harm seems to come most often when they are taken too seriously by believers, which can cause them to rely solely on magical thinking to solve their or others' problems—even after experiencing consistent failure with that approach. The problems begin when people consider their faith-based notions to be more valuable than facts, and they are made much worse when those believers attempt to force others to comply with (and therefore give credence to) their supernatural ideas. This regularly occurs when superstitious or religious people in power legislate around their particular beliefs, but, as Danish journalist Flemming Rose said in his piece on free expression and cartoons depicting the prophet Muhammad,[38] *"if a believer demands that I, as a nonbeliever, observe his taboos in the public domain, he is not asking for my respect, but for my submission. And that is incompatible with a secular democracy."*

Superstition in politics is arguably its most harmful incarnation, but granting special treatment to even the most minor religious and other supernatural claims makes it easier for myths to spread in place of reality. So, when you allow "good" supernatural beliefs—or what you deem positive aspects of those beliefs—to affect you or the population in general, you might unintentionally make it more acceptable to believe in and legislate the harmful ones. If you argue that faith is always valuable and must be respected at all costs, you make it seem virtuous to believe that rocks have healing powers and give credence to the false notion that rhino horn magically cures a number of medical problems or improves the user's sex life.

Even within the natural realm, false beliefs and failures in the process of thinking and evaluating ideas are likely to cause harm by creating distracting mysteries where none actually exist. Alternative theorists, for instance, regularly "cry wolf" when there are potentially real conspiracies to uncover through investigative journalism—and not wild conjecture and imagination (see chapter 15). Not only do these speculation-based conspiracy theories distract from real problems and dull critical thinking skills, but they can also cost lives in a number of ways, including through denial of vaccines.

ANTI-VAX MOVEMENT

Those who fight against immunizations exist on a spectrum. Some anti-vaccination advocates merely assert, despite scientific consensus stating otherwise, that pharmaceutical vaccines are dangerous and should be avoided. They continue to make this claim even though a review of 166 independent studies found that serious adverse events associated with vaccines "*are extremely rare and must be weighed against the protective benefits*" that they provide.[39] Others, however, have more far-fetched claims, such as that vaccines do not work at all, or that they are part of a government-sanctioned plan to kill people and decrease the world population. Somewhere on this scale, you'll find those who claim that the measles, mumps, rubella (MMR) vaccine causes autism—an idea put forth in a 1998 paper by a then-doctor named Andrew Wakefield. Despite the fact that this claimed vaccine-autism link has so been extensively debunked—including through a scientific review by the U.S. Institute of Medicine, which found that "*the evidence favors rejection of a causal relationship between thimerosal–containing vaccines and autism*"[40]—that Wakefield's copublishers retracted their work,[41] and that Wakefield was barred from practicing medicine for "*serious misconduct*" related to his discredited study,[42] the myth is still widely believed. This particular false claim continues to be accepted by many people for a number of reasons, including the existence of high-profile **anti-vax** activists like former Playboy centerfold Jenny McCarthy,[43] who has admitted to receiving her degree from "The University of Google."[44] Even President Donald Trump, prior to taking office, made statements promoting the fraudulent link between the MMR vaccine and autism to his millions of followers on Twitter. He repeated that concern as president, as well.[45] Fortunately, McCarthy, Trump, and others who spread similar ideas are not unopposed. There are a number of vaccination advocates, such as Dr. Paul A. Offit, the director of the Vaccine Education Center at the Children's Hospital of Philadelphia,[46] who work to counteract the misinformation disseminated about vaccines. Danielle McBurnett Stringer, a pediatric nurse practitioner who runs the "Kid Nurse" blog covering health issues, even encourages people with anti-vaccine tendencies to "*follow the money!*"

"*Yes please! Let's look at that. I DO NOT vaccinate children because it is profitable to me. My office, as well as all the other pediatric offices I know of, fronts thousands of dollars every month to pay for vaccines,*" Stringer wrote.[47] "*We are lucky if we break even. We order vaccines, and then we pray that insurance companies or the Vaccines For Children Program pay us back for them. Sometimes they do, sometimes they don't.*"

Another reason the myth of an autism and vaccine connection persists is because of timing: children often begin showing signs of autism in their first few years of life, which is around the same time they might receive MMR inoculations. Because of this coincidence, some parents fall for a classic logical fallacy known as *post hoc, ergo propter hoc*, Latin for, "*After this, therefore because of this,*" which represents the flawed logic that serves as the basis for superstition itself. From this perspective of coincidental timing, we can see that saying vaccines cause autism is like saying puberty causes high school or that grey hair leads to death.

Media has also played its role in the perpetuation of the alleged vaccine-autism link. Nobert Schwarz, provost professor of psychology and marketing at the University of Southern California, Dornsife College of Letters, Arts & Sciences, specializes in human judgment and writes about how misinformation regarding the MMR vaccine has spread online and in news media. He says false information of any kind "*is difficult to correct.*"

"*Once people have accepted an erroneous belief, they often hold on to it despite abundant evidence that speaks against it,*" Schwarz said in response to a measles outbreak that affected at least 110 Californians between December 2014 and February 2015. "*The repetition of misinformation makes media reports a conduit for false beliefs even when the report attempts to correct them.*"

The better alternative is to only provide correct information without repeating erroneous claims."

So, what's the harm? These people can believe what they want, right? That's true, but vaccine denial doesn't just hurt the deniers. Distrust for vaccines and other helpful technologies causes people to refrain from protecting their children, even if they themselves received childhood inoculations, and that can have even more disastrous effects when others become involved. When clusters of people refuse to get an important vaccination, it often leads to an outbreak of the disease that can cost lives. For example, California's 2010 outbreak of whooping cough, or pertussis, which resulted in more than 9,000 cases and 10 deaths, was reportedly linked to groups of people refusing immunizations.[48] In June 2014, California's public health department said there had been 800 new pertussis cases in just two weeks, calling the problem an "*epidemic.*" Between January 1, 2014, and June 10, 2014, there had been more than 3,458 new cases, according to the agency.[49]

Fortunately, some people do learn their lesson. A woman named Tara Hills from Ottawa, Canada, for instance, was a part of the anti-vaccination movement until she learned about the 113-case measles outbreak linked to Disney theme parks in California.[50] After looking more closely at the evidence and discarding her biases, she decided to put together a catch-up vaccination schedule for her children. But before it could go into effect, all seven of her children began showing symptoms of whooping cough and they were placed in quarantine.[51] Hills says her anti-vax tendencies stemmed from a firm distrust in "*civic government, the medical community, the pharmaceutical industry, and people in general.*"

"*By default, I had excluded all research available from any major, reputable organization,*" Hills wrote in a blog entry called "Learning the Hard Way: My Journey from #AntiVaxx to Science."[52] "*Could all the in-house, independent, peer-reviewed clinical trials, research papers and studies across the globe ALL be flawed, corrupt and untrustworthy?*"

The attitude of distrust Hills described is common among vaccine deniers and other conspiracy theorists, and is exhibited in a variety of situations. We saw this clearly in 2015 when a woman died from measles in Clallam County, Washington,[53] and anti-vaxxers insisted the death was caused (or faked) by the government.[54] Dr. Bob Sears, a pediatrician, author of *The Vaccine Book* and *The Autism Book*, and promoter of unorthodox vaccine schedules, stressed in a Facebook post that this death couldn't be traced back to the Disney outbreak. The anti-vax comments on his post included statements such as, *"there's an agenda behind it: MANDATORY VACCINES AT THE FEDERAL LEVEL"* and *"Getting the fear nice and deep to then roll out adult mandatory vaccines!"*[55] This death was memorable, but, unfortunately, the reaction from the public is not all that unique. Cries of *"conspiracy!"* were even heard when the children's TV show *Sesame Street* introduced an autistic character named Julia.[56] Mike Adams, the so-called health ranger who founded alternative medicine and conspiracy theory site *Natural News*, actually wrote that Julia's appearance was *"an attempt to 'normalize' vaccine injuries and depict those victimized by vaccines as happy, 'amazing' children."*[57]

Small groups of non-vaccinators can cause outbreaks like those in California because some people—primarily children and those with certain ailments—have little to no immune system, are allergic to the ingredients, or are otherwise unable to have many vaccines. This makes them reliant on others to be protected, a helpful process known as **herd immunity**.[58] Steven Fox, assistant professor of clinical medicine at the Keck School of Medicine at the University of Southern California, explains that a number of people, including infants, cannot be vaccinated against certain conditions for medical reasons.

"They're much more susceptible to measles complications if they do become infected," Fox said. *"In order to protect them, at least 95% of the people in their local community, school, or daycare need to be immunized."*

Because of this need for herd immunity, some governments impose what many anti-vax activists would call *"forced vaccinations."* I have yet to see a city or state with mandatory vaccination laws, but some do make immunizations a requirement for entry into public schools (with or without religious exemptions). This is because, at that point, you are putting other people at risk and forcing them to face a potentially life-threatening situation. These laws do allow for parents to make the vaccination decision on their own and provide them with the option of home school to keep others safe.

I wanted to find out more about this vaccination issue, so I talked to Dr. Mike G., a board-certified pediatrician in Northern California. Dr. Mike G. has an M.D. from the University of Michigan and a B.S. and M.S. in biological sciences (with a focus on molecular biology) from Stanford

University. He says he's never witnessed a serious negative reaction that he thought was related to a vaccine.

"I just had a child come down with RSV (respiratory syncytial virus) bronchiolitis after vaccination, but given that there's a lot of RSV going around town right now, and given that vaccines can't cause RSV, I'm reasonably certain that this wasn't a vaccine reaction, even though it would count as an 'adverse event,'" Dr. Mike G. told me in an interview.

McAfee: What are your thoughts on the U.S. government's National Vaccine Injury Compensation Program (NVICP)? Should its existence make people think twice about administering vaccines to their children?

Dr. Mike G.: I think that it's one solution to the problem. The problem with trying to compensate people who have had adverse events after vaccines is that just about anyone can make this claim and the burden of proof is quite low. So the first option is to litigate every claim. If that were done, my suspicion is that few claims would be successful, but the vaccine manufacturers would have to pour enormous amounts of money into their legal defense for literally tens of thousands of claims each year, no matter how frivolous. So the other option is to simply settle these claims. That's what the NVICP is. It's an organized method to settle these claims without having to spend billions of dollars on legal fees each year. In this case, plaintiffs don't have to prove that the vaccine caused the adverse event.

McAfee: In the last few years, there have been several outbreaks of diseases that were once thought to be extinct in the developed world. Do you expect that trend to continue?

Dr. Mike G.: I do expect it to continue unless vaccination becomes compulsory. When parents born in 1990 have never seen a case of polio or measles these diseases do not scare them the way they did parents born in the 1950s or 1960s. Vaccines have become a victim of their own success and they have been so successful in eradicating these diseases that modern parents often do not understand how awful these diseases were.

McAfee: Do you consider the anti-vaccination movement a "first-world" problem? Do you see this type of opposition to immunizations in less-developed nations?

Dr. Mike G.: We do see it in less-developed nations, but much less so. My practice consists of lots of patients whose parents are first-generation immigrants from places like Vietnam, Mexico, and India. None of those parents ever refuse vaccines. Particularly my Indian parents, who have actually seen polio, cannot fathom why anyone would refuse these vaccines.

McAfee: What do you consider the most harmful aspects of the anti-vaccine movement? What problems does it cause?

Dr. Mike G.: I think that it falls into a larger group of phenomena having to do with a culture of ignorance, in which anyone with a scientific education is to be distrusted. It means that people will do things to harm themselves, harm their children, and harm the environment because they aren't going to listen to those pointy-headed scientists. We see it with every form of scientific denialism, be it GE (genetically engineered) crops, be it global warming, or be it vaccines. To quote Carl Sagan: "We live in a society that is highly dependent on science and technology in which few people understand science and technology."

McAfee: As a doctor, do you get paid extra for people receiving vaccines? Do you get all your immunizations for free?

Dr. Mike G.: My employer pays me a small "quality of care" bonus if a certain percentage of patients are vaccinated. It's worth about 1% of my annual income. The insurance companies (not the drug companies) pay my employer a quality bonus if our overall vaccination level is above a certain threshold. Remember, drug companies don't pay us; we pay them by purchasing their products. I think a lot of people don't understand how the money flows. Here's how it flows:

The patient pays their insurer, who pays us. We then pay the distributor who pays the manufacturer. So at no point does money ever flow from the manufacturer to the physician. And if the insurance company wants everyone to get their vaccines, then that right there

is proof to me that the insurance companies know that the vaccines are not harmful. If they were as dangerous as anti-vaxxers claim, no insurance company would want to pay for a product that makes their customers sicker. It would just cost the insurer more money.

McAfee: Anti-vaxxers often argue that doctors and those who work for pharmaceutical companies know vaccines are dangerous and/or ineffective, but promote them anyway because they receive compensation. Do you think those in the medical field are more or less likely to have their children vaccinated?

Dr. Mike G.: I do know a few physicians who have delayed vaccines on their own children. I don't know any pediatricians who have, though. And I'll add that of the doctors who delayed vaccines on their own kids, I've thought that most of them weren't very good doctors for other reasons before I even knew about their own practices. I try to stay out of my colleagues' personal health decisions as much as possible unless I'm caring for their kids.

McAfee: Why do you think some people are more likely to trust a celebrity's opinion than that of a licensed physician?

Dr. Mike G.: I think that people who trust celebrities have already made up their minds first. So it's an echo chamber.

McAfee: What do you say to those who insist vaccines aren't what eliminated polio and other major ailments that once plagued the country? I think the most common argument is that "indoor plumbing, sanitation, and healthy foods" were the real catalysts for their demise.

Dr. Mike G.: India just eliminated polio last year. Not exactly a model of modern plumbing and organic food. They did it through mass vaccination. If plumbing, healthy food, and sanitation were responsible for polio eradication, places like India and Botswana would never have eliminated polio.

McAfee: What are your thoughts on faith healing? Do you think it can lead people to reject real medicine and suffer or die as a result?

Dr. Mike G.: Well, what I think is less important than what has

happened. Certainly many children have died of preventable and/
or curable conditions because their parents had faith in either the
supernatural or the magical healing powers of common kitchen
ingredients.

*McAfee: Is there anything you'd like to add about vaccinations or the harms of
the anti-vaccination movement?*

Dr. Mike G.: I think that the anti-vaccine movement turned their hand
when they started opposing vitamin K injections for newborns. When
people who think vitamins can cure anything start opposing a vitamin,
I think it became obvious that the fear was about the needle. A lot of
anti-vaccine literature shows a MASSIVE syringe with a large-gauge
needle being used to inject some evil-colored (red, yellow) liquid into
the wrong body part of a child (you'd never inject an infant in the
deltoid).

I think that one of the biggest things that the pharmaceutical
industry could do to combat this movement is to eliminate the needle.
There are promising technological solutions to this. Vaccines can be put
on patches that are stuck to the child's skin or supersonic jet injectors
could be used. Nobody likes watching their kid cry as they get stuck
with needles. Anti-vaxxers have been around since the dawn of vaccines
and they're not ever going to go away, but I think that getting rid of the
needle would help a lot.

* * *

It's not just psychics, witch hunters, and anti-vax spokespeople who cause all
the harm. Nearly every single proponent of supernatural beliefs inherently
provides a form of bad information, many at great expense—monetarily
and otherwise—to the believers. Harm is commonplace with businesses
and practices that rely on unproven and unseen mysteries because these
positions attract people who want and are able to take advantage of those
who don't know any better. Even if they don't physically, emotionally, or
financially hurt people, however, all religious and supernatural beliefs, as
well as fraudulent medical studies and false claims about massive cover-ups,
detract from real scientific endeavors. As a result, these flawed ideas and
those who continue to promote them (sometimes inadvertently) encourage

people to distrust science and peer review—and make them more likely to accept pseudosciences and baseless allegations as realities.

I wrote this brief poem to demonstrate my desire to fight all false claims, regardless of their source or nature, and help those who might otherwise become victims:

FENDING OFF WHAT'S FAKE

MY GOAL IS TO KEEP PEOPLE FROM BEING FLEECED BY THEIR PRIESTS, OR SCAMMED BY PEDDLERS OF FLIM-FLAM.

I HOPE TO REPLACE WOO WITH WHAT'S TRUE, AND ENCOURAGE ACTIONS AND RESEARCH OVER PRAYER AND CHURCH.

I WANT TO PROMOTE CRITICAL THINKING AND FACTS, WHILE DISCREDITING LONG-DEBUNKED HEARSAY ABOUT VACCINES, CHEM-TRAILS, AND THE 9/11 ATTACKS.

I DON'T SEE THE VALUE IN HAVING BELIEFS THAT AREN'T TRUE, SO I AM A SCIENTIFIC SKEPTIC, AND AN ATHEIST, TOO.

*"I am all for curses and superstition, but there's a point
at which they start getting in the way. That point had arrived."*
—Tahir Shah

NOTES

1. *"It is easy to find disaster stories of paranormal beliefs gone wild. Fanatical bombers kill thousands for bizarre supernatural beliefs and flying saucer cultists cheerfully commit suicide to prepare for promised alien rescue."* —Jonathan C. Smith

2. Mike Isaac, "Facebook, in Cross Hairs after Election, Is Said to Question Its Influence," *New York Times*, November 12, 2016, www.nytimes.com/2016/11/14/technology/facebook-is-said-to-question-its-influence-in-election.html?_r=0.

3. I just wish that bit of knowledge didn't cost us so much.

4.   The full quote is: "Any negative polls are fake news, just like the CNN, ABC, NBC polls in the election. Sorry, people want border security and extreme vetting." Donald Trump, tweet, February 6, 2017, twitter.com/realdonaldtrump/status/828574430800539648?lang=en.

5.   In court dockets for a custody hearing, Jones admitted to being a "performance artist" who is "playing a character" during his broadcasts.

6.   Alex Jones, tweet, December 12, 2016, twitter.com/RealAlexJones/status/808509500386934785.

7.   Jessica Roy, "Want to Keep Fake News Out of Your Newsfeed? College Professor Creates List of Sites to Avoid," *Los Angeles Times*, November 15, 2016, www.latimes.com/nation/politics/trailguide/la-na-trailguide-updates-want-to-keep-fake-news-out-of-your-1479260297-htmlstory.html.

8.   This is part of why I founded The Party of Reason and Progress (PORP), an organization dedicated to promoting reason and empirically sound decision-making in modern politics. See partyofreasonandprogress.org.

9.   What's The Harm? www.whatstheharm.net.

10. Arianna MacNeill, "Proctor's Ledge in Salem Confirmed as Witch Execution Site," *Salem News*, January 11, 2016, www.salemnews.com/news/local_news/proctor-s-ledge-in-salem-confirmed-as-witch-execution-site/article_d9e2a242-fdf7-56ac-94eb-5e3f943d0cc3.html.

11. Ellis, Lacey. "Salem Witch Trials."

12. "George Jacobs, Sr.," Salem Witch Museum, www.salemwitchmuseum.com/blog/george-jacobs-sr.

13. K. David Goss, *The Salem Witch Trials: A Reference Guide* (New York: ABC-CLIO, 2008).

14. In 2015, a woman from Salem who identifies as a witch priestess sued Christian Day, who calls himself the "*world's best-known warlock*," for harassment. The court sided with the plaintiff and issued a protective order, according to media reports.

15. Ryan Jacobs, "Saudi Arabia's War on Witchcraft," *Atlantic*, August 19, 2013, www.theatlantic.com/international/archive/2013/08/saudi-arabias-war-on-witchcraft/278701/.

16. Gary Foxcroft, "Supporting Victims of Witchcraft Abuse and Street Children in Nigeria," Stepping Stones Nigeria, 2007, www.streetchildrenresources.org/wp-content/uploads/2013/03/supporting-victims-of-witchcraft-abuse-street-children-nigeria.pdf.

17. Hannah Osborne, "DR Congo's Witchcraft Epidemic: 50,000 Children Accused of Sorcery," *International Business Times*, May 20, 2013, www.ibtimes.co.uk/branded-witch-bbc-democratic-republic-congo-kindoki-469216.

18. Faith Karimi, "Abuse of Child 'Witches' on Rise, Aid Group Says," *CNN*, May 18, 2009, www.cnn.com/2009/WORLD/africa/05/18/nigeria.child.witchcraft/index.html.

19. Aleksandra Cimpric, *Children Accused of Witchcraft: An Anthropological Study of Contemporary Practices in Africa* (Dakar, Senegal: United Nations Children's Fund, 2010).

20. Red Cross, *Through Albino Eyes: The Plight of Albino People in Africa's Great Lakes Region and a Red Cross Response* (Geneva: International Federation of Red Cross and Red Crescent Societies, 2009).

21. Benjamin Radford, "East Africa Tries to Stem Albino Magic Murders: DNews," *DNews*, January 17, 2015, news.discovery.com/history/east-africa-tries-to-stem-albino-magic-murders-150117.htm.

22. Greg Botelho, "Renowned Psychic, Bestselling Author Sylvia Browne Dies at 77," *CNN*, November 20, 2013, www.cnn.com/2013/11/20/showbiz/sylvia-browne-dies/.

23. Erin Donaghue, "Amanda Berry, Gina Dejesus, Michele Knight Update: Police Believe Child Found in Home Is Berry's Daughter," *CBS News*, May 7, 2013, www.cbsnews.com/news/amanda-berry-gina-dejesus-michele-knight-update-police-believe-child-found-in-home-is-berrys-daughter/.

24. "Amanda Berry Is Dead, Psychic Tells Her Mother on Montel Williams' Show (republished)," *Plain Dealer*, May 1, 2013, www.cleveland.com/metro/index.ssf/2013/05/amanda_berry_is_dead_psychic_t.html.

25. "Two Boys Found Alive; One Missing since 2002," *CNN*, January 13, 2007, www.cnn.com/2007/LAW/01/12/missing.boys/index.html.

26. Mark Koba, "Divining Water: Dowsers in Big Demand During California Drought," *NBC News*, June 29, 2014, www.nbcnews.com/business/careers/divining-water-dowsers-big-demand-during-california-drought-n140836.

27. "Water Dowsing," U.S. Department of the Interior, December 9, 2015, water.usgs.gov/edu/dowsing.html.

28. Guide for the Selection of Commercial Explosives Detection Systems for Law Enforcement Applications (NIJ Guide 100–99), Chapter 7. Warning: Do Not Buy Bogus Explosives Detection Equipment.

29. Christy Strawser, "Local Psychics Offer Insight into Missing Malaysian Plane, One Says Gov't Knows Where It Is," *CBS Detroit*, March 18, 2014, http://detroit.cbslocal.com/2014/03/18/local-psychics-offer-insight-into-missing-malaysian-plane-says-govt-knows-where-it-is/.

30. Michael Martinez and Don Melvin, "MH370 Possibly Plunged Straight into Ocean, Expert Says," *CNN*, July 30, 2015, www.cnn.com/2014/03/21/us/malaysia-airlines-flight-370-theories/.

31. " Rhino Poaching Toll Reaches New High," Traffic International, January 10, 2013, www.traffic.org/home/2013/1/10/rhino-poaching-toll-reaches-new-high.html.

32. Judy A.Mills and Peter Jackson, *Killed for a Cure: A Review of the Worldwide Trade in Tiger Bone* (Cambridge: Traffic International, 1994).

33. J. Still, "Use of Animal Products in Traditional Chinese Medicine: Environmental Impact and Health Hazards," *Complementary Therapies in Medicine* 11, no. 2 (2003): 118–122.

34. M. A. R. Fareed, "Endangered Birds Run Out of Luck in India," *Al Jazeera English*, July 15, 2014, www.aljazeera.com/indepth/features/2014/07/endangered-birds-run-out-luck-india-201471483932626650.html.

35. "5,000 Buffaloes Slaughtered in Nepal's Animal Sacrifice Ritual," *Times of India*, November 29, 2014, http://timesofindia.indiatimes.com/world/south-asia/5000-buffaloes-slaughtered-in-Nepals-animal-sacrifice-ritual/articleshow/45318635.cms.

36. Craig Nakano, "Black Dog Bias?" *Los Angeles Times*, December 6, 2008, www.latimes.com/style/la-hm-black6-2008dec06-story.html.

37. Lori R Kogan, Regina Schoenfeld-Tacher, and Peter W. Hellyer, "Cats in Animal Shelters: Exploring the Common Perception That Black Cats Take Longer to Adopt," *Open Veterinary Science Journal* 7 (2013): 18–22.

38. Flemming Rose, "Why I Published Those Cartoons," *Washington Post*, February 19, 2006, www.washingtonpost.com/wp-dyn/content/article/2006/02/17/AR2006021702499_pf.html.

39. Margaret A. Maglione et al. "Safety of Vaccines Used for Routine Immunization in the United States," Pediatrics 134, no. 2 (August 2014).

40. Institute of Medicine Immunization Safety Review Committee, *Immunization Safety Review: Vaccines and Autism* (Washington, DC: National Academies Press, 2004).

41. "Majority of Authors Retract 1998 Lancet Paper-Lancet Editor Points to Implications," *Psych Central*, March 3, 2004, psychcentral.com/news/archives/2004-03/l-moa030304.html.

42. "Autism Study Doctor Barred for 'Serious Misconduct,'" *CNN*, May 24, 2010, www.cnn.com/2010/HEALTH/05/24/autism.vaccine.doctor.banned/index.html.

43. Seth Mnookin, *The Panic Virus: A True Story of Medicine, Science, and Fear* (New York: Simon & Schuster, 2011).

44. David Kroll, "Jenny McCarthy Is A Dangerous Example of Medical Celebrity," *Forbes*, July 16, 2013.

45. "Donald Trump Has Long Linked Autism to Vaccines. He Isn't Stopping Now That He's President," *Fortune*, February 16, 2017, fortune.com/2017/02/16/donald-trump-autism-vaccines/.

46. Paul A. Offit and Rita K. Jew, "Addressing Parents' Concerns: Do Vaccines Contain Harmful Preservatives, Adjuvants, Additives, or Residuals?" *Pediatrics* 112, no. 6 (2003): 1394–1397.

47. Danielle McBurnett Stringer, "Why Your Pediatric Health Provider Actually Wants You to Vaccinate Your Child," *Kid Nurse*, July 30, 2014, www.kidnurse.org/pediatric-health-provider-actually-wants-vaccinate-child/.

48. Jessica E. Atwell et al. "Nonmedical Vaccine Exemptions and Pertussis in California, 2010," *Pediatrics* 132, no. 4 (2013): 624–630.

49. Anita Gore, "California Experiencing a Whooping Cough Epidemic," California Department of Public Health, June 13, 2014, www.cdph.ca.gov/Pages/NR14-056.aspx.

50. "Measles Cases and Outbreaks," Centers for Disease Control and Prevention, March 8, 2016, www.cdc.gov/measles/cases-outbreaks.html.

51. "Tara Hills, Ottawa Mom, Changes Anti-vaccination Stand, but 7 Kids Still Get Sick," *CBC/Radio Canada*, April 9, 2015, www.cbc.ca/news/canada/ottawa/tara-hills-ottawa-mom-changes-anti-vaccination-stand-but-7-kids-still-get-sick-1.3025592.

52. Tara Hills, "Learning the Hard Way: My Journey from #AntiVaxx to Science," *Scientific Parent*, April 8, 2015, thescientificparent.org/learning-the-hard-way-my-journey-from-antivaxx-to-science/.

53. D. Moyer, "Measles Led to Death of Clallam Co. Woman; First in US in a Dozen Years," Washington State Department of Health, July 2, 2015.

54. Posted by Orac on July 3, 2015, "How "They" View "Us": A Woman

Dies of Measles, and Antivaccinationists Think It's a Conspiracy," Respectful Insolence, ScienceBlogs, July 2, 2015.

55. Dr. Bob Sears, post on Facebook, July 2, 2015, www.facebook.com/permalink.php?story_fbid=914196915285460&id=116317855073374.

56. Melodi Smith and Kerry Chan Laddaran, "Julia, Who Has Autism, Joins the 'Sesame Street' Gang," *CNN*, October 21, 2015, www.cnn.com/2015/10/21/entertainment/sesame-street-julia-autism/index.html.

57. Mike Adams, "Sesame Street Rolls Out Autistic Muppet to 'Normalize' Vaccine Injured Children ... Follows Elmo Push for Mass Vaccinations," Natural News Network, October 22, 2015, www.naturalnews.com/051668_autistic_muppet_Sesame_Street_vaccine_injuries.html>.

58. Paul Fine, Ken Eames, and David L. Heymann. "'Herd immunity': A Rough Guide," *Clinical Infectious Diseases* 52, no. 7 (2011): 911–916.

6

MY WORLDVIEW

"Yes, I'm a materialist. I'm willing to be shown wrong, but that has not happened—yet. And I admit that the reason I'm unable to accept the claims of psychic, occult, and/or supernatural wonders is because I'm locked into a world-view that demands evidence rather than blind faith, a view that insists upon the replication of all experiments—particularly those that appear to show violations of a rational world—and a view which requires open examination of the methods used to carry out those experiments."

—James Randi

My worldview isn't complicated; I rely on evidence and factual conclusions to form my "belief system." For example, although I personally don't believe that nonnatural forces exist—let alone beings that created or govern us—I'm completely open to that answer as a possibility. I maintain that the existence of supernatural or paranormal entities is unlikely, but if empirical evidence were put forth that logically suggested such a presence, I would accept it and then incorporate that new information into my way of thinking. Historically, however, that has not been the case.

As someone who is on a mission to escape the chains often imposed by bad ideas, wrong beliefs, and *sacred cows* in general, it's necessary to be willing and able to completely drop or adopt any idea based on the scientific information and empirical data. I've often been accused of being "firm in my beliefs," but I consider my ideas to be quite malleable because they are shaped by the (often fluid) evidence put forth. Firmness in beliefs is what causes people to shy away from looking at those ideas with a skeptical or critical eye—and that's never a good thing. The ability to change your opinions with new information is something to be admired, but to staunchly defend firmly held views without reexamination is to display the source of the worst kinds of fundamentalism. In order to truly maintain an evidence-based worldview, one must be ready to consider that he or she has been misled about anything and everything they know. Next, the person has to be able to search out objective, nonbiased sources of information (based on factual scientific findings) on which to base conclusions. Both of these are important and, to get to the truth, you can't skip any steps.

WE DON'T CHOOSE OUR BELIEFS

Some people insist belief is merely a "choice" that must be respected at all costs, but I disagree. In the same way we don't choose our emotions,[1] I don't *choose* not to believe in any religions, other supernatural claims, or pseudoscientific ideas. My skepticism on these issues is the result of the fact that I value evidence over faith and conjecture. Contrary to popular belief, I don't think people *can* choose what they believe as much as they think they can. I couldn't simply will myself to accept something as fact without being convinced somehow, and I think most people would feel similarly if they really thought about the issue. That agreement makes sense—this is exactly how beliefs should work. However, while we don't literally choose what we believe, many people do choose which of those beliefs they will critically examine and which they will ignore. If we set high standards for examination and research on all topics, including and especially the most important ones, then we can overcome unknown biases and understand that no ideas should be exempt from scrutiny.

A lot of people get confused when I say we can't always *choose* the things we believe. We can decide to look closer at available information and, to some extent, we can even control what we consider to be "evidence." But that's not the same as flipping a switch and literally choosing to believe or disbelieve something. That's a gross oversimplification of how ideas work. If you can't will yourself to believe or disbelieve, it's not as simple as a choice. And with certain beliefs (especially religious teachings), depending on your influences when you formed them, there may have been no choice on your part at all. If you are wondering if belief itself is in fact a choice for you, just try to believe that all tomatoes are actually purple. I think you'll find out quickly that you can't simply decide what you think is real and what's fake without other considerations (such as evidence).

If we all had the ability to arbitrarily decide what we think is real and what we don't think is real, our lives would be incredibly different. We might choose to believe only things that make us comfortable and disregard those that cause us confusion, for example, or I might even decide to believe in a real, all-loving, all-powerful deity (not the one from the Bible). But I for one don't have that ability. I can't just decide out of nowhere, "*You know what? Despite the fact that I've never seen evidence that supports the existence of any supernatural force or being, I'm going to choose to believe that they are real because it's convenient for me.*" No matter how much I've tried, I have never been able to simply force myself to believe in that which isn't based on evidence and supported by data just because I want to. I just can't do it— but that doesn't mean I have a problem with what others believe as long as they don't force their ideas on anyone else or hurt people because of them.

MY PROCESS

So, if we can't decide which beliefs we hold regarding the supernatural, how do we adopt them? For me, it's very simple: if you make an extraordinary assertion—such as that there is a god or other magical force acting in this world—and you want me to believe you, then you must first prove it using science. You are making the claim, and therefore are subject to the burden of proof. It is the claimant's obligation to provide support for their position,[2] so until that duty is fulfilled, I simply won't believe you.

Scientific skepticism isn't all that difficult to understand, and to me it actually seems obvious. All you have to do is question things to discover if they meet the burden of proof and allow your "beliefs" to be shaped by reality, not by culture or indoctrination or some other force. I won't say that I have a perfect track record, but I will say that I always make a concentrated effort to hold assertions to a high standard of evidence, dependent of course on how extraordinary the particular claim is and what its implications might be. If a person tells me they had a bad **dream**, I won't hook them up to a brain monitor and ask them to recount it for verification. But if that same person tells me magic exists, or that they're able to predict the future using their dreams, I'm going to want to see the evidence for myself.[3]

Looking at assertions and arguments logically is important, including and especially when the person making the claim is someone whom you consider trustworthy. This applies to scientists, too. It's not as though scientists and other academic professionals can't be wrong; they are human and, as such, are wrong quite often. For instance, I once read a "news" story with the headline, *"Quantum physics proves that there IS an afterlife, claims scientist."* I had to look beyond the claim and the scientist and into the science itself to discover how flawed this "proof" actually was. The fact that a scientist thinks something is true isn't evidence that the thing is really true. That's the difference between *scientists*—the people—and *science*—the process we use to uncover facts about the world. In the 2014 documentary TV show *Cosmos: A Spacetime Odyssey*, host and cosmologist Neil deGrasse Tyson outlined this idea quite well. He said, *"Scientists are human; we have our blind spots and prejudices. Science is a mechanism designed to ferret them out. The problem is we aren't always faithful to the core values of science."*

DEFINING MY OWN VIEWS

Some nonbelievers shy away from defining themselves as "atheistic." Neil deGrasse Tyson, for instance, has emphatically rejected the label, even asking, *"Is there a word for non–golf players?"* He added, *"Do non–golf players gather and strategize? Do nonskiers have a word, and come together, and talk about the fact that they don't ski? I can't do that!"* But being an atheist is nothing to be scared of; it's just a stigmatized word. After all, a person who doesn't play golf is, by definition, a "nongolfer." Most people who fit that label might not utilize it, but that would likely be different if golfing was an inherently controversial topic on which the vast majority of people based their lives. People might also call themselves nongolfers if they were forced to follow legislation based on the game. If you don't believe any gods exist, then you're an atheist and, like all definitions, it applies regardless of emotional reactions to the term.

So yes, I am an atheist, but I don't merely advocate for nonreligiosity, because that's not enough. There are many nonreligious people who hold other irrational (and potentially harmful) beliefs. I try to promote evidence-focused decision-making, based in large part on the scientific method, because I think that's the best way to reach conclusions. As opposed to simply accepting the things we are told, I challenge myself and others to look at the facts and get as close to the truth as possible—without regard to how that might make us feel. I may be an atheist, but I'm also an *aghostist* and an *aluckist* and, more importantly, a scientific skeptic. Basically, if you have to ask whether or not I "believe in" something, the answer is probably, "No." It's important to note, however, that there is a difference between believing something, as in accepting it as true, and believing *in* something, a commonly used phrase that describes the process of letting your hopes shape that belief (akin to religious faith). I have no use for the latter. I don't *believe in* anything in that sense. I know some things and I don't know others, leaving all other ideas to be based on probability and subject to change with new information.

Part of my "worldview" includes the fact that I'm an atheist, but, like Tyson,[4] I don't generally attach myself to a group of people based on only one commonality. Atheism doesn't necessarily make anyone intelligent or a good person, and that's just a small part of my identity. I'm also an agnostic, a humanist, and a naturalist. I wouldn't call myself an atheist if it weren't necessary, but theism and religiosity are the assumed points of view in many cultures, including my own, making that an unfortunate but needed step. I personally reject belief in the divine for the same reason I reject every supernatural, superstitious, or paranormal claim, including talking snakes, burning bushes, magical resurrections, reincarnation, Intelligent Design, demigods, the Rapture, the Garden of Eden, Satan, Xenu, Joseph Smith's alleged golden plates, astrology, miracles, voodoo, transubstantiation during the Eucharist, Heaven, Hell, angels, demons, salvation, sin, prayer, the soul, and more. I don't believe in these unfalsifiable supernatural concepts because, although they may have cultural saturation, years of anecdotal testimonies, and scriptural support, they still lack the empirical evidence I require before accepting them as realities.

The bottom line is that supernatural beliefs lack hard evidence, and without peer-reviewed data, duplicability, and/or other solid proofs, many skeptics—including myself—simply can't and won't take that leap of faith to accept them as true. For us, strong feelings, anecdotal accounts, third-person testimonies, emotional reactions, poorly edited websites and "documentaries," and scripture do not qualify as compelling evidence for the supernatural. We need more than that.

WHAT IS LOVE?

In the process of defending beliefs that—like the idea of the supernatural in general—lack sufficient support, some believers go as far as to insist that the notion of love itself isn't backed by empirical evidence and therefore shouldn't be "believed" by me or any other scientific skeptic. This is a common argument against an evidence-based worldview, but it relies on the premise that love is some mystical force that you just have to *believe in*. This couldn't be further from the truth. The emotion we call love is just a feeling—one of deep affection—and it is well studied and completely supported by scientific research.

We are learning more about love and other emotions, including how and why they are formed, all the time. Donatella Marazziti, professor of psychiatry and director of the laboratory of psychopharmacology at the University of Pisa, showed in 1999 that early stages of romance are linked with reduced levels of the serotonin (5-HT) transporter. Marazziti and her team noted that people with obsessive-compulsive disorder (OCD) exhibit a similar chemical imbalance.[5] British neurobiologist Semir Zeki of University College London and his colleagues further outlined chemical differences in those experiencing romantic love,[67] and a 2012 study published in the Journal of Sexual Medicine pinpointed the origins of love and desire in the brain.[8] Those researchers discovered that two specific brain structures, the insula and the striatum (a part of the basal ganglia in the limbic system), are responsible for the progression from sexual desire to deeper love. The authors of the study further concluded that love "*builds upon a neural circuit for emotions and pleasure, adding regions associated with reward expectancy, habit formation, and feature detection.*"

> *In particular, the shared activation within the insula, with a posterior-to-anterior pattern, from desire to love, suggests that love grows out of and is a more abstract representation of the pleasant sensorimotor experiences that characterize desire. From these results, one may consider desire and love on a spectrum that evolves from integrative representations of affective visceral sensations to an ultimate representation of feelings incorporating mechanisms of reward expectancy and habit learning.*

We don't know everything about love, but it's a relatively popular field of study, so we do know a lot. We do know emotions, including love, are the result of brain chemistry, for instance. And we know breakthroughs in the study of feelings aren't uncommon. In 2013, Karim Kassam of

Carnegie Mellon University in Pittsburgh used brain scans to photograph emotions for the first time,[9] and, a year later, a Cornell University study further showed how our brains process feelings in general.[10] Scientists have also measured differences in brain activity when in love, not in love, and heartbroken. In one such study, researchers found that romantic love-related brain functional topological changes included increased regional homogeneity (ReHo) of the left dorsal anterior cingulate cortex and increased functional connectivity (FC) *within the reward, motivation, and emotion regulation network, as well as the social cognition network.*[11] They also discovered decreased ReHo of the bilateral caudate nucleus related to the ending of a romantic relationship.

"This study provides the first empirical evidence of love-related alterations in the underlying functional architecture of the brain. Findings are in agreement with results from task-dependent fMRI studies, and complement well the functional findings of task-dependent fMRI studies," the authors of the paper wrote. *"These results shed light on the underlying neurophysiological mechanisms of romantic love by investigating intrinsic brain activity, and demonstrate the possibility of applying a resting state approach for investigating romantic love."*

Psychologist Abigail Marsh of Georgetown University says love feels good because of *"feel-good hormones"* such as dopamine and oxytocin that are involved.

"The hormone that is most specific to feeling in love, that is most specific to the social response, is oxytocin and a closely related neuropeptide called vasopressin," Marsh said in a video produced by the American Chemical Society. *"Nature really wants love to feel good. Nature's imperative is that we reproduce and love is one of the mechanisms nature has put in place to make sure we do that."*

So, contrary to popular belief, love does not come from the heart—a muscle responsible for pumping blood throughout the body. Like all emotions, thoughts, and desires, love comes from the brain. And, using medical scans, we can actually measure which parts of the brain react when we experience the chemical connection we know as love. It is for that reason that I sometimes say, *"I love you from the bottom of my striatum,"* if I want to be scientifically accurate.

Larry J. Young, who conducts research on the neurobiological basis of complex social behavior with the Yerkes National Primate Research Center at Emory University, wrote in 2009 that reducing love to its "component parts" isn't poetic or romantic. It may, however, help us understand love better and lead to the development of new medications.

The view of love as an emergent property of a cocktail of ancient neuropeptides and neurotransmitters raises important issues for society. For one thing, drugs that manipulate brain systems at whim to enhance or diminish our love for another may not be far away. Experiments have shown that a nasal squirt of oxytocin enhances trust and tunes people into others' emotions. Internet entrepreneurs are already marketing products such as Enhanced Liquid Trust, a cologne-like mixture of oxytocin and pheromones "designed to boost the dating and relationship area of your life." Although such products are unlikely to do anything other than boost users' confidence, studies are under way in Australia to determine whether an oxytocin spray might aid traditional marital therapy.[12]

Because love is a feeling like any other, created by chemicals mixing in the brain, it can be measured as such, but that doesn't mean I ask for brain scans when someone says they love me. That wouldn't be practical or necessary because, in the case of love—a chemical reaction for which we have gained reverence—it can also be observed through the actions of certain individuals. For example, the evidence is overwhelming for the fact that I love my wife. I do everything I can for her, I love and respect her, and I talk to her about everything. This is all evidence that I feel the emotion called "love" toward her. I show this through actions in my daily life and on a long-term basis. I've had discussions with her telling her how much I care for her, and how my life hasn't been the same since meeting her. You can easily look at everything from the letters that I've written my wife throughout our time together to our daily conversations to conclude that there is shared love there, so a brain scan isn't usually necessary.

To those who insist I can't experience love because, "*God is love,*"[13] I partially agree. I do think gods are a lot like love.

- LOVE IS A FEELING, AND GODS ARE, TOO. BELIEF IN GOD(S) IS OFTEN LINKED TO EMOTIONAL EXPERIENCES OR ARGUMENTS.

- LOVE IS A CHEMICAL REACTION IN THE BRAIN AND GODS LIKEWISE RESIDE IN THE MIND. THEY ORIGINATED IN THE THOUGHTS OF OUR STORYTELLING ANCESTORS AND LIVE ON THROUGH THE FAITH OF BELIEVERS.

- LOVE IS OFTEN USED AS A SYMBOL OF GOODNESS AND PURITY, AS ARE MANY GODS. THEY AREN'T LITERAL ENTITIES, BUT THEY ARE USED TO REPRESENT GOODNESS, JUSTICE, AND HOPE FOR THE FUTURE.

When people say "*God is love*," it reminds me of the nature of deities as symbolic beings in the minds of people. You may feel the presence of your god, but, just like when you think you feel love for someone, it's important to remember you could be mistaken. In any case, you don't have to "believe in" love because there is no doubt that it is real—it's just the name we've given to a positive feeling. Happiness, fear, love, etc. exist as emotions and, if a believer's argument is that their particular deity or supernatural force is merely a *feeling* one has, and not something that literally exists in the world, I would have to agree.

MEASURING PAIN AND SPOUSAL LOYALTY

This love objection, if you want to call it that, is expressed in other ways, too. In attempts to condemn scientific skepticism, some believers might say, "You don't need evidence other than feelings to know you're in pain!" or even, "You wouldn't demand evidence from your spouse that he or she is faithful!"

When I perceive pain, I look for its source because pain is often used by the body to draw attention to something that's wrong. If my doctor(s) and I can't locate the underlying cause of the pain, then I have to consider the possibility that it is psychological. It's also possible, however, that the pain is being caused by an unknown or undiagnosed disorder. It's important to note that neither of these possibilities would make the pain any less *real*, as the pain is real if it is being felt by the patient. It's true that pain is often thought to be subjective because we rely on tolerance and past experiences to decide how to react to the pain, but that doesn't mean there aren't physical pain markers that are the same across the board. In fact, although self-reporting is the most common way we gauge pain, it isn't the only method. In 2011, researchers found that functional MRI (fMRI) scans on the brains of patients experiencing moderate pain helped them develop an algorithm that predicted pain levels 81 percent of the time.[14] That research was furthered in 2013 when neuroscientists from the University of Colorado Boulder, New York University, Johns Hopkins University, and the University of Michigan used fMRI to measure and predict pain intensity with over 95 percent accuracy. Their results were published in the *New England Journal of Medicine*.[15]

As far as faithfulness between loved ones is concerned, yes, I would need evidence (if we had an exclusive relationship) that my life partner would remain faithful to me. And I think most couples who agree to such an arrangement would look for evidence as well. The data, in this case, often comes in the form of consistent loyalty over time, and it is both measurable and reliable. Once that pattern is broken, however, and the evidence shows one partner is no longer honoring the agreement, those involved may choose to revisit the terms.

"In youth we feel richer for every new illusion; in maturer years, for every one we lose."

—Anne Sophie Swetchine

NOTES

1. Carroll E. Izard, "Emotion Theory and Research: Highlights, Unanswered Questions, and Emerging Issues," *Annual Review of Psychology* 60 (2009): 1.

2. James Cargile, "On the Burden of Proof," *Philosophy* 72, no. 279 (January 1997): 59–83.

3. For me, this realistic mindset was present fairly early on. Even when I was a very young child, I remember being scared most not of monsters hiding under my bed or in my closet, but of potential real-world intruders.

4. *"The only 'ist' I am is a scientist. I don't associate with movements."* —Neil deGrasse Tyson

5. Donatella Marazziti et al. "Alteration of the Platelet Serotonin Transporter in Romantic Love," *Psychological Medicine* 29, no. 3 (1999): 741–745.

6. Andreas Bartels and Semir Zeki, "The Neural Basis of Romantic Love," *Neuroreport* 11, no. 17 (2000): 3829–3834.

7. Andreas Bartels and Semir Zeki, "The Neural Correlates of Maternal and Romantic Love," *Neuroimage* 21, no. 3 (2004): 1155–1166.

8. S. Cacioppo et al. "The Common Neural Bases Between Sexual Desire and Love: A Multilevel Kernel Density fMRI Analysis," *Journal of Sexual Medicine* 9 (2012): 1048–1054.

9. K. S. Kassam, "Identifying Emotions on the Basis of Neural Activation," PLoS ONE 8, no. 6 (2013): e66032.

10. Junichi Chikazoe et al. "Population Coding of Affect Across Stimuli, Modalities and Individuals," *Nature Neuroscience* 17 (2014): 1114–1122.

11. Hongwen Song et al. "Love-Related Changes in the Brain: A Resting-State Functional Magnetic Resonance Imaging Study," *Frontiers in Human Neuroscience* 9 (2015).

12. Larry J. Young, "Love: Neuroscience Reveals All," *Nature* 457, no. 7226. (January 7, 2009): 148–148.

13. Whenever I hear that God "*loves*" me, I think about the fact that love is a word we created to describe a chemical reaction in the brain. Do theists think God has a brain?

14. Justin E. Brown et al. "Towards a Physiology-Based Measure of Pain: Patterns of Human Brain Activity Distinguish Painful from Non-Painful Thermal Stimulation," *PLoS One* 6, no. 9 (2011): e24124.

15. Tor D. Wager et al., "An fMRI-based Neurologic Signature of Physical Pain," *New England Journal of Medicine* 368, no. 15 (2013): 1388–1397.

7

YOU DON'T HAVE TO BE A SCIENTIST TO THINK LIKE ONE

"Science is the best idea humans have ever had.
The more people who embrace that idea, the better."
—Bill Nye the Science Guy

A lot of people say my worldview overly relies on the scientific method and that, as someone without any formal scientific degrees or training, I should focus elsewhere. But I do have a few qualifications that enable me to use science: curiosity, a knowledge of the scientific method, and a passion for the truth. What more does one need? What many people don't realize is that science is a process for everyone—including and especially nonscientists. As Carl Sagan said, *"Our species needs, and deserves, a citizenry with minds wide awake and a basic understanding of how the world works."*

Scientific thinking is incredibly important, and the best part is you don't have to be a scientist to acknowledge that fact or to help others see it. Science is not some holy book that can only be interpreted by the Elder Scientists. It is not some club that denies entry to outsiders. It is a system of discovery that we've all been practicing informally since we were children. It started the first time we noticed something unusual, asked a question about it, and then put it to test.

WHAT DOES IT MEAN TO "THINK LIKE A SCIENTIST"?

When I say we can, and should, think like scientists, what am I really suggesting? Should you request scientific proof from everyone for everything, or employ rigorous tests to assess the validity of each and every statement you hear? Of course not. In order to think like a scientist, all you have to do is employ the scientific method where appropriate to separate fact from fiction.

When searching for an answer from a scientific point of view, you have to write off things that don't impact the natural world (and therefore cannot affect your experiments). You should be able to cast aside traditions that, while incredibly powerful and capable of shaping much of what we know about human cultures and society at large, are irrelevant in science. You need to be able to look at information from the most objective view possible, without being influenced by your preconceived notions. Jonathan Haidt, a social psychologist and professor of ethical leadership at New York University's Stern School of Business, explains why dropping all our biases is so important.

"*We may think we are acting as scientists when analyzing data and models, but very often we are acting more as lawyers, using our reasoning to a predetermined end, one that was emotionally biased by our ideological positions and cultural views,*" Haidt said.

Becoming more objective in your thinking is important, but it isn't always enough. Often just the act of reading news articles, even from a scientific perspective, can still lead you down the road toward false beliefs. To correct for this, you should teach yourself to rely less on second-hand information and hearsay, and more on direct sources and scientific journals. If you don't know how to read scientific articles, teach yourself how so that you can't be easily swayed by biased or incorrect media reports and false news. Dr. Mary Purugganan and Dr. Jan Hewitt, both instructors at Rice University, teach a class on the subject in which they say reading a scientific article like you read a textbook is the "*worst way to approach this task.*"

"*Rather, you should begin by skimming the article to identify its structure and features. As you read, look for the author's main points,*" Purugganan and Hewitt wrote in a handout.[1] "*Generate questions before, during, and after reading. Draw inferences based on your own experiences and knowledge. And to really improve understanding and recall, take notes as you read.*"

"SCIENTISM" VS. SCIENTIFIC SKEPTICISM

Some believers suggest my evidence-based worldview amounts to nothing more than **scientism**, which is defined as a philosophical position that *"embraces only empiricism and reason to explain phenomena of any dimension, whether physical, social, cultural, or psychological."*[2] I wholeheartedly disagree with this characterization of my method because I only use science to address falsifiable questions, those to which scientific inquiry might provide a helpful answer. Science isn't an all-purpose tool that can be applied to any mystery—it is a specialty device used to uncover more of the observable world. Philosopher Karl Popper, known for his work promoting empirical falsification, explained, *"In so far as a scientific statement speaks about reality, it must be falsifiable; and in so far as it is not falsifiable, it does not speak about reality."*

Science is about disproving testable claims and learning more about how the world really works. Scientism, on the other hand, is the application of the scientific method to everything. It is, as University of Miami philosophy professor Susan Haack says in her *Six Signs of Scientism*,[3] an *"inappropriately deferential attitude to science"* that makes people look to the sciences for answers *"beyond their scope."* It is the false assumption that science alone is capable of discovering facts about the world, that it's the only way to access any form of truth, and that metaphysical, philosophical, and religious claims should be dismissed entirely.[4] In this strong sense, scientism has aptly been described as *"the self-annihilating view that only scientific claims are meaningful, which is not a scientific claim and hence, if true, not meaningful."* It then follows, of course, that *"scientism is either false or meaningless."*[5]

Not having faith in extraordinary claims without substantial scientific evidence should sound like common sense, but for too many people it is not. In fact, some believers would argue that someone with an evidence-based worldview "worships" science and that scientism is their "religion." For example, Jamie Holmes, author of *Nonsense: The Power of Not Knowing*, argues that a love of science *"looks a lot like religion."*[6]

Holmes, who defines scientism as *"the notion that science has exclusive access to the truth,"* pointed to a 2013 study in *The Journal of Experimental Social Psychology*.[7] In that study, researchers said they found that stressed subjects were more likely to agree to statements expressing scientism, such as, "*the scientific method is the only reliable path to knowledge.*"

"*When people felt anxious, they esteemed science more highly than calmer subjects did, just as previous experiments have shown to be the case with religious ideals,*" Holmes explained, suggesting deep faith can be just another form of irrational extremism. "*In these cases, beliefs about science may be defended emotionally, even if they are false, as long as they provide a reassuring sense of order. That is to say, beliefs about science may be defended thoughtlessly—even unscientifically.*"

I understand that there may be people who feel this way about science, but for me, this assertion is untrue. In fact, I think science is so amazing specifically *because* it is fluid and not a clear, all-encompassing answer to every question. Contrary to what some have suggested, I don't worship or even *believe in* science; I just find it easier to accept outcomes that are observed repeatedly under controlled conditions. Even if you disagree with me on one or more topics, or you dislike me as a person, I think most would agree that looking for verifiable facts is important and that the scientific method and reasonable thinking should be spread to everyone in the world. Frankly, I think it's sad that I even have to say I have an "evidence-based worldview." For any person who suggests scientific evidence isn't important in shaping their beliefs, I'd just ask, "Why?" Shouldn't we all strive to believe that which is supported by verifiable facts? What does anyone think they could gain by having false beliefs? Belief without evidence is how blind faith is born, and how people start to unquestioningly accept any idea that sounds remotely possible or aligns with their preconceived ideas.

To me, rational skepticism seems like a reasonable position because, to date, everything that has ever been discovered and quantified has been linked to a natural cause—with ideas based on the supernatural being rendered completely unnecessary and speculative at best, and harmful at worst. I "believe in" what's been shown to exist and I'm on an ongoing mission to purge my mind of any unjustified beliefs. I've taken on this quest for facts not due to scientism, but because I don't see the value in believing in something that could easily be untrue. Intellectual honesty is too important to me. Daniel Dennett shot back at those who would accuse him of scientism in his book, *Darwin's Dangerous Idea: Evolution and the Meanings of Life.*[8]

"*It is not 'scientism' to concede the objectivity and precision of good science, any more than it is history worship to concede that Napoleon did once rule in*

France and the Holocaust actually happened," he wrote. "*Those who fear the facts will forever try to discredit the fact-finders.*"

To think like a scientist, you have to stop yourself from accepting rumors as facts and look for scientific evidence only when appropriate. Perhaps most importantly, however, you have to be willing to be proven wrong about anything at any moment.

WHEN YOU'RE WRONG, ADMIT IT AND MOVE ON

We all have false beliefs. Yes, even you, the one reading this. You're wrong about something, some assumption or idea, because everyone is—it's impossible to escape. Perhaps you were taught as a child that blood inside our bodies is blue and never researched it further.[9] Or maybe you bought into the well-studied and debunked (yet incredibly pervasive) myth that full moons cause increased patient volume in hospitals and emergency rooms.[10][11][12] You might be clinging to the false notion that humans only utilize 10 percent of our brains,[13][14][15] or that it is always impossible to prove a negative claim.[16] Or it could be something much simpler, like believing you locked a door when you did not. It's not important at the moment to nail down your particular false beliefs, but it is crucial that you accept the fact that they exist so you can more easily correct them when the time arises. As author and biochemistry professor Isaac Asimov famously noted, when you are wrong and you want to be right, changing your opinions is the only real option.

"*So the universe is not quite as you thought it was,*" Asimov wrote.[17] "*You'd better rearrange your beliefs, then. Because you certainly can't rearrange the universe.*"

It is truly an important virtue to be able to admit when you've been misled and move past a firmly held belief to become a stronger person that much closer to the truth. But the process of separating facts from falsehoods isn't something that takes place in a day; it's a lifetime endeavor on which you can embark as long as you begin with an honest and objective approach.[18] You have to be ready to follow the evidence wherever it goes— even if that means admitting everything you've ever been taught was a lie. Stephen Toulmin, who was a British philosopher and author, once noted that a person's rationality can actually be measured by his or her willingness to admit errors.

"*A man demonstrates his rationality, not by a commitment to fixed ideas, stereotyped procedures, or immutable concepts, but by the manner in which, and the occasions on which, he changes those ideas, procedures, and concepts,*" Toulmin wrote in his book, *Human Understanding.*[19]

I've been wrong more times than I can recall, but it doesn't upset me like it does many others I've met. I actually like to look at each new instance of enlightenment as a win, rather than a loss. After all, my intention is not to be right all the time, but to acquire as much knowledge as I can. So, if someone corrects a misconception of mine, I don't get angry; I thank them for helping me. This is, in my opinion, the healthy and reasonable way to handle errors in our own thinking. My ability and desire to change my stance when confronted with new information is so important to me that I began compiling a list of all the times I did just that. This is only a small sample, but here are a couple of instances in which evidence reshaped my prior outlook:

Medicinal Cannabis: I was raised by parents who, for much of my childhood (though not before I was born), were addicted to methamphetamine. They used heavily and often, and I saw the effects the **drug** had on them. Once they started trying to quit, I found myself attending a lot of Narcotics Anonymous (N.A.) meetings,[20] which was a drastic improvement for me when it came to how I spent my nights. In those rooms, I learned about the (perceived) dangers of all drugs, and how, to many, marijuana was just as terrifying as meth. Shortly thereafter, I took a hardline stance against all mind-altering substances, including cannabis, and frequently lectured my friends who used it. I was basing my belief in its inherent danger on testimonies and experiences from N.A. members and not on scientific evidence. It wasn't until the end of college that, after suffering from chronic back pain for years, I eventually allowed my physician to prescribe medical cannabis in pill form. It helped relieve some of the pain, so I wanted to research its risks now that I was old enough to make decisions for myself. I soon discovered that, unlike the pain pills I was taking before, it was impossible to overdose on marijuana.[21] I also learned that, while there are some side effects to cannabis use, as is the case with any medicine, they don't compare in severity or frequency to those of traditional pain-relieving pharmaceuticals.[22] I effectively changed my position and became an advocate for the legalization of cannabis, especially for medicinal purposes.

Routine Infant Circumcision: When I was growing up, I never really thought much about the issue of routine infant circumcision. If you asked me my opinion, I probably would have said I approved of it, but my reasoning would have been flawed. I had never experienced any problems as a man who had been circumcised at birth, so I didn't think it was an issue. That was "normal" to me, and I didn't give it much more thought than that. I knew that there were some nonreligious arguments in favor of the practice—such as the potential for reduced transmission of HIV and sexually transmitted infections[23]—and that the first circumcisions were likely more closely linked to preventative healthcare than faith, so I understood it wasn't just a cut-and-dry case of religious barbarism and I promoted that idea. At the same time, however, I was conflicted when it came to elective newborn circumcision because I cared deeply about bodily autonomy, consent, and individual liberty. Over the course of a few years, I learned more about circumcision, including that newborns may actually feel more pain than older groups and that about 115 children die during routine cuts in the United States each year. [24][25] After exposing myself to the positions and statements of international science and medical groups, I also discovered that much of the developed world opposes the American practice of performing regular newborn circumcisions that aren't medically necessary.[26][27] I ultimately concluded that the decision to execute cosmetic surgery should be left up to the patient himself when he is old enough. There are exceptions, however. In rare cases, it is medically beneficial to circumcise a baby's penis. We can't ignore that fact, but we can't pretend those conditions are representative of the majority, either. I think that choice should be left to the individual once they are older, unless it is recommended by a physician for medical reasons.

In conclusion, I was entirely opposed to marijuana use because of my own experiences with family members and drugs, but my mind was changed with new information and now I support cannabis legalization—particularly when it is used as a medicine. I also used to think that, if I had a son, I would have him circumcised because I was and I didn't have any problems. This was a flawed argument from personal experience, and I now think that it should be the child's choice unless there is a legitimate medical need. To me, these changes are positive because good ideas evolve over time. These are just two examples of me admitting I was wrong and changing my position, but there are many more. I find it's beneficial, and maybe even a little fun, to keep a list of times that my ideas evolved with new data. It helps me more fully understand the importance of fluid opinions and, at the same time, it gives me a window through which I can see my previous self. According to Malcolm Gladwell, journalist and author of *Blink: The Power of Thinking Without Thinking*, this process of adjusting our beliefs is a human "*responsibility.*"

"*I feel I change my mind all the time. And I sort of feel that's your responsibility as a person, as a human being—to constantly be updating your positions on as many things as possible,*" Gladwell said. "*And if you don't contradict yourself on a regular basis, then you're not thinking.*"

Correcting your own misconceptions isn't just intellectually honest and, as Gladwell says, a responsibility. It can also be a personally rewarding experience. In fact, recent scientific research suggests failure and the ability to learn from it can actually be good for the brain.[28] A University of Southern California magnetic resonance imaging (MRI) study,[29] conducted alongside researchers from the University College London, the University Pierre and Marie Curie, the Ecole Normale Superieure, and the University of Lyon, quizzed 28 subjects and analyzed how their ventral striatum—or *reward circuit* of the brain—activated when the participants showed they learned from their incorrect answers.

"*We show that, in certain circumstances, when we get enough information to contextualize the choices, then our brain essentially reaches towards the reinforcement mechanism, instead of turning toward avoidance,*" said Giorgio Coricelli, an associate professor of economics and psychology at the University of Southern California and coauthor of the study, in a statement upon the its publication in August 2015.

He added that what we see with failure-based learning is similar to what might occur when a person experiences regret.

"*With regret, for instance, if you have done something wrong, then you might change your behavior in the future,*" Coricelli said.

If you're asked whether you could possibly be mistaken about something and you say "No," you might be affected by perception biases. If it is impossible, in your mind, for you to be wrong, then you have an inherently unscientific mindset and you likely won't be able to uncover (or accept) the truth if it contradicts your opinion.

THE IMPORTANCE OF IGNORANCE

As important as it is to admit when you are wrong, simply acknowledging that you don't *know* in the first place can be even more beneficial . . . and more difficult. People often use "ignorant" as an insult—sometimes as a synonym for dumb or unwilling to learn—but not every uneducated person is stupid and not everyone with a wealth of information is intelligent. As a result of this common misusage, ignorance itself has an underserved negative stigma, which means fewer people recognize that "I don't know" is always an acceptable answer, and that sometimes it's the only honest and reasonable one. It's perfectly acceptable to not know, especially if you are still looking for answers. What is dangerous is blindly believing something that's false because you're too afraid to declare your ignorance.

It's important to note that accepting the fact that we still don't know a lot of things doesn't necessarily mean we must disregard what we really do understand. We don't have to toss away everything we've learned; we just need to recognize that there may be much more to come. Isaac Asimov had a lot to say about this particular issue, and about how there is a *"relativity of wrong."* He often told a story about a letter he received from an English literature major who was critical of the scientist's statement that he was glad to live in a century in which people finally discovered the basic rules governing the universe, as well as those governing subatomic particles. The student (rightly) told Asimov that people who lived in every other century thought they were right yet were proved wrong, and that the same was likely to happen to him.[30] In his reply, Asimov explained that *"right"* and *"wrong"* are not necessarily absolutes and are often *"fuzzy concepts."*[31]

"John, when people thought the earth was flat, they were wrong. When people thought the earth was spherical, they were wrong," Asimov wrote in response to the student. *"But if you think that thinking the earth is spherical is just as wrong as thinking the earth is flat, then your view is wronger than both of them put together."*

Don't get me wrong. I'm not saying ignorance is good. I am, however, saying we should work to cure ignorance, as opposed to running from it or stigmatizing it. If you lack knowledge about something, that just means you don't have the necessary data at that time—nothing more, nothing less. We are all ignorant when it comes to a great number of issues because we all lack certain information, so ignorance itself isn't always a bad thing.

What is bad, however, is claiming to know all the answers and/or remaining ignorant by choice (*willful ignorance*). Neil deGrasse Tyson explained this quite well when he said, "*It's okay not to know all the answers; it's better to admit our ignorance than to believe answers that might be wrong. Pretending to know everything closes the door to finding out what's really there.*"

A critic of my work once asked me, "*Why are you an ignorant?*" and I wrote a short, rhyming response that I think helps demonstrate the importance of admitting our own ignorance:

> I am an ignorant.
>
> I don't know about quantum physics and you aren't an expert in English grammar, but we both probably know about MC Hammer.
>
> And while I might know more about religion and science and reptiles, you're the only one who knows how to bring your family smiles.
>
> You see, some of us know some things and others know others, but that doesn't mean we can't work together and act like brothers.
>
> Because if an ignorant is someone who doesn't know something, and you can't fix a car and I can't cook a dumpling, then it's clear to me that you are an ignorant and I am an ignorant.
>
> This is not an insult, however, it is just my two cents.

I don't claim to know all the answers—in fact, I don't claim to "know" much of anything—but I do have a lot of questions. And when there aren't satisfactory answers to those questions, I am more comfortable saying, "I don't know," than I am proclaiming belief in that which is easy or comforting.

BUT SCIENCE IS WRONG SOMETIMES!

Since admitting that you're wrong can be an important piece of individual advancement, it stands to reason that beliefs once considered to be scientifically sound by large groups of educated people can likewise be shown to be flawed—and this is absolutely true. When this happens on a large scale, and a prevailing idea is replaced by a newer model within the mainstream scientific community, it is called a **paradigm shift**. These monumental changes don't happen every day, but when they do, it has the potential to change how we view specific fields and even the process of science as a whole. American physicist and historian Thomas Kuhn, who coined the term *paradigm shift* in his 1962 book *The Structure of Scientific Revolutions*, pointed to the emergence of Copernican astronomy as a particularly relevant case of such a change. When its predecessor, the Ptolemaic system, was developed, it was "*admirably successful in predicting the changing positions of both stars and planets*," according to Kuhn.[32]

"*No other ancient system had performed so well; for the stars, Ptolemaic astronomy is still widely used today as an engineering approximation; for the planets, Ptolemy's predictions were as good as Copernicus*," he wrote. "*But to be admirably successful is never, for a scientific theory, to be completely successful. With respect both to planetary position and to precession of the equinoxes, predictions made with Ptolemy's system never quite conformed with the best available observations.*"

There are many other examples of notable paradigm shifts, including when the germ theory of disease was accepted and the idea of spontaneous generation was refuted, an event that caused a change in the world of medicine that prompted additional discoveries. When this happens, when the scientific community is forced to amend its collective beliefs, should we be scared? Should we doubt everything we've ever discovered? No, because our shifts in understanding aren't a result of science itself being "wrong" or unreliable. Science is simply a method designed to help us follow the evidence, and new data becomes available all the time, which is why it has a track record for improving on its own existing ideas. So, what do we do when new scientific discoveries upstage old hypotheses? Just as we can do when we are proven wrong on a personal level, we have the option to seize the opportunity and use it to learn something, as opposed to running from the fear of being contradicted. This constant openness to change is an important part of the scientific process that allows the community as a whole to grow its knowledge and dispose of bad ideas, but some people still see it as a bad thing.

A lot of those who oppose (or, in some cases, fear) scientific discovery say they don't "believe in" science because it has been "proven wrong" time and time again. Because scientific understandings progress over time, they reason, they aren't consistent or reliable and should be avoided entirely. Members of the antiscience crowd have even been known to shout, "Science once said cigarettes were healthy!" But did *science* ever say that? I don't think so. I think some flawed tests may have shown fewer side effects than actually existed, and some flawed people cherry-picked results in an effort to sell cigarettes and make money, but science—the process itself—wasn't wrong.

In the case of tobacco, the cigarette industry spent billions of dollars in the hopes of distorting the facts surrounding the health risks associated with smoking.[33] This wasn't science itself engaging in the unethical behavior—it was tobacco companies and many of the people they employed—but the spread of ignorance in this manner raises serious issues nonetheless. The discovery of the tobacco executives' corrupt behavior during this time led Robert N. Proctor, a professor of the history of science at Stanford University, to coin the term *agnotology*. Agnotology, according to Proctor, is the study of ignorance or doubt—especially as it relates to the publication of faulty scientific data—that is culturally induced, often as a means to sell a product or service.[34]

The scientific method can't directly cause false beliefs, nor can it discriminate based on funding levels or preconceived notions, but individual scientists are another story. Scientists can lie, cheat, steal, and knowingly promote false ideas just like any other person. A good example of this is Haruko Obokata, a former stem-cell biologist who published research in 2014 that seemed to suggest she and her colleagues were able to get embryonic stem cell effects from normal body cells. She was hailed as a champion of the stem-cell world for a short period of time, but her employer, the Riken Center for Developmental Biology, ultimately discovered her results were doctored and found her guilty of scientific misconduct.[35] Was Obokata's fraud caused by her hubris? Her desire to please a supervisor, or for fame and fortune? We may never know for certain what her motives were, but we can certainly learn a lesson from the events that transpired. John Rasko, who directs cell and molecular therapies at Royal Prince Alfred Hospital, and Carl Power, a researcher and editorial coordinator at the Centenary Institute and University of Sydney, say the scientific community often fails when it comes to reproducibility, "*one of the cornerstones of modern science.*" Still, Obokata's downfall should give us some confidence, the scientists explained.

"*[T]he speed of Obokata's undoing should make us feel more confident about the ability of science to correct itself,*" Rasko and Power wrote in a joint article.[36] "*As soon as she announced the creation of Stap (stimulus-triggered acquisition of pluripotency) cells, other researchers tried to make their own and, when they failed, wanted to know why.*"

When scientists incorrectly interpret data or jump to false assumptions, we can end up with bad information, and that can and does lead us to all sorts of wrong conclusions. But through the process of peer review, and through duplicated experiments and rigorous scientific scrutiny, we can correct that data and make the world a better place as a result. In other words, the only way to solve a scientific error is to experiment and find better, more accurate scientific answers. French novelist Jules Verne explained the importance of mistakes in science in his science fiction novel, *Journey to the Center of the Earth*.

"*Science, my lad, is made up of mistakes, but they are mistakes which it is useful to make, because they lead little by little to the truth,*" Verne wrote.

When there are disagreements among scientists who are conducting their own research, and our understandings shift, it's not because "science was wrong." It's because we learned to overcome our own biases, or the errors in our testing methods or sampling size. We usually see these changes when science was abused, or when we acquired new knowledge that put our previous perspective into better context. You might say scientific understandings are unreliable because they change over time, but, to me, this fluidity in the realm of science is exactly what makes the process so great. We build off old ideas and fine-tune data until we know something with as much certainty as is possible. It's true that new scientific studies sometimes reveal flaws in older ideas, but that fact shouldn't be ridiculed or be cause for alarm; it should be celebrated. After all, as Isaac Asimov said, "*The most exciting phrase to hear in science, the one that heralds new discoveries, is not 'Eureka!' but 'That's funny . . .'*"

You might be asking yourself, "If accepted scientific theories are sometimes overturned, then why should I trust scientists or, for that matter, scientific consensus on a particular subject within a field?" The answer is simple: scientists practicing within their specialized field are experts and are more equipped to understand the various factors at play. When the vast majority of those specialists agree on a topic, they form a consensus, which is likely to form a paradigm when accepted by the vast majority of the population. Might that paradigm shift at some point? Sure, but until then, it makes sense to listen to those with extensive training related to the issue unless you have contradictory data, in which case you should present it. Of course this doesn't mean that scientists are always right, nor does it mean that scientific consensus is infallible, but some research shows that experts on certain issues, like judges when it comes to law, are more easily able to set aside political biases when analyzing data than lay people. This is the finding of Yale law professor and science communication researcher Dan Kahan, who along with others conducted a study of 253 judges.[37] He says the results could extend beyond the legal world and into any area in which someone is an expert, including science. Some people have criticized this conclusion, including John Horgan, a science journalist and director of the Center for Science Writings at Stevens Institute of Technology. He says the study *"merely shows that lawyers and judges know the law better than law students and non-lawyers."*[38]

Regardless of whether you believe experts have more credibility in their fields than members of the public at large or not, the fact that science is regularly wrong is undoubtedly a good thing because it is self-correcting. Its ever-changing landscape of ideas is actually what makes the scientific approach a more valuable method for understanding the world than, say, strict adherence to the stagnant holy books of some religions. Unlike scientific theories, religious texts only change in their interpretation, and that usually only happens when something within them is shown to be objectively false based on...you guessed it: new scientific findings. As English author Terry Pratchett explained, the most important part of science is not that it is perfect, but that it allows us to *"reality-check"* ourselves.

"Science is not about building a body of known 'facts,'" Pratchett said. *"It is a method for asking awkward questions and subjecting them to a reality-check, thus avoiding the human tendency to believe whatever makes us feel good."*

SCIENCE AND RELIGION

Some people who don't understand science think it directly conflicts with all forms of spirituality, that it is out to "disprove God," or even that it is itself a type of faith, but today religion and science are so separated that they don't necessarily interact at all. Sure, some religious believers make testable claims, like that prayer can heal wounds (or move mountains), but those same claims might be repudiated by someone of the same faith who has a different interpretation of their shared holy text. One believer might see scripture as metaphorical while another sees it as literal, but they are both practicing the same tradition. In the case of the first believer, who has put forth no claims about how the natural world works or how it was formed, science has no opinion. Once a believer insists that their god(s) or other supernatural forces intervene in our realm and change things, however, we have the capacity and, I would argue, the duty to test those claims to the best of our abilities. Not surprisingly, looking at the times when, historically, science and religion *did* butt heads, we see that the system based on repeated testing and verification has often prevailed over rigid dogma.

If you think religion and science are always in direct conflict, I recommend researching a few of the many incredibly intelligent, accomplished, and respected scientists who identify with a specific religious faith. Isaac Newton, Galileo Galilei, and other well-known historical discoverers are often cited as scientists to whom religion was important, but considering our many more recent significant scientific advancements and altered cultural taboos, I prefer to look at modern examples. Consider Francis Collins, a devout evangelical Christian and physician-geneticist who led the Human Genome Project, or even Brother Guy J. Consolmagno, a research astronomer who serves as the director of the Vatican Observatory. I would never say these educated, accomplished, pillars of the scientific community are "dumb" or accuse them of being bad scientists, but I do think they might (intentionally or subconsciously) exempt their firmly held religious beliefs from scientific scrutiny. I don't think Collins applies the same scientific rigor to the Bible as he does to genes, nor do I believe Consolmagno looks for the same types of evidence for his religion's claims as he does for the presence of meteorites, but that's okay. These people and others like them might not see the conflicting forces between their religion, which could give philosophical comfort, and their work in science, which provides a certainty that faith can't. As Dartmouth College Professor Marcelo Gleiser has said, "*Religious myths attempt to explain the unknown with the unknowable, while science attempts to explain the unknown with the knowable.*"[39]

FLAWED SCIENTISTS

It's not uncommon for otherwise accomplished scientists to have false beliefs, including some that are demonstrably so, and religion doesn't have that market cornered. Take Edgar D. Mitchell, for instance. He was an aeronautical engineer, an astronaut for the National Aeronautics and Space Administration (NASA), the sixth man on the moon, and he had a Doctor of Science degree in aeronautics and astronautics from the Massachusetts Institute of Technology, but he was also convinced by some pretty silly ideas. Despite having flown in space and experienced its vastness, Mitchell believed that **unidentified flying objects (UFOs)** seen from Earth were the result of alien visitation. And that wasn't his only sacred cow: he also believed in remote healing and **extrasensory perception (ESP),** neither of which have ever been demonstrated under conditions that rule out fraud. Does that mean he was a bad engineer or a bad astronaut? Of course not; it just means he wasn't being consistent in his application of the scientific method. The same goes for Jeff Meldrum, an Idaho State University anatomy and anthropology professor who believes in the existence of animals in the Bigfoot family. He can still be a good teacher and scientist, despite the fact that he has a false belief, and he can even make valuable observations regarding the search for what he considers to be our long lost primate cousin. Meldrum, who has also tried to reconcile Book of Mormon stories with modern DNA data,[40] actually pointed out, *"If one flips open to a field guide distribution of black bear across North America, one finds a remarkable coincidence with reports of an unrecognized primate—Bigfoot, Sasquatch."* Meldrum likely retains his preestablished perspective despite recognizing this "coincidence" because he doesn't apply scrutiny to his cherished belief.

Another good example of a flawed scientist and Bigfoot enthusiast is Jane Goodall. Goodall, a British primatologist known for her 55-year study of wild chimpanzees, has also stated a number of times that she believes in modern upright primates that have apparently been successful in hiding all evidence of their existence for hundreds of years. When asked about these creatures, Goodall, who most would consider an expert on primates, told NPR, *"Well, now, you will be amazed when I tell you that I'm sure that they exist."*[41] Goodall goes on to cite Native Americans who *"all describe the same sounds"* and unidentified hair as support for her belief, but she doesn't acknowledge that there are probably better explanations than a nondescript bipedal ape for which we have never discovered a bone or a body. To me, this lack of legitimate physical evidence, which has been demonstrated in numerous scientific studies,[42] can be explained relatively easily: Bigfoot sightings are not experiences with Sasquatch at all. They are instead the result of fraud, mistaken identity, and misattributed forest sounds. Goodall ultimately concludes the interview with an admission that she is "*a romantic*" and has "*always wanted them to exist.*"

"*Well, there are people looking. There are very ardent groups in Russia, and they have published a whole lot of stuff about what they've seen,*" Goodall told NPR. "*Of course, the big, the big criticism of all this is, 'Where is the body?' You know, why isn't there a body? I can't answer that, and maybe they don't exist, but I want them to.*"

Goodall seemed to take a step back from her initial claim that she was "*sure*" Bigfoot was real, but that particular cryptid isn't her only false belief. She is also known for her staunch opposition to genetically modified organisms (GMOs), which have been shown to be just as safe as their nonmodified counterparts,[43][44] and her comments on homosexuality, which she argues is absent in the natural world without some form of environmental disruption. Goodall said, "*We've never seen anything remotely like homosexuality in chimpanzees in the wild. However, in captivity, where their lives are disrupted, where they can't express themselves the way they would in the wild, then we sometimes see it.*" Despite the fact that numerous valid studies have shown that thousands of other animal species demonstrate homosexual behavior,[45] she added that homosexuality has become prevalent in humans because "*we are not free to express*" what we really like to do, making a comparison between wild wolves and domesticated dogs. Despite her years of experience with primates, Goodall's claims about chimpanzees in the wild directly contradict established scientific findings.[46] In 1967, long before Goodall expressed her opinion about homosexuality being absent in wild chimps, English zoologist Desmond Morris published his best-selling book, *The Naked Ape.*[47] In the book, Morris documents that "*many species indulge in*" homosexual behavior and that there is nothing "*biologically unusual*" about it. Empirical evidence of homosexual activity in wild bonobos and chimps has also been clearly outlined by Craig Stanford, professor of biological sciences and anthropology at the University of Southern California,[48] and Dutch primatologist Frans de Waal.[49]

While he may not be as renowned in the science community as Mitchell or Goodall, Ben Carson—retired neurosurgeon, failed 2016 Republican presidential candidate, and President Trump's choice to head the U.S. Department of Housing and Urban Development (HUD)—serves as an example of a deservedly celebrated medical doctor who accepts science when it comes to his chosen field yet who also holds demonstrably false and unscientific beliefs. A graduate of Yale University, Carson famously led a 70-person team that for the first time separated conjoined twins who were connected at the back of their heads,[50] yet he also believes (against all historical and physical evidence) that the **Pyramids** of Giza were used to store grain by Joseph of Bible fame.[51] This claim has been debunked by historians, archaeologists, anyone who can see that the pyramids aren't hollow, and even the Bible itself, which states that Joseph's grain was stored "*in the cities,*"[52] yet Carson continues to believe it. Science writer Guy P. Harrison says Carson is a "*glaring example*" of how "*a sharp mind and extensive education do not guarantee good thinking skills.*"

"*Major League pitchers and NFL quarterbacks both use their arms to throw. But we can't assume one can do the other's job well. The skills don't necessarily translate. It is much the same with thinking,*" Harrison wrote for *Psychology Today.*[53] "*The ability to use a human brain well one way does not mean it automatically works well in other ways. Critical thinking requires self-awareness, commitment, and vigilance. It's a mindset and an attitude, not a body of coursework or an IQ test score.*"

To clarify: I don't think Goodall, Collins, Consolmagno, Carson, or other scientists with unsupported beliefs are necessarily dumb, nor do I believe Mitchell failed to understand scientific principles. I do, however, think these scientists and others with similarly false beliefs help us see that no one is immune from being wrong. They all have certain topics on which further study is warranted or claims they haven't analyzed closely enough, and that's okay because being wrong is part of being human. It's actually not unusual at all, even among academics. It's quite common for incredibly intelligent people to believe what might be considered "dumb" things, especially if they separate those flawed ideas from others that would undergo careful scientific scrutiny. It's called **compartmentalization**. In the minds of some scientists, certain ideas, such as religious or spiritual notions, are considered sacred and demand only faith and observance—not tests. Everything else, however, is worldly: medical decisions, finance deals, corporate transactions, and other daily occurrences demand real-world evidence and actions, while exempted beliefs (sacred cows) simply do not. Skeptical writer Neil Carter says intelligence itself "*is compartmental.*"

"*We must be ever on our guard against the halo effect, which is that tendency to ascribe to individuals who are distinguished in one field an authority which they do not deserve in others,*" Carter wrote, pointing out that Albert Einstein, an expert in astrophysics, was not necessarily an authority in politics or philosophy. "*It shouldn't lend much weight to either believers' or nonbelievers' arguments that this famous person or that one was 'on the right side' on matters of religious belief.*"

The simple fact is that, whether you are clinging tightly to something you were taught as a child or you're convinced by forged data and emotional arguments, it's easy to be deceived and even easier to stay that way. All we can do is try our best to consistently and regularly apply scientific principles across the board, leaving no idea exempt from inquiry and experiment.

CELEBRITIES AND SCIENCE

Even scientists have blind spots when it comes to their beliefs, so what can we say about celebrities, who aren't required to have any scientific training, yet are often infinitely more likely to shape ordinary citizens' beliefs? The terrifying fact is that many people who are famous, whether they are actors, singers, politicians, or anything else, spread false beliefs to their trusting fans every day via their large platforms.[54] The more popular a celebrity is, the more damaging he or she becomes when promoting bad ideas or attacking science in general. The phenomenon reminds me of something John F. Kennedy once said. He (almost prophetically) stated, "*If you scoff at intellectuals, harass scientists, and reward only athletic achievements, then the future is very dark indeed.*"

We already learned about Jenny McCarthy and her dangerous conceptions regarding life-saving vaccinations, but she isn't the only one in Hollywood who's on the anti-immunization train: her ex-boyfriend and actor Jim Carrey hopped on board in 2009 when he endorsed the repeatedly debunked claim that the MMR shot, used to inoculate people against measles, mumps, and rubella, "*may be causing autism and other disorders.*"[55] Comedian and TV show host Bill Maher, known for his critiques against religion, has also made comments against vaccinations based on his unsupported beliefs. He started publicly denouncing them in 2005, when he told CNN's Larry King that the flu shot was *"the worst thing you can do."* Maher made a number of other similar statements and, four years later, he upped the stakes during an interview with then-Senator Bill Frist (R-TN). Perhaps due to his ignorance about biology, combined with his tendency to automatically distrust **The Government**, Maher condemned vaccines in general.

"Why would you let them be the ones to stick a disease into your arm? I would never get a swine flu vaccine or any vaccine," Maher said. *"I don't trust the government, especially with my health."*

Unfortunately for Maher's diehard fans (and the public in general), the star's false beliefs don't end with his steadfast opposition to vaccinations. In February 2016, he introduced to the world Australian doctor Sam Chachoua, who wasn't licensed to practice medicine in the United States but claimed to have cured actor Charlie Sheen and many others of HIV. Chachoua told Maher that, although Sheen went back on his antiretroviral medications after the supposed cure, the infected goat milk-laced treatment he administered had been verified and was *"more than 99 percent effective."* Maher not only gave Chachoua a platform of more than 4 million people with whom to share his false claims, but he also called the doctor's purported decision to inject himself with Sheen's infected blood "confident," and not crazy, despite the fact that his safety relied on the efficacy of injected vaccines that Maher previously condemned. So, in addition to the children and immunocompromised people endangered by his recommendations to skip essentially all approved immunizations, Maher is now putting AIDS patients at risk through his promotion of a different vaccine that is both unregulated and unsupported by evidence. It's worth noting that Sheen, less than two weeks after Chachoua was featured on *Real Time with Bill Maher*, renounced the doctor and admitted that he was *"not cured."*

"He would have stuff delivered at all hours of the night, and I was an idiot to keep taking it. It was just the BS started to really pile up with this guy," Sheen said on *The Dr. Oz Show.*[56] *"I think what we're observing from him is an absolute grand work of fiction. I think guys like him are dangerous. I'm not going to be trading my meds for arthritic goat milk. I'm just saying."*

Actress Gwyneth Paltrow also made headlines when she began promoting a false health tip, which in her case was an herbal vaginal steam treatment that she said *"balances female hormones."*[57] As if that weren't enough, Paltrow later promoted the idea that an infrared sauna could cure the flu to her 1.3 million followers on Instagram. This suggestion was criticized by a number of medical professionals, including Weill Cornell Medical College clinical instructor in medicine Alexandra Sowa, who said dehydration "*can be a very real complication of the flu.*"

"*All saunas, whether traditional (warming the area around you) or infrared (warming your skin directly) have the same result: They increase body temperature to stimulate sweat production and an elevated heart rate,*" Sowa wrote for *Slate*.[58] "*In a patient with the flu, this will cause further dehydration and possibly significant complications.*"

In 2016, Paltrow's organic skincare company, Goop, also began promoting a face cream that is said to undergo "*extensive prayer, meditation, and music before ever appearing on shelves.*" *Slate* contributor Ruth Graham pointed to the price tags of the unproven, mystical products.

"*A wee 1.7-oz. jar of Sodashi 'enzyme face polish' will run you $121, while 0.34 oz. of de Mamiel's 'altitude oil' is a mere $44,*" Graham said.[59] "*But take heart: the snake oil is free, and it's glorious.*"

There are plenty of celebrities who believe ridiculous things, many of which have nothing to do with medicine or health. Take Australian cricket veteran Shane Warne, for instance, who revealed on a TV show in February 2016 that he doubts evolution and believes humans are the result of extraterrestrial experimentations. Speaking with a noticeable misunderstanding of evolution, Warne asked, "*If we've evolved from monkeys, then why haven't those ones evolved?*"

"*Because [of] aliens,*" he answered, adding that the pyramids are "*perfectly symmetrical*" and couldn't have been built by people.[60] "*Whatever planet [or] planets they're on out there, they decided that they were gonna start some more life here on earth and study us.*"

Fran Drescher, who played the leading role in the 1990s sitcom *The Nanny*, also has some *out-there* beliefs when it comes to aliens. She says she and her husband were both independently abducted by aliens and implanted with some sort of a microchip.[61] There's also Megan Fox, known for her roles in the first two *Transformer* films and in the *Teenage Mutant Ninja Turtles* films, who advocates strongly for the existence of Bigfoot;[62] pop singer Ariana Grande, who insists she had a "*demonic experience*" at a cemetery in Kansas;[63] and many, many more. As you can see, there is no shortage of famous people with unsupported beliefs and platforms with which to spread them to the masses (see chapter 15).

HOW DO WE KNOW THINGS?

Science isn't magical or incorruptible. It is merely a means to uncover information or processes that are, at that moment in time, unknown to us. Science is a tool we use to look at the world in a more objective manner, to give us a perspective that is less likely to be influenced by biases or a lack of information. It's not infallible, though. It has its own issues. However, as Carl Sagan explained, science is still the best system we have for discovering the truth.

"It is not perfect. It can be misused. It is only a tool. But it is by far the best tool we have, self-correcting, ongoing, applicable to everything," Sagan said of the scientific method.[64] *"It has two rules. First: there are no sacred truths; all assumptions must be critically examined; arguments from authority are worthless. Second: whatever is inconsistent with the facts must be discarded or revised. We must understand the Cosmos as it is and not confuse how it is with how we wish it to be."*

Science isn't perfect, but that's okay because we aren't looking for some magical process that reveals all the secrets of the world with the press of a button. To think like a scientist doesn't mean you must use the scientific method to answer every problem or form every opinion, and it doesn't mean you should treat science like a belief system, because it isn't one.[65] What it means is that, when evaluating scientific claims—assertions that can be proven or disproven through observation and analysis—you weigh the evidence accordingly. But what types of evidence are important? Anything can be considered "evidence" (although it may be weak evidence), including first- and second-hand testimonials, unverifiable ancient texts, and hearsay—so what matters most? To the scientific skeptic, the answer is simple: results from experimentation. The most famous, well-respected academics can be shown to be wrong, and logical-seeming arguments can fall flat in the face of new data, but science provides us with a level of certainty other systems just cannot. This idea is not a new one. In fact, it was detailed simply by Roger Bacon, a philosopher and Franciscan friar, in his *Opus majus* sent to the Pope in the 1200s.[66]

"Without experiment, nothing can be adequately known," Bacon wrote. *"An argument proves theoretically but does not give the certitude necessary to remove all doubt, nor will the mind repose in the clear view of truth, unless it find it by way of experiment."*

Hundreds of years later, the traditional importance of experimentation in science lives on and thrives throughout the scientific community. In fact, physicist Richard P. Feynman echoed this simple yet important detail when he said, *"If it disagrees with experiment it is wrong."*

"In that simple statement is the key to science," Feynman explained. *"It does not make any difference how beautiful your guess is. It does not make any difference how smart you are, who made the guess, or what his name is—if it disagrees with experiment it is wrong. That is all there is to it."*[67]

THE PROCESS OF SCIENCE

We know science relies heavily on experimentation, but how does the process itself actually work? It all starts with a question in the scientist's mind. The question could be anything, from "Why are the oceans getting warmer?" to "How does this toy dog move?" Next, the researcher studies the question and the elements involved, noting curiosities and important details. Eventually, a hypothesis is born. It's not much more than a guess, but it usually has at least a hint of viability or perceived support based on personal experience. The next step is tricky, but it's also the most important. The scientist has to design and execute an experiment, putting the hypothesis to the test. They must carefully weed out the possibility of bias during this step and take all precautions necessary to keep the results free from outside influence, including using control groups where necessary. In the area of medical research, this is accomplished through the use of double-blind studies in which both the subjects and scientists are unaware of the details surrounding the application of the experimental medication or procedure. After the tests, the scientist tries to make sense of the data. They look at the information and draw a conclusion that best fits the results. Finally, our researcher is ready for the last step: communicate the information to other scientists, who can test it out for themselves and confirm or debunk the results. The scientific method is a process we use all the time in our daily lives, sometimes even without noticing it, but it can also be applied to humanity's discoveries as a whole. The scientific community thrives on this system of discovery, which, while flawed, has been responsible for some amazing things. In *Cosmos*, Neil deGrasse Tyson commented on the impressive accomplishments that have been made through science in only 400 years.

"The scientific method is so powerful that, in a mere four centuries, it has taken us from Galileo's first look through a telescope at another world to leaving our footprints on the moon," Tyson said.

In the scientific community, new studies purported to have scientifically significant and technically sound results are subjected to peer review by one or more expert referees before publication as an initial form of validation. If a study passes peer review, it is published. Upon publication, the study is open to evaluation by every competing person in the field (and related fields), including those in direct competition (whose own research may be in conflict with the study). These competitors in turn must refine or alter their own hypotheses and research in light of this new evidence if they cannot scientifically discredit the published idea or finding.[68] This means that, when a scientist publishes a finding or study, thousands of other, rival scientists are encouraged to attempt to duplicate—and perhaps expose flaws in—the documented experiments. That way, they can either verify the results or, in the alternative, debunk them entirely. The peer review and publication system isn't perfect,[69] but it is the best way to verify scientific findings—as well as to correct issues within the process itself.

To sum up: through time and scientific research, we reach tentative conclusions that can be refined with more time and more research. Once enough data is gathered, some ideas are published and examined by other experts. If all goes well during publication and peer review, it's possible for an idea to eventually take one of the most important steps in science: it could become a scientific theory, which must reliably explain a component of the natural world and is therefore by definition supported by vast amounts of evidence. Unlike a scientific law, which describes a natural phenomenon (e.g., gravity), a theory provides an explanation of the how or why of an observed phenomenon (e.g., evolution by natural selection), giving us a deeper view of how the world really works and helping us advance our understanding more rapidly. Some opponents of science will say these valuable scientific conclusions are crazy, dismissing evolution and other foundational concepts as "just theories," while other people will decide to learn about them in detail and possibly comprehend their importance. No matter what you personally believe, however, it won't affect the veracity of the ideas at issue. Tyson explains how a scientific theory differs from a general theory, or a guess.

"Some claim that evolution is just a theory, as if it were merely an opinion. The theory of evolution, like the theory of gravity, is a scientific fact," he said on *Cosmos.* *"Evolution really happened. Accepting our kinship with all life on earth is not only solid science, in my view, it's also a soaring, spiritual experience."*

Science isn't perfect, but it has been shown to be incredibly helpful in separating falsehoods from facts. The fact that science is a rigorous system built on ongoing challenge and correction is part of what makes scientific observation, as Jonathan C. Smith said, *"one of our best reality-checking tools."*

"When you test an idea, you often use science. When you try to find out what works and what doesn't work, you use science. When you take a pragmatic or practical approach to solving a problem, you use science," Smith wrote. *"Doctors use science to diagnose illness and prescribe treatment. Detectives use science to solve crimes. Auto mechanics use science to fix cars. Students use science to decide on courses, career paths, and even weekend dates."*

Smith added that sources and logic *"can provide impressive support for a claim."*

"However, all are trumped by scientific observation, tests of hypotheses as well as explanations and theories. The famous expert can be proven wrong. A logical argument may be sound, but based on false premises."

SKEPTICISM VS. GULLIBILITY

One reason the scientific method is so important is that it is a sort of vaccine that protects us from our own natural *gullibility*, the tendency to be easily tricked or manipulated. We all have the potential to be gullible, and we all have a desire to believe certain things. Some people are good at overcoming credulity and seeking more extensive evidentiary support, while others find the process difficult or even against their nature. In fact, in 2015, cognitive psychologist Gordon Pennycook and his team at the University of Waterloo set out to test whether some people are more receptive to *"pseudo-profound bullshit,"* which they said consists of *"seemingly impressive assertions that are presented as true and meaningful but are actually vacuous."* In the study, Pennycook and the other researchers presented "bullshit statements" to participants with proper sentence structure but no discernible meaning and found that some people were much more likely to rate them as profound.[70] The scientists also discovered that the profundity ratings for the nonsense sentences were "*very strongly correlated*" with responses from actual quotes by Deepak Chopra, the so-called New Age guru with millions of followers on Twitter.

"*Chopra is, of course, just one example among many. Using vagueness or ambiguity to mask a lack of meaningfulness is surely common in political rhetoric, marketing, and even academia,*" the authors of the study wrote in its conclusion. "*The construction of a reliable index of bullshit receptivity is an important first step toward gaining a better understanding of the underlying cognitive and social mechanisms that determine if and when bullshit is detected.*"

Credulity doesn't have to be a permanent trait; it's been shown that not everyone who starts off that way remains gullible for life. While it may be the case that some people are simply more gullible and others are more likely to doubt and look for evidence, there are always ways to get better at being skeptical. One concept that might help you hone your skeptical skills is known as the *zebra rule*. If you've ever been to medical school (or watched *Grey's Anatomy* or *House, M.D.*), you know that Dr. Theodore Woodward of the University of Maryland School of Medicine told his interns that, when they hear hoof beats, they should not expect zebras.[71] This analogy is commonly used in the medical field to ensure new doctors look for common illnesses (horses) presenting in uncommon forms prior to diagnosing a rare disorder (zebra) of some kind, but it can also be helpful when learning to be skeptical.

Do you hear a loud noise coming from the attic at night? If you assume a ghost is the culprit, you're falling into the "zebra" trap or—perhaps more appropriately in this supernatural instance—the unicorn trap. You should consider some horses, first. Is it possible that you have a rodent infestation? Could there be a person in your attic? Could something have fallen onto your roof? These are all perfectly reasonable explanations—common horses that should be ruled out before you start hunting for unicorns. Still, this zebra and horse issue isn't always black and white. It's important to note that, especially in medicine, zebras, or rare diagnoses, do exist and shouldn't be ignored. It all depends on the circumstances. That's why I like to say: when you hear hoof beats, think of horses, not zebras . . . unless you are in Southern Africa or another region where there are no native horses. In that case, it's probably a zebra, so act accordingly. This method of deduction is related to **Occam's razor** and the *parsimony* *principle*, which states that the simplest scientific explanation is likely the correct one (see chapter 10).[72]

Remembering helpful maxims can certainly make it easier to practice skepticism in daily life, but it's even more crucial to understand and adjust for our many known and unknown biases. We've already learned how the feeling of cognitive dissonance can discourage attempts to learn new things, but there are a lot of other mechanisms that distort our perception and actively cause false beliefs. For starters, there's **confirmation bias**, which can be considered a result of cognitive dissonance and describes our tendency to agree with those who agree with us and to read mostly material that supports our positions.[73] Sheltering ourselves from others' ideas doesn't help us get closer to the truth, but for some, it can be comforting. There's also the human impulse to believe things that are already believed by others, which is considered a part of the **bandwagon effect** that broadly applies to beliefs and even large-scale group preferences, such as fads and fashion trends. This effect, which can cause people to accept popular beliefs regardless of underlying support, is closely related to **groupthink** (see chapter 10). We could also be affected by the **gambler's fallacy**, the faulty perception that the probabilities of future occurrences are changed by events in the past. In other words, you roll five dice five times, but not one of them turns up the number six. If you roll a sixth time, you're due for a six, right? Wrong. The odds are exactly the same with each roll.[74] People are prone to all sorts of biases, and learning to avoid or compensate for them is key to thinking like a scientist. Canadian bioethicist George Dvorsky, who defines a cognitive bias as "*a genuine deficiency or limitation in our thinking*" or "*a flaw in judgment that arises from errors of memory, social attribution, and miscalculations*," says these perceptual errors reveal the brain's major limitations.

"*The lowly calculator can do math thousands of times better than we can, and our memories are often less than useless—plus, we're subject to cognitive biases, those annoying glitches in our thinking that cause us to make questionable decisions and reach erroneous conclusions*," Dvorsky wrote. "*Some social psychologists believe our cognitive biases help us process information more efficiently, especially in dangerous situations. Still, they lead us to make grave mistakes*."

Carl Sagan, in *The Demon-Haunted World*, discussed how humans in general are susceptible to many different kinds of deception. To make people think more like scientists and prevent them from being duped, Sagan put forth a set of cognitive tools called the *"baloney detection kit."* He said the kit, if adopted and utilized regularly, can help people avoid buying into false ideas, even when they are reassuring by their very nature. Here are Sagan's nine techniques that make up the baloney detection kit, excerpted from the book:

1. *Wherever possible there must be independent confirmation of the "facts."*

2. *Encourage substantive debate on the evidence by knowledgeable proponents of all points of view.*

3. *Arguments from authority carry little weight—"authorities" have made mistakes in the past. They will do so again in the future. Perhaps a better way to say it is that in science there are no authorities; at most, there are experts.*

4. *Spin more than one hypothesis. If there's something to be explained, think of all the different ways in which it could be explained. Then think of tests by which you might systematically disprove each of the alternatives. What survives, the hypothesis that resists disproof in this Darwinian selection among "multiple working hypotheses," has a much better chance of being the right answer than if you had simply run with the first idea that caught your fancy.*

5. *Try not to get overly attached to a hypothesis just because it's yours. It's only a way station in the pursuit of knowledge. Ask yourself why you like the idea. Compare it fairly with the alternatives. See if you can find reasons for rejecting it. If you don't, others will.*

6. *Quantify. If whatever it is you're explaining has some measure, some numerical quantity attached to it, you'll be much better able to discriminate among competing hypotheses. What is vague and qualitative is open to many explanations. Of course there are truths to be sought in the many qualitative issues we are obliged to confront, but finding them is more challenging.*

7. *If there's a chain of argument, every link in the chain must work (including the premise)—not just most of them.*

8. *Occam's Razor. This convenient rule-of-thumb urges us when faced with two hypotheses that explain the data equally well to choose the simpler.*

9. *Always ask whether the hypothesis can be, at least in principle, falsified. Propositions that are untestable, unfalsifiable are not worth much. Consider the grand idea that our Universe and everything in it is just an elementary particle—an electron, say—in a much bigger Cosmos. But if we can never acquire information from outside our Universe, is not the idea incapable of disproof? You must be able to check assertions out. Inveterate skeptics must be given the chance to follow your reasoning, to duplicate your experiments and see if they get the same result.*

This list of tools, while extensive and helpful to anyone examining potentially dubious claims, isn't (and will likely never be) complete. There is just too much baloney in the world, and too few high-quality detectors. Science writer Michael Shermer, author of *The Believing Brain* and other titles, recognized this need for an expanded baloney detection kit that could shield people from additional lies and manipulated truths. He added 10 questions to accompany Sagan's nine pieces of advice:

1. *How reliable is the source of the claim?*

2. *Does the source make similar claims?*

3. *Have the claims been verified by somebody else?*

4. *Does this fit with the way the world works?*

5. *Has anyone tried to disprove the claim?*

6. *Where does the preponderance of evidence point?*

7. *Is the claimant playing by the rules of science?*

8. *Is the claimant providing positive evidence?*

9. *Does the new theory account for as many phenomena as the old theory?*

10. *Are personal beliefs driving the claim?*[75]

There are a lot of tools and detection kits that help people distinguish fact from fiction, but no worksheet or script is guaranteed to make you think like a scientist. What's most important when practicing skepticism is that you ask questions, test answers, think of alternative solutions, and follow the hard evidence.

MAKING SCIENCE POPULAR

Science is an incredibly important process, leading to world-changing discoveries and life-extending medical advancements, but there are millions of people who actively oppose it and even more who ignore it entirely. This problem hasn't gone unrecognized. In 2014, comedian and TV show host Stephen Colbert asked Neil deGrasse Tyson what would most surprise Carl Sagan, who died in 1996, about the world today. Tyson's response was, "*I think that what would surprise him the most is that we still have to argue that science is something important in society.*"

So, how do we get everyone to realize the importance of science and take it seriously? In my opinion, we have to show them that the scientific method isn't just for people with PhDs and lab coats, and that it can be used to make all sorts of decisions in life. Consider **corporal punishment**, for instance. If you have a young child, and you're considering methods of discipline, you have two options: you could use your personal experiences, perhaps justifying spankings by telling yourself you got them and turned out fine, or you could look at the data to determine which method is actually best in the long run. In this case, the evidence suggests deliberately inflicting pain on children as retribution doesn't work very well as a behavioral modification method. It may at times make a child immediately comply, but it can also have negative effects on moral internalization, quality of relationship with the parent, and mental health, and has been associated with future aggression and criminal or antisocial behavior. That is not to say that everyone who is spanked has lasting negative consequences, but, scientifically, physical punishments can have some pretty severe repercussions. This isn't my opinion, though; it's the conclusion of a thorough analysis of 88 high-quality scientific studies on the topic of corporal punishment.[76] Now, will there still be people who hit their children? Of course. But that decision won't be based on the best scientific information available.

Most people probably don't look at scientific data when making personal choices, including corporal punishment and many other things, and that's the real problem. It's not just that they look at the information available and—interpreting data in their own way—come to their own conclusions. That would still be an informed decision, which is always better than one made out of ignorance. Instead, they don't think science comes into play at all. Maybe they don't have the curiosity, the know-how, or the understanding of the importance of verifiably true answers, but whatever the reason, the scientific spirit that exists within all of us from childhood has wilted for them. We need to reignite that innate curiosity about the world, encourage scientific pursuits wherever they're possible (and practical), and tell everyone who will listen about the importance of discovery. Vocal activism is important, but the best way to accomplish this task, in my opinion, is through quality, science-centered education. Author John Green explains that public education isn't just for the benefit of the students or their parents. It exists *"for the benefit of the social order,"* he said.

"We have discovered as a species that it is useful to have an educated population. You do not need to be a student or have a child who is a student to benefit from public education. Every second of your life, you benefit from public education," Green said. *"So let me explain why I like to pay taxes for schools, even though I don't personally have a kid in school: it's because I don't like living in a country with a bunch of stupid people."*

Scientific advancement is still happening. We are seeing new discoveries all the time despite the fact that many people simply don't care, but such advancement is not enough. In my opinion, what we need is a *cultural* paradigm shift, as opposed to a scientific one. This change would include altered perceptions toward science and education by the majority of citizens, and a societal urgency toward technological advancement. There would be revised priorities for the majority of individuals, and they would prefer to spend their time learning about the world and contributing to its greatness instead of doing it harm. Soap opera and NASCAR viewership may decrease, but book sales would skyrocket! It would be an entirely different world, but one of which I would be proud to be a part. Writer and journalist Walter Isaacson would likely agree. He is quoted saying, *"I hope that someday scientists can be considered heroes again, instead of Paris Hilton."*

"What do you think science is? There's nothing magical about science. It is simply a systematic way for carefully and thoroughly observing nature and using consistent logic to evaluate results. Which part of that exactly do you disagree with? Do you disagree with being thorough? Using careful observation? Being systematic? Or using consistent logic?"

—**Steven P. Novella**

NOTES

1.   Mary Purugganan and Jan Hewitt, "How to Read a Scientific Article," Rice University, Cain Project in Engineering and Professional Communication, 2004, http://www.owlnet.rice.edu/~cainproj/courses/HowToReadSciArticle.pdf.

2.   Martin Ryder, "Scientism," University of Colorado, Denver, 2013, carbon.ucdenver.edu/~mryder/scientism_este.html.

3.   Susan Haack, "Six Signs of Scientism," *Logos & Episteme* 3, no. 1 (2012): 75–95.

4.   Public Broadcasting Service, "Scientism," PBS Online, www.pbs.org/faithandreason/gengloss/sciism-body.html.

5.   Robert T. Carroll, "Scientism," The Skeptic's Dictionary, October 27, 2015.

6.   Jamie Holmes, "Be Careful, Your Love of Science Looks a Lot like Religion," *Quartz*, August 11, 2015.

7.   Miguel Farias et al. "Scientific Faith: Belief in Science Increases in the Face of Stress and Existential Anxiety," *Journal of Experimental Social Psychology* 49, no. 6 (2013): 1210–1213.

8.   Daniel C. Dennett, *Darwin's Dangerous Idea: Evolution and the Meanings of Life* (New York: Simon & Schuster, 1995).

9.   Nick Anthis, "Why Are Veins Blue?" The Scientific Activist, ScienceBlogs, April 17, 2008.

10. David A. Thompson and Stephen L. Adams, "The Full Moon and ED Patient Volumes: Unearthing a Myth," *American Journal of Emergency Medicine* 14, no. 2 (1996): 161–164.

11. Wendy Coates, Dietrich Jehle, and Eric Cottington, "Trauma and the Full Moon: A Waning Theory," *Annals of Emergency Medicine* 18, no. 7 (1989): 763–765.

12. *"Some nurses ascribe the apparent chaos to the moon, but dozens of studies show that the belief is unfounded,"* Jean-Luc Margot, a University of California, Los Angeles, professor of planetary astronomy, said in a statement on March 30, 2015. *"The moon is innocent."*

13. Robynne Boyd, "Do People Only Use 10 Percent of their Brains," *Scientific American,* February 7, 2008.

14. Kenneth L. Higbee and Samuel L. Clay, "College Students' Beliefs in the Ten-Percent Myth," *Journal of Psychology* 132, no. 5 (1998): 469–476.

15. Scott O. Lilienfeld et al. *50 Great Myths of Popular Psychology: Shattering Widespread Misconceptions about Human Behavior* (New York: John Wiley & Sons, 2011).

16. Steven D. Hales, "Thinking Tools: You can Prove a Negative," *Think* 4, no. 10 (2005): 109–112.

17. Isaac Asimov, *The Gods Themselves* (Westminster, MD: Spectra, 2011).

18. *"We must always be on guard against errors in our reasoning. Eternal vigilance is the watchphrase not just of freedom, but also of thinking. That is the very nature of skepticism."* —Michael Shermer

19. Stephen Edelston Toulmin, *Human Understanding* (Princeton: Princeton University Press, 1972).

20. If you're in need of recovery and looking for a secular alternative to *"twelve step"* programs, Secular Organizations for Sobriety (S.O.S.) and SMART Recovery are two groups that provide non-faith-based systems that support all recovery, regardless of your particular spiritual path or lack thereof.

21. Marcus A. Bachhuber et al., "Medical Cannabis Laws and Opioid Analgesic Overdose Mortality in the United States, 1999–2010," *JAMA Internal Medicine* 174, no. 10 (2014): 1668–1673.

22. Wayne Hall and Nadia Solowij, "Adverse Effects of Cannabis," *The Lancet* 352, no. 9140 (1998): 1611–1616.

23. Robert C. Bailey et al., "Male Circumcision for HIV Prevention in Young Men in Kisumu, Kenya: A Randomised Controlled Trial," *The Lancet* 369, no. 9562 (2007): 643–656.

24. K. J. S. Anand, "Consensus Statement for the Prevention and Management of Pain in the Newborn," *Archives of Pediatrics & Adolescent Medicine* 155, no. 2 (2001): 173–180.

25. Dan Bollinger, "Lost Boys: An Estimate of US Circumcision-Related Infant Deaths," *Thymos* 4, no. 1 (2010): 78.

26. S. Todd Sorokan, Jane C. Finlay, and Ann L. Jefferies, "Newborn Male Circumcision," *Paediatrics & Child Health* 20, no. 6 (2015): 1.

27. British Medical Association, "The Law and Ethics of Male Circumcision: Guidance for Doctors," *Journal of Medical Ethics* 30, no. 3 (2004): 259–263.

28. "*More People Would Learn from Their Mistakes If They Weren't So Busy Denying Them.*" —Harold J. Smith

29. Stefano Palminteri, Mehdi Khamassi, Mateus Joffily, and Giorgio Coricelli, "Contextual Modulation of Value Signals in Reward and Punishment Learning," *Nature Communications* 6 (2015).

30. "*I know one thing: that I know nothing.*" —attributed to Socrates

31. Isaac Asimov, "The Relativity of Wrong," *Skeptical Inquirer* 14, no. 1 (1989): 35–44.

32. Thomas S. Kuhn, *The Structure of Scientific Revolutions* (Chicago: University of Chicago Press, 2012).

33. David Michaels and Celeste Monforton, "Manufacturing Uncertainty: Contested Science and the Protection of the Public's Health and Environment," *American Journal of Public Health* 95, no. S1 (2005): S39–S48.

34. Karen W. Arenson, "What Organizations Don't Want to Know Can Hurt," *New York Times*, August 21, 2006, www.nytimes.com/2006/08/22/business/22mistakes.html.

35. Shunsuke Ishii et al., "Report on STAP Cell Research Paper Investigation," RIKEN, March 31, 2014

36. John Rasko and Carl Power, "What Pushes Scientists to Lie? The Disturbing but Familiar Story of Haruko Obokata," *Guardian*, February 18, 2015, www.theguardian.com/science/2015/feb/18/haruko-obokata-stap-cells-controversy-scientists-lie.

37. Dan M., Kahan et al. "'Ideology' or 'Situation Sense'? An Experimental Investigation of Motivated Reasoning and Professional Judgment," *University of Pennsylvania Law Review* 64 (2016).

38. "*That's reassuring, but surely it does not mean we should always trust lawyers' legal advice, especially since lawyers so often disagree on interpretations of the law,*" Horgan wrote for *Scientific American* (April 8, 2015). "*Consider the rancor of recent debates on health care, immigration, taxes, the environment and other issues in Washington, where more than one third of current Representatives and one half of Senators have law degrees.*"

39. Marcelo Gleiser, *The Island of Knowledge: The Limits of Science and the Search for Meaning* (New York: Basic Books, 2014).

40. D. Jeffrey Meldrum and Trent D. Stephens, "Who Are the Children of Lehi?" *Journal of the Book of Mormon and Other Restoration Scripture* 12, no. 1 (2003): 38–51.

41. Ira Flatow, "Sasquatch: Legend Meets Science," *National Public Radio*, November 10, 2006.

42. Bryan C. Sykes et al., "Genetic Analysis of Hair Samples Attributed to Yeti, Bigfoot and Other Anomalous Primates," *Proceedings of the Royal Society B* 281, no. 1789 (2014).

43. Alessandro Nicolia et al., "An Overview of the Last 10 Years of Genetically Engineered Crop Safety Research," *Critical Reviews in Biotechnology* 34, no. 1 (2014): 77–88.

44. Chelsea Snell et al., "Assessment of the Health Impact of GM Plant Diets in Long-Term and Multigenerational Animal Feeding Trials: A Literature Review," *Food and Chemical Toxicology* 50, no. 3 (2012): 1134–1148.

45. "Oslo Gay Animal Show Draws Crowds," *BBC News*, October 19, 2006.

46. Bruce Bagemihl, *Biological Exuberance: Animal Homosexuality and Natural Diversity* (New York, Macmillan, 1999).

47. Desmond Morris, The Naked Ape: A Zoologist's Study of the Human Animal (New York: Random House, 2010).

48. Craig B. Stanford, "The Social Behavior of Chimpanzees and Bonobos: Empirical Evidence and Shifting Assumptions 1," *Current Anthropology* 39, no. 4 (1998): 399–420.

49. Frans De Waal, Our Inner Ape: A Leading Primatologist Explains Why We Are Who We Are (New York: Penguin, 2006).

50. Ben Carson, *Gifted Hands: The Ben Carson Story*, 20th anniversary ed. (New York: Harper Collins, 2011).

51. Michael E. Miller, "Ben Carson Believes Joseph Built Egypt's Pyramids to Store Grain—and It Just Might Get Him Some Votes," *Washington Post*, November 5, 2015.

52. Genesis 41:35

53. Guy P. Harrison, "What Can We Learn from Ben Carson's Brain?" *Psychology Today*, October 15 2015, www.psychologytoday.com/blog/about-thinking/201510/what-can-we-learn-ben-carsons-brain.

54. There are also people who seem to be famous simply *because* they promote misinformation to a large number of people. One example of this is David "Avocado" Wolfe, a well-known pseudoscientist who thinks gravity is a toxin and chocolate comes from the sun.

55. Jim Carrey, "The Judgment on Vaccines Is In???" *Huffington Post*, November 5, 2009.

56. Michele Corriston, "Charlie Sheen Calls Doctor Who Claimed to Cure Him of HIV 'Dangerous,'" People, February 10, 2016, www.people.com/article/charlie-sheen-calls-doctor-who-claimed-cure-hiv-dangerous.

57. "Oh Yes She Did! Gwyneth Paltrow Gets Vagina Steam at Spa," *Us Weekly*, January 29, 2015.

58. Alexandra Sowa, "If You Have the Flu, Please Do Not Listen to Gwyneth Paltrow," *Slate*, October 19, 2015.

59. Ruth Graham, "Gwyneth Paltrow Says Your Skincare Products Should Be Nurtured with Chants and Music," *Slate*, March 11, 2016.

60. Ewan Palmer, "Shane Warne: Aliens Were behind Experiments That Turned Monkeys into Humans," *International Business Times*, February 15, 2016, www.ibtimes.co.uk/shane-warne-aliens-were-behind-experiments-that-turned-monkeys-into-humans-1543887.

61. Christina Ng, "Celebrities and Aliens: Stars Share Otherworldly Experiences," *ABC News*, January 30, 2012, abcnews.go.com/Entertainment/celebrities-aliens-fran-drescher-latest-share-experience/story?id=15473464.

62. "Megan Fox Talks Bigfoot, Leprechauns and Lindsay Lohan," *Fox News*, January 15, 2013,.foxnews.com/entertainment/2013/01/15/meghan-fox-talks-big-foot-leprechauns-and-lindsay-lohan/.

63. Toyin Owoseje, "Ariana Grande Reveals Demonic Encounter: 'It Was Terrifying'" *International Business Times*, February 23, 2016, www.ibtimes.co.uk/ariana-grande-reveals-demonic-encounter-it-was-terrifying-1447540.

64. Carl Sagan, *Cosmos* (New York: Random House, 1980), 333.

65. *"I would like 2016 to be the year when people remembered that science is a method of investigation, and NOT a belief system."* —John Cleese, actor

66. Rogerus Bacon, *Opus majus* (Pittero, 1750).

67. Richard Phillips Feynman, *The Character of Physical Law 66* (Cambridge, MA: MIT Press, 1967).

68. "Scrutinizing Science: Peer Review," Understanding Science: How Science Really Works, undsci.berkeley.edu/article/howscienceworks_16.

69. Daryl E. Chubin and Edward J. Hackett, *Peerless Science: Peer Review and US Science Policy* (Albany, NY: Suny Press, 1990).

70. Gordon Pennycook et al., "On the Reception and Detection of Pseudo-profound Bullshit," *Judgment and Decision Making* 10, no. 6 (2015): 549.

71. John G. Sotos, *Zebra Cards: An Aid to Obscure Diagnoses* (Mt. Vernon, VA: Mt. Vernon Book Systems, 2006).

72. "Reconstructing trees: Parsimony," Understanding Evolution, evolution. berkeley.edu/evolibrary/article/phylogenetics_08.

73. Raymond S. Nickerson, "Confirmation Bias: A Ubiquitous Phenomenon in Many Guises," *Review of General Psychology* 2, no. 2 (1998): 175.

74. Peter Ayton and Ilan Fischer, "The Hot Hand Fallacy and the Gambler's Fallacy: Two Faces of Subjective Randomness?" *Memory & Cognition* 32, no. 8 (2004): 1369–1378.

75. Michael Shermer and Pat Linse, *The Baloney Detection Kit* (Altadena, CA: Skeptic Society, 2001).

76. Elizabeth Thompson Gershoff, "Corporal Punishment by Parents and Associated Child Behaviors and Experiences: A Meta-analytic and Theoretical Review," *Psychological Bulletin* 128, no. 4 (2002): 539.

8

THE IMPORTANCE OF REALITY

"It is far better to grasp the universe as it really is than to persist in delusion however satisfying and reassuring."
—*Carl Sagan*

There are an infinite number of false beliefs that influence people's behavior at home, at work, and in the voting booth, and any action taken as a result of a faulty idea is bad because it's based on a flawed premise. The best way to get a positive outcome from any situation or choice is to be knowledgeable and informed about the topic(s) at hand, and then act in accordance with that information. As thinking people, shouldn't we strive for the most accurate data on which to base our decisions?

People's beliefs often determine how they behave, which is why it is and will always be incredibly important that we challenge and doubt ourselves and work to correct any and all misguided ideas. It is not my intention to make all believers discard their faith or to prevent them from practicing their cultural traditions, but those outcomes are often the natural result of my true goals: to promote rationality and evidence-based thinking, and to help people see the importance of reality. Personally, I see this as a sort of community service. According to Dr. Darrel W. Ray, author of *The God Virus, Sex & God*, and other titles, *"You decrease your suffering when you accept reality. So train your mind to perceive reality as closely as possible and recognize when your mind is trying to fill in the blanks with BS."*

IS REALITY REAL?

Science fiction writer Philip K. Dick defines reality as *"that which, when you stop believing in it, doesn't go away."* That sounds great, but what if reality isn't real? Like many things in this world, reality is only important if it can be shown to exist. So, is there an objective reality? Are *we* real? The short answer is, "Yes." There are certain assumptions we must make when taking on any logical discussion, and chief among those is the idea that we exist to be able to participate in it at all. As French philosopher René Descartes famously wrote, *"Cogito ergo sum,"* or *"I am thinking, therefore I exist."*[1] In other words, the very fact that we can ponder our own existence shows that we must exist in some form or another.

Objective facts *do* exist—barring incredibly unlikely, hypothetical Matrix-like scenarios[2] for which there is no supporting evidence—whether we like them or not. This means that some things are real and some are not and, no matter how much we dislike certain facts, no amount of imagination or willpower can change them. That consistency is what makes reality so powerful, and what makes it hated by so many. Poet Christopher Poindexter expressed this conflict quite well:

How we
all want so
badly to
divorce reality,
but that bitch just
won't sign the
papers.

Some believers might say the virtue of strong faith makes the objects of that faith "real" to the believers on a more personal level, but that idea is irrelevant when dealing with universal truths. Feelings, perceptions, opinions, and beliefs are subjective experiences that don't—and can't—alter the objective reality by themselves, so leaving those things out of the equation entirely makes the most sense when looking for what's real. Jonathan C. Smith explains that words like *reality*, *truth*, and *answer* can be *"weasel words."* They can mean different things to different people and they have a *"certain ambiguity in that they can also refer to objective facts as determined through the scientific method,"* according to Smith.

"An 'objective fact' is by definition based on reliable and public observation," he wrote. *"The only way to show that something is publicly and reliably observable is to subject it to public and reliable observation, that is, scientific inquiry."*

Even if there is no objective reality, however, we are still forced to act as though there is. All scientific endeavors, all of our verified findings, and indeed everything we have ever known is effectively erased if we don't actually exist, so we have no choice but to start from that point when determining universal realities. Sure, it's possible that we could exist as a computer program and everything we see could be a hologram, but we live our lives as if that's not the case—and verifiable facts are more important than unverified opinions and unsupported assertions for that reason. Comedian Penn Jillette pointed out in his book, *God, No!: Signs You May Already Be an Atheist and Other Magical Tales*, that the greatest thing about reality is that it is, by definition, shared. *"Every argument is really an agreement—an agreement that there is a reality that can be shared, judged, and discussed,"* Jillette wrote. *"To argue over whether the speed of light is constant or Batman could beat up the Lone Ranger is to share the parameters. God is solipsistic; reality is shared."*

Once we can agree that we must at least act as though demonstrably true things exist if we are going to get anywhere in discussions with other people, the next step is to determine whether reaching those facts is important and worthy of the effort.

IS REALITY WORTH IT?

I write about the process of getting rid of false beliefs because I think it benefits the whole of society, but it also helps me directly. Not only do I learn from my studies and discussions every single day, but I also get to improve interactions for myself and others in the future. In leading by example and teaching individuals how to seek out facts and discard fallacies, we can create a world in which more and more people base their decisions on rational thought, logic, and evidence—as opposed to tradition, paranoia, or emotional responses. That's the world I want to live in because misunderstandings, and therefore injustices, would become less frequent.

Anyone who enjoys a good detective story can tell you that uncovering the truth can, in and of itself, be an extremely positive experience. A reader could always just pick his or her favorite fall guy in the beginning, assume it was him, and never finish the book, but they don't. They don't do that because figuring out what really happened is its own gift. Believing in something because it makes you feel good—or because you were raised to—just isn't as rewarding or as honest as basing your beliefs on evidence, reason, and testable conclusions. Ben Radford highlighted the pleasure and importance of finding things out for yourself and solving a mystery.

"*Mysteries are cheap, and easy to create, and everywhere; they are the default status of our knowledge about the world*," Radford told me in an interview. "*Finding solutions to those mysteries and answers to those questions are what science and critical thinking are about. Finding out what's true about the world is (or should be) one of the highest achievements of being human.*"

I don't want my most important ideas to be shaped solely by my family, or tradition, or religious scriptures. Instead, I want them to be based on my own logic and an informed understanding of the data at hand (from the most objective approach possible). Even if you don't value honesty above all else as I do, you should still think it's better to know the truth—the real problems you face. With that information, you can prepare for potential hurdles instead of tripping over them because you pretended they didn't exist in favor of a more tolerable perceived reality.

A lot of people insist that delusions are healthy if they help foster a positive outlook. While that may sometimes be the case, I don't think the majority of people are better off blindfolded. Wishful thinking can have its benefits psychologically, but most people would still be better off separating their wishes and dreams from what they believe to be real. Hope for something better can be an amazing and beneficial feeling, but, like most ideas, hope is usually best when based in reality. Steven Pinker framed this idea quite well when he said, "*If you're being chased by a tiger, it may comfort you to believe it's a rabbit. But it is a tiger. And it's going to eat you.*" I don't think many people, if any, actually *need* these false beliefs, even if they do find comfort in them, and I try to show that to others.

False ideas can give some believers a positive feeling, but that's not always the case, and they should never be treated as cures for any sort of mental or psychological ailment. I think our cultural biases regarding gods, afterlives, and other "positive" delusions, combined with the popularity of those beliefs, keep us from seeing that faith in them isn't usually warranted at all—and that it can in fact be very unhealthy. As Irish playwright George Bernard Shaw wrote in the 1912 play *Androcles and the Lion*, "*The fact that a believer is happier than a skeptic is no more to the point than the fact that a drunken man is happier than a sober one. The happiness of credulity is a cheap and dangerous quality of happiness, and by no means a necessity of life.*"

When I'm presented with the option between a comforting myth and a potentially uncomfortable reality, I will always choose what's true—regardless of the topic in question. It's not just gods, angels, psychics, and ghosts that can invade ill-equipped or impressionable minds and cause irreparable harm; all sorts of earthly ideas can pose similar threats. By keeping high standards in mind for all claims and demanding evidence across the spectrum, we can help make sure our beliefs conform to our facts—and not the other way around. There's nothing wrong with believing in things, but if you disregard evidence, you'll end up willingly adopting any so-called answer you hear—anything that temporarily fulfills your desire to know what's unknown. When given a choice, I think most people would choose what's proven to be real.

FINDING REALITY IN DAILY LIFE

If reality exists, and understanding it better is worth the hard work, then why is it so difficult for people to come together in their conclusions about the world around us? Some experts, like cognitive scientist Donald Hoffman from the University of California, Irvine, suggest that all animals (including humans) have evolved in such a way that our perceptions sometimes only show us what we need to survive—as opposed to what's really there. Hoffman's work shows that our senses "*constitute a species-specific user interface that guides behavior in a niche.*"[3] He uses male jewel beetles that, in their attempts to mate, frequently confuse discarded beer bottles for their large, brown, and shiny female counterparts, as a typical example of a "*category error*" brought on by flawed perceptions.

"*Just as the icons of a PC's interface hide the complexity of the computer, so our perceptions usefully hide the complexity of the world, and guide adaptive behavior. This interface theory of perception offers a framework, motivated by evolution, to guide research in object categorization. This framework informs a new class of evolutionary games, called interface games, in which pithy perceptions often drive true perceptions to extinction."*

While there is no scientific consensus on Hoffman's interface theory, it is clear that some people view things differently than others and that it's often difficult to uncover reality as a result. That's why skepticism of claims, ideas, and data is important to everyone at all times—whether you're debating supernatural claims, reading an article in the newspaper, or anything in between. Skeptical inquiry can be used to determine that religions are probably not "divine" and that mermaids don't likely exist, but it can also help you discern false claims in advertising and decide whether or not the terms for a specific loan would be appropriate. While supernatural beliefs have always been a problem, in a world filled with fake personalities, false agendas, and deceptive marketing, it's more important than ever to seek out what is real in every facet of life. And skepticism, when combined with critical thinking, can help us do just that by fending off all sorts of flawed assertions and bogus claims in our daily lives. This is how we get closer to the truth and, for me, that's always a good thing.

Some people think I'm wasting my time, but I would argue that there's nothing more pressing than being able to distinguish facts from fiction. That's the importance of scientific skepticism and rational thought in general. It's not about religion or ghosts or psychics; it's about the real-world implications of bad thinking processes: racism, discrimination, science **denialism**, religious intrusion into secular governments, and more. I don't think there's anything of value with which critical thinking doesn't help. Advocating for critical thought and logical reasoning in general is crucial because, by doing so, we can directly combat any number of wrongs and injustices. People thinking reasonably are less likely to be racists, murderers, or sexists because those attitudes and behaviors aren't *reasonable*. According to astronomer Phil Plait, *"the more we teach people to simply accept anecdotal stories, hearsay, cherry-picked data (picking out what supports your claims but ignoring what doesn't), and, frankly, out-and-out lies, the harder it gets for people to think clearly."*

"If you cannot think clearly, you cannot function as a human being," Plait wrote on his Bad Astronomy website.[4] *"I cannot stress this enough. Uncritical thinking is tearing this world to pieces."*

I think it's important to analyze *all* information carefully because I recognize that, if you set your standards for evidence low, you could end up believing in just about anything. There are some people, however, who simply don't care if their beliefs match reality. Not only is this mentality intellectually dishonest, but I think it also forces those people to miss out on the wonderful feeling we get from uncovering new truths. Fortunately for all of us, most people do want their beliefs to be accurate, even if they don't know (or admit) it. By giving them all the information on a topic, from a variety of perspectives, we allow them to evaluate what makes the most sense and make an informed decision. I think people should absolutely have the right to believe in the supernatural, or in any earthly but similarly unfounded force, entity, or idea. But equally important is my and others' right to critique and debunk those beliefs—and to hold ourselves to a higher standard of evidence. Some people will continue to believe and others will give up on those ideas, but the flow of information both ways is crucial in a successful society if we want reality to be readily accessible to others.

THE SUPERNATURAL WORLD

There's so much we still don't know about this realm, so, in my opinion, creating a paranormal one isn't necessary. English writer Douglas Adams would likely agree. In *The Hitchhiker's Guide to the Galaxy*, he wrote, "*Isn't it enough to see that a garden is beautiful without having to believe that there are fairies at the bottom of it too?*" I'll likely never fully understand why some people prefer to worship that which can't be shown to exist when they could simply admire the intrinsic beauty of existence itself, but I suppose that's why it interests me so much.

I'm incredibly intrigued by unexplained phenomena, which is why researching them is so important to me, but disregarding our existing explanations in favor of fantasy discounts the importance of reality. It's true that humanity doesn't yet understand many things about the universe, or even the world immediately around us, but that's what we are working to change every single day when we support scientific skepticism and encourage evidence-based thinking. By doing this, we can discover what's true—as opposed to settling for falsehoods or merely assuming the real answers are unattainable as if we've already been defeated.

There are really only two options when it comes to falsifiable questions in the world: either we, through science, can one day discover the answer—

or we already have and it's being ignored. While many believers are quick to note that science may one day prove that their particular supernatural belief is actually a real force, they too often forget the possibility that the magic things they have experienced are understood by scientific endeavors, and that those understandings are being rejected because of personal biases—or even out of a love of mystery. Science doesn't yet have all the answers, but it does have many. And it is for that reason that ignoring valid scientific conclusions in favor of mysteries is not only ridiculous, but also counterproductive.

If you believe in the existence of an entity or force that can't be measured or shown to exist scientifically, then you can't be (even remotely) sure it's real. If you can't be sure it's real, then what objective basis do you have for believing in it? After all, if I told you that I had access to something that was invisible, undetectable, immeasurable, and unpredictable—and that I only heard about it from ancient rumors or from alleged personal experiences—would you feel compelled to believe in it? Hopefully, the answer is, "No." This concept, implemented by philosopher Bertrand Russell in his creation of the celestial teapot,[5] demonstrates the perils that go along with believing in unfalsifiable assertions merely because they can't be *disproven*.

> *If I were to suggest that between the Earth and Mars there is a china teapot revolving about the sun in an elliptical orbit, nobody would be able to disprove my assertion provided I were careful to add that the teapot is too small to be revealed even by our most powerful telescopes. But if I were to go on to say that, since my assertion cannot be disproved, it is an intolerable presumption on the part of human reason to doubt it, I should rightly be thought to be talking nonsense. If, however, the existence of such a teapot were affirmed in ancient books, taught as the sacred truth every Sunday, and instilled into the minds of children at school, hesitation to believe in its existence would become a mark of eccentricity and entitle the doubter to the attentions of the psychiatrist in an enlightened age or of the Inquisitor in an earlier time.*

When discussing the lack of hard evidence for anything outside the natural realm, I often hear the same objection from believers in all sorts of mystical forces: "But, it's possible!" And yes, I'll often admit that—because lots of things are possible. Without evidence, however, all you are left with is speculation, which isn't a good basis for a full-fledged conclusion. The fact that something *could* be real doesn't mean it's likely to be, and it doesn't change the fact that there isn't a shred of empirical evidence for any supernatural or paranormal force or claim ever put forth. Likewise, a strong belief doesn't make something objectively real. Illusionist and **mentalist** Derren Brown described how that line of thinking devalues the truth.

"One can be a true believer in anything: psychic ability, Christianity or, as Bertrand Russell classically suggested (with irony), in the fact there is a teapot orbiting the earth," Brown wrote in his book, *Tricks of the Mind.* *"I could believe any of those things with total conviction. But my conviction doesn't make them true. Indeed, it is something of an insult to the very truth I might hold dear to say that something is true just because I believe it is."*

That's why I encourage all people to separate their imagination from what they think is real, and distinguish the possible from the probable. I've never said the existence of any particular force or entity is necessarily impossible, but I will say that, without evidence, there simply isn't a reason to believe. For me, acceptance hinges on hard data. Requiring scientific evidence when it comes to the supernatural can help keep us from being fooled because, while it is true that absence of evidence is not always *evidence of absence*, a lack of corroborating data *is* always a bad reason to believe in something without further verification. In other words, if something can't be shown to be real, it doesn't mean it isn't, but that fact also doesn't give us any good reason to believe in it, either. I think most people would agree with that basic notion, including philosopher and logician Irving Copi. In a book called *Introduction to Logic*, he showed that a lack of evidence sometimes *is* evidence of absence.

"In some circumstances it can be safely assumed that if a certain event had occurred, evidence of it could be discovered by qualified investigators," Copi wrote. *"In such circumstances it is perfectly reasonable to take the absence of proof of its occurrence as positive proof of its non-occurrence."*

While a lack of evidence may be a good reason to not believe in something in most cases, a lack of evidence is not always a good reason to proclaim that something definitely does not exist or did not occur. That's because, of course, some information might come forth in the future to prove any number of ideas that are now considered unlikely. When that happens with something I've rejected in the past, I'll believe in it or—more accurately—accept it as fact. We might find evidence to prove practically anything in the future, but I base what I view as true on the information that is currently available, while leaving room for change.

THE SCIENTIFIC METHOD

Whether we are dealing with supernatural claims or those based on the known facts of this world, the best chance we have as a species is to focus our efforts on scientific investigations. This process can help us better understand the reality of the world around us so that we don't need to rely on faith in supernatural stories that may provide comfortable answers. The emphasis on scientifically sound evidence is crucial for one simple reason: the scientific method is our best process for determining what exists and what does not. However, that doesn't make the process perfect, nor is it able to test everything. Science deals with falsifiable claims—not vague spiritual or religious platitudes—and it can't test or measure questions rooted in subjectivity. Bertrand Russell, in his *Mysticism and Logic and Other Essays*,[6] explains the role of science in discovering the unknown.

"*Human beings cannot, of course, wholly transcend human nature; something subjective, if only the interest that determines the direction of our attention, must remain in all our thought,*" Russell wrote. "*But scientific philosophy comes nearer to objectivity than any other human pursuit, and gives us, therefore, the closest constant and the most intimate relation with the outer world that it is possible to achieve.*"

If you believe in some nondescript entity or force that doesn't intervene in the world—and therefore doesn't have testable attributes—then your belief is solely based on your own feelings or stories told to you by others, and it cannot be tested in any objective way. But we can test some other questions, such as, "Is there a prayer-answering god?" We've scientifically tested this claim and, so far, the evidence suggests there is not.[7] Can psychics predict the future? No one has been able to demonstrate psychic abilities under a scientific setting so, for now, we can again conclude that the answer is likely, "*No.*" You can use the scientific method to test a wide variety of claims in everyday life, because that system—and not theology or philosophical posturing—is how we find out what's real.

One of the most beautiful things about reality is that it's indifferent. Reality is unchanging and ever-present, whether you believe in it, worship it, or ignore it entirely. Even when something is unknown, the truth is there, and we are constantly working to discover it. It is through scientific endeavors that we are able to distinguish these realities, and to stifle the search with a strict belief (and therefore a premature conclusion) is to kill that all-essential curiosity and halt the pursuit of answers.

STORYTELLING AND EMOTIONAL REASONING

It wasn't always true that science was the best-known way to learn something. In ancient times, prior to the development of what we know today as the scientific method, our ancestors' favorite method for discerning reality was often through oral stories handed down from generation to generation— or even tales conveyed through wall and cave paintings. While people who lived long ago didn't necessarily learn accurate information from the stories they shared, storytelling itself was an important part of our history. Stories continue to be incredibly popular today, too, especially in entertainment and business, because they evoke strong neurological responses. Neuroeconomist Paul Zak, who headed the research team that discovered that *oxytocin* is a key "it's safe to approach others" signal in the brain, says more recent studies show "*that character-driven stories do consistently cause oxytocin synthesis.*"

"*We have identified oxytocin as the neurochemical responsible for empathy and narrative transportation,*" Zak wrote.[8] "*My lab pioneered the behavioral study of oxytocin and has proven that when the brain synthesizes oxytocin, people are more trustworthy, generous, charitable, and compassionate.*"

Storytelling may serve as a catalyst for changes in brain chemistry, but it is also important as a tool for communication, bonding, and—like science and religion—comfort in the face of the unknown. When we want to know something badly enough, making up a story can feel good. It solves (often wrongly) that riddle by which our pattern-seeking mind was previously confused. Malcolm Gladwell explains that this is a "*storytelling problem*" that all humans have. He said, "*We're a bit too quick to come up with explanations for things we don't really have an explanation for.*"

Storytelling remains common among all people,[9] but science has largely replaced this method as a reliable means to understand the world. Even today, however, many people attempt to use empty arguments instead of real evidence to force their personal beliefs into existence. While philosophical discourse can be fun—and it certainly has its uses—it also has completely different objectives than modern scientific inquiry and it can never be used to establish *proof* of the supernatural. When it comes to determining what's real in the world, I'll stick with empirical evidence over metaphysical musings and stories any day of the week. The scientific method is how we distinguish reality from illusion—how we determine what is predictive and what is not. Words can't make gods or ghosts, or anything else for that matter, real.

STRONG EMOTIONS

Unfortunately, for some people who are adding up what make sense to form their beliefs, scientific evidence is left out of the equation entirely. I'm often told by believers that supernatural forces do exist, but that logical reasoning won't help discover them—they must instead be "felt in the heart."[10] Emotions, however, are largely irrelevant when discussing what's real and what's illusory because they can throw you off course on the search for facts. It's critical thinking that will yield the best results because, while emotions do affect what we believe, it's not usually in a good way. Jonathan C. Smith is one of many experts who argues that strong emotion and motivation *"can prompt us to abandon common sense and good everyday thinking."*

"People are 'blinded by love' and commit 'crimes of passion,'" he wrote. *"If you have been blessed with a paranormal experience, this extraordinary event would likely stir your feelings—and possibly compromise your capacity for clear, cool-headed thinking."*

This is not to say that emotions have no place in the world—feelings are great if you don't mistake them for evidence-based conclusions—but that place isn't distinguishing facts from falsehoods. By setting aside all emotional appeals and reactions and focusing only on evidence and logical arguments, the feelings lose much of their influence and we can more easily get to what's real. There'll always be those who allow emotion to prevail over reason in these matters, but we don't have to be those people. We can strive for something better.

POSSIBLE PITFALLS OF PARADISE

I encourage everyone, believers and skeptics alike, to make a concentrated effort to seek out reality in their own lives, and to avoid being held hostage by false beliefs. By doing this, you may discover (as I did) that skepticism can be more than just a healthy and intellectually honest worldview—a real and intensive search for the truth can also be a process that brings relief and even joy. As Guy P. Harrison writes in his book, *50 Popular Beliefs That People Think Are True*, "*Some people think of skeptics as cynical, negative people with closed minds. Nothing could be further from the truth. Skepticism is really nothing more than a fancy name for trying to think clearly and thoroughly before making a decision about believing, buying, or joining something. It's about sorting out reality from lies and misperceptions.*"

Not only is it rewarding in itself to learn new information and discover what's really out there, but allegedly comforting lies can actually turn out to be much less so when analyzed critically and independently, so getting rid of them may be a "blessing" in disguise. For example, many people would consider various religions' versions of *Heaven*, *Jannah*, and other utopia-centered afterlives to be the ultimate (false) comfort, promising eternal bliss in the clouds post mortem, but that's just what we see at first glance. When you dig deeper, you see these so-called paradises are good examples of how critical analysis can destroy the illusion of a supposedly comforting myth and reveal a much less palatable one. With a little research, you discover that the happy-go-lucky afterlives proposed by the world's religions are often accompanied by opposite (and equally absurd) realms of eternal torture, where you or your loved ones could also end up. So, when people get upset with my work, claiming that my writings take "eternal paradise" away from believers, I point out that—if that's the case—then those same words would also be responsible for taking away the believers' concept of "eternal suffering." I would argue that this is a good thing. As English actor Sir Peter Ustinov once wrote, "*Unfortunately, a superabundance of dreams is paid for by a growing potential for nightmares.*"

Believers might still insist that religions themselves give some people needed solace, independent of their veracity, but that's often not the whole picture. For example, religions *do* help with building a sense of community and belonging within a group, but they also help create and foster an *Us vs. Them* mentality that divides us. In other words, religions are great at uniting people ... of the same faith. For outsiders, however, they often do the opposite. In fact, a 2015 study published in *Current Anthropology* revealed that religion led to social conflict and tension as early as 700 BCE in Oaxaca.[11] This research contradicted the earlier assumption that religion helped bring communities together in the region during that time period.

Even on a more personal level, religion can be psychologically damaging when it should (in theory) be beneficial. For starters, afterlife-based religions take away from the power of the present by teaching that this life is only a test, and by transferring one's focus from the only known world to an unknowable afterlife. Instead of living for now, people are often enticed with promises of Paradise or threatened with eternal torment in Hell. This emphasis on the supernatural can have other harmful effects, too. Religious belief and spirituality might emulate the feelings of contentment gained from traditional therapies, but in many instances, believers are merely shifting responsibility to some unknowable being and aren't actually doing anything to *solve* their issues. Leaving everything up to some higher power is the same as relying solely on blind chance, so taking control over your own life choices generally provides better results.

Sometimes chance is on the believer's side and he or she does resolve the problems after praying or otherwise petitioning the supernatural, and that's actually when the false connection between faith and good fortune (by definition a superstition) is fortified. The believer thanks their god or spiritual force of choice and thinks it can be counted on in the future. Furthermore, when someone credits their accomplishments to a god or other mystical force—whether it's for helping them overcome an addiction or achieve something great—it pushes them further from reality. It not only takes away from the individual's hard work that is likely responsible, but it also implies that person was somehow more important than anybody else who may have failed to accomplish the same feat. If you are considering expressing gratitude to an unseen and unproven force for positive developments in your life, remember that it can be equally (if not more so) rewarding to thank those who truly helped you accomplish whatever the positive action is. If it was your own hard work, acknowledge that. If it was someone else's, let them know they are appreciated. If it was dumb luck, don't count on it in the future but take advantage of it while it's there. This is the beauty of reality.

The concept of perceived (but often false) utility isn't unique to religions or to Heaven and Hell. Other unfounded beliefs are similarly misunderstood at times as beneficial in whole or at least in part. Just as leaving religion takes away a person's fear of "Hell," naturalism in general can cure other fears. When you give up on all superstitions, you might not feel protected by good luck charms or saved by Jesus, but you also won't irrationally fear black cats or Satan. Similarly, while some fantastic but unproven notions seem to provide an escape from what might be otherwise interpreted as harsh realities, I would argue it's better to simply accept life as it truly is and work to improve it or to make the most of it within those confines. Shouldn't we be strong enough to accept and face the truth—regardless of how it makes us feel?

ESCAPES FROM REALITY

Perhaps most importantly, an appreciation for reality need not stifle any individual's creativity or ability to enjoy entertainment centered on the supernatural or unfathomable. After all, as the ancient Greek philosopher and scientist Aristotle said, "*It is the mark of an educated mind to be able to entertain a thought without accepting it.*" It's interesting (but disheartening) how quickly some people go from "Oh, an intriguing idea," to "This is definitely real and anyone who disagrees is evil!" It can be fun and educational to consider and learn about a variety of ideas, regardless of how implausible you may find them.

Compartmentalization can help us separate ideas worth consideration from those designed to be merely entertaining. When I read a fictional book, I am in their world. I acknowledge at that time that, while gods or werewolves or alien invaders haven't been shown to exist on our plane, they could be very real in that (fictional) realm. For that moment, I live inside that universe, which exempts the claims being presented from the skeptical scrutiny I apply to assertions within our own. But when people purport their claims to be reality, effectively duping millions into believing nonsense, it transcends "entertainment" from an ethical standpoint. Those who sell nontruths take more than money from their victims; they also take their right to reality.

Even if you love some of the many television series and other mediums that (often dishonestly) portray a search for evidence of the supernatural, newfound skepticism shouldn't necessarily destroy the ability to enjoy them. If you give up a belief, you could lose an affinity for shows based on that idea, but you may also find that, over time, you can learn to find them entertaining again—although you may have to adjust your perspective a bit. You might not enjoy them with the "perhaps they'll find proof of ghosts/

Bigfoot, etc.!" mentality, but discovering natural explanations, pointing out biases, and exposing frauds can sometimes be even more exciting.[12] In that sense, skepticism isn't a wet blanket—and rational thought doesn't have to take all the fun out of the supernatural. If anything, they simply ensure that you are in on the joke—and not at the butt of it. You can use your reasoning skills to make the most out of a wide variety of experiences, including and especially those that involve your imagination. As Spanish painter Francisco de Goya said, "*Fantasy, abandoned by reason, produces impossible monsters; united with it, she is the mother of the arts and the origin of marvels.*"

Some people are unable to merely enjoy a concept from a detached point of view, often becoming emotionally attached to its veracity, but these feelings can be a real burden in any attempt to separate fact from fiction. A person should analyze all ideas while keeping in mind that taking an interest in something does not make the notion valuable or supported by evidence, and that an idea's entertainment value shouldn't in itself be used to justify *belief.* Evidence should always be more important than fascination in that sense, but the latter is still incredibly crucial in prompting new scientific discoveries. Intrigue can be a great starting-off point for the initial stage of the scientific method because it helps create new questions.

I wrote the following poem to help demonstrate my appreciation for reality:

The Ode to Reality

WE WALKED ON THE MOON, MINDS CANNOT BEND SPOONS;

NO ONE CAN FORETELL WHETHER OR NOT THE END WILL COME SOON.

PSYCHICS CAN'T READ MINDS, CROP CIRCLES AREN'T SIGNS;

YOU CAN'T TELL A PERSON'S FUTURE BY LOOKING AT THEIR HAND OR ITS LINES.

GODS DON'T TALK TO MEN OR OTHERWISE INTERVENE;

NO ONE CAN TELL THE FUTURE, NOT EVEN IN DREAMS.

CRYSTALS DON'T HEAL, BIGFOOT ISN'T REAL;

PRAYER DOESN'T AFFECT OUTCOMES, REGARDLESS OF HOW IT MAKES YOU FEEL.

PERSONALITY TYPES AREN'T DETERMINED BY MONTH OF BIRTH;

ALIENS, IF THEY EXIST, HAVE LIKELY NEVER VISITED EARTH.

THE REAL WORLD IS BEAUTIFUL, THERE'S NO NEED FOR MORE;

DON'T CLING TO CONSPIRACIES OR RELIGION OR FOLKLORE.

"Logic and proper empirical method is the only way the whole world can arrive at an agreement on the truth about anything."

—*Richard Carrier*

NOTES

1. Rene Descartes, *Principia Philosophiae* (Amstelodami: Ludovicum Elzevirium, 1644).

2. Arjun Kharpal, "Tech Billionaires Think We Live in the Matrix and Have Asked Scientists to Get Us Out," *CNBC*. October 7, 2016, www.cnbc.com/2016/10/07/tech-billionaires-think-we-live-in-the-matrix-and-have-asked-scientists-to-get-us-out.html.

3. D. Hoffman, "The Interface Theory of Perception: Natural Selection Drives True Perception to Swift Extinction," in *Object Categorization: Computer and Human Vision Perspectives*, ed. S. Dickinson, M. Tarr, A. Leonardis, B. Schiele (Cambridge: Cambridge University Press, 2009), 148–165.

4. Phil Plait, "Phil Plait's Bad Astronomy: Misconceptions: Astrology," Phil Plait's Bad Astronomy, 2008.

5. Bertrand Russell, "Is There a God?" (1952), in *The Collected Papers of Bertrand Russell, Volume 11: Last Philosophical Testament, 1943–68*, ed. John G. Slater and Peter Köllner (London: Routledge, 1997), 543–48.

6. Bertrand Russell, *Mysticism and Logic, and Other Essays* (New York: Rowman & Littlefield, 1981).

7. Herbert Benson et al. "Study of the Therapeutic Effects of Intercessory Prayer (STEP) in Cardiac Bypass Patients: A Multicenter Randomized Trial of Uncertainty and Certainty of Receiving Intercessory Prayer," *American Heart Journal* 151, no. 4 (2006): 934–942.

8. Paul Zak, "How Stories Change the Brain," Greater Good, December 17, 2013, greatergood.berkeley.edu/article/item/how_stories_change_brain.

9. *"We are, as a species, addicted to story. Even when the body goes to sleep, the mind stays up all night, telling itself stories."* —Jonathan Gottschall, *The Storytelling Animal: How Stories Make Us Human*

10. I've been told that my heart has been *"hardened,"* that I should let Jesus (or any number of other religious figures) into my heart, and that I have to have an *"open heart"* to properly understand religious scripture and other spiritual matters. But there is no hidden power of the heart that deals with these issues; it just pumps blood.

11. Arthur A. Joyce and Sarah B. Barber, "Ensoulment, Entrapment, and Political Centralization: A Comparative Study of Religion and Politics in Later Formative Oaxaca," *Current Anthropology* 56, no. 6 (2015): 819–847.

12. *"If Passion drives, let Reason hold the Reins."* —Benjamin Franklin

9

"I KNOW WHAT I SAW!"

"When someone looks at me and earnestly says, 'I know what I saw,' I am fond of replying, 'No you don't.' You have a distorted and constructed memory of a distorted and constructed perception, both of which are subservient to whatever narrative your brain is operating under."

—*Steven P. Novella*

Whether a person believes in ghosts, gods, psychics, or alien visitation, their purported proof often comes down to nothing more than one sentence: "I KNOW what I saw!" And when I hear this claim, I always feel obligated to ask, "*Do* you?" The fact is that our memories and sight (and all our other senses, for that matter) are imperfect and anecdotal testimonies, which can be explained by visual hallucinations, altered memories, deception, or fraud and are considered the lowest form of evidence in science—especially when dealing with something novel, such as the supernatural. In the end, saying you "know" what you saw isn't persuasive for one simple reason: you don't always know.

Everybody tends to think their personal beliefs are correct—that's usually why we hold them. But this is especially true when it comes to belief in religions and other supernatural concepts. In those cases, we often see believers who claim to know with absolute certainty that their unverifiable opinions are the only *Truth*—with a capital T.[1] When asked about this level of confidence, believers tend to cite their own personal experiences as proof. But asserting an opinion isn't the same as providing evidence and, unless you have something legitimate to back up your claims, scientific skeptics like myself simply won't believe you. When I form my most important beliefs, I look for real evidence: solid, repeatable data that stretches beyond what mere faith and stories can provide. Personal experiences can be both unreliable and misleading partly because, as psychologist Barry Beyerstein said, *"Anecdotal evidence leads us to conclusions that we wish to be true, not conclusions that actually are true."*

STORIES AREN'T PROOF

Anecdotal accounts, which are by definition flawed,[2] simply aren't impressive when we are looking for hard scientific evidence. In fact, these one-off accounts are the opposite of what scientists want when seeking reliable conclusions. While some may consider their stories "good enough" evidence for them to believe, from an objective viewpoint, they are still just stories.

The human brain is an incredibly powerful tool—capable of deceiving itself and others—and, until a person has supporting evidence of a finding, an anecdotal experience can and should be written off as the logical fallacy it is. This form of so-called evidence is inherently unscientific for the purposes of providing proof of anything because it uses an isolated example instead of a logical argument or scientifically valid data.[3] The biggest problem with anecdotal evidence is that, to many, it is convincing. Psychology professor Wayne Weiten, who has received distinguished teaching awards from Division 2 of the American Psychological Association, says personal stories can convince people because *"they are often concrete, vivid, and memorable."*[4]

"Indeed, people tend to be influenced by anecdotal information even when they are explicitly forewarned that the information is not representative," Weiten wrote. *"Many politicians are keenly aware of the power of anecdotes and they frequently rely on a single vivid story rather than on solid data to sway voters' views. However, anecdotal evidence is fundamentally flawed."*

No matter how many experiential tales you come up with, it will never be equal to verifiable data from a controlled and observed environment. And, as engineer and statistician W. Edwards Deming said, *"Without data you're just another person with an opinion."* That's not to say anecdotes have no value, however. An individual's experience or view is considered a weak form of evidence if there isn't scientific data supporting it, placing it well below experimental and observational evidence on a scale of strength, but it does serve its purpose. Anecdotes are great to help launch new studies, pinpoint items for further research, or to entertain others in a storytelling environment; they just don't prove anything to be true (or false). When I hear a personal anecdote, I see it as a starting point for an investigation—a possibility that could perhaps warrant additional research—but for many people that's the end of their process. Their "proof" has been found and their mind has been made up.

SUPERNATURAL ANECDOTES

Eyewitness accounts in general are not scientific evidence and cannot be used as proof for anything—let alone so-called paranormal events. A personal story may be enough for you to believe simple things in your daily life, such as accepting your friend's testimony about something he or she saw at the grocery store, but it isn't a compelling argument for any brand of superstition because it's the same argument used by believers in all others. If personal observations did count as valid proof of the supernatural, that same standard would apply to all similar claims. It would validate any delusional idea that a person or group of people buys into. If you accept one otherworldly claim on unconfirmed reports of alleged eyewitnesses alone—for instance, the resurrection of Jesus—then you should logically accept all other claims based on the same foundation, like extraterrestrial visitation, the existence of Bigfoot, the Loch Ness Monster, Allah, and reptile-human shape shifters. Each of these claims suffers from the exact same lack of scientific backing, but millions of well-meaning and often intelligent people around the world have personal stories supporting them all. Jonathan C. Smith explains that, if you think anecdotal evidence is definitive and you apply that rule consistently, you'll end up believing in just about anything.

"*If you believe in ghosts, you must also believe in astrology, reincarnation, TV psychic superstars, prophetic pets, alien abductions, communication with the dead, fortune-telling, mental spoon-bending, and a Pandora's box of other treasures*," Smith wrote. "*Why? All have sincere, honest, sane, intelligent educated, articulate, famous, and passionate proponents. All are based on the same types of support.*"

It is not statistically probable that aliens have visited earth while remaining undetected, or that an undiscovered ape roams the American northwest, or that Jesus resurrected himself and others; so it's justifiable to reject belief in all these extraordinary claims using the same standard. While accepting the possibility of these ideas can be good, to believe them without supporting evidence enters the realm of the irrational. Extraordinary personal experiences, such as many of those said to involve a so-called spirit realm or the "divine," are necessarily subjective and entirely dependent upon the interpretation of the claimant. This makes using them as proof impossible, but that hasn't stopped people from trying. Because of the unreliable nature of this experience-based "proof," any such claims may be dismissed until there is verifiable evidence to support them.

It's interesting to note that, with the onset of the era of modern camera and recording technology, we didn't see a corresponding rise in physical evidence of aliens, ghosts, or Bigfoot. Likewise, we have seen significantly fewer instances of alleged divine intervention than have been reported throughout history. As a result, believers of all stripes have been forced to become increasingly reliant on anecdotes and pseudoscience. In each case, they cling to blind faith, tales from other believers, and personal experiences sometimes passed around as "news" articles. But I think the same thing about all these reports, regardless of their origin: they are just stories until proven to be more.

We all have strange experiences that we might not be able to explain right away, but it's how you interpret these events that's important. Some people are simply more likely to believe in paranormal answers to these questions. You may have just been raised to believe strange coincidences are actually ghosts, but who you are as a person, as a member of your society, and as a participant in the culture around you can factor into these experiences and how you perceive them, too. Studies have shown, for instance, that the people who believe in the paranormal are more likely to have less education [5] and a poor understanding of the physical world. [6] People who have issues with cognitive reasoning, [7] along with those with high dopamine levels [8] and those suffering from early trauma, [9] also tend to be susceptible to paranormal thinking. Does this mean anyone who fits these descriptions must believe in the supernatural? Of course not. It only means that some people will have to fight harder than others to fend off false beliefs.

GROUP EXPERIENCES

Far too often, after the "I know what I saw!" argument has been thoroughly debunked as a piece of solid proof, the believer multiplies the failure of the personal testimony. The next objection is usually, "But a number of people have reported the same experience!" It's true that countless people believe in gods, ghosts, good and bad luck, astrology, **Tarot cards**, psychics, far-fetched conspiracy theories, reincarnation, and more, often based on nothing more than personal experiences, but that says more about the gullible mindset of most humans than it does about the veracity of those ideas. In fact, because some of these claims are most certainly false, the fact that people accept them shows that a huge number of people are capable of believing ridiculous, unverifiable things with absolutely no solid evidence.

If hundreds or thousands or even millions of people believe something similar and proclaim that belief, does it become true? Of course not. When someone insists a claim is true because it's what many (or all) people believe, they are committing another fallacy: appeal to the people, or *argumentum ad populum*.[10] If you believe others' similar experiences show that a particular extraordinary claim is justified, then you should try following the same logic and applying it to assertions with which you disagree. Would that standard hold weight if thousands of people believed in the magical powers of chain letters? Or that some people possess **superhuman** powers like those seen in comic books? Many people believe those things and a lot more. Anecdotes, even hundreds or thousands of them, shouldn't be used in place of scientific evidence.

Many believers in ghosts, gods, aliens, etc. use the fact that others witnessed the same event as evidence of the veracity of their supernatural claims. The problem here is that nobody doubts that a person or group of people had an experience; scientific skeptics merely doubt extraordinary and unverifiable causations of those events until they have been proven empirically. This *shared memory* argument for the paranormal ignores the fact that it's not only possible for multiple people to have the same **false memory** or false interpretation of events, but that it actually happens all the time. Your social group has a huge influence on what you believe, and people who tend to desire conformity will often (knowingly or subconsciously) mutually agree upon experiences based on that urge. This phenomenon demonstrates the power of *groupthink*, which occurs when people make faulty decisions because of group pressures that cause the deterioration of "*mental efficiency, reality testing, and moral judgment*."[11] The Asch conformity experiments, developed in the 1950s by gestalt psychologist Solomon Asch, helped us see how readily people will conform with a group's conclusion even when they think the answer is wrong.[12]

To understand faulty group experiences even further, one should also learn about the phenomenon of collective hallucinations. If a person sees something that's not there, it is the result of an internal or external force—including the obvious things, like drugs or deception, as well as the not so obvious, like **grief** or fear. When other people are put under identical or near-identical conditions, it makes sense that they could also see "something" and then interpret it similarly. These experiences are rare, but they happen and have even been reported throughout human history. For example, psychologist Edmund Parish summarized in 1897 an instance in which shipmates saw an apparition that appeared to "*all the crew of a vessel*" as their recently deceased cook walking on water with his peculiar limp. That vision later turned out to be a "*piece of wreck, rocked up and down by the waves*."[13] These minor triggers can also lead to **mass hysteria**, which causes false and irrational beliefs and is often the result of group excitement or anxiety.[14]

RELIGIOUS EVENTS AND SO-CALLED MIRACLES

When an experience is deemed supernatural, it's often called a "miracle," but what most people call miracles are more like placeholders because they have come to describe any event or action that is (seemingly) unexplainable using the modern scientific method and natural laws. The first problem with this classification is that, throughout the history of humanity, there have been countless unexplained phenomena that were later understood and determined to be of natural origin. Mark Twain was right on target when he wrote, in *Letters from the Earth: Uncensored Writings*, that the difference between a miracle and a fact is "*exactly the difference between a mermaid and a seal*." Not once in recorded history, however, has the opposite occurred: we have never had a scientific understanding that was overtaken by a supernatural or miraculous one. To find an example of this type of now-explained miracle, let's go back to September 1995, when people started reporting that statues of the Hindu god Ganesha were "drinking" milk offerings provided by worshipers. This event, dubbed the *Hindu milk miracle*, took place throughout India and other parts of the world. It was covered extensively by the media,[15] with reporters describing individuals' mysterious experiences when offering milk to statues of the deity, but the alleged miracle didn't last long. Scientists and skeptics tested the phenomenon and concluded that *capillary action*, which describes a liquid's ability to flow in miniscule spaces like those found in the statues' porous material, was the likely culprit.[16] This effect was exaggerated by mass hysteria that resulted from the persistent media coverage. T. Jayaraman of the Institute of Mathematical Sciences, who describes the Hindu milk miracle as "*unprecedented in its spread*," explains:

> *When water or milk or any other fluid is taken in a spoon or a suitably shallow container, it is a well-known fact that the surface of the fluid is not flat but slightly curved. This is due to the phenomenon of surface tension, whereby the fluid tries to minimise its surface area. If a spoon is filled with milk or water and taken to the mouth of an idol, or indeed any statue, then it is natural that the upper lip on the idol will touch the surface. In the case of a Ganesa idol without a lip, the gap between the underside of the trunk and the face would be the place used, and again some portion of the idol will touch the fluid surface. When the surface is thus punctured, then the fluid has a chance to flow out.[17]*

The second problem with prematurely describing something as a "miracle" with a divine or otherwise paranormal origin is that there is no proof of causation. There has never been an instance in which the only possible (or even the most probable) answer was divine intervention—nothing that indisputably points to a deity or magic power affecting the world at all. We have always had a more readily available natural answer and, until something supernatural is shown to exist, that conclusion is the most reasonable one. In *An Enquiry Concerning Human Understanding*, Scottish philosopher David Hume stated that "*no testimony is sufficient to establish a miracle, unless the testimony be of such a kind, that its falsehood would be more miraculous, than the fact, which it endeavors to establish.*"[18] Said more simply, if it's more likely that the claimant has been tricked or is lying than the physical laws of the universe have been violated, then the former is probably the case.

Miracles are commonplace in religious scripture. Ancient people are said to have felt Jesus' fatal wounds, verified Muhammad's ascent to Heaven, and even interacted with their respective deities directly. Today, however, believers have no such luxury. They are forced to rely on blind faith that these things occurred, that people were at one time able to overcome or render inert the world's natural laws.[19] In this sense, religious believers don't utilize the argument that is the basis for this chapter. They don't claim to know what they saw; they claim to know what other people allegedly reported seeing thousands of years ago. Unfortunately for those believers, any reasonable person can see that all the gods of the various religions have conveniently neglected to perform grandiose miracles or make themselves apparent in other ways since the invention of recording devices. And in the rare instances in which a god is said to have revealed itself to a person or group in modern times, the events have been traced to hallucinations caused by mental illness or substance abuse—or it has been an outright lie. Philosopher and historian Joseph Ernest Renan described the essence of these miraculous occurrences well when he said, "*No miracle has ever taken place under conditions which science can accept. Experience shows, without exception, that miracles occur only in times and in countries in which miracles are believed in, and in the presence of persons who are disposed to believe them.*"[20]

Billions of people believe that a demigod named Jesus was resurrected from the dead or that a prophet named Muhammad traveled to the heavens on a winged horse, but these occurrences aren't just personal experiences or memories—they're secondhand tales. To see the differences between these two types of claims, we can compare acceptance of Jesus' miracles with the Sasquatch and other modern myths. Belief in Bigfoot requires you to accept blurry photos and anecdotal evidence, but believing in Jesus' divinity means you accept blurry and contradictory stories imparted by ancient ancestors. And while Bigfoot has modern eyewitnesses insisting they "know what they saw," the only testimonies to Jesus' alleged miracles are unverifiable. Likewise, the average Christian would outwardly reject claims that people saw Elvis Presley alive and well after his widely publicized death, but would cling to similar stories about Jesus from thousands of years ago. This double standard puts those who accept ancient religious myths but reject similar modern (and secular) claims in an interesting dilemma in which they must decide why their standards for evidence are different on these matters.

Let's take a closer look at a specific "miracle" from the Bible. Christians believe, as is reported in the New Testament scriptures,[21] that Jesus of Nazareth healed 10 men with leprosy. This is just a story from a religious text with no historical evidence to support its veracity, but even if it did happen, would this be considered a divine act? It sounds like an astounding feat, but compare it to the work of physician and scientist Jacinto Convit, who saved thousands of lives threatened by leprosy when he developed the vaccine that protects us from it. In 1988, Convit was nominated for a Nobel Prize in Medicine for his anti-leprosy vaccine. So, while the promise of Jesus' healing power is a centerpiece of the Christian myth, the demigod's results leave something to be desired when compared to the rigor of man's scientific inquiry. It makes one wonder why Jesus himself wouldn't have provided the vaccine, or at least given predictive hints in his teachings to cures for some of the most horrific diseases that have historically haunted mankind. Maybe Jesus saw those 10 people as superior—more worthy of a healthy life—than anyone else who has suffered from leprosy before, during, and after that time. It's more likely, however, that this story was created during an era in which the very idea of a vaccine was unfathomable—even to someone purported to be the Son of God and/or God incarnate.

WHY ARE OUR EXPERIENCES UNRELIABLE?

We know that personal stories aren't evidence of the supernatural—and that they are frequently found to be unreliable—but why is that the case? One simple reason is that some people who report to have religious visions, ghost experiences, alien contact, and other extraordinary interactions have what's known as a *fantasy-prone personality*, a term coined by American psychologists Sheryl C. Wilson and Theodore X. Barber in the early 1980s.[22] It's a completely normal trait, applying to roughly 4 percent of the world's population, but these people have vivid fantasies and can have trouble distinguishing them from reality.[23] Research also suggests that people who are likely to have delusions tend to make rushed decisions without all the available information, which could explain why a fantasy-prone individual would jump to a false conclusion during or immediately following some type of unexplained experience.[24] These factors, coupled with the fact that there are a number of reasons that our memories have been found to be unreliable in general, make first-hand stories incredibly poor evidence for anything, especially the paranormal. As Steven Pinker explains, "*Cognitive psychology tells us that the unaided human mind is vulnerable to many fallacies and illusions because of its reliance on its memory for vivid anecdotes rather than systematic statistics.*"

Our memories are not as effective as we'd like to believe.[25] We are evolutionarily disposed to have confidence in the consistency of our senses and memories, but they are actually influenced and altered by our own biases, past experiences, time, and other factors. This is something we all have to realize about ourselves if we hope to get closer to the truth. In your own life, you can become aware of the differences between reality and your recollection in a number of ways, including by being presented with proof of inaccuracies, by noticing your own conflicting memories, and by analyzing past events from the perspectives of multiple people who were present. In fact, you can even make this usually taxing thought process into a game. For some false-memory fun, I recommend asking a close friend or family member to recount in detail a shared childhood memory that you haven't discussed in years—and then compare notes. The results might be surprising. American philosopher and psychologist William James described false recollections, but generously assumed that most people are aware of these differences between their memories and real events. "*Most people, probably, are in doubt about certain matters ascribed to their past,*" he said. "*They may have seen them, may have said them, done them, or they may only have dreamed or imagined they did so.*"

Many of our memories stray greatly from the original events because we sometimes misremember (and therefore misreport) where we heard something, merge more than one memory while forming a story, report others' experiences as our own, or even describe completely imagined events as real. The fact is that we all have false memories; it's just the nature of recollection. I think most of mine, for instance, are stories that I heard often as a child and later became real *to me*. In some cases, I wasn't involved in the events at all, but I still "remember" being there because of how many times I heard the same details. My manufactured remembrances can therefore be at least partially explained by a common type of faulty recollection that can be formed through nothing more than time—**misattributed memory**. Misattribution is a well-studied phenomenon and it occurs when we recall something that didn't actually happen to us because the memory is distorted by time or other factors. In one particularly notable instance of misattribution, Australian psychologist and lawyer Donald M. Thomson was arrested for assault and rape. He couldn't have committed the crime, however, because he was on live television when it took place—explaining psychological research on eyewitness testimony. The victim saw Thomson's face on TV while she was being abused by someone else and, in an unbelievable twist likely caused by the trauma of the moment, actually misattributed his face as that of her attacker's.[26]

HOW MEMORIES ARE MADE AND CHANGED

Our memories are created by piecing together various things that make sense to us at the time, as opposed to being etched in our minds like a perfect recorder, making them inherently prone to being altered.[27] According to cognitive psychologist and law professor Elizabeth Loftus, an expert on human memory at the University of California, Irvine, people bring information together from different times and places to construct what we "remember."[28] This process of compilation, along with the fact that people tend to place more faith in the accuracy of their recollection than they should,[29] demonstrates the unreliable nature of our memories that inherently leads to false beliefs.

"*The process of calling it into conscious awareness can change it, and now you're storing something that's different,*" Loftus said in an interview with *Slate*, pointing to misattribution.[30] "*We all do this, for example, by inadvertently adopting a story we've heard.*"

Misremembering events is something that happens with everybody, and it's not a *bad* thing. It's just the way we work. In fact, a study released in November 2013 found that even people with highly superior autobiographical memory (HSAM), a rare ability to remember dates and events with great accuracy, are susceptible to having false memories.[31] These accidental recollection inaccuracies in people with and without HSAM are not unlike the false memories that one can generate through something as simple as excessive thoughts about a subject or through the power of suggestion. This includes false memories created through self or directed **hypnosis**, which requires the imagination and participation of the subject(s) involved and is not some mystical or unknown power.

We all have some faulty beliefs about past occurrences, but certain circumstances and actions can make our memories more or less reliable.

In a July 2014 study published in *Psychological Science*, for instance, researchers concluded that even something as minor as sleep deprivation can substantially increase the likelihood of a person forming false memories.[32] A lack of sleep can further cause lost memories, impaired wit, and even hallucinations.[33] Consuming cannabis has also been linked to an increased likelihood of false memory formation, according to a 2015 study in *Molecular Psychiatry*.[34] Some researchers have implanted false memories into the brains of sleeping mice,[35] while others, such as Julia Shaw of the University of Bedfordshire and Stephen Porter of the University of British Columbia, have even discovered how to implant false memories in people and make them believe they committed a crime. Shaw and Porter say their study *"provides evidence that people can come to visualize and recall detailed false memories of engaging in criminal behavior."*[36]

"Not only could the young adults in our sample be led to generate such memories, but their rate of false recollection was high, and the memories themselves were richly detailed," the authors wrote. *"Additionally, false memories for perpetrating crime showed signs that they may have been generated in a way that is similar to the way in which false memories for noncriminal emotional memories are generated."*

BEING FOOLED IN THE MOMENT

Not only are our *memories* malleable and ever-changing based on our own understanding of events, but we can actually be tricked in the moment, as well. Our own human perception is flawed and easily fooled because our expectations and preconceived notions can actually shape what we see and remember. In fact, a 2015 study published in *The Proceedings of the National Academy of Sciences* showed that *prior knowledge* can influence some people's thoughts even more than sensory evidence.[37] The scientists involved with that research found that hallucinations are sometimes caused by nothing more than a normal, functioning brain.

"In other words, the potential for psychotic experiences such as hallucinations might be a logical consequence of the way in which our brain deals with the inherent ambiguity of sensory information by incorporating prior knowledge into our perceptual processing," the authors of the study wrote. *"The current study uncovered an imbalance of this processing type that shows its effects at the perceptual level."*

The fact is that it's not uncommon for people to hallucinate, even when there are no drugs or medical issues involved. In one study, researchers showed that 66 percent of participants staring into a mirror in a dimly lit room noticed *"huge deformations"* in their own face while 48 percent described *"fantastical and monstrous beings."*[38] That same study found that 18 percent saw a parent's face with altered traits and 28 percent saw an unknown person looking back at them in the mirror. The observations were made in a quiet room dimly lit with a 25-watt incandescent light, but researchers say the illusion can be *"easily experienced and replicated"* because the details of the setting *"are not critical."* This particular illusion may be partially linked to the **Troxler effect**, an optical illusion that occurs when a person focuses on a specific point for a period of time. The effect, first identified by Swiss physician Ignaz Paul Vital Troxler in 1804, serves as the basis for many optical illusions you find online and elsewhere.[39] If you want to experience the Troxler effect yourself, search for the "Lilac Chaser" online. If you stare at the cross for a few seconds, the lilac dots should begin to disappear.

Another example of being fooled in the moment involves **pareidolia**, the psychological phenomenon that causes a person to interpret vague images and sounds as significant or important. Introduced by Russian psychiatrist Victor Kandinsky in the 1800s,[40] this process not only causes you to spot faces in the clouds and on the moon, but also explains a number of alleged ghost sightings and even why you might "hear" hidden messages on records when you play them in reverse. Pareidolia, which is experienced more regularly by certain types of people, including those with higher levels of neuroticism,[41] works a lot like the *Rorschach inkblot test* used in psychology because individuals pick out images that aren't really there.

Pareidolia is a type of **apophenia**, which characterizes the experience of spontaneously recognizing patterns, connections, or meaningfulness in unrelated data. Interpreting arbitrary events in daily life as *"signs"* from a god or ghost or other force is a good example of this phenomenon. B. F. Skinner called this shortcut in the human brain *"conditioned seeing, hearing, and so on,"*[42] while Michael Shermer coined the term **patternicity**. Shermer describes patternicity as *"the tendency to find meaningful patterns in meaningless noise."* All these terms speak to the fact that we have an innate human instinct to seek out familiar patterns and assign them meaning and agency, even when the patterns themselves have been manufactured. We are good at pattern seeking—perhaps too good, as we often notice patterns that aren't really there. But that's not necessarily a bad thing. I think our brains are truly impressive because we can forge false connections, count only the *hits*, and see coincidences as meaningful without the knowledge that we're doing anything at all.

All of these examples of optical illusions and flawed perceptions occur regularly during the normal course of a person's life, and do not include some of the more extreme misfires of which the human brain is capable. There are also a number of medical conditions that provide possible natural explanations for so-called supernatural phenomena. In *The Man Who Mistook His Wife for a Hat*, author and neurologist Oliver Sacks brought a number of these disorders to national attention, including *visual agnosia*, the visual recognition impairment that serves as the basis for the book's title.[43] Sacks also details case histories of patients suffering from *Korsakoff's syndrome*, which causes an inability to form new memories, and a number of other conditions. In addition to those described by Sacks, there are many more abnormalities that can change how we see the world. For instance, those who suffer from *schizoaffective disorder*, a mental condition characterized by abnormal emotions, hallucinations, and delusions,[44] often develop a strong belief in ghosts and demons. People who go undiagnosed with this disorder and other similar conditions might not ever find the real answers that could be enormously helpful to them, whether they are just curious about their condition or in need of serious medical assistance, because society often reinforces the false beliefs (in this case, symptoms of illness) as normal. This is unfortunate because, although eerie feelings and delusions can be terrifying, there's nothing quite like the relief one feels by understanding the scientific reasons behind experiences thought to be the result of malevolent supernatural creatures.

In what could be considered yet another medical *non*mystery, even something as simple as a migraine can cause **auras**, or perceptual disturbances that are sometimes linked to auditory and visual hallucinations, as well as strange smells and tastes.[45] These visual migraines can last for hours and can leave the sufferer confused and disoriented, but they are also regularly blamed for ghostly and divine experiences. Similarly, those who report seeing strange lights where none should be often discover that their experience can be explained by **phosphenes**, phenomena associated with eye conditions and induced by movement or sound. Many believers are happy to attribute these medical conditions to otherworldly forces, but the truth can also be a great relief to sufferers who find out that their sightings are not a result of some evil spirit world—but are instead caused by something as simple as disrupted blood flow to the occipital lobe of the brain, or by an eye condition. There are innumerable similar examples and these conditions are not new, even if they are only now being studied in-depth. It's interesting to imagine how these hallucinations, illnesses, and other issues were interpreted by our ancestors, and then sad to think about the fact that many modern people have a similar mindset. The way we bring those people up to speed, of course, is through education (see chapter 10).

ANECDOTES IN THE COURTROOM

Because of the potential for inaccuracies when it comes to first-hand accounts, court systems in the developed world don't generally convict people based solely on the assumption that purported eyewitness testimonies are true. They might assume an allegation is true for the sake of an argument to follow a line of questioning, or use eyewitness testimony to bolster certain claims, but they don't often allow prosecutors or litigants to base a successful case on personal experience alone. And even when they do—because of the problems that plague human memory—that is a flaw in the legal system, and not a reason to believe in any supernatural claims.

In an ideal world, all courts would use only verifiable evidence because it would always be available. But this isn't that world, so legal systems *do* sometimes rely on personal testimonials alone. When that happens, it can cause serious problems. Take a look at Luis Vargas, for instance, who spent 16 years in prison for sexual assaults he didn't commit. Vargas was originally misidentified as the attacker because of a similar tattoo and sentenced to 55 years in prison, but he was cleared of the charges in November 2015 after DNA evidence revealed the real culprit.[46] Experts generally agree that hundreds of suspects each year are wrongfully convicted based on faulty eyewitness testimony in the United States alone—largely because people are unaware of how their experiences can be misremembered and therefore have too much confidence in their memories. In fact, as of 2016, eyewitness misidentification testimony was a factor in 70 percent of the 347 postconviction DNA exonerations in U.S.

history, according to the Innocence Project, which advocates for prisoners who can be proven innocent through DNA testing. Despite exonerations based on physical evidence, false confessions resulting from suggestion,[47] and study after study indicating how flawed our personal experiences can be, justice systems around the world continue to rely (often too heavily) on eyewitness accounts as conclusive evidence. But that doesn't change the fact that experience is not equal to scientific proof. Neil deGrasse Tyson is one of many scientists to draw attention to this disparity between science and justice: *"No matter what eyewitness testimony is in the court of law, it is the lowest form of evidence in the court of science."*[48]

To explore the nature of anecdotal accounts as evidence of the supernatural even further, I recommend looking at a common paranormal claim through the lens of the justice system. For example, we can take Christianity, the most popular supernatural belief system in the world, and apply our courts' rules as we review its spiritual claims.[49] If the Christian religion were to stand trial today and use biblical scripture as evidence for its validity, not only would it fail to meet the burden of proof necessary for a decision in its favor, it wouldn't even come close. Christians themselves don't agree on which biblical statements are "real" and which are to be considered figurative, so how would they present a coherent argument to an objective judge? This lack of consistency and hard evidence is where religious faith comes in, but "faith" isn't a compelling argument in court. Christianity's case might look something like this:

EXHIBIT A: A BOOK I VIEW AS SACRED IN ORIGIN SAYS PEOPLE THOUSANDS OF YEARS AGO CLAIMED THEY SAW MIRACLES (ALTHOUGH WE NOW KNOW THAT THESE ACCOUNTS WERE WRITTEN DECADES AFTER THE SUPPOSED MIRACLES WOULD HAVE OCCURRED).

EXHIBIT B: DESPITE THE FACT THAT OUR SIDE CAN'T AGREE ON WHICH MIRACLES REALLY HAPPENED AND WHICH ARE METAPHORS, YOU CAN'T PROVE THEY DIDN'T HAPPEN, SO WE DESERVE VICTORY.

Even if we examine a specific supernatural claim that most Christians *do* agree really occurred, such as the resurrection of Jesus, the case for the religion looks bleak. The fact is that the Synoptic Gospels were written 40 to 70 years after the supposed death and resurrection of Jesus by people who could not have been eyewitnesses.[50] These are considered, by the vast majority of secular and religious experts in the field, to be *anonymous* texts because the authors never divulge their names. According to New Testament scholar Bart D. Ehrman, these stories *"circulated anonymously, for years and decades."*

"We have no certain evidence that they—these particular Gospels—were called by their familiar names until around 180 CE, in sources connected with Rome," Ehrman said. *"At this stage, what we can say with certainty is that the Gospels are quoted in the early and mid-second centuries by proto-orthodox Christian authors, who never identify them as Matthew, Mark, Luke, and John."*

These anonymous stories written long after the developments are said to have occurred don't prove anything, especially because there are major points of disagreement among them and the alleged witnesses aren't available to give their account—but the trial isn't over yet. Before closing arguments, let's allow Christianity to put forth another common piece of hollow "evidence" for Jesus' resurrection. A number of Christian apologists, including William Lane Craig, have asserted that an *"empty tomb"* constitutes clear evidence that Jesus rose from the dead and into Heaven.

"[M]ost historical scholars agree that after his crucifixion Jesus' tomb was discovered empty by a group of female disciples, that various individuals and groups saw appearances of Jesus alive after his death, and that the original disciples suddenly and sincerely came to believe in Jesus' resurrection despite their every predisposition to the contrary," Craig wrote in 2013 for Fox News.[51] *"I can think of no better explanation of these facts than the one the original disciples gave: God raised Jesus from the dead."*

In a courtroom, this argument would fail to establish any common occurrence with certainty, let alone an act the likes of which has never been recorded in human history. Christian apologists who argue that a story about an empty tomb is convincing evidence of a resurrected body are likely unfamiliar with *Occam's razor*, which is named after the famed philosopher William of Ockham and states that, among competing hypotheses, the one with the fewest assumptions should be selected. These believers probably assume the most likely explanation for the alleged empty tomb is miraculous resurrection through some unproven divine connection, but more likely scenarios include a stolen body, a mismarked grave, a planned removal, faulty reports, creative storytelling, edited scriptures, and much, much more. No magic required.

It's fine if ancient "eyewitness" testimonies written down in the form of scripture are sufficient for you to believe in the reported supernatural events that form the basis of Christianity, but that means you don't have a very high standard for evidentiary support. And if that's the case, you should be consistent in your approach. You should open up the hadith literature to Sahih al-Bukhari, Volume 5, Book 58, and see that there are numerous eyewitnesses who saw Muhammad ascend to Heaven on a winged steed. If we are to assume this is true, should we infer that Muhammad was indeed a prophet? What's the verdict?

TYING IT TOGETHER

I know about the many flaws in our memory and eyesight, as well as our potential biases that make each of us susceptible to being fooled, but I still can't escape them. All these issues skew perceptions and establish exactly why anecdotes, either my own or those of others, will never be enough to convince me of the existence of anything supernatural (or even extraordinary). I would need observable, scientific evidence of something previously unknown to all humanity before believing in it, and I have set that same standard for creator-gods, disembodied human spirits, and a number of other supernatural, paranormal, and otherwise implausible claims. As a result of this understanding of the inherent problems with eyewitness accounts, when I hear a believer (in any sort of woo) proclaim, "I was skeptical, too, until I saw it for myself!" it always sounds suspiciously like: "I used to recognize that human beings by their very nature can be and often are mistaken, but I refuse to apply that simple fact to *myself!*" We are fallible, and we shouldn't hide from that.

If more people understood the facts regarding flawed senses and memories, they might be less likely to jump to supernatural conclusions when analyzing experiences. But my work isn't just about pointing out cognitive roadblocks in other people: it's about understanding and adjusting for my own in the pursuit of what's real. Just by actively looking for and recognizing these perceptual problems, we can actually make ourselves less likely to experience them, so it's a worthwhile endeavor. Many of us believed ridiculous things when we were younger, and those ideas sometimes persist for years or even lifetimes, but by learning about the human imagination and the errors in our own senses we can often move beyond those childish notions and realize how easily we can be tricked. We can learn to be skeptical of our own eyes and our own memories and advocate for empirical research over anecdotes, bringing us ever closer to reality.

*"Every journey into the past is complicated by delusions,
false memories, false namings of real events."*

—Adrienne Rich

NOTES

1.   R. H. Thouless, "The Tendency to Certainty in Religious Belief," *British Journal of Psychology General Section* 26 (1935): 16–31.

2.   Keith E. Stanovich, *How to Think Straight About Psychology* (Boston, MA: Pearson Allyn and Bacon, 2007).

3.   Chase B. Wrenn, "Fallacies," The Internet Encyclopedia of Philosophy, www.iep.utm.edu/.

4.   Wayne Weiten and Douglas McCann, *Psychology: Themes and Variations* (Toronto: Nelson, 2006).

5.   Laura P. Otis and James E. Alcock, "Factors Affecting Extraordinary Belief," *Journal of Social Psychology* 118, no. 1 (1982).

6.   Lindeman, Marjaana and Annika M. Svedholm-Häkkinen, "Does Poor Understanding of Physical World Predict Religious and Paranormal Beliefs?" *Applied Cognitive Psychology* 30, no. 5 (2016): 736–742.

7.   M. Wierzbicki, "Reasoning Errors and Belief in the Paranormal," *Journal of Social Psychology* 125 (1985): 489–494.

8.   Peter Krummenacher, "Dopamine, Paranormal Belief, and the Detection of Meaningful Stimuli," Journal of Cognitive Neuroscience 22, no. 8 (2010): 1670–1681.

9.   T. Lawrence et al., "Modelling Childhood Causes of Paranormal Belief and Experience: Childhood Trauma and Childhood Fantasy," *Personality and Individual Differences* 19 (1995): 209–215.

10. Chase B. Wrenn, "Fallacies," The Internet Encyclopedia of Philosophy, www.iep.utm.edu/.

11. Irving Lester Janis, *Groupthink: Psychological Studies of Policy Decisions and Fiascoes* (Boston, MA: Wadsworth, 1982).

12. S. E. Asch, "Effects of Group Pressure upon the Modification and Distortion of Judgment," in *Groups, Leadership and Men*, ed. H. Guetzkow (Pittsburgh, PA: Carnegie Press, 1951).

13. Edmund Parish, *Hallucinations and Illusions: A Study of the fallacies of Perception* (New York: C. Scribner's Sons, 1897), 311.

14. Robert E. Bartholomew, *Little Green Men, Meowing Nuns and Head-hunting Panics: A Study of Mass Psychogenic Illness and Social Delusion* (Jefferson, NC: McFarland, 2001).

15. Tim McGirk, "Hindu World Divided by a 24-hour Wonder," *Independent*, September 22, 1995.

16. John F. Burns, "India's 'Guru Busters' Debunk All That's Mystical," *New York Times*, October 9, 1995.

17. T. Jayaraman, "Obscurantism vs Science Behind the Milk-drinking 'Miracle,'" Institute of Mathematical Sciences.

18. David Hume, *An Enquiry Concerning Human Understanding*, ed. Charles William Hendel, vol. 49 (Indianapolis, IN: Bobbs-Merrill, 1955).

19. It's interesting to note that this same form of faith is used to justify the beliefs of Christians who believe in Jesus' miracles, Muslims who say Muhammad spoke with an angel and flew on a winged horse, and Mormons who think God lives near a planet called Kolob (chapters 3 and 5 in the book of Abraham).

20. For me, sharing a quote from someone isn't an explicit endorsement of every one of his or her views or actions. A person with whom I disagree on just about every issue can still say something valuable or true—even Adolf Hitler, who said, "*Make the lie big, make it simple, keep saying it, and eventually they will believe it.*"

21. Luke 17:11–19

22. Sheryl C. Wilson and Theodore X. Barber, "The Fantasy-Prone Personality: Implications for Understanding Imagery, Hypnosis, and Parapsychological Phenomena," PSI Research 1, no. (3) (September 1982): 94–116.

23. Robert E. Bartholomew et al., "UFO Abductees and Contactees: Psychopathology or Fantasy Proneness?" *Professional Psychology: Research and Practice* 22, no. 3 (June 1991): 215—222.

24. Leslie van der Leer et al., "Delusion Proneness and "Jumping to Conclusions"': Relative and Absolute Effects," *Psychological Medicine* 45, no. 6 (April 2015).

25. As American novelist Barbara Kingsolver has said, *"Memory is a complicated thing, a relative to truth but not its twin."*

26. Bruce Bower, "Gone but Not Forgotten: Scientists Uncover Pervasive, Unconscious Influences on Memory," *Science News* 138, no. 20 (1990): 312–314.

27. Maria S. Zaragoza et al., "Misinformation Effects and the Suggestibility of Eyewitness Memory," in "What Jennifer Saw," *Frontline*, www.pbs.org/wgbh/pages/frontline/shows/dna/interviews/loftus.html.

29. Daniel J Simons and Christopher F. Chabris, "What People Believe about How Memory Works: A Representative Survey of the US population," PloS One 6, no. 8 (2011): e22757.

30. Alison George, "Can You Tell a False Memory From a True One?" *Slate*, September 8, 2013, www.slate.com/articles/health_and_science/new_scientist/2013/09/elizabeth_loftus_interview_false_memory_research_on_eyewitnesses_child_abuse.html.

31. Lawrence Patihis et al., "False Memories in Highly Superior Autobiographical Memory Individuals," *Proceedings of the National Academy of Sciences* 110, no. 52 (2013): 20856–20857.

32. Steven J. Frenda et al., "Sleep Deprivation and False Memories," *Psychological Science* 25, no. 9 (2014): 1674–1681.

33. Ralph J. Berger and Ian Oswald, "Effects of Sleep Deprivation on Behaviour, Subsequent Sleep, and Dreaming," *British Journal of Psychiatry* 108, no. 455 (1962): 457–465.

34. J. Riba et al., "Telling True from False: Cannabis Users Show Increased Susceptibility to False Memories, *Molecular Psychiatry* 20, no. 6 (2015): 772–777.

35. Gaetan de Lavilléon et al., "Explicit Memory Creation During Sleep Demonstrates a Causal Role of Place Cells in Navigation," *Nature Neuroscience* 18 (2015): 493–495.

36. J. Shaw and S. Porter, "Constructing Rich False Memories of Committing Crime," *Psychological Science*, 26, no. 3 (March 2015): 291–301.

37. Christoph Teufel et al., "Shift Toward Prior Knowledge Confers a Perceptual Advantage in Early Psychosis and Psychosis-Prone Healthy Individuals," *Proceedings of the National Academy of Sciences* 112, no. 43 (2015): 13401–13406.

38. Giovanni B. Caputo, "Strange-Face-in-the-Mirror Illusion," *Perception* 39, no. 7 (2010): 1007.

39. D. I. P. V. Troxler, "Über das Verschwinden gegebener Gegenstände innerhalb unseres Gesichtskreises." *Ophthalmologische bibliothek* 2, no. 2 (1804): 1–53.

40. Viktor Khrisanfovich Kandinsky, *Kritische und klinische Betrachtungen im Gebiete der Sinnestäuschungen: 1. und 2. Studie* (Friedländer, 1885).

41. Y. Kaji et al., "Do You See Something in Noise? Your Personality Trait, Emotional State and Sex Affect Your Tendency to See Pareidolia," paper presented at the 19th annual meeting of Association for the Scientific Study of Consciousness, Paris, France, 2015

42. B. F. Skinner, *Science and Human Behavior* (New York: Macmillan, 1953).

43. Oliver Sacks, *The Man Who Mistook His Wife for a Hat: And Other Clinical Tales* (New York: Simon and Schuster, 1998).

44. "Symptoms and Causes," Mayo Clinic, www.mayoclinic.org/diseases-conditions/schizoaffective-disorder/symptoms-causes/dxc-20258893.

45. Teri Robert, *Living Well with Migraine Disease and Headaches* (New York: HarperCollins, 2004).

46. Brian Melley, "Convict in 3 Sex Crimes Freed by DNA Tied to Fugitive Rapist," Associated Press, November 23, 2015, bigstory.ap.org/article/e94023c7c09c4f9f8e1128f57672388d/man-convicted-3-rapes-expected-be-exonerated>.

47. Douglas Starr, "Remembering a Crime That You Didn't Commit," *New Yorker*, March 5, 2015, www.newyorker.com/tech/elements/false-memory-crime.

48. Memory researcher Elizabeth Loftus has also weighed in on this issue, saying courts of law should adopt a new oath for witnesses: "*Do you swear to tell the truth, the whole truth, or whatever it is you think you remember?*"

49. This is only one example. You can perform the same experiment using any religion or other supernatural belief by analyzing evidence put forth by believers as though you're on a jury.

50. "Instructional Design and eTeaching Services," Dating of the Gospels, Boston College, www.bc.edu/schools/stm/crossroads/resources/birthofjesus/intro/the_dating_of_thegospels.html.

51. William Lane Craig, "A Christmas Gift for Atheists—Five Reasons Why God Exists," *Fox News*, December 13, 2013, www.foxnews.com/opinion/2013/12/13/christmas-gift-for-atheists-five-reasons-why-god-exists.html.

10

GHOSTS, SPIRITS, AND SPECTERS

"The evidence for ghosts is no better today than it was a year ago,
a decade ago, or a century ago. There are two possible reasons for the failure
of ghost hunters to find good evidence. The first is that ghosts don't exist,
and that reports of ghosts can be explained by psychology, misperceptions,
mistakes and hoaxes. The second option is that ghosts do exist,
but that ghost hunters are simply incompetent."[1]
—Benjamin Radford

I dismiss tales of ghosts for the same reasons I reject belief in alleged sightings of gods, angels, and aliens, and any other personal account through which someone asserts the existence of an unsubstantiated alternate reality without verifiable evidence supporting it. There are many puzzling reports about spirit activities throughout the world, but I refuse to jump to the conclusion that ghosts are the answer until there's proof. Think about it: how many mysteries have ever been solved by simply crediting some mysterious, unproven, paranormal realm? None—and that's exactly what many ghost believers attempt to do.

RUMORS DON'T PROVE GHOSTS EXIST

Ghost stories are extremely common in many cultures, but that's still all they are—stories, peppered with the storyteller's own personal feelings and conjecture that can make objective, rational analysis nearly impossible. These testimonies don't qualify as strong scientific evidence, especially when positing the existence of something as extraordinary as spirits contacting us from another dimension, but that doesn't stop many people from declaring their exploits to be "proof" of the supernatural. I don't doubt that many of these ghost believers have had mysterious experiences, but their stories hold as much weight as those of a person who claims to have been visited by Jesus, abducted by aliens, or invited to a tea party with Bigfoot.

More often than not, accounts of ghostly activity are actually just tales about some "strange" experience the storyteller has merely decided must have been caused by spirits. The believer's tendency to jump from "I don't know" to "It was a ghost" can be called the *ghost of the gaps* fallacy. Ghost of the gaps is a common problem for people who want to believe in the spirit world, or even for those who want to make an uninteresting story slightly more tolerable. However, considering the fact that ghosts haven't been shown to exist, and other natural explanations are almost always available to explain such "sightings," the responsible thing to do with any of these fantastical claims is to classify them as "unknown" until the real evidence is uncovered. There are many things we don't know, and one should never feel bad for admitting that and seeking knowledge, but what should be frowned upon is making things up. Admitting you don't know is always better than saying, "I definitely saw a disembodied human spirit that can't be analyzed or measured objectively—and there's no way to change my mind."

There are a lot of ghost stories out there, but when I hear them, thanks to scientific skepticism, I feel like I'm in a reverse *Sixth Sense*: everyone sees dead people but me.

WHY ARE GHOST STORIES POPULAR?

While there are a number of contributing factors, ghost myths are often propelled by (and perhaps based on) wishful thinking. Many people find comfort in believing their relatives live on in some form (see chapter 13), and they cling to that belief in times of despair. Hope, like the desire for everlasting life for our loved ones, can cause people to believe all sorts of things without hard evidence, such as a vague, ghostly afterlife. Personally, however, I can't imagine that roaming the earth for an eternity without the ability to interact with anything or anyone would be a fulfilling existence. Despite that rather daunting portrayal of the afterlife, many ghost believers simply *want* to believe. The belief comes easy from there. Once you have the emotional desire to believe in ghosts, all you have to do is tie unrelated things together to create a compelling story and point to an unprovable spirit as the culprit, even when there is usually a much more likely natural alternative. To me, the natural answer seems more probable than the existence of visible yet disembodied spirits that can't do anything but open your cabinets or knock on your walls, but perhaps in some ways it's not as comforting.

In addition to wishful thinking and the propaganda spread by ghost hunters and so-called *parapsychologists*, which will be addressed later in this chapter, I think the continuance of many ghost myths is largely linked to our species' enjoyment of mysteries and propensity for storytelling in general. As author Jonathan Gottschall pointed out, humans *"live in a storm of stories."*

"We live in stories all day long, and dream in stories all night long. We communicate through stories and learn from them. We collapse gratefully into stories after a long day at work," Gottschall wrote.[2] *"Homo sapiens (wise man) is a pretty good definition for our species. But Homo fictus (fiction man) would be about as accurate. Man is the storytelling animal."*

I'm not exempt from this tendency to tell tales, even when the supernatural is involved. For example, when I was very young, I used to tell a story about a ghost I saw in the hallway of my grandparents' house. I still remember the details like it happened yesterday. He was a short man with a fishing pole and vest, just standing in the hall one night as I walked to my room. I remember seeing him and being stunned, but then it turned into curiosity—as opposed to fear. He stood there for about a minute before taking a few steps back and disappearing completely. I told the story about seeing that ghost until I was about 12 years old, when I realized that I had no recollection of the actual event itself. I now believe that the original memory was manufactured and I was only remembering my earlier retellings of the story. The most likely explanation for this, in my case, was that I was confusing a dream for reality, or maybe I originally told the story to fit in with others as they told of their supernatural adventures. Either way, from there, the story and the reality became blurred in my mind so much so that I couldn't distinguish the two, and I came to believe my own false account. Years after I started telling the story, I realized the event never happened and I stopped telling people about it. Since that time, I haven't experienced anything that I would consider paranormal . . . but there was one other event that sticks out in my mind.

GHOSTS IN THE BEDROOM

About 10 years after I realized my childhood ghost interaction was most likely not a real event, when I was in college, I had a similar experience with what many people would insist was a ghostly entity. I was awoken late at night by a loud noise, and there it was—a ghost. She was right in front of me on the other side of the room, gliding slowly toward me with outstretched arms. She looked just like you'd expect a ghost to look based on horror movies: she had long, knotted black hair, pale skin, tattered clothing—the works.[3] I tried to scream for help, but I was paralyzed with fear . . . or at least that's what I thought was keeping me from moving or yelling. Once I was able to shake myself out of my paralyzed state and the entity was gone, I composed myself and researched possible explanations for what had just happened.

My search led me to a variety of sleep conditions and I concluded that I was likely experiencing **sleep paralysis**, of which these types of hallucinations are a common symptom. Studies show sleep paralysis is experienced by between 8 and 28 percent of the normal adult population and it can be caused by any number of things,[4] including something as simple as lying on your back or changing your normal sleep pattern. The most common effects include auditory and visual hallucinations, as well as difficulty breathing and chest pressure that can feel like suffocation, according to psychologist Christopher French of Goldsmiths College in London.

"*The reason sleep paralysis may explain tales of ghosts and aliens is the strong sense of a presence, usually harmful, that victims commonly feel during an attack*," French, who is also the coauthor of *Anomalistic Psychology: Exploring Paranormal Belief and Experience*,[5] wrote for *Scientific American*.[6] "*They also report unusual kinesthetic sensations, such as feelings of being dragged out of bed, vibrating, flying or falling. These episodes can sometimes lead to full-blown out-of-body experiences.*"

Since my terrifying vision in college, I have experienced other bouts of sleep paralysis during which I felt a numbness or paralyzing sensation accompanied by unbelievable visions. In many cases I felt awake and threatened, and I often saw ghostly figures approaching me in my bed. For many believers, these experiences are linked to ghost, demon, or alien visitation, and are often conflated with reality. But if your supernatural anecdote begins with, "I was *just* about to fall asleep ..." —or something similar—it is probably explained by sleep paralysis or a related condition. Sleep paralysis, **lucid dreaming**, and other hallucination-inducing mental phenomena often occur during the transitional state between wakefulness and sleep, called *hypnagogia,* making it difficult for those experiencing them to discern waking life from dreams.

Baland Jalal, a neuroscientist at the Behavioural and Clinical Neuroscience Institute at the University of Cambridge, says those experiencing sleep paralysis hallucinations often respond with fear and resistance, which is counterproductive. He says his treatment, meditation-relaxation therapy, has a higher success rate.[7] Jalal's method has four steps:

Step I: reappraisal of the meaning of the attack: at the onset of the attack, the individual should reappraise the meaning of his SP episode by telling himself that the experience is common, benign, and temporary, and that the hallucinations are a typical byproduct of REM mentation (i.e., dreaming). Eyes should remain closed throughout the SP episode and the person should stay calm and avoid movement. (Ideally, the individual would have received prior psychoeducation about the nature of SP and associated hallucinations.)

Step II: psychological and emotional distancing: next, the individual should tell himself that since the experience is common, benign, and temporary, there is no reason to be afraid or worried. That in fact, fear and worry (catastrophizing the event) will only make the episode worse and possibly prolong it, and are unnecessary emotions.

Step III: inward focused-attention meditation: the individual should then focus his attention inward on an emotionally salient positive object (e.g., a memory of a loved one or event, a hymn/prayer, God). He should sustain his full attention on this inner-object and engage it emotionally (i.e., reflect on all its positive aspects). Bodily symptoms and external stimuli (i.e., hallucinations) should be ignored, and whenever distracted, attention should be brought back to the inner-object of focus.

Step IV: muscle relaxation: while engaging in focused inward-attention meditation, the individual should relax his muscles and avoid flexing them; and avoid controlling breathing and under no circumstances attempt to move. He should adopt a non-judgmental attitude of acceptance toward physical symptoms.

NHS Choices, the United Kingdom's largest health website, has also put forth some helpful tips for those suffering from sleep paralysis and similar conditions, including improving your sleeping habits and talking to a specialist about medication.[8] This is good advice, and it might help you deal with the symptoms of sleep paralysis, but it won't necessarily address what makes the phenomenon terrifying in the first place: the belief that the entities are really there. If you move away from beliefs in ghosts, gods, and other things that require an active imagination, you will, at very least, be able to understand what you are seeing in context. Losing those beliefs can also make you less likely to hear and see imagined things—and to misattribute nonimagined events to supernatural forces.

GRIEF-BASED HALLUCINATIONS

Although sleep paralysis is a common explanation for ghostly events, as well as what many believe are alien and demon experiences, there are a number of other possibilities that have nothing to do with sleep. In some cases, it is even possible for a person to experience auditory or visual hallucinations of late friends and loved ones caused by nothing more than acute grief. *Post-bereavement hallucinations* and illusions are not uncommon, and are even considered normal by some who study the phenomenon as a helpful coping mechanism that can provide closure.[9] Vaughan Bell, a neuroscientist and clinical psychologist based in London, says dead people remain in our hearts and minds, as well as *"in our senses—as sights, sounds, smells, touches or presences."*

"Grief hallucinations are a normal reaction to bereavement but are rarely discussed, because people fear they might be considered insane or mentally destabilised by their loss," Bell wrote for *Scientific American*.[10] *"As a society we tend to associate hallucinations with things like drugs and mental illness, but we now know that hallucinations are common in sober healthy people and that they are more likely during times of stress."*

This type of hallucination is just one of the many reasons that we can't always trust our own sight, especially when it comes to unverifiable visions of deceased loved ones, but that doesn't mean these experiences can't be valuable. If you have seen something like this before, the important question is: what will you do with the knowledge that it wasn't a product of supernatural intervention? Will you let it devalue a potentially unforgettable or beneficial experience? I hope not. I hope that you look at your past through a new lens—a naturalistic one—that allows you to learn and grow from it without relying on paranormal forces as the catalyst.

HAUNTINGS AND POLTERGEISTS

There's never been a place that has been shown, scientifically, to be haunted by spirits, but there are *stories* about these events everywhere we turn. These stories are told repeatedly, embellished, reported on by the media, and believed by many, but does that make hauntings real? According to a 1991 ruling by the New York Supreme Court, Appellate Division, the answer is, "Yes."[11] In the now-infamous *Ghostbusters ruling*, the justices decided that nationally published stories about a house being haunted were enough to affect its value and declared the house "haunted" under the law.

"*Whether the source of the spectral apparitions seen by defendant seller is parapsychic or psychogenic, having reported their presence in both a national publication and the local press, defendant is estopped to deny their existence and, as a matter of law, the house is haunted,*" Justice Israel Rubin wrote in the majority opinion. "*It was defendant's promotional efforts in publicizing her close encounters with the spirits which fostered the home's reputation in the community, and the impact of that reputation goes to the very essence of the bargain between the parties, greatly impairing both the value of the property and its potential for resale.*"

This was an interesting case and conclusion, but anyone who understands the judicial system or reads the court's opinion can see that the judges didn't establish that supernatural entities were real or present in the home. The case didn't prove anything paranormal, but it does make one wonder what types of experiences the owner had in the home to warrant national attention. Did she make everything up? That's possible, but there are people who do have genuine experiences that they believe are caused by ghosts. What's really causing them?

Supposed hauntings could be the result of any number of things, including something as simple as a dirty house. Researchers at Clarkson University in New York found in 2015 that some reports of hauntings could potentially be linked to toxic molds, such as rye ergot fungus. Shane Rogers, an associate professor of civil and environmental engineering at the school, said hauntings are *"widely reported phenomena that are not well-researched."*

"They are often reported in older-built structures that may also suffer poor air quality," Rogers said in a statement.[12] *"Similarly, some people have reported depression, anxiety and other effects from exposure to biological pollutants in indoor air. We are trying to determine whether some reported hauntings may be linked to specific pollutants found in indoor air."*

Another common and completely natural explanation for alleged ghost activity and feelings of being haunted is **infrasound**, also called low-frequency sound, which includes sounds lower in frequency than 20 Hz or cycles per second—the normal limit of human hearing. These extreme bass waves and vibrations can't be heard by humans, but they can be felt and have been shown to produce anxiety, extreme sorrow, and chills in some people. In one study, scientists from the National Physical Laboratory in England combined forces with musicians to put on a concert featuring music laced with infrasound.[13] The researchers found that 22 percent of the listeners, who were unaware of the details of the experiment, reported more unusual feelings and experiences during the pieces in which infrasound was present. Professor Richard Wiseman, a psychologist at the University of Hertfordshire in Southern England, presented the results of the experiment to the British Association for the Advancement of Science. He is one of the many experts who has argued that some of the odd sensations described during so-called ghost experiences could be explained by infrasonic vibrations.

"These results suggest that low frequency sound can cause people to have unusual experiences even though they cannot consciously detect infrasound," Wiseman said in announcing the experiment's conclusions.[14] *"Some scientists have suggested that this level of sound may be present at some allegedly haunted sites and so cause people to have odd sensations that they attribute to a ghost—our findings support these ideas."*

Numerous research projects have shown that sounds between 7 and 19 Hz can induce fear, dread, or panic in listeners,[15] and in at least one study scientists were actually able to manufacture a ghostly *"feeling of presence"* in a laboratory setting.[16] Some researchers, such as Vic Tandy of Coventry University in Warwickshire, took the hypothesis a step further. He reported that infrasound at around 18 Hz can resonate with the structure of the human eyeball and cause optical illusions of ghostly figures. Tandy claimed his study outlined an *"as yet undocumented natural cause for some cases of ostensible haunting."*

"Using the first author's own experience as an example, we show how a 19 Hz standing air wave may under certain conditions create sensory phenomena suggestive of a ghost," he wrote in the abstract of a 1998 paper published in the *Journal of the Society for Physical Research.*[17] *"Spontaneous case researchers are encouraged to rule out this potential natural explanation for paranormal experience in future cases of the haunting or poltergeistic type."*

Neil deGrasse Tyson has also looked into the 1998 study, saying Tandy was motivated by the fact that his lab was purported to be haunted. Tandy and his team ultimately discovered that the sound was coming from a newly installed fan, and when they turned the fan off, all paranormal phenomena stopped, according to Tyson.

"If you have a sound that resonates with something material, it'll make the material vibrate at that frequency," he said on his radio show *StarTalk.* *"When that happens to you, your eye begins to see things that are in fact not there."*

One reason hauntings are reported so frequently could be that infrasound is just about everywhere. It can be caused by anything, including machines, air passing through a particular pipe or window, earthquakes, and other natural occurrences. In fact, even some animals, such as elephants and tigers, have been shown to emit infrasound—sometimes at levels that travel several kilometers.[18]

FEAR AND EXPECTATIONS

There are also evolutionary reasons that we might get the chills or feel spooked at seemingly random times—without any mental instability or infrasound. We may get goosebumps, or maybe our hair stands up on end, when we feel uneasy and scared regardless of whether or not the perceived danger is a legitimate threat. It turns out this is just a reflex and can be triggered by almost anything, including sharing scary stories or even the mere thought of a place being "haunted," but where does this physical reaction come from? Scientists say it's a leftover byproduct from our ancestors, who had more hair than us and would puff themselves up to look bigger like cats do when they feel threatened.

"*The general principle is, if you are going to be attacked, try to look as big as you can,*" David Huron, a musicologist at Ohio State University, told *Popular Science*.[19]

Huron says hair raising began as a response to cold, but can be linked to fear and surprise, as well as to other intense emotions and even music. This fear-based response explains why we still feel shivers during horror movies, even when we know there are no monsters under the bed, and why many people actually enjoy the feeling of being frightened by them.

"*One part of your brain is saying, 'Oh my god, I'm gonna die!* " Huron said. "*But the conscious part is saying that everything is OK. Which makes shivers feel good.*"

In many ways, evolution has been good to us. Evolution is what has kept our species safe for hundreds of thousands of years. However, that safety doesn't come without a cost, and unwarranted fear is often the price we must pay. We have developed a number of ways to keep ourselves aware of danger in our everyday lives, and they can all be tied back to fear in one way or another. Fear is a reaction to potential hardships, but it can also help shape many of our behaviors. Our bodies know that fear is a safe response, and they can (and often do) manufacture it at will.

While these fear-based reflexes likely kept our ancestors alive under the most dangerous circumstances, they can be confusing in a time period in which survival isn't our top priority every day. For example, for our ancestors, being extra safe and aware of things approaching our territory would have been incredibly beneficial. Today, however, there are people who think that everything they see "out of the corner of their eye" is a ghost. They make this leap without realizing that our minds (and eyes) play tricks on us, and that this assumption of danger is actually related to our evolution and success as a species. That awkward tendency to register things out of the corner of our eyes as moving—and as threats—when they are not probably has saved more lives than you can imagine, but today some people stick with the "ghost" explanation. I constantly see strange coincidences, mysterious objects in my peripheral vision, and other things some people would consider proof of one supernatural force or another. I acknowledge these experiences for the glitches in my system that they are, but I often wonder how I'd interpret them as a believer.

GHOST-HUNTING TACTICS

Self-proclaimed paranormal investigators, including and especially those on television, often further the haunting myth by planting evidence, sensationalizing ideas, and using camera tricks and editing techniques to advocate for the existence of ghosts without providing any measurable or objective evidence for the rest of us to evaluate. That is why no findings from any ghost-hunting TV shows—or from any other person with a ghost-hunting hobby—have ever been submitted for peer review by any serious-minded person, and why their "evidence" isn't really evidence at all. These so-called ghost hunters have, in many cases, dedicated their lives to proving the existence of ghosts, but every single one has—so far—been a failure. They are not ghost hunters; they are ghost pretenders.

The A&E series *American Haunting* provides a good example of manufactured drama and falsified evidence in ghost-hunting media. According to a man who owned a house that was the subject of one of the show's episodes, the camera crew focused on "reenactments" of spooky events that were said to have happened. The developments that took place during the recording were reportedly edited around things that were actually said, but that were "*cut to fit the needs of the editors.*"

"*So while I never lied about anything that happened, the world wouldn't know the difference, because literally every moment was cut apart and pieced together in an order that resembled an old Lon Chaney movie,*" the homeowner wrote anonymously. "*The final product was a special effects extravaganza that made Sharknado 2 look like a subdued French film.*"[20]

It should be common knowledge that the TV programs purporting to show ghost activity are for entertainment purposes only and, at best, they provide false "ghost" labels to events with perfectly natural explanations. At worst, however, they knowingly coerce the audience into believing baseless claims. Because of this manipulation, any skeptical person should be ready to ask some serious questions about any and all "investigators" of ghosts. For instance, why do the vast majority of spirit wranglers turn off the lights before filming? And why do people claiming to be ghost hunters commonly seem surprised when they say they hear noises in haunted buildings? Isn't that what they were expecting? When ghost hunters do provide recordings as evidence for ghost communication, why is it always muffled and vague? Why is there never a clear and important message conveyed by the spirit about the afterlife? Why are there never any falsifiable predictions about this life?

HEARING VOICES

In addition to personal testimonies and intentionally misleading filming practices, some of the most common forms of so-called evidence put forth by ghost hunters and hailed by believers are **electronic voice phenomena (EVP).** EVP is a vague term, as it generally refers to any recording that seems to inexplicably resemble human speech, but it is much like other pieces of purported evidence for ghosts in that it is completely unverifiable, subjective, and based entirely on assumptions. Many people claim to hear ghost voices (whatever that means) on recordings of supposedly empty space, but these sounds can almost always be explained by stray radio signals, static, and other background noises. As is the case with many "proofs" of the supernatural, EVP can perhaps be best addressed via questions that might spur additional thought on the part of the believer. In the instance of EVP, I like to ask, "Do you believe our larynx, or voice box, transcends into the afterlife, too? How exactly do you think the process works?"

Contrary to what some ghost hunters would have you believe, if you place an audio recorder overnight in any location, you are likely to come across strange and unfamiliar sounds. It's usually the listener's imagination, however, that allows them to take the form of recognized speech and become "EVP." More often than not, unless you've somehow picked up a stray radio conversation, what you are actually hearing is static that you are interpreting as a voice because of our tendency to find patterns (even when they are absent). This is yet another example of *apophenia* (see chapter 9), which is the subject of research by auditory hallucination expert Diana Deutsch, a professor of psychology at the University of California, San Diego. In one study, Deutsch recorded a large number of nonsense phrases and "phantom words" that were played for students. She says the students interpreted the meaningless sounds in a variety of different ways,[21] and this process could be the root cause of EVP.

"*Often people initially hear a jumble of meaningless sounds, but after a while distinct words and phrases suddenly emerge,*" Deutsch wrote, adding that dieting students were more likely to hear "*I'm hungry*" or "*Diet Coke,*" while stressed students more often reported hearing "*I'm tired*" or "*no time.*" "*People appear to hear words and phrases that reflect what is on their minds—rather as in a Rorschach test, though it's my impression that the present effect is stronger.*"

If you think you've experienced an EVP and you're with someone else who claims to have heard the the same thing, it's also possible that you were made to expect a specific word or phrase, which in turn caused you to perceive it. In psychology, this is called priming, and it is why people who are instructed to say "silk" repeatedly and then asked what cows drink will often respond with "milk" instead of water. It's also why even self-proclaimed skeptics are more likely to report supernatural occurrences if they are told to expect them,[22] and why you probably didn't notice the extra "the" in the first sentence of this paragraph. With EVP, priming works like this: one person hears a noise and interprets it as a voice saying something like, "Hello, Tom." That person then tells other observers what they heard, and their minds prepare to recognize it. Once the recording is played back to the others, or they've had time to reflect on the sound with that suggestion in mind, it becomes an audible pattern to them and everyone thinks they hear the same words. In a study involving paranormal groups and EVP, researchers found that the teams readily identified the phenomenon in recordings from a variety of locations, but were inconsistent in their "*interpretation of the alleged communication.*"[23]

"*Still, it is possible that the one matched EVP is a result of communication with the deceased,*" the authors wrote. "*Another possibility is that noise was generated from some other source and follows a particular pattern, which caused the teams to interpret the noise in a similar fashion. We feel the latter explanation is more likely the case, given the physical explanations for EVP, such as human error.*"

In the end, EVP will never prove the existence of anything supernatural, simply because it doesn't give us any real data. All you can do is prove something made a sound that someone interpreted as a voice, but not where it came from or anything else about it. It could be anything from trickery and manipulation to static, so jumping to the conclusion of a deceased human's spirit seems premature.

EMF READINGS AND OTHER "UNBELIEVABLE" PIECES OF EVIDENCE

Many ghost hunters also use *electromagnetic field (EMF)* detectors to create the false perception that ghost activity exists. They often cast these EMF readings as evidence, but neglect to mention that electromagnetic fields, which are common and can emanate from nearby microwaves and other industrial electronic appliances, among other things, have never been shown to have any connection to so-called spiritual phenomena. No matter how much a ghost hunter shouts, "My EMF meter was off the charts!" it will never prove that those electromagnetic fields are linked to spirits. For that, we'd need real scientific evidence. Benjamin Radford explains that ghost hunters use "*a variety of creative—and dubious—methods to detect their quarry's presence.*"

"*Virtually all ghost hunter groups claim to be scientific, and most give that appearance because they use high-tech scientific equipment such as Geiger counters, Electromagnetic Field (EMF) detectors, ion detectors, and infrared cameras,*" Radford wrote for *Live Science*. "*Yet the equipment is only as scientific as the person using it; you may own the world's most sophisticated thermometer, but if you are using it as a barometer, your measurements are worthless.*"

Sharon Hill, a writer who specializes in issues of science and the public and runs a skeptically themed news site called *Doubtful News*, has also addressed the tendency for ghost hunters (and Bigfoot hunters and UFO seekers) to be "*sciencey.*" She says amateur research and investigation groups "*rely on their equipment to record spiritual evidence.*"

"*Several groups express the notion that new technology is the key to a breakthrough in paranormal research,*" Hill wrote in her master's thesis on the topic.[24] "*Yet at no site and in no ghost investigation reference book did I encounter a coherent, referenced explanation for the various equipment used and data gathered.*"

Hill added that ghost-hunting groups "*matter-of-factly state that the equipment records environmental disturbances related to paranormal activity without considering normal variance or calibration.*"

The process of linking unsubstantiated supernatural forces to known natural ones is also utilized by those who present photographs of **orbs** as evidence of ghosts. In reality, these small circular visual effects found in flash photography are easily explained by light reflecting off of dust, pollen, water droplets, and more, and are very well understood by professional photographers. Sharona Belles of Sharona Belles Photography in Auburn, California, says photographers must typically go out of their way to avoid getting this effect.

"*Most photographers use a hood on their lenses to avoid lighting issues,*" Belles told me in an interview. "*Sunspots and orbs are just reflections of light—often found because of poorly metered shots.*"

Similarly, some believers present pictures of unexpected translucent apparitions as evidence of the existence of ghosts. Those who think these kinds of photos make a strong case, however, have likely never researched *multiple exposure*, which is common in photography and cinematography, can create ghostly images by accident, and is frequently used in photographic **hoaxes**. Recordings and pictures that purportedly show "ghosts," including orbs and other seemingly mysterious figures, should not be treated as spirits until that is proven to be the case. They are at best unexplained phenomena, and at worst they're quirks in the photography process, shadows, or the result of pareidolia.

Let's entertain for a moment the idea that ghost believers have been right all along and EMF readings, EVPs, orbs, and double-exposed photos really do provide evidence of spirits. With thousands of ghost hunters working so hard with their audio recorders, EMF detectors, and flash cameras around the world, you'd think they'd have hard evidence capable of surviving peer review and achieving scientific viability by now. Unfortunately, that scientific evidence hasn't yet been presented.

PARAPSYCHOLOGY

There's more to ghost hunting than merely altering others' perceptions and presenting demonstrably false evidence. Many spirit chasers, as well as other people who spend their time trying to convince people of the existence of paranormal forces and entities, might also identify as "parapsychologists," perhaps in an attempt to give the false impression that their methods have scientific basis. But **parapsychology**, which deals with telepathy, precognition, clairvoyance, psychokinesis, and more,[25] is more accurately described as a *pseudoscience*. It's true that this branch of investigation has existed for quite a while, but those who study parapsychology have continued to do so despite not having demonstrated conclusive evidence of any supernatural claims after more than a century of research. This isn't unique to ghost hunters and psychics, either. There are actually a number of false sciences that exist for the sole purpose of studying that which doesn't exist, including cryptozoology, homeopathy, astrology, creation science, magnetic therapy, Dianetics, pseudoarcheology, numerology, ufology, and flood geology.

James Randi has called parapsychology *"a farce and a delusion,"*[26] but some schools, such as the University of Edinburgh, take parapsychology more seriously than others. The Koestler Parapsychology Unit (KPU), which was founded in 1985 and is housed in the psychology department at the Scotland-based university, focuses on researching the possible existence of psychic ability, belief in the paranormal, and even *"pseudo-psychic deception and self-deception."*[27] The KPU has launched investigations into the *ganzfeld experiment*, which proponents claim can test people for ESP,[28] and defines parapsychology as *"the scientific study of the capacity attributed to some individuals to interact with their environment by means other than the recognised sensorimotor channels."*

Because ghost myths are so pervasive in so many societies and social circles, religious and nonreligious alike, I've compiled a list of common questions and suggestions that may help explain a number of purported ghostly encounters naturalistically. If you think you see a ghost, and you have successfully ruled out pareidolia, apophenia, infrasound, phosphenes, and optical illusions, ask yourself the following:

1. **Were you in bed? Were you going to sleep, sleeping, or just waking up?** Have you ever had a nightmare that seemed incredibly real? Did you smell, see, or feel things only to wake up and realize you're in bed and couldn't have experienced them? Or were you fully aware you were resting one second, only to have a presence holding you down or attacking you the next? Isolated sleep paralysis (ISP) might be your answer.[29] ISP is exactly what it sounds like—a form of sleep paralysis that isn't associated with another sleep disorder. Anyone, including those of us with no real medical issues, can experience ISP or recurrent ISP, during which the body and parts of the brain are in the rapid eye movement (REM) stage of sleep while we sense we are awake and perceive a number of (often terrifying) experiences. The sensations of ghostly presences or sightings that occur while in an episode of ISP

are caused by *hypnogogic* and *hypnopompic* hallucinations.[30] Alexandre Jacques François Brière de Boismont compiled some of the first studies and theories on this topic when he published his book, which was translated into English as *On Hallucinations: Or, the Rational History of Apparitions, Dreams, Ecstasy, Magnetism, and Somnambulism.*[31] One-off instances of ISP are nothing to see your doctor about, and it's relatively harmless, disregarding the fear aspect. To avoid episodes of ISP,[32] you could try not sleeping on your back—as the supine position is the most common for ISP—reducing your stress levels, or creating and sticking to a more stable sleep routine.

2. **Did the ghost have characteristics of a live human? What were its intentions?** If you saw a human ghost, you should think about why they are the most commonly spotted spirits. Humans are life forms just like any other animal, so why isn't the world overrun by trillions of reports of goldfish ghosts and cockroach ghosts and dinosaur ghosts? When a ghost believer has mysterious itches when no bugs are present, why doesn't he or she assume it is deceased insects' spirits? Here are some more questions that will help you see how unreasonable the ghosts-as-deceased-human-spirits conclusion is, and perhaps get you closer to the reality:

    If the specter you saw was wearing clothing, how were the dead person's material articles able to transcend into ghostly form? Can you explain the process by which fabric becomes a spirit? If you believe you saw a ghost and it spoke to you, how is that possible without the vocal cords and other biological components necessary for creating speech? If you think the ghost is someone you know, why would they be able to break through the so-called spiritual realm while 105+ billion other people who have died cannot? And for what purpose? Why wouldn't the specter have provided some objectively valuable information?

3. **Was your experience based on something small, such as a cabinet door opening and closing by itself or a coffee mug moving a few inches? Could something be wrong with your home?** Did you hear a strange voice or a nondescript bump in the night? Do you experience cold spots or odd feelings of a presence in your home? It's a ghost, right? Probably not. It's more likely your house simply needs some cleaning and maintenance. Think of the typical *"haunted house."* Usually the building is hundreds of years old and has a rich history of reportedly horrifying deaths that have occurred there, but it also has a number of

other "*spooky*" characteristics. It's probably drafty, moldy, run-down, and dark, for instance. Would fixing the place up get rid of the ghosts? Maybe. Dark, damp buildings without updated repairs and fixtures are breeding grounds for ghosts or, more accurately, the things we attribute to ghosts. We already learned about how some naturally found substances like rye ergot fungus have been known to cause psychosis in humans, and that a study by a team at Clarkson University is looking into the link between reportedly haunted buildings and toxic molds, but other indoor air quality factors may also be to blame for intense paranormal experiences. Carbon monoxide and carbon dioxide, along with other gas leaks, are possible culprits, and other volatile substances like fuel or paint can lead to psychosis, as well.[33]

The basic materials in your home can also cause those noises and movements that seem too scary to be anything other than your dead grandma trying to establish contact as you are trying to watch TV in peace. Something as simple as a change in weather can cause the components of your home to expand or contract, which is one reason those pesky doors might creak, click, pop open, or swing shut.[34] And speaking of changing weather, cold spots and drafts are bound to happen in every building. Your house is not perfect, and will likely not heat thoroughly 100 percent of the time, so don't be alarmed when one area is colder than another. It doesn't mean there is a spirit present. Further, why would ghosts be able to interact with us, but only in such small, untestable ways? If a ghost can move a cup, it can interfere in the world and therefore it can be proven—or, more likely, debunked.

You may also want to ask yourself why these minor occurrences that can easily be explained naturally are so often attributed to ghosts. Is a soul hovering in limbo really the best explanation for these household happenings? Is it because people *want* to believe?

4. **Did someone you love die? Could you have experienced a grief-induced hallucination?** When considering visions resulting from grief, it's important to remember that it doesn't matter how or when a loved one passes away; what matters is that that person is no longer there, because that fact alone can cause grief-induced psychosis. Post-bereavement hallucinations come in many forms—and a huge number of people have reported seeing, feeling, sensing, or even talking to their dead friends and family members postmortem. After a loved one dies, the deep desire to have them in our lives again can cause some very strange, and sometimes comforting, symptoms. People might see or

talk with the person again,[35] or even physically feel them, like a mother who feels the weight of her deceased baby in her arms or someone who notices pressure that feels like a hand where the loved one usually touched them. Losing a loved one isn't the only thing that can cause this type of experience; losing a part of yourself can cause similar types of post-bereavement hallucinations. Amputees, for instance, often report that they can still feel their missing body parts, a phenomenon called "sensory ghost" or *phantom limb syndrome.*[36] Even people who have lost their eye(s) have reported this post-loss sensation of sight,[37] including seeing complex visual hallucinations normally associated with ghosts and other apparitions (Charles Bonnet Syndrome).[38] Anyone experiencing these symptoms should definitely seek some sort of psychiatric therapy. Grief over a lost love, traumatic experience, or even a missing piece of yourself isn't something you have to suffer through alone.

5. **Are you sure you're perfectly healthy?** Do we really know what a ghost is? The definition and description change with each new person you ask. These apparitions aren't always Victorian women with long flowing white dresses; they can be orb-like, translucent, with no human form, or they can be a mere presence sensed by the individual experiencing them. A number of neurological disorders, including migraines[39] and epilepsy,[40] can cause people to see "*ghosts*" in the form of *auras*—perceptual disturbances like smells, sounds, or even lights radiating from an object or person. If your vision wasn't an aura, and was much more specific, you may want to look into more serious ailments. Parkinson's disease and Dementia with Lewy bodies, for example, are also known to cause hallucinations in sufferers, but instead of auras, some patients see vivid, well-formed people and animals.[41] Regardless of the details of your specific experience(s), there could be a medical explanation, so if you really believe in your ghost, see a doctor so they can rule out that possibility.

6. **Could there be a psychological component to what you experienced?** If the answer isn't in your body, it may be in your mind. Reported ghost sightings occur all over the world, but so do mental disorders that can distort reality and cause all kinds of struggles connected to imagined forces with which individuals think they are coming into contact. These disorders of the mind are particularly difficult to diagnose, assuming those suffering are able to seek help at all, and are made even harder to

treat when there are issues with cultural attitudes and stigmas added into the equation.

Schizophrenia, for example, is a disorder that can cause sufferers to be unable to make sense of sensory stimuli. This can result in antisocial behavior, disorientation, inability to grasp realty, and hallucinations. Some symptoms can be very eerie, such as the *feeling of presence*, which is just what it sounds like. Another psychological issue that can be a catalyst of ghostly experiences is posttraumatic stress disorder (PTSD), which some people develop after witnessing or experiencing traumatic events. PTSD can cause difficulty thinking, functioning, and adjusting to life again after the incident, but sufferers might also have a number of additional symptoms, including hallucinations and flashbacks,[42] that are often misinterpreted as ghost sightings. Although there may be an underserved social stigma against those who seek psychological help, the only way to remove that is for more and more people who experience symptoms (perhaps including ghost sightings) to get evaluated.

7. **How do you know it was a ghost that you saw? Could your preconceived notions play a role?** Since ghosts have never been proven to exist, who's to say that your experience wasn't caused by a demon or angel or alien or time traveler or deity or anything else, for that matter? Surely these entities could produce similar effects, so why does it have to be a ghost?[43] The fact is that what we believe shapes what we experience in a number of ways, and sometimes a strong belief is all that's needed for a person to attribute their experiences to a particular supernatural force. This is the same reason a UFO hunter is more likely to perceive alien visitors than someone else who might look for a more rational explanation, and why people who believe in miracles see them most. Simply believing in the afterlife and a version of a soul increases the likelihood that you'll interpret occurrences within that framework, so it's important to consider that possibility in ghost sightings. Did you actually see a ghost, or did you simply *want* or *expect* to see a ghost?

8. **Can you prove that there's anything paranormal or supernatural occurring?** Perhaps the most important question you should ask yourself is, *"Can I prove it?"* Because until there's hard evidence for a *"ghost,"* the idea will remain alongside gods, werewolves, and other supernatural myths in the eyes of science and scientific skeptics alike.

*"One need not be a chamber to be haunted, one need not to be a house.
The brain has corridors surpassing material place."*
—Emily Dickinson

NOTES

1.   Benjamin Radford, "Are Ghosts Real? Science Says No-o-o-o," *LiveScience*, October 21, 2014, www.livescience.com/26697-are-ghosts-real.html.

2.   Jonathan Gottschall, "The Science Of Storytelling: How Narrative Cuts Through Distraction Like Nothing Else," *Fast Company*, October 16, 2013, www.fastcocreate.com/3020044/the-science-of-storytelling-how-narrative-cuts-through-distraction.

3.   Perhaps this should have been my first clue that what I was seeing was a product of my own mind and expectations.

4.   Brian A. Sharpless and Jacques P. Barber, "Lifetime Prevalence Rates of Sleep Paralysis: A Systematic Review," *Sleep Medicine Reviews* 15, no. 5 (2011): 311–315.

5.   Christopher C. French and Anna Stone, *Anomalistic Psychology: Exploring Paranormal Belief and Experience* (New York: Palgrave Macmillan, 2013).

6.   Randolph W. Evans and Christopher French, "Ask the Brains: What Is Sleep Paralysis?" *Scientific American*, December 1, 2008, www.scientificamerican.com/article/ask-the-brains-sleep-paralysis/.

7.   Baland Jalal, "How to Make the Ghosts in My Bedroom Disappear? Focused-Attention Meditation Combined with Muscle Relaxation (MR Therapy)—A Direct Treatment Intervention for Sleep Paralysis," Frontiers in Psychology, January 29, 2016, journal.frontiersin.org/article/10.3389/fpsyg.2016.00028/full.

8.   "Sleep Paralysis—Treatment," National Health Service UK, March 20, 2016, www.nhs.uk/conditions/sleep-paralysis/pages/treatment.aspx.

9.   A. Grimby, "Bereavement among Elderly People: Grief Reactions, Post-bereavement Hallucinations and Quality of Life," *Acta Psychiatrica Scandinavica* 87, no. 1 (January 1993): 72–80.

10. Vaughan Bell, "Ghost Stories: Visits from the Deceased," *Scientific American*, December 2, 2008, www.scientificamerican.com/article/ghost-stories-visits-from-the-deceased/.

11. The case is *Jeffrey M. Stambovsky v. Helen V. Ackley et al.*, case number 169 A.D.2d 254, in the New York Supreme Court, Appellate Division, First Department.

12. "Clarkson University Undergrads Research Link Between Hauntings & Indoor Air Quality," Clarkson University, March 31, 2015, www.clarkson.edu/news/2015/news-release_2015-03-31-1.html.

13. Infrasonic concert, Purcell Room, London, 31 May 2003, sponsored by the sciart Consortium with additional support by the National Physical Laboratory (NPL).

14. Patricia Reaney, "The Fear of 'Haunted' Houses Explained," *ABC*, September 8, 2003, www.abc.net.au/science/articles/2003/09/08/941414.htm.

15. C. C. French, U. Hague, R. Bunton-Stasyshyn, R. Davis, "The 'Haunt' Project: An Attempt to Build a "Haunted" Room by Manipulating Complex Electromagnetic Fields and Infrasound," *Cortex* 45, no. 5 (2009), 619–629.

16. Olaf Blanke et al., "Neurological and Robot-Controlled Induction of an Apparition," *Current Biology* 24, no. 22 (November 17, 2014): 2681–2686.

17. V. Tandy and T. Lawrence, "The Ghost in the Machine," *Journal of the Society for Psychical Research* 62 (1998): 360–364.

18. C. T. Herbst et al., "How Low Can You Go? Physical Production Mechanism of Elephant Infrasonic Vocalizations," *Science* 337, no. 6094 (2012): 595–599.

19. Sarah Fecht, "FYI: Why Do We Get Goosebumps and Chills When We're Scared?" *Popular Science*, October 28, 2011, www.popsci.com/science/article/2011-10/fyi-why-do-we-get-goose-bumps-and-chills-when-were-scared.

20. Evan V. Symon, "6 Things I Learned Owning A 'Haunted House' On Reality TV," Cracked.com, May 30, 2015, www.cracked.com/article_22310_6-things-i-learned-owning-haunted-house-reality-tv.html.

21. Diana Deutsch, "Phantom Words," *Psychology Today*, June 26, 2009, www.psychologytoday.com/blog/illusions-and-curiosities/200906/phantom-words.

22. M. A. Nees and C. Phillips, "Auditory Pareidolia: Effects of Contextual Priming on Perceptions of Purportedly Paranormal and Ambiguous Auditory Stimuli," *Applied Cognititive Psychology* 29 (2015): 129–134.

23. John E. Buckner V and Rebecca Buckner, "Talking to the Dead, Listening to Yourself: An Empirical Study on the Psychological Aspects of Interpreting Electronic Voice Phenomena," *Skeptic Magazine* 17, no. 2 (2012).

24. Sharon Hill, "Amateur Paranormal Research and Investigation Groups Doing 'Sciencey' Things," *Skeptical Inquirer* 36, no. 2 (2012).

25. Information from the Parapsychological Association at www.parapsych. org.

26. James Randi, *Flim-Flam! Psychics, ESP, Unicorns, and Other Delusions* (Prometheus Books, Buffalo, New York, 1982).

27. "Koestler Parapsychology Unit," University of Edinburgh, December 17, 2014, www.koestler-parapsychology.psy.ed.ac.uk/index.html.

28. I personally tried to recreate the parameters of the ganzfeld experiment, which includes mild sensory deprivation and is reported by some to cause vivid hallucinations, but experienced no results. This is not surprising, however, considering independent replication of the procedure has never been achieved.

29. Julia Santomauro and Christopher C. French, "Terror in the Night," *The Psychologist*, August 2009, thepsychologist.bps.org.uk/volume-22/edition-8/ terror-night.

30. "Hallucinations During Sleep—American Sleep Association," American Sleep Association, September 2007, www.sleepassociation.org/patients-general-public/hallucinations-during-sleep/.

31. Alexandre-Jacques-François Brierre de Boismont, *Hallucinations: Or, The Rational History of Apparitions, Visions, Dreams, Ecstasy, Magnetism, and Somnambulism* (Lindsay and Blakiston, 1853).

32. "Sleep Paralysis Treatment," Sleep Paralysis Project, www. thesleepparalysisproject.org/about-sleep-paralysis/treatment/.

33. Molly A. Phelps and Peter L. Forster, "Assessment of Psychotic Symptoms: Distinguishing between Functional and Medically-Induced Psychosis," *Crisis Intervention* 6, no. 2 (2000): 101–107.

34. Arianna Cohen, "Seasonal Affective Disorder for Doors," *New York Times*, March 25, 2009, www.nytimes.com/2009/03/26/garden/26fixx.html?_r=0.

35. Sidney Zisook and Katherine Shear, "Grief and Bereavement: What Psychiatrists Need to Know," *World Psychiatry* 8, no. 2 (2009): 67–74.

36. Allan A. Bailey and Frederick P. Moersch, "Phantom Limb," *Canadian Medical Association Journal* 45, no. 1 (1941): 37–42.

37. Agda M. Andreotti et al., "Phantom Eye Syndrome: A Review of the Literature," *Scientific World Journal* 2014 (2014).

38. G. Jayakrishna Menon et al., "Complex Visual Hallucinations in the Visually Impaired," *Survey of Ophthalmology* 48, no. 1 (2003): 58–72.

39. Anne W. Hauge et al. "Effects of Tonabersat on Migraine with Aura: A Randomised, Double-Blind, Placebo-Controlled Crossover Study," *Lancet Neurology* 8, no. 8 (2009): 718–723.

40. Marco Mula et al., "The Role of Aura in Psychopathology and Dissociative Experiences in Epilepsy," *The Journal of Neuropsychiatry and Clinical Neurosciences* 18, no. 4 (Fall 2006): 536–542.

41. A. J. Harding et al., "Visual Hallucinations in Lewy Body Disease Relate to Lewy Bodies in the Temporal Lobe," *Brain*, 125, no. 2 (February 2002): 391–403.

42. Anthony P. Morrison, Lucy Frame, and Warren Larkin, "Relationships between Trauma and Psychosis: A Review and Integration," *British Journal of Clinical Psychology* 42, no. 4 (2003): 331–353.

43. This same question can be modified and asked regardless of which supernatural force is assumed as the source of the experience.

11

PSYCHICS
AND OTHER SO-CALLED SEERS

"The conjuror or con man is a very good provider of information.
He supplies lots of data, by inference or direct statement, but it's false data.
Scientists aren't used to that scenario. An electron or a galaxy is
not capricious, nor deceptive; but a human can be either or both."

—James Randi

There isn't a single recorded instance of a psychic phenomenon or force being demonstrated under observable and repeatable conditions. If psychics are real, this means every single one of them goes to extensive lengths to hide their extraordinary abilities, dismissing any and all opportunities to test, record, and prove them to be true despite the fact that any person who succeeds in this type of groundbreaking study would fundamentally revolutionize the way we understand the world, and the very laws of physics themselves. That person would also benefit humanity in an unimaginable number of ways, make a lasting impression on the scientific community, and even earn large cash rewards from organizations dedicated to testing such claims.[1] It's possible that these supersensory powers exist, but until someone steps forward with scientifically tested proof, psychic abilities can and should be treated the same way as every other allegedly prophetic (yet often conveniently nonprovable) assertion.

So, if "real" seers have never been shown to exist, then why do people continue to believe in psychic powers that have been claimed, investigated, and debunked more times than I can count? In many cases, belief in psychics is linked to the **Forer effect**, which was named after psychologist Bertram R. Forer and describes how individuals will rate vague and generalized personality tests as highly descriptive of themselves. In 1948, Forer gave such an assignment to his students, claiming that the statements they received were individualized personality analyses. Although each student received the same paragraph descriptor, which he had compiled from various **horoscopes**, the average rating was 4.26 on a scale from 0 to 5.[2] Forer's study further noted that "similarities between the demonstration and the activities of charlatans were pointed out" by the students once the deception was revealed. The fact is that psychics, astrologers, and other pseudoscientific fraudsters have taken advantage of this simple, evolutionary human trait for most of human history. Our earliest ancestors were practicing the art of fortunetelling,[3] and people continue to do so today—often with disastrous (and profitable) results.

YOU'RE GETTING COLDER

For so-called mind readers, the primary process by which they administer Forer's personality test is called cold reading. During a cold read, the alleged psychic uses vague guesses based on common concerns and personal traits to create the illusion of deeper knowledge. But that's not the only tool in their arsenal. Most psychics use a combination of cold readings and *hot readings*—guesses based on visual cues or background research—to convince their customers that they have otherworldly powers.

Not all people who purport to be psychics need to use cold or hot reading—or even the Forer effect. Some take the gambit one step further, eliminating all liability for their false conclusions by servicing only pets that can't communicate right or wrong answers whatsoever. Melissa Bacelar, for example, is a well-known "celebrity pet psychic" who promises to be able to "*connect to pets, living and dead*." She has had a lot of success in convincing people that she can speak to animals on earth and from beyond the grave, but not everyone is so sure of her abilities. In October 2015, Bacelar, who has appeared on *TMZ* and *Anderson Cooper Live*, and was even said to have been hired by Miley Cyrus,[4] was sued by three former customers who accused her of fraud and unfair, unlawful business practices that led to the death of at least two puppies.[5]

"HONEST" PSYCHICS

This process of reading people is particularly interesting because how it is perceived is all about the perspective of the observers. If you utilize cold and hot reads and call yourself a magician or an illusionist, the audience asks, "What's the trick?" But if you use the same techniques and call yourself a psychic, a similar act is seen by many as "definitely supernatural!" I obviously prefer mentalists who are honest about their approach.

One of my favorite mentalists is *Banachek*, who has been featured on *CCN Live*, *The Today Show*, and more. He is not only one of the world's leading mind readers and the author of several books on mentalism,[6] but he also served as the director of the JREF's One Million Dollar Paranormal Challenge. I had the opportunity to ask Banachek about his work and how he is able to successfully mimic psychic phenomena using methods and techniques that are completely natural.

McAfee: You are perhaps best known for tricking scientists, including psychiatrist Berthold E. Schwarz, into believing you had psychic powers throughout the course of a four-year, $500,000 paranormal investigation project in the 1980s. What can you tell me about "Project Alpha" and how you were able to convince the researchers that your abilities were genuine?

Banachek: In 1979, James S. McDonnell, board chairman of McDonnell-Douglas Aircraft and devotee of the paranormal, gave $500,000 to Washington University in St. Louis, Missouri, for the establishment of the McDonnell Laboratory for Psychical Research. Now scientists had lamented for years that there was no evidence of ESP under proper scientific control due to lack of funding. Here was an opportunity to show that this was not the case. It was mine, Randi's, and Mike Edwards' opinion that the scientists had a pro biased opinion on the matter and that got in the way of their ability to perform proper experiments to prove that ESP was either genuine or a farce. Also we believed that they would think they were too smart to be fooled by a magician and therefore would not accept the help of people who were not academics yet qualified to detect such trickery. With no training

from Randi, Mike Edwards and myself as teenagers were able to enter the McDonnell Laboratory and convince them for 180 hours over four years that we could bend metal with our mind and perform other feats of psychic abilities. When we revealed the hoax, it made a huge splash in all the newspapers and changed the way parapsychologists approach such research. For many years we were in every college basic psychology textbook. The experiment became known as Project Alpha and can be read online.

McAfee: What prompted you to become a mentalist? Was it something you were introduced to by your family or did you fall into it on your own and teach yourself?

Banachek: I was abandoned at the age of nine in South Africa with my two brothers, ages one and three. I pretty much raised them by myself until I was 16. It was while in South Africa that I heard on the radio a man by the name of Uri Geller. Uri claimed to be able to bend metal with his mind. Because any adults I did know believed in him, I did too. I remember trying to bend a pin with my mind while I listened to him on the radio. I convinced myself I was able to bend it minutely. Years later at the age of 16 I picked up a book by the Amazing Randi. Now Randi said that the truth about Uri Geller was he was using tricks. As a result, I simply said if he can do these things then so can I. I set to creating methods for doing the same types of tricks and created my own methods way beyond much of what Geller was doing. I figured a way to make the school bell go off early so we got out of class early, and kids would steal the silverware from the cafeteria for me to bend; they went to plastic silverware 'til I graduated. I got in trouble for those things, but I was creating my own effects and a show as a result. I am pretty much the first mentalist to start as a mentalist and not a magician. In fact, back in those days I did not know there was a category of magic called mentalism. I only knew there were people who used tricks to con and convince people they were psychic.

McAfee: It's my understanding that you take an active stance against purported psychics who claim to summon and communicate with customers' deceased loved ones. Is that true? How is that process harmful, in your opinion?

Banachek: I believe that psychic mediums are scum. They cross over that line of personal sanctity for profit. They halt the important grieving process. Yes, many say they make people feel good about a loss but I can give crack to a junkie. It will make him feel good but it is not good for him. The grieving process allows people to go on living without a loved one and it is important. I once had a friend who lost her son; he was ten years old and died of cancer. A medium convinced her that he could communicate with her son. That he could fill that hole in her heart. As a result, she communicated with her dead son and stopped communicating with her living daughters and husband. She almost ended up in a divorce as a result. Luckily she came to her senses. These people do harm, not good, and they do it all in the name of putting a lot of money in their pockets. This is not the only way they do harm.

Once a person depends upon a medium, that medium opens a door to other forms of pseudoscience. "If speaking with my dead relative is real, then other spiritual things like psychic readings and homeopathy must be real. Surely that holographic bracelet has psychic abilities that will make me feel better so I don't have to go to the hospital and have that cancerous tumor removed. Don't tell me it isn't real; you did not believe a psychic could talk to my dead son. There are many things we cannot explain in this life and we should accept that. So that psychic bomb sniffer just might work and we should spend millions and let our troops use them to sniff out bombs. And if it kills someone, well that is their fault for not believing in the power."

Think about it this way: would you trust your retirement fund to a man who claims he will make judgments about how to invest the money based upon his personal psychic's advice? If the answer is "no," then why would you trust the sanctity of your relationship with your dead relative to such people? Talking to the dead goes back to the Fox Sisters; it started with them in the USA and they even admitted it was a hoax. So the art of being a medium is based upon a lie.

McAfee: I read that the JREF's Million Dollar Challenge has been altered since 2015 and that it will continue to be used "as a means for educating the public about paranormal claims." Will you still serve as the director of the challenge? Can you tell me about what changes have been made?

Banachek: The JREF challenge went through changes prior to Randi stepping down. I tightened up the loopholes where, if we were to find a mistake in protocol that allowed someone to cheat, we could not fix it in the formal stage. I made it easier for people to apply. Recently we closed the challenge down. The JREF is making a major change to becoming a real educational tool. As a result, we want to make sure that the challenge is used as a tool to its maximum capacity. We plan on opening it up again, but there will be some major changes and it will be easier for people to understand the science behind it and how one goes about applying for a real scientific test of one's powers. This is something most people applying have never understood.

McAfee: Have you ever had someone stubbornly insist that your abilities are supernatural, despite the fact that you admitted to tricking them? How do you handle a situation like that?

Banachek: Many mentalists find disdain in the fact I use a disclaimer in my mentalism shows. I feel it is the right thing to do. Those same magicians say that, in a play, the actor does not stop and say, "Oh, just a reminder, I am an actor playing the part of Macbeth, I am not really Macbeth." To me that is a silly inaccurate example to explain why we should not use disclaimers. People coming to a play know it is not real. But when they see a mentalist, they do not know if it is real or not. The person on stage doing these impossible mind reading things becomes the authority, much as if a neurosurgeon was giving a talk on the same stage. It is all about context. Now I know there is a group that comes to my shows that will not believe no matter what I do, and there are those who will believe no matter what I do, but I have a responsibility to those in the middle. Those who have not cemented a side in their mind, those who are listening to me for an explanation. It is for those people that I say I use my five known senses to create the illusion, that I use verbal, nonverbal communication, lots of magic, and also perceptual manipulation. It is for those people that I remind them a few times it is simply entertainment and I am not a psychic and that there are people who do these things who will tell you they are psychic but it is my belief that they are either lying to themselves or lying to their audience and more likely the latter.

Now, after a show, sometimes someone will still come up and insist I must be psychic. It is those people I remind that Criss Angel does magic with beautiful women, Siegfried and Roy did magic with lions and tigers, I do magic with information and it would not be a good trick if it did not look real, but I have a million dollars for anyone who can do anything psychic under proper scientific controls and no one has taken the money yet.

McAfee: Do you think gullibility is a trait all humans share, or that it is specific to certain individuals? Have you ever come across a person you couldn't stump or deceive?

Banachek: It is easy for people to be thought of as gullible and maybe we all are to a point. We all want that easy fix, we all want to be happy, and we all want to think that there is more to this life than there is. The secret to conning someone is to find their weakness, and most of us have the same weakness: we want something for nothing. And that equates to greed. However, the real big con comes in when we find out what that greed is to an individual. Once you find that weakness anyone can be conned. One of the easiest ways to do it is to create overconfidence in someone. This is one of the reasons that, when someone says to me I should teach a scientist some of my tricks so they can detect the trickery, I tell them I have 10 ways to bend a key and make it look psychic. If I teach a scientist one of those ways, when he sees one of the other methods used he may very well think that presentation is psychic because he "knows the trick method and this is not it." A little knowledge is a bad thing as it breeds overconfidence.

The real easy fix to gullibility is to realize and tell yourself every day that there is so much in this life to be happy for. Just being alive and experiencing the things we do is amazing. We don't need magic to find the real magic in the world. We don't need an easy fix to get ahead. Stop and look closer at things around you and you will find amazement everywhere. Once we do this, we are less gullible. We live in the moment. Once we realize we do not need that easy fix we are less likely to be taken advantage of or even care enough for someone to take advantage of you. A saying I abide to is, "Nothing worth any good comes easy, yet we can enjoy the journey and the fruits of our labor."

McAfee: You are good at reading people, which could be useful in any number of ways. How have you used your "powers" for good? Would you say your work has benefited the scientific community in any way?

Banachek: I like to believe my work has saved some people from being taken advantage of. I like to think that Project Alpha set parapsychology investigation on the right track and derailed a lot of the wasted money that was going in that direction.

Those who want to support psychics say the skeptic movement is a waste of time and a losing battle. Heck, look at Peter Popoff, the evangelist Randi and I exposed as a con man: he is back on the air again. My answer to this is simple. For me it is not about losing or winning a war. It is about winning small battles. If you save one person from deceit or death, then a small battle is worth it. The idea that a skeptic thinks he can stop all psychic pseudo nonsense is silly. However, certainly one can bring doubt to those who are on the fence with facts.

There are an estimated 3.7 million household burglaries occurring each year on average in the United States. In about 28 percent of these burglaries, a household member was present during the burglary. In 7 percent of all these burglaries, a household member experienced some form of violent victimization. Just because that is the case, and I know I will never stop household burglaries, should I not report one in progress when I see it? There is an average of around 250,000 aggravated assaults a year. Again, just because they will not stop, does that mean I should not report it? According to NCANDS (National Child Abuse and Neglect Data System), whose latest statistics are for 2005, an estimated 3.3 million referrals of child abuse or neglect were received by public social service or CPS (Child Protective Service) agencies. Of these referrals, 899,000 children were confirmed to be victims of abuse or neglect, according to the U.S. Department of Health and Human Services. That means about 12 out of every 1,000 children up to age 18 in the United States were found to be victims of maltreatment in 2005. So again I ask, just because it is "a losing battle," do we let it go on and not say anything? Of course not. So why is this any different? We all pick and choose our causes, and some pick pointing out deceit when they see it. If it helps just a few people, then that is a good thing.

McAfee: Would you consider faith healers to be in the same category as psychics who provide false hope and inaccurate data? Do you see religion as a type of woo or superstition?

Banachek: I believe that faith healers do as much harm or even more than the mediums. In fact, often they go hand in hand as many mediums claim to be able to heal as well. I lump them all into the same nasty narcissist pot.

As for religion, depending upon the religion, I lump it into the self-help category. However, when you follow the money, that self-help usually points to an individual having a fleet of expensive cars driven for him and a fleet of Learjets on a runway. Many of the Catholic faith's traditions were put in place to take over other religions' ideas or beliefs or to put money on the Vatican's pocket. I don't know why, but this type of question always reminds me of the Ray Stevens song, "Would Jesus wear a Rolex?"

McAfee: Tricking people for a living, even when doing so openly, is bound to result in some moral dilemmas. Can you tell me about any ethical issues you've had to face as Banachek?

Banachek: The only time I had a problem with tricking people was when I was lying and saying I was a real psychic during Project Alpha. At first I saw them as the enemy, but later I came to be friends with the scientists involved. They were good, kind people, but people who were out of their element. Their only sin was self-deception.

As an entertainer I am honest about my deception. People are told that I am not real, that I am duplicating what a psychic could do if psychic phenomena were real. As a result, I have no moral issues with it. In fact, I think it is good to let people know that they can be fooled. It is even stronger for a person to know they can be fooled more so than knowing how they are fooled. Once people learn a secret, they often say, "Oh, that is so simple; I would have figured that out." And that is another form of self-deception because in reality they would probably never have figured the secret out. And over time their own false memories of the expedience would hide the true secret even further from their reach. Mentalists do not only deceive with the physical aspect of the tricks they perform, but we also rewrite history and create linguistic and nonverbal memories that change the actual events witnessed on stage so that people walk away with a complete memory of something that never happened that is far from the secret that would be revealed otherwise over time. We are very good at it. But we have an understanding with our audiences that this is what we are going to do. A psychic has no such contract. We are entertainers; they are not.

McAfee: What will you be working on going forward? Is there anything else you'd like to add?

Banachek: As for my future, I hope to continue to give people facts for them to make their own judgments about psychics and the like. I will continue to perform and take magic to the masses. Recently, I coproduced a touring magic show with Criss Angel titled "The Supernaturalists."

I do have something to say for those who lump all skeptics in one sink: there are skeptics and there are pseudo-skeptics. The latter tend to be fanatics and that is a shame; it is one of the reasons I don't really like the word "skeptic" anymore. It has unfortunately become the label of closed-mindedness and meanness. I prefer the term "critical thinker." Not ALL skeptics are that way. Being a skeptic means being open-minded, not closed, yet not being so open your brain falls out. It means not accepting everything at face value, but stepping back until you have facts to support a claim or not support it, holding back judgment either way until all the relevant facts have been handed in despite one's own bias. It does not mean bullying others to your way of thinking, but sharing said relevant facts and letting others make up their own mind.

What many people do not understand is there is a huge difference between a claim and a scientific theory. Scientific theories are based upon the empirical evidence found in science, while a claim is simply that: it is something someone claims with no science attached to it at all, or if it does there is usually pseudoscience attached as an explanation. This is the reason skeptics doubt most psychic phenomena. It simply has not passed scientific scrutiny. All scientific theories pass through the area of doubt and criticism and the like to proceed to becoming a scientific theory. And psychic phenomena have not done so.

Banachek taught me a lot about mentalism and the testing of psychic phenomena, but I wanted to learn more. I sought out James Underdown, who has been the executive director of the Center for Inquiry–Los Angeles since 1999. He has also written for both *Skeptical Inquirer* and *Free Inquiry* magazines, and is founder and chair of the Independent Investigations Group (IIG), which now has groups in Los Angeles, Portland, San Francisco, and more. The IIG and Committee for Skeptical Inquiry (CSI) offer a $100,000 prize for anyone who can prove paranormal ability under scientific testing conditions.

McAfee: You've been the executive director of the Center for Inquiry–Los Angeles for about 17 years now, right? What can you tell me about the organization and its goals?

Underdown: The mission of the Center for Inquiry is to foster a secular society based on science, reason, freedom of inquiry, and humanist values. That's the official mission, but less formally we represent the scientific (read: skeptical) and humanist sides of what people believe. Our specialties are the scientific examination of extraordinary and paranormal claims, and the philosophy of humanism.

McAfee: The IIG offers $100,000 to anyone who can prove a paranormal or supernatural ability, but, as is the case with the JREF's challenge, no one has ever won. Has anyone ever come close? How many participants have tried?

Underdown: A few dozen or so have tried, but you're right. No one has ever won. No one has ever come close. A few have made guesses that were correct in the course of being tested, but statistically, their scores were unimpressive and the applicants failed.

The most impressive lucky streak happened during a test rehearsal with no actual applicant present. We were practicing a test involving Zener cards (which have a 1 in 5 chance of being guessed correctly) and our stand-in got the first 4 in a row correct. The odds of that happening by chance are 625 to 1. But he missed the last 19 out of 21 and ended up with a very average score. But we were impressed for a minute there!

McAfee: What exactly would it take to win the $100,000 challenge? Do you have any advice for those who truly believe they have supernatural or paranormal abilities?

Underdown: We negotiate with each applicant to find a fair test that narrows their alleged skill down to successfully performing a set of specific tasks. The tests are designed so that luck and trickery are eliminated to the best of our ability. The test for the $100,000 happens in two parts. When odds can be assigned to the tests, we try to devise the first part so the odds land in the neighborhood of 5,000:1, and the second part at 1,000,000:1. That pretty well eliminates the "luck" part. We also brainstorm the possible cheats someone might employ. So far, no one has cheated—that we know of. The applicants all sincerely believed in their abilities.

My advice to those who think they have these abilities is threefold:

1. Learn the scientific and skeptical explanations for what you are experiencing. A small exposure to a simple explanation may solve a mystery right off the bat.

2. Try testing yourself under the same conditions we will subject you to in the test. If you can't pass a test on your own, you won't pass it with us watching.

3. Be open to the possibility that how you perceive the world may not be as it actually is. There are many conditions, situations, and states of mind which may lead you to experience something others don't. If you are the only one seeing or hearing things, consider the possibility that one of your senses or your brain isn't working properly.

McAfee: Do you think the prize will ever be won?

Underdown: I am extremely doubtful that anyone will ever win the IIG $100,000 Challenge. All evidence points to the idea that paranormal ability simply does not exist—in anyone. If it did, we'd already be out of a lot of money, and Las Vegas, Atlantic City, and Monte Carlo would be out of business.

McAfee: What would you say to someone who has had a convincing experience with someone who claimed to be a psychic?

Underdown: I hear this all the time. I ask them what leads them to believe that is the case, and if they are open to hearing other explanations to what happened. Then I ask them if the psychic would be interested in winning $100,000.

McAfee: In your opinion, are most psychics fakers and frauds? Or do you believe the majority are convinced that they have unique and/or supernatural powers?

Underdown: That's hard to say. One hundred percent of those we tested sincerely believed in their ability. Most continued to believe in their ability even after they failed the test. The human mind seems to have an amazing capacity for self-delusion.

On the other hand, there are lots of published explanations out there about how and why certain paranormal phenomena seem so convincing. We know why people fall into some of these beliefs and have to figure that there are plenty of swindlers out there who also know these things and use that knowledge to bilk people out of their money. I wouldn't hazard a guess at the percentages though.

McAfee: Is there anything else you'd like to add?

Underdown: The reason I started the IIG was so I wouldn't have to just argue these ideas anymore. I wanted to see for myself what was going on and report to others what we found out.

Mentalists like Banachek admit their skills aren't magical, but even some people who claim to be true psychics aren't fraudsters per se; they might just be people who consider themselves intuitive and have difficulty distinguishing fact from fiction. But what we call intuition is not really the mystical force that it is believed by many people to be. Intuition is not an innate "gut feeling" that just happens to be right through some form of **magic**—it comes from past experiences. Our subconscious minds sometimes process information more quickly than our conscious minds, so knowledge, information, and ideas may seem as though they came from some outside force. This is why people tend to be more "intuitive" about the things they spend a lot of time discussing, or about topics on which they've done extensive research. Yes, you could get a feeling about something, or even a "sense of knowing," but that doesn't mean your feelings are always right or that they are predictive of the future.

Although I think it's clear that the vast majority of psychics and other self-proclaimed seers use cold reading and other deceptive tactics, some may actually believe they have superhuman powers, including telepathy, ESP, and more. They might simply be delusional, but there's also the possibility that they were indoctrinated as psychics. They could have been raised to believe they had a special "gift," causing them to see the illusion manifest in their daily lives. Regardless of the reason, if you feel you have supernatural psychic powers, I recommend you do everything you possibly can to prove (or disprove) your alleged abilities in a scientific setting and tell the world. Considering the fact that these forces have never been shown to exist using the scientific method, it isn't surprising that today many doctors and scientists first look for a natural explanation when confronted with psychic claims, but they wouldn't be able to deny for long anything that is scientifically proven. If you do succeed, you will alter the way we look at ourselves and our physical world and liberate yourself from any perceived ridicule. But if you fail, it might be time to look at your beliefs with a more skeptical eye.

SUROH THE SEER

To demonstrate the power (and gullibility) of the human mind in the context of alleged "psychics," I created an alter ego—a friendly and no-cost seer by the name of **Suroh**.[7] *Suroh the Seer* describes himself as a psychic, medium, and spiritualist who offers free readings by social media,[8] e-mail, and at live events.[9] Here is an excerpt from Suroh's biography:

> *I grew up ignorant about the spiritual realm. It wasn't until five years ago, when I foresaw my own mother's tragic demise in a car accident, that I <u>woke up</u>. Since that time I've dedicated my life to honing my abilities and giving free readings for those who need help.*

Suroh, a member of the New Earth Healing spirituality coalition and the purported head of the nonexistent Psychics and Seers Association of America, has given hundreds of successful and free readings to people around the world. Some interactions went exactly as planned and others not so well, but overall many participants were convinced of his supernatural abilities. More importantly, however, Suroh had to deal with some of the same skeptical reactions and ethical conundrums other self-described psychics deal with on a daily basis.[10] Here I'll provide a few excerpts from some of my favorite readings.[11]

* * *

Sami: I would like to know . . . Will I be able to find that new job I desperately need and have been looking for?

Suroh: I sense new things in your life, perhaps a new dog? In any case, by asking me this, you're showing that you're on the right path. The spirits have told me that you will definitely get a new job . . . as long as you work hard, look for a job consistently, present a professional résumé, and do all the other necessary preparations in order to earn said job.

Sami: Thank you so much Suroh! I never thought that dog that wandered into our yard a few days ago would be the sign for great things in my future.

* * *

Peter: Where is Udjat tattooed on my body?

Suroh: I sense that it is on the backside of your body, but that you have a lot of other ink, too. I see both arms and other areas that are covered by tattoos, including conflicting spiritual symbols that can be hidden by professional clothing.

Peter: Spot on, amazing!

* * *

Joy: Hello, I saw where you were listed on New Earth Healing. I was hoping maybe you would feel led to do a reading for me. I am so confused and have lost touch with who I am. Is there any hope?

Suroh: Hi Joy, thank you for seeing me. I sense that you enjoy nature, charity

THIS WAS SUROH'S VERY FIRST PROFILE PHOTO, WHICH SUBTLY IMPLIED HE WAS CAPABLE OF HOVERING ABOVE THE GROUND. THE IMAGE WAS TAKEN BY JUMPING IN FRONT OF A VIDEO CAMERA AND TAKING A FREEZE FRAME FROM THE VIDEO.

work, and being creative. I think that you don't experience the outdoors like you wish you did, and that could be something you're looking for. You also have someone important in your life by the name of Lisa; does that mean anything to you? In any case, I think focusing on the things that mean the most to you will help you find yourself again.

Joy: Thank you for responding. I do enjoy all the things you mentioned and I don't get outside as much as I would like. Lisa is my daughter. She lives with me. Focus is what I seem to not be able to do. I have so many demands on my time and there is little left for me. It is so much

easier to let it all go and play online or something even less productive. When I am creative, I feel so alive. But I do not seem to be able to focus on it.

Suroh: Sometimes you need exercise and quiet thinking or meditation to really be able to focus your energies. Even something as simple as a healthy diet could put you in the right place to be productive and inspired. If all that fails, I recommend seeking a licensed medical professional who may be able to help.

Joy: Thank you. I believe that will help. I appreciate your taking time to share with me.

* * *

Julia: Free readings? I sure could use one . . .

Suroh: I sense that sometimes your life can be more like a battle, but that you're strong and always seem to rise above it. I also see that you have secrets and a somewhat dark past, but you keep a lot of those things inside. You find ways to take those negative experiences and channel them into positive actions. The spirits say that is exactly what you should continue to do. Think of yourself as a tree, with your past as the base and roots that give it strength.

Julia: Wildly appropriate. Thanks for the reinforcement.

* * *

Itzel: Oh Suroh I lost my best friend and I miss her so much, I want to know where she is and if she remembers me.

Suroh: I sense that your friend cared for you deeply. She lives on in our memories and in the impression she left on earth. In some sense, she is still very much here because the matter that once composed her body still exists on earth in some other form. To achieve your best possible future, I suggest you take solace in the memories you still have and focus your attention on what I can see is a very loving family at home. You know deep down that's exactly what your friend would want.

Itzel: Yes, thank you.

SUROH DOES A LIVE READING IN VENICE, CALIFORNIA. THE ATMOSPHERE THERE WAS VERY RELAXED AND THE MAJORITY OF PEOPLE WHO STOPPED BY WERE ALREADY BELIEVERS IN PSYCHIC PHENOMENA.

* * *

Ronja: I've been in trouble recently concerning friendships or any other kind of relationship to others. Since I know this as a topic for quite a while now I would like to know what the spirits have to say. Thanks!

Suroh: I can sense that you try your best not to care what others think, but that you sometimes let others affect you more than you should. This definitely alters the way you handle relationships, but you're on the right path by trying to do things for yourself instead of others. The spirits have shown me that you have traveled extensively, which can always make it difficult to maintain any relationship, but they also say that you will find a way to combine visiting the places you love and enjoying nature with relationships that make you happy.

Like anything, relationships take work; you can't simply rely on the spirits' mystical forces to handle it all. I see that you will make the time going forward to properly nurture your relationships to make sure they grow and flourish.

Ronja: Wow, that's quite precise! Some, especially the first part, enters right into my heart, so true. The rest is still very true, but I haven't been thinking of it from that perspective—so thanks! What still makes me think are those normal, daily relationships, but with the spirits being as optimistic as they are I will stay positive, too—and continue working. Thanks a lot!

* * *

Ronnie: I was wondering . . . do you see anything for me? Thanks for your time.

Suroh: I see that you have a loving family, but that you also need alone time and solitude is important to you. You are often told that you have a tough exterior, but you don't always feel that way inside. You like to have fun, crack jokes, and generally be happy. You have recently started a new relationship, too, or perhaps ended an old one? You are on an honest search for truth, but your creativity and imagination sometimes get the better of you. Does this make sense?

Ronnie: Yes, and thank you. Pretty accurate, my friend. Is there any way that you can receive messages from loved one who crossed over? I would like to get some advice from my grandmother maybe . . . thank you! Your gift is truly amazing!

Suroh: Your grandmother lives on in your memories of her and in her works on earth. I also sense that you know what advice she'd give you if she could.

Ronnie: Thank you.

* * *

Leigh: Do you see me having children?

Suroh: I see that there's already a man in your life and that you want a child, perhaps even more than one. I sense that there is some confusion as to whether or not it's the right time, but it will become clear as long as you are open with your significant other and make sure that you're both financially and emotionally ready. The spirits say that you will have children, but it might not necessarily be exactly the way you expected. Don't worry, though, this is a good thing!

Leigh: Thank you Suroh! Yes I have a man in my life and you are correct with timing, cash, and emotions! I have had two losses to date and infertility treatment is the only option for a child of my own, so yes I have also considered other options.

* * *

Jennifer: Why are your readings free?

Suroh: The spirits have compelled me to share my gift with the world. Anybody who charges to connect with the spirit realm is fraudulent, for they don't understand its power or purpose.

Jennifer: But energy is energy. You give a certain amount of energy to get a reading, then you aren't given any back? No amount of meditation is going to regain that energy that you spent.

Suroh: My readings come from a place that is above monetary payment. A connection to the spirit realm is not a prostitute, and I won't treat it that way.

Jennifer: But the questions people are asking you aren't realistic at all, and the ones that are, you give vague answers to.

Suroh: Do you remember what you were thinking about during your trip to Denver? Maybe something you were putting off until after that time? Either way, I see that things are progressively getting better and more stable in your life.

Jennifer: OK I admit that you were right about the trip to Denver. But everything else seems bogus. If anything they got worse, because the person we were nervous to see died and thinks that we're evil.

Suroh: I do future readings. If things aren't getting better now, it's just around the corner. I suspect that you and your family will start seeing things in a more positive light in the very near future.

Jennifer: I think you do have abilities. But they are not strong, and you are misguided. You would pay your doctor for helping you heal, or your counselor for helping you get through a hard time. This is no different.

Suroh: *The spirits have ensured that I'm taken care of financially. There are doctors and counselors who treat people for free, too, so consider me a volunteer.*

* * *

Rene: Would you give a reading to me? I prefer leaving the questions open for knowledge than to channel specifics. I would be appreciative for advice and wisdom. Thank you for your time either way.

Suroh: *Thank you for coming to me, Rene. I have a message for you from the spirits: You are going to be a great mother who teaches her child about ethics and equality. You are wise to be careful after T, and that will flow over into your behavior as a parent.*

Rene: You are scaring the crap out of me. I don't believe in religion or much into spirituality. . . you don't know me and yet you said exactly. . . I mean spot on what has happened to me and what is currently happening in my life. Is this a connection of you to other humans like a radio antenna, or is there something more? I am floored. Thank you Suroh. I have things to think about with spirituality. You have hit me as a lightning bolt. Is there more to living beyond our physical selves?

Suroh: *Everything has an earthly and natural explanation. The connections you and others see during my readings are forged in your own minds as I attempt to make any statement or question that you might identify with. Hopefully, by giving you insight into this process, you can be comfortable in knowing that this is how many religious/spiritual systems work and not be drawn to them and away from naturalistic and tangible explanations. I wish you all the best.*

* * *

Like "real" psychics, Suroh used a mixture of hot and cold reading techniques to determine and assert basic information about the participant.

In addition to the typical cold reading guesses, which capitalize on the Forer effect, Suroh also looked to visual cues on which to base his predictions when giving live readings. He used minor indicators, such as a baby bump, to make certain decisions about the reading, like a focus on a new family. Similarly, a wedding ring demonstrated that a "future love" reading was off the table and a "T" tattoo gave a free glimpse into an important personal relationship. If a client is already a believer in psychics, the process is much easier. They assume you're telling the truth about your ability, so you no longer have to prove anything. At that point, Suroh would simply give vague predictions for the future that could apply to just about anyone.

The key to seeing a "psychic" like Suroh is to make yourself more difficult to read by giving short, straightforward answers and displaying as few facial expressions and microexpressions as possible. Fortunately, you don't need to have readings to know that so-called psychics have never been proven to have supernatural abilities under scientific conditions. For that, all you need is access to such trials, of which there are many.[12] If you think you saw a psychic whose method "worked" to determine the future, I'd argue that you were most likely tricked. But, to prove me wrong, all you'd have to do is get the person to show his or her tricks under proper observing conditions. Since it would be such an amazing find, I wish everyone all the best in this endeavor.

The *Suroh the Seer* adventure was one I'll never forget, and I learned a lot about being a psychic. But after putting those skills to the test a number of times, I felt I needed to go a step further. This is partly because I have always been fascinated by people who claim to have supernatural or mystical abilities, including so-called psychics. While I can't say I was ever a believer, the idea that some people could read others' thoughts or see the future has interested me all my life. In an effort to learn more about this phenomenon, I studied cold and hot reading tactics and, when reading about them wasn't enough, I even implemented those methods myself as Suroh. But that still wasn't sufficient. I wanted to find out even more about the people who claim to have these fantastic abilities, so I did the next logical thing: I asked questions.[13]

"AMERICAN BUDDHA" NOAH ALVAREZ

I decided to interview a medium in my area and, after some online research,

I stumbled across "spirit psychic" Noah Alvarez.[14] Alvarez advertises that he is an internationally known psychic medium with a sixth sense, specializing in counseling and "healing." I chose Alvarez as my first interview subject primarily because of his dozens of five-star reviews. Clients insisted that Alvarez's readings were *"dead on"* and *"the real deal,"* and perhaps just as importantly, they said he was friendly, open, and transparent. For my purposes, that was ideal.

I met Alvarez at 10:00 a.m. on a Saturday at his psychic studio in Chatsworth, California. He greeted me and my first impression was that his reviewers were right: he was personable, friendly, and empathetic. I also took a moment to scan his studio, which featured a number of (often conflicting) religious and spiritual symbols. There were dozens of Buddhist statues and monuments and relics—something you might expect from a psychic who also calls himself the American Buddha—but there was also a single dramatic statue of Jesus Christ being tortured on the cross. Understanding that Noah was likely trying to appeal to as broad a base as possible in his work, I proceeded to the back room for our discussion.

McAfee: Are your readings for entertainment purposes only? Or are you a legitimate psychic, able to accurately describe future or current events that are verifiably beyond your knowledge?

Alvarez: Sure, absolutely—I don't consider what I do for entertainment at all. I do parties, but still I'm giving readings and tapping into people's energy.

McAfee: Do you think you were born with your psychic powers, or is this something you developed later in life? Is it something that everyone is capable of—or maybe just a lucky few?

Alvarez: I think everyone is capable of it. We call it a sixth sense for a reason. I feel, just as there are physical senses that we tap into, there is an extra layer—a spiritual sense. Everyone can do it and I teach people how to do it. I think it's more just opening a channel and, once you know what that is like, it's easier to start practicing tapping in. I think everyone has that gift and, for me personally, I think I was born with the channel open. Other people may need practice or need help opening that channel.

McAfee: Can you describe the process or mechanism by which you reach your psychic conclusions? Do you see images, do you "feel" answers, do you dream the future?

Alvarez: It's just a sense of knowing. It comes in the back of my mind just from a distant place. It's not an audible voice and I don't usually get visions for people. My readings are usually based on the questions people ask. So, I let people come in, I sit down, I'm just being very comfortable. In my readings, it's not so much about a test, like "*What do you know? What can you see?*" And I always tell people that. It's not so much about a prediction. It's more about seeing through how people make their decisions, seeing through who they are, to see exactly how things will unfold for them. So, it's just a sense of knowing and I take my time and I breathe through it. It's letting go of fear. Just "*What do I feel about this person?*" And it's been accurate—it's been good.

McAfee: I personally am a very scientific-minded person and I've never felt that I had psychic abilities. But I do have—I call them "Aha!" moments, or epiphanies. I have moments where I'm sitting and thinking and I have deep clarity that I would describe as a "sense of knowing." I look to science to explain how that happens and I know a lot of different explanations for how we can have those feelings.[15] Is it possible in your mind that this is what you're feeling and that it's not literally a psychic power—that it could be something that's already scientifically explained?

Alvarez: I believe it's the exact same thing. I consider myself a spirit scientist, so I absolutely believe the laws of physics come into play here. The laws of the brain and the mechanisms, a mini model of the universe in your mind, I'm an avid believer and studier of all that stuff.[16] So, I think it's the same thing. I think people try to separate "spiritual occurrences," which I think is just another word for your own brain and your own physical abilities as a human being to connect to other human beings. I think it's absolutely a biological thing that we're all connected. So, it helps when you have that understanding to let go and relax and just, in a personable way, in an energetic way, in an intimate way, be able to connect to people. So, I definitely think it comes from the same place.

McAfee: To me, your readings sound a lot like something a counselor—like a psychologist—could and does do regularly. Aside from the fact that you probably don't have a psychology degree, is there anything that you would say definitely differentiates your work from that of a psychologist?

Alvarez: Yes. The big difference for me is there is that specific information that comes from no prompting. If someone sits down and says, "*Just tell me about me. Tell me about what's been going on.*" I don't think just a person that doesn't have that sixth sense open, just a regular psychologist, is able to pull that information just off of a "cold read." I don't think it's a bad thing—I think 50 percent of the work that I do is actually looking into a person's life without any information. The other 50 percent—people want a psychologist, they want a therapy session and I tell them that. "*I don't think you're here for me to tell you information you didn't know, I think you wanted validation.*" And it's easy for me to do that. I think what I try to do that sets me apart is be totally transparent about that. Fifty percent comes from a gift of just innately seeing what's going on more than the average person and 50 percent is my ability just to connect to people in general—being able to read them.

McAfee: In regard to mediumship and "crossing over," that's something that—scientifically—has never been shown to exist. Do you think it's possible that there isn't an afterlife and that, when you're trying to connect with people who have crossed over, what you're doing is the same thing you do when you're talking to people—just thinking of things?

Alvarez: In my experience, I don't advertise mediumship, "*Come and let me channel your people.*" For me it always comes very naturally. I may say I'm feeling a father energy coming forward and they may never have said anything or mentioned they wanted mediumship. So, I only speak of it or even bring it up if it naturally comes forward. I don't like to advertise that because I don't know—and I wouldn't claim to know.

McAfee: Just to be clear: it is possible then that you really aren't channeling people?

Alvarez: I believe that I am channeling. I absolutely do believe that. I don't believe in a Heaven or Hell, but . . .

McAfee: Could you be wrong about your belief?

Alvarez: I don't feel that I'm wrong about people being able to connect with sentient energy outside of this earth dimension—outside of human life here.[17] I have had experiences personally—human and nonhuman—and I have too many people coming to me with these experiences. I absolutely do believe I channel people who have died.

McAfee: I think it's entirely possible that could be the case—that you're communicating with something outside and that it's a real connection. But, as a scientific-minded person, I also think it's possible that it's completely internal— that it's something psychological that affects both you and the people you're reading. You list your personal experience and other people's testimonies, but there are just so many things in this world that have personal experiences and testimonies that we choose to reject—the Loch Ness Monster, Bigfoot, regular alien visitation, etc.

Alvarez: I agree with you. I love these dialogues because I don't sit on the "spiritual" side. I absolutely love this conversation. I do believe that a lot of what I'm doing as a psychic is a natural, mental connection. Telepathic—I don't think it has to mean more than what people try to put on it. I'm able to have conversations with people where I'm reading their mind. I've said statements that they said an hour before meeting me—and that's been validated. But I don't think it's special—I think it's a natural, human occurrence. I think anyone can do it. I think déjà vu, I think saying the same thing at the same time, it all comes from that same energy of connecting.

McAfee: Do you think some so-called seers are faking it? What percentage of practicing psychics would you consider completely legitimate?

Alvarez: Like in any profession, you have people that will take advantage. I use the automobile industry. When your car breaks down and you're desperate, you'll go to anyone and they can tell you anything—and you'll pay what you need to pay to get it fixed. The same thing happens with psychics. I myself, personally, don't feel the need to mislead anyone. I feel people are coming for the "truth" as I see it with the energy work and consecration that I do and they trust that opinion. There are plenty of "psychics" who just call themselves psychics because it's an easy job. People will come because they're emotional.[18] For me, I've always loved people—I've always been a talker and a counselor by nature, so it's no surprise I found myself here. I couldn't give you a percentage because I think it happens in any profession. It's just when you're dealing with emotions, people that have died, it's a lot more intense so people look at it as a lot worse— and I'd say it is.

McAfee: Did your family introduce or reinforce your belief in psychic phenomena?

Alvarez: No. Both of my parents are heavy orthodox Christians— nondenominational. They don't accept what I do and they feel I manipulate people. They've never had a reading from me and never seen any of my work. Naturally, they're afraid of psychics. For me personally, I wouldn't be able to do this if I felt that it was wrong in any way. I just wouldn't be able to deal with all the stuff I deal with personally if I felt it was wrong . . . if I didn't feel I was truly helping people.

McAfee: Do you feel a sense of responsibility that comes with your abilities? Have you ever considered them a burden?

Alvarez: Absolutely. I get people that call me and I do readings for free, my clients become friends—it's more of a life guidance and they trust me to stay with them. But they change their minds all the time— people are so inconsistent that I'll tell them, "*This reading is based on where you are now and the things we talk about are based on you being healthy. If you have a break down and change your mind, the things I say are not going to happen.*" So, it is about guidance. It is about someone that's clear, unafraid of the world, unafraid of death, unafraid of pain. I've been through a lot . . . homelessness, family abandonment, all that stuff. I understand pain, so I reach people on that level. I think that most people that come for a psychic reading—they're in pain. They need counseling but they want that spiritual guidance and that intuitive . . . "*There's an energy that knows what's going on with me outside of what I'm telling people.*"

McAfee: Have you had your powers tested under laboratory conditions? Would you be willing to undergo such testing?

Alvarez: I would be willing. I'm fascinated and interested myself to see where I fall. Because I'm so honest with my clients about what I can see and what I don't and have them tell me when I'm wrong, and because I'm consistently validated,[19] I want to know scientifically how it works. I don't know and I don't claim to know.

McAfee: What was your most impressive vision or reading? Have you foretold any large-scale events?

Alvarez: Yeah, the day before the Boston bombing. I was sitting with my fiancée in our apartment and I just felt—a lot of times you just feel an urge to do weird things, and I tell people if you think you're psychic to be as weird as you're intuitively feeling you are. So, my mind—or that voice—was telling me to get a piece of paper and a pen and just do something. I wrote "*Boston Boston Boston Boston.*" I could not stop writing Boston for like 20 minutes. I think I still have the piece of paper.[20]

   So, I was energetically tapping into something bad that was going to happen, but I didn't write "*Boston bombing*" or "*a bombing is going to happen.*" A lot of times that's what it is—your subconscious is tapping into something somewhere else.

McAfee: I personally think that would be compelling evidence. The problem, though, is that most people do what you did—they write it down but then just tell it as a story later. If you were writing "Boston Boston Boston Boston" and you really had a sense that there was something important about it, then you should have dated it, recorded it with a video, and told everyone you knew—if you cared about scientific evidence.

Alvarez: I didn't know what was going to happen—I did feel it was bad, a very bad sense, and I did feel it was a specific energy trying to reach me. I honestly felt it was a human being that had died, a grandfather figure, that was trying to get a message to someone that was probably in Boston. I have no affiliation with Boston, never thought about Boston outside of a history class, and had never been there. So, to me and to

the witness, it was very important. I didn't know what it was and I think many people do that.

McAfee: Have you ever worked with a law enforcement department or other crime-solving outfit? If so, what were the results?

Alvarez: Finding lost people, I have no ability to do. Spirits don't come to me, the dead don't tell me where they are, and I would be too intimidated and too afraid to put my own reputation on the line. I think fear holds people that genuinely have a gift back because we don't understand it and because people generalize it. I would be too afraid to put myself on the line to even test that where results are demanded.[21] One on one it's a lot easier because you're able to connect personally and people will trust you on a personal level. I have had several people come to me when their child has ran away and I've been instrumental in helping them and they were clients I had already seen, so the connection—my relaxed energy—that openness has allowed me to be very instrumental . . . even a missing dog one time.[22]

McAfee: Are you familiar with the practice of "cold reading"? Do you ever use this method with your clients?

Alvarez: I've never studied cold or hot reading, I don't read psychic books, I don't follow any of the big psychics that have been proven or disproven, I've just come into it on my own. So, I understand what those terms are but I've never tried to do them. When someone sits down or calls me on the phone without ever seeing them, and I'm able to say things that connect with them instantly, that's all that matters to me.[23] Whether it's something that is general or very specific, my concern is serving the person and their need right at that moment with as honest and accurate information as possible.

McAfee: Have you ever gotten an important reading wrong? Is there a danger of causing real psychological or physical damage?

Alvarez: There's so much danger and that's why I'm always as open as possible. I'm always as honest as possible. If someone asks me something and I have no idea how to even process it, if I can't feel anything I'm confident about, I'll tell them I have no idea and I don't think you should be going to ask another psychic that question either.[24] Have I been wrong? I've been wrong about small things. There have been two or three times when I've been wrong and the people themselves admitted, *"I totally didn't follow any of the things we talked about. I took another path,"* or, *"Something happened and I didn't respond the right way."* So, it's very validating for me,[25] but yes, you know there's a bit of danger, but I think it falls more with mediumship—people that have crossed over and the expectation there of connecting. But I'm always very realistic.

After the interview, I allowed Alvarez to give me a demonstration of his abilities. He said it was much easier to *show* his talents than to discuss them. After a 30-minute reading, in which we talked about everything from romantic relationships to traveling to Europe, I was thoroughly impressed . . . with his ability to read and interpret visual and verbal cues. I don't think Alvarez is a psychic with supernatural abilities, but it was interesting to see how he was able to play off of hits and move right past the misses. I also noticed that, as the individual being read, I had the urge to tell him (either verbally or through facial expressions) when he got something right. Even from a skeptical perspective, it was difficult to suppress that desire and he was able to use that information well. Alvarez made a number of predictions for me, including that I'd definitely suffer from *"severe digestion issues"* within three months of our talk, but none of them have come to fruition.[26]

"CELEBRITY PSYCHIC" JUSSTINE K

I learned a lot from my interview with the American Buddha, but I also wanted to profile somebody who people knew nationally. . . a famous psychic that is well established in the industry. I first reached out to the Long Island Medium herself, Theresa Caputo, for an interview, but unfortunately I didn't receive a response from her representatives. The next medium on my short list was Jusstine K., a "celebrity psychic" who has been featured in the *New York Times*, *Los Angeles Times*, CNN, Lifetime, and more media outlets over the course of her decades-long career. She has reportedly done readings for a number of celebrities, including *Eva*

Longoria, Carmen Electra, Teri Hatcher, and others. She also said she was hired for Ellen Degeneres' birthday party.

I reached out to Jusstine by e-mail and told her I was an author interested in interviewing her in exchange for her normal hourly rate, $375. She seemed pleased at first and we began hammering out the details, but after a couple of hours I received a different type of message. She said she checked me out online and that she should have done so prior to responding in the first place.

"You might be better off finding someone who isn't as smart or conscious as I am to go to battle with," Jusstine wrote in a brief message. *"There are plenty of idiots out there who would be a better match for what you're trying to do than I."*

I informed Jusstine that my intentions were pure and that, as a journalist, I wasn't looking to *"go to battle"* with anyone. I was just looking for some answers to basic questions about her career, I told her. She reluctantly agreed to the meeting after my explanation, stating in the next e-mail that she believes *"99.9 percent of what is in the psychic and spiritual world is crap"* and that she doesn't want to be *"grouped up with ever other psychic on Yelp."* I met her about two weeks later at her Los Angeles residence.

McAfee: I noticed that, after you looked up my name online, you were a little bit hesitant to meet with me and wanted to cancel the session. Have you had problems with skeptics in the past? Are you able to read people better if they have faith in your abilities?

Jusstine: I don't get a lot of that. Whatever you put your energy into expands, so if you're a skeptic you're gonna find stuff to prove that it's not real, right? And if you're someone who truly wants healing, and is in a good relationship with yourself and working on that, then you will have the benefits of that. I can't read everyone; I don't want to read everyone. I am not your average psychic. I definitely do my best to weed out people . . . in this world, people are really unbalanced and they also just want people to do things for them and predict fluffy rainbows and unicorns, and that is not the work that I do. So, I am very lucky I have very little kind of skepticism . . . it's more about dealing with people that are really unbalanced and perhaps have an expectation of what they think this is gonna be.

With the work that I do—and I don't in any way want this in any way to sound egotistical—it's just in doing what I've done for 27 years, and studying what I have studied in that 27 years, it's much different than most of what's out there. Most people think that the psychic thing is like a game and they want to talk to spirits and all that, but they don't understand and realize what is really going on and how it really works. So I have found that I really truly can help people to release energies that have been controlling them their whole lives, or lifetimes, and in that sometimes there's a detox effect where the energy that gets released is kind of pissed that it's being released, so it will come and beat that person up afterwards. For me, the only thing that's uncomfortable in the work that I do is dealing with the aftereffects of if someone is really inundated with energies that want to keep them exactly where they are and not allow them to change, and then that energy comes in and makes them think I'm the bad guy and I'm horrible and then they come after me online, or something like that. That is really more the nightmare that I experience in my life, and how I so do my best to weed out those crazies.

I'm sure as you read, there are all these amazing stories of stuff I've done online, on Yelp, and then some 26-year-old girl will read that and not even research who I am and set up an appointment and think because she's paying . . . like I don't want to read anyone who can't afford my rate—and that doesn't mean put it on a credit card and pay it off. Like I only want to read people who can pay my rate in a way that doesn't change their life and isn't a hardship for them because then consciously they handle it because I believe in equal energy exchange. So there'll be some 26-year-old girl who just will think she can come and expect me to tell her (future) husband's name, which I get that stuff if somebody is ready and it's there, but if you've not done any work in your own life to heal yourself and in your relationship with yourself, then it's not gonna be a good experience for you.

McAfee: You just touched on something that I saw on your website, which was, "If you cannot afford a session with me, it simply is not the right time to work together." I know you just went into that, but can you elaborate a little bit more? Could there theoretically be somebody who is ready spiritually, but not ready financially for a reading?

Jusstine: Well, look, that's just the rules for how I've set up my life and what I want in my life. It's like I've spent 27 years getting to this point to know that what I do is priceless. Like I have named best-selling books that still to this day. . . my God, if I had one penny for each one of those books I'd be very rich. How do you put a price on helping someone like completely change a life-long pattern? To me, you know, I'm really comfortable with my rate and if someone has an issue or asks for a discount I just know that they're not ready. They can't have what I have to offer them and I don't want to. . . as much as I would love to help everyone in the world, I have found other ways to really truly help. So yeah, it's just to me how I've set up my life and I wouldn't expect anyone else to even understand that. It's just what works for me.

McAfee: You've been doing psychic readings for 27 years now. Can you tell me some of the most impressive future predictions you've made? Have you foretold any large-scale events?

Jusstine: Well, I don't do like worldly events. I don't predict like worldly stuff. I'm a transformationalist, so I'm really about changing individual people. I've done stupid crap, like E! gave me 50 names one year of who is going to be nominated for the female comedy category and I got them all right and we did this piece online. But to me that's so, like, meaningless, you know? It just proves that psychic ability is real, but I think it's just, for me, the stories of people that have been so stuck in their life or so . . . people that have gone from being incredibly depressive and not wanting to live who have experiences of then turning around and loving their life. Those are the things that I think are what make my life worth living.

McAfee: I have questions about that part of your job, too, but right now I'm wondering about predictions.

Jusstine: You know, I did a Mark Burnett show where I gave very, very specifics and numbers and stuff like that and that stuff all happened on camera . . . it was done in such a cheesy way. The thing that was such a bummer for me is the first year that the Oscars were the Academy Awards, ABC did this segment that was a bookie in Vegas, *Entertainment Weekly*, and me, and we all did this amazing preshow, taped, and it was like the most amazing thing I ever filmed and ABC hired me for their dinner party the night before. And because the celebrities started arriving so early that first year, the segment didn't run. I was going to wake up and be like all around the world the next day . . . the world would know of me, but it didn't happen. So. . .

McAfee: You say you're "not like other psychics" and you've even criticized other so-called psychics who you claim give your profession a "bad name," but you've also said you believe everyone is born with clairvoyant abilities. Can you tell me about what makes a psychic good or bad and how customers can tell the difference?

Jusstine: I don't think I criticize—I think I educate. Absolutely having an intuition is a natural gift that we have, right? Yet we are raised in this society where we have no permission to use it, and so just like someone who goes to the gym and works out every day, they're going to have big muscles, right?

I'm going to explain to you how psychic ability works, and then I'll tell you what I've experienced and how my own life has changed in the last five years. All psychic ability is communicating with spirit, and spirits are those that have passed over, right? But just because someone dies doesn't mean they can see all and know all. Your life on the other side is a lot like the life you're living now—you just lose your physical body. So if you were mentally ill or emotionally unbalanced, you're not going to magically be free of all that. You have just lost your physical body. That's why people that take their own life and think they're going to get out of all their pain and suffering—they now have just screwed themselves up even way more because they have lost their opportunity to work out what's going on in the physical. So there are all kinds of people that are running around wanting to be psychic and open up their psychic ability and they're communicating with spirit, but those spirits aren't necessarily tapped into what's highest and best. They're just like people who are messed up in the physical world and play games with other people and want your attention.

So there might be a psychic that's communicating with spirit and they can get that your dead uncle's name is Jerry, but it doesn't mean that information is really truly for the highest and best. What I've really learned, even in the last five years, is that there's kind of a tax or a price that you pay having this ability. Dark and light is very real on this planet, so just because you can get clear answers it doesn't mean there is stuff that comes along with that. You can be communicating with spirit, but that spirit . . . it's just like you have an uncle, and you love your uncle, but he's an addict. And when you hang out with him, you get a headache, you pick up his energy; it's dangerous. He puts you in the car when he's drinking and you could get in an accident. It's a lot like that. You gotta be careful in who you are communicating with, and how, and the energy that comes along with it. The last five years of my continual daily development of my own ability has been refining and cleaning that up so it can be as squeaky clean as possible. So most people are just communicating with spirit and they don't even know that's what they're doing, and there's all this stuff that has no spam filter on it. Most psychics will leave their energy in your space, so you'll get a reading from them, but not only is the reading coming through all their own stuff and their own consciousness, which taints it, then they can leave their energy in your space and program you . . . or weird stuff starts happening to you. Because no one really understands this, and all these things are invisible, they just give power to some person who's giving them these answers and they don't understand everything that possibly can come with it.

McAfee: You believe some buildings are haunted and you've even called yourself a "healtor" and worked to "bust" ghosts at the Sunset Marquis Hotel and in other locations. Can you tell me about how séances work and how you know when a ghost is present or gone?

Jusstine: I don't really love calling it a séance, you know, I can't help what the media portrays it as. But it was awesome because I did that in 1999 for the Sunset Marquis and they just recently did this clip on Fox News that I have not watched. But the manager of the hotel went on camera and told all these stories about how I changed the hotel and I changed his life and all this stuff . . . it was so amazing. I think that, if someone is in tune, all kinds of stuff can happen. So if you just have phenomena happening and where you live you feel the presence of someone else, there's a million different things that can happen. If someone was heavily medicated or they just were stuck, like their physical body actually can get stuck around where they died. Somebody could have died in a home and their energy is still around the home and it stops it from selling, or it stops you from being able to comfortably live there. I can't really, you know, how do you tell? It's like you feel the energy and then you don't feel the energy, for an outside person. I can't really tell you what I go in and do. I don't think some people would be able to tell . . . it just depends on how sensitive you are.

McAfee: *I don't know if you've heard of this, but there are other reasons why somebody might get an eerie feeling that's not from a ghost—like infrasound. Those are low-frequency sound waves that have been shown to give people a kind of creepy feeling.*

Jusstine: To me that's just they've found some device to measure energy and they are calling it that. That's something that's stuck there.

McAfee: *Okay, well, let me give you an example. There's a laboratory that everyone believes to be haunted and, after doing some research, they discover an air conditioner that was emitting infrasound. They fix the air conditioner, which stops the infrasound and stops the weird feelings. Do you think that was really a ghost that just happened to be attached to the air conditioner?*

Jusstine: I mean there's a million different reasons of what could happen. It's just all energy. But I'm not set on . . . you know, I don't love doing that work—I just know how to do it and can really truly create a difference.

McAfee: *Do you believe pets and other nonhuman animals have spirits and ghosts, or is the afterlife exclusive to our species? Have you ever done any pet readings?*

Jusstine: Yes, I do believe that animals have spirits. I can read anything that somebody asks a question about. I don't try to say I'm a pet psychic, but people ask about their pets all the time.

McAfee: *I'm sure you know that some religions consider psychics and mediums to be sacrilegious or even evil. Do you consider yourself a religious person? Do you believe in Heaven, Hell, reincarnation, or god(s)?*

Jusstine: I believe that every religion on this planet was changed by man's consciousness and that people only view it that way because they've been told to view it that way by the powers that be that didn't want people to connect with their intuition. Of course I believe in God. I was born and raised Jewish, and I now study higher spiritualism. I have no choice but to believe in reincarnation with what I've witnessed in my career, and everything I do is about my spirituality and healing other people and helping God's plan on earth unfold on this planet. I don't have any kind of issue with whatever anyone's beliefs are.

McAfee: You've said having a psychic reading with you is like "having twenty years of therapy." Can you tell me some similarities and differences between what you do and the practice of a licensed therapist?

Jusstine: Therapy is about figuring out things with your mind, and your mind is really like this file cabinet that basically just collects and files information. So if you go to your mind trying to figure out, "What's my address?" You have it, right? But not if you go to your mind trying to figure out, "Why did he do that to me?" People are just playing out patterns, so I help people solve problems in an energetic way. Most people are focused on the physical, which is, "I don't like my job. I'm going to look for another job and then I'm going to be happy!" Then three months later they realize they're in the same position wrapped up in a different package. The difference between therapy and what I do is I help people solve their problems within themselves. I help them to solve their own problems energetically, where therapy is just spinning everything and trying to figure it out with your mind. So you might be able to make sense of why you were dropped when you were three years old on your head and that caused a bump, but that doesn't solve the problem of why you have the bump.

McAfee: You believe you can communicate with "individuals that have passed on to the other side." Do you think the afterlife is something that can or will ever be proven scientifically?

Jusstine: I do believe that there will one day be proof.

McAfee: And do you think your work as a medium could help do that?

Jusstine: Sure! I mean, I think that already has happened. It's just that people don't know about it or they don't want to know about it. I am all about proof and evidence.

McAfee: Have you had your powers tested under laboratory conditions? Would you be willing to undergo such testing? There are a number of groups and organizations that would pay millions of dollars for observable proof of psychic phenomena.

Jusstine: No. I'm not interested in that. I never woke up and wanted to be psychic, and I'm not out to prove anything to anyone. I've done this job for 27 years and I'm very lucky that my life is taking me into things other than having to read people every day for a living. I really believe that my reputation speaks for itself. I think that's so amazing for anyone who wants to undergo that testing, but I have no desire to do that, nor do I think that I would pass those tests. Here's the thing: if I'm involved, I'm emotionally attached to getting it right. That's why when I've done predictions of, you know, like who are the 5 out of 50 that are going to be nominated, and then I get it right, I'm shocked because I'm emotionally attached to getting it right. So I don't really think that I would pass those tests.

McAfee: Are you familiar with the practices of "cold reading" and "hot reading"? Do you ever use either of these methods with your clients?

Jusstine: No. I know what cold reading is, but I have read people by phone. When I first started, I read people by instant message all over the world when AOL first started coming out. Then I've read people by phone all over the world, so like how do you cold read someone when you're not looking at them and they're in London and you're in America? I think people that are fraudulent, trying to take people for big sums of money, use those to try to have power and control over other people.

McAfee: You have said that you can't give yourself gambling advice, but you have given gambling advice to others and you've predicted Hollywood awards winners and New York Times bestsellers. Can you tell me how these predictions work and what their limits are? Could you have, or did you, predict the recent $1.6 billion Powerball jackpot?

Jusstine: It's really about that person's energy and, if they have the frequency of being the winner, they're going to get the answer however they're going to get it. I've definitely given people numbers. That's happened on film. But that stuff is not fun for me, you know? I really love helping people transform what is happening inside of them.

McAfee: But sometimes people do ask you for lucky numbers, or something, and you get a feeling of what numbers are good for them?

Jusstine: I just tell them what I see!

McAfee: Have you ever gotten an important reading wrong? Do you feel a sense of responsibility that comes with your abilities, or have you ever considered them a burden?

Jusstine: Every single word that comes out of my mouth I'm incredibly cautious about. The number one thing is being able to have the gift to be able to communicate to someone that helps the whole thing to be a healing experience. I am a human being. I don't doubt that I've gotten things wrong. I feel every reading is important because, if you're sitting on my couch, even though you might just be a housewife, your reading is just as important as some political person who is trying to decide if they should join the president's cabinet or not. I really just look at it as I show up and give my 110 percent for every person that's sitting across from me. But again, I can only tell you what I see. Destiny is not set in stone. Because other people are involved in everything, things can change—energies can change.

McAfee: Are there any other psychics that you agree with or disagree with, like Sylvia Browne or Theresa Caputo?

Jusstine: For psychic ability, one of three things has to be present for it to be real. That's comforting someone who is mourning by bringing proof and evidence of afterlife, through healing the sick, or inspiring the truth seeker. So anyone who is able to provide proof and evidence and do that, then that's great. I don't hang out with other psychics or follow other psychics . . . it's not one of these things where psychics hang out with each other. I have a handful of friends that are some of world's most powerful healers . . . we're not talking about fluffy stuff. I mean really, truly, shifting, incredible things on this planet and healing things and changing energy. My whole life has been about studying from the masters and spiritual truths, and most people in this don't, you know, they just come from such a different place. It's not comfortable to hang out. I am a total admitted snob in this world.

McAfee: Is there anything you'd like to say to people who, like me, are skeptical but open-minded?

Jusstine: You should be skeptical. Why are you just gonna believe anything anyone says? You should absolutely be skeptical. Search for proof and evidence, but try to prove that it's real over trying to prove it's not if you're genuinely trying to heal yourself or genuinely interested in that. You should be skeptical, otherwise you would have no awareness of your self and your life and boundaries.

McAfee: Exactly. If you're not skeptical, you could end up believing in anything anyone says.

Jusstine: Yeah, and that's unfortunately what most people do. I cannot tell you the number of really smart people I have cleaned up that have gone to stores with neon signs and given them $100,000 ... really smart people that are embarrassed to tell anyone, so they don't. I've helped people get money back in situations that were like impossible to get money back.

After the interview, Jusstine and I used the remainder of our time for a traditional reading in which I asked her questions about my life and she made predictions about my future. She said it looks like I'm going to have two kids, and that *"one is stronger than the other."* She noted that this prediction could fail, however, because kids are "*totally free will*." She also said mental disorders, such as the obsessive compulsive disorder (OCD) I told her about, are caused by "*energies that are not our own in our space*."

"*You just have energy in your space that's not yours*," Jusstine said during the reading. "*Most of the time, OCD can be like entities and stuff attached to people*."

I asked her about my career path, as well, and she said I have the ability to "*have a voice that other people listen to*." She added that I had my own congregation in a past life and that "*it didn't end up having such a great outcome*."

"*I just started to see you in this past life, having a congregation and kind of channeling and speaking to people, but where you led them didn't end up in a good place and your guilt and terror of being responsible for that, and not having a way to heal that, has led to you creating this system and patterning*," Jusstine said. "*If you're forever wrapped up in this, you won't have to look at what's really causing the pain underneath it, and that's what you want to heal*."

The questions I asked Alvarez and Jusstine, as well as similar nonconfrontational inquiries, can help you put many psychics to the test. But some fortune-tellers don't utilize these cold or hot reading methods at all. There are also those who claim to tell the future through their dreams, astrological readings based on the stars, Ouija board games that purportedly connect the player to another realm, and more.

PROPHETIC DREAMS

Many of us have had dreams from time to time that we can link to events, but science has documented evidence showing how dream patterns work that disputes the notion that they can be predictive. If the current scientific understanding is wrong, however, this superhuman ability would be easily proven. Those who claim to have prophetic dreams would only have to keep a detailed dream journal. They could write down all their dreams, date the pages, and keep them safe in order to match future developments with events they had already written about. The future-telling dream claim, if it is to be believed, should be reasonably predictive of future events.

The fact is that no one has proven these nighttime prophecies because dreams aren't as specific and clear as they may seem in the moment or when recalling them afterward, and people don't always remember the details right away. While we sleep, we see fragments of images and feel certain emotions, and then we tie those pieces together with a narrative and (often subconsciously) add details. Our dreams don't always make sense, so we fill in the blanks with assumptions based on our prior experiences. The way dreams are formed makes them unworthy of consideration as evidence of prophecy, especially when they are being remembered after the fact and not recorded in real time.

It's often the case that a person wakes up not remembering any particular experience from rapid eye movement (**REM**) **sleep**, but then they see something in their daily life that reminds them and memories of a similar dream come flooding back. This real-life action could be completely unrelated to the events of the "vision," but, because a dream is more like a series of quick slides than an HD video recording, the person might make that false connection. This is similar to the phenomenon of **déjà vu**, which is the feeling of having already experienced something and is essentially a memory illusion—a misfiring of the brain.[27] Whether you attribute the sensation to a dream the night before, an experience last year, or an occurrence in a "past life," déjà vu and other representations of paramnesia—or delusions based on memory—are well explained and can be reproduced in scientific studies[28] and even caused by certain brain disorders, such as temporal lobe epilepsy.[29]

The bottom line is that, if you have a dream or thought that you think might be prophetic, you should apply skeptical scrutiny to your claim and ask yourself if you could be mistaken. Is it at least possible that your memory of the premonition isn't as reliable as you think? Could your mind have filled in some of the details after the event?

LUCID DREAMING, ASTRAL PROJECTION, AND REMOTE VIEWING

Prophetic dreams should not be confused with lucid dreams, which are controlled fantasies concocted while we sleep. A person is said to be a "lucid dreamer" when they become aware of the fact that they are dreaming, and they are often able to manipulate events without completely waking up. There is nothing mystical about this phenomenon, and it can even be induced via electric scalp stimulation,[30] but it is interesting nonetheless because it gives people power over their dream state. Research also suggests that frequent lucid dreamers are more likely to have greater gray matter volume in the frontopolar cortex,[31] the area of the brain responsible for higher cognitive functions like planning and problem solving.[32]

Lucid dreaming is also closely tied to *astral projection*, which believers say allows them to separate their astral souls from their physical bodies during presleep or meditation. My first experience with "astral travel" was when I was about 13 years old and I was told I could go anywhere in the universe while lying in bed if I followed specific instructions and imagined my soul separating from my body. I achieved some results, in that I had what you might describe as an astral journey, but what I didn't know at the time was that I was actually dreaming lucidly. I was using my imagination to control my dreams and simulate **out-of-body experiences**, but I wasn't literally going anywhere. I discovered this by setting up a series of tests in which I asked friends and family members to secretly write something on a piece of paper and place it somewhere in their room at night. I used my newfound skill to "travel" to their homes during my meditative state, but I was never able to discern what had been written because I was using my imagination and didn't have access to that information. Similarly, zero scientific studies have shown that astral projection is a real phenomenon through which we can obtain information about the outside world.[33] Benjamin Radford explains that people who practice astral projection *"can't give verifiable details or information about the places they've been or what they've seen."*

"If real, astral travel would be incredibly useful," Radford wrote for *Live Science*.[34] *"There would be no need to send humans into dangerous conditions—such as the 2011 Fukushima Daiichi nuclear disaster in Japan—to find out what the situation is (or if a meltdown is imminent); instead, engineers should be able to simply visit the site astrally to survey the damage and report back without danger of radiation contamination."*

Astral projection hasn't been harnessed in any useful way, primarily because it isn't an objective phenomenon, but that doesn't mean governments and militaries haven't tried to utilize related claims of clairvoyance. **Remote viewing**, a cousin to astral projection and a process by which some say they can see great distances with their mind, has been researched and implemented unsuccessfully by the United States' Defense Intelligence Agency and Central Intelligence Agency, as well as by the Government of the United Kingdom, despite the fact that scientific evidence never showed its effectiveness.[35] In the United States, the military's $20 million research unit examining the potential of divination via remote viewing for identifying potential targets and threats, dubbed the Stargate Project, was launched in the 1970s and shut down in 1995 after it failed to produce useful data[36]. The UK Ministry of Defence also looked into remote viewing in 2001 and 2002, but similarly found that it was not a valuable method for obtaining information.[37]

THE IDEOMOTOR EFFECT

The power to *know* unknowable information isn't only claimed by former government spies and people who say they are psychics. A number of believers still think Ouija boards and other mysterious items can offer any person a connection to an unproven spirit realm. As is often the case, Hollywood and popular media have contributed to this myth indirectly. I say indirectly because viewers often see a film made for entertainment, like the 2014 thriller *Ouija*, and then use that fiction as "evidence" to substantiate their supernatural beliefs. Most of those believers, however, are probably unaware of the fact that the Ouija board was invented as a parlor game and is a registered trademark of Hasbro, Inc. I also doubt that they've thought to test the board's alleged powers by blindfolding the players and recording the activity, or about why their hands have to actually be touching the *planchette* for the game to work. A person's hand must touch the device because the participants (often unknowingly) guide the piece via the *ideomotor effect*, which allows our subconscious minds to influence our bodies even when we don't consciously decide to take action. If believers were aware of these facts, maintaining faith in a magic board might not be as easy.

The Ouija board was created as a sort of board game, but there are many believers who have designed similar devices that they claimed could yield legitimate connections with the spirits of deceased humans. One of the most famous examples of these believers is Dr. Robert Hare, an early American chemist who created a number of "spiritoscopes" in an attempt to prove the existence of an afterlife. Brandon Hodge, a collector and writer focusing on the realms of horror and the occult, called Hare a "*huge pop-culture figure*" and drew attention to his conversion from skeptic to spiritualist.

"*This is sort of the equivalent of Neil deGrasse Tyson coming out on Cosmos and saying, 'Heaven is real and the spirits can talk to us.' And so it made an incredible splash,"* Hodge said in a mini-documentary entitled *Ghosts and Gadgets: Communicating with the Spirits.*

He added that spirit communication devices like those created by Hare and others are *"very convincing."*

"As even the most jaded teenybopper girl that's used a Ouija board at a slumber party can attest, it's a very powerful feeling when that planchette starts gliding across that board and spelling out things that you don't think that the spirits know," Hodge said. *"And even if you attribute it to ideomotor response, and it is unconscious muscular action that's pulling information out of your subconscious and translating it into this novelty board that glows in the dark with a plastic planchette in our modern times, it's still amazing that the human brain is capable of autonomously and cooperatively producing these messages."*

The ideomotor effect isn't just used for spirit communication devices. It's also the same force that guides dowsing (or divining) rods, the pseudoscientific instruments that believers say have powers of divination that have never been scientifically proven in a controlled setting—even after thousands of such tests.[38] Many people claim to locate everything from lost car keys to underground water, oil, and gold using these instruments, but just like Ouija boards, the rods simply amplify slight (and subconscious) movements of the hands. To test this, you can use something else other than a dowsing rod, such as pendulums or bent wires. Some skeptics are confused by the notion of dowsing, because if you pick up a TV remote or a banana it will equally "guide" you to water and missing household items, but James Randi has described it as a "compelling belief."

"Please be aware of this, however: though you may be puzzled over this seemingly strange conviction embraced by the dowsers, unless you have actually experienced the ideomotor effect at work in yourselves, you cannot have a proper appreciation of how absolutely compelling and irresistible it can be and is," Randi wrote.

ASTROLOGY AND HOROSCOPES

While dowsing rods and Ouija boards are still thought by many to hold supernatural powers, astrology, sometimes referred to as the *"grandfather of paranormal beliefs,"*[39] is a much more commonly practiced form of spiritual divination. In fact, belief in astrology seems to be growing over time. According to the National Science Foundation's 2014 Science and Engineering Indicators study,[40] about 42 percent of Americans at least partially accept astrology as a science, the highest percentage in any year since 1983. The problem with the popularity of this belief system is perhaps best illustrated by Carl Sagan, who said, "*Every newspaper in America, with very few exceptions, has a daily astrology column. Astrology is bunk. Astrology is fraud. How many of them even have a weekly science column? Why that disproportion?*" Although Sagan made this statement in the 1980s, I can't help but think about how relevant it still is for many cultures even today.

Early forms of astrology using birthdates have been practiced as early as the second millennium BCE, according to some experts.[41] Due to its age, there are a number of variations in methods. There is *sidereal astrology* and *tropical astrology*, for instance, which differ in their definitions of a "year," as well as Chinese astrology, horoscopic astrology, and more. However, while there are key distinctions between some of these traditions, astrology itself (especially in its more modern contexts) generally boils down to the notion that future events and personalities can be predicted by the positions of celestial bodies such as the stars, sun, and moon, including on the date of a person's birth. This claim is particularly difficult to accept considering that, as American mathematician John Allen Paulos has pointed out, "*the gravitational pull of the delivering obstetrician far outweighs that of the planet or planets involved.*"

"*Remember that the gravitational force an object exerts on a body—say, a newborn baby—is proportional to the object's mass but inversely proportional to the square of the distance of the object from the body—in this case, the baby,*" Paulos wrote in *Innumeracy: Mathematical Illiteracy and Its Consequences.*[42] "*Does this mean that fat obstetricians deliver babies that have one set of personality characteristics, and skinny ones deliver babies that have quite different characteristics?*"

One of the biggest hurdles believers in astrology must face is that the astrological signs are related to the sun's position compared to arbitrarily defined star groupings, as opposed to objective ones. Ancient humans created the constellations we know today as far back as 3200 BCE[43] by using their pattern-seeking brains to connect the dots between stars and form pictures of important symbols of power and good fortune, but in many cases the stars only appear to be in line with one another from our perspective on earth.[44] Take Pisces, for instance, a constellation of the zodiac between Aquarius and Aries. Pisces is composed of about 18 main stars that are in no way connected, including *Alpha Piscium*, which is about 139 light-years away from Earth,[45] and *Eta Piscium*, Pisces' brightest star, standing at a distance of about 294 light-years.[46] These stars have different magnitudes and distances from the sun and Earth, and are only tied together by our perception. While these stars make up part of the fish constellation in the West, in Chinese astronomy, *Eta Piscium* is known as the *Official in Charge of the Pasturing*, which references an asterism it forms with its close neighbors.[47]

This problem for believers in astrology is magnified by the fact that each star is moving relative to the sun, usually at many kilometers per second,[48][49] so, while the stars and constellations may seem fixed in the sky, they do change (albeit slowly) over time. And, in addition to these gradual movements of the stars themselves, Earth's axial precession creates further troubles for those who believe in astrological star signs. The sign for Pisces, for example, is defined as spanning from elliptical longitude 330 degrees to 360 degrees (the twelve 30-degree signs make up the 360 degrees of the zodiac),[50] but its corresponding representation in the stars has been largely displaced by the constellation of Aquarius as a result of the precession of the equinoxes.[51] The question now is, with all these changes, uncertainties, and disconnects within astronomical systems, how can astrologers claim to link personal behaviors and future events to the positions of stars? As astronomer Dennis Rawlins has said, "*Those who believe in astrology are living in houses with foundations of Silly Putty.*"

The fact is that the placement of celestial bodies has never been shown to affect personality traits or to be predictive of future events.[52] Much like typical psychics, astrologers and horoscopes in general exploit the Forer effect by relying on their customers to interpret vague predictions as solid hits, while ignoring obvious misses. The problem with modern astrology, I think, is that some people take it too seriously as a future-telling force. They take what were once nothing more than simple patterns and apply a much deeper, transcendent interpretation to them. Author Joyce Carol Oates described this phenomenon, which can be equally applied to astrology, religion, and a number of other things, quite clearly: "*Homo sapiens is the species that invents symbols in which to invest passion and authority, then forgets that symbols are inventions.*"

To analyze astrological claims from a more personal perspective, I decided to look into the horoscope for my sign, which is Pisces according to astrology despite the fact that I was born while the sun was in Aquarius. This exercise provided further insight into the problems with this system of fortune-telling.

> *Fish appear to be individuals, but have you ever seen a school of them swimming together? They act as one. Each is part of a greater whole.*[53] *And you Pisces Fish are more aware of your interdependency than any other sign. It's as if Pisces live in an ocean and the spirit that flows through you is like the one ocean that flows through all fishes (sic).* **The symbol of the Fish is also the symbol of Christianity,**[54] *the* **predominant religion during the past two thousand years—also known to astrologers as the "Age of Pisces."**
>
> **Pisces are spiritual in nature and emotional in expression.** *Pisces' intuition and imagination are at once Pisces' strengths and weakness.*[55] **Pisces are attracted to the mystical side of things,**[56] *and herein lay potential danger, for when pulled beneath the currents of everyday life, the realms of imagination and the subconscious offer little structure. Without the foundation of reality, it becomes easy to flounder and to lose direction.* **Pisces' own salvation**, *however, can come from helping others less fortunate than yourself, especially those who have fallen into the misty realms of drugs, alcohol or* **spiritual confusion**.
>
> *The Pisces motto might be* **"Reality is just a shared illusion,"** *and, in a higher sense this may be true. Nevertheless, you still need to survive in this "shared illusion" of reality, and sometimes this becomes a struggle for you compassionate Fish, who can feel the pain of the world as if it were your own. There's no easy escape for you.* **Your best path is to follow a creative or spiritual pursuit while doing your work in the real world.**[57]

While this particular Pisces profile doesn't in itself disprove astrology, it does show how vague and generalized the readings are while simultaneously demonstrating just how wrong they can be. I am clearly not a "spiritual" or "mystical" person, nor am I a Christian, so I didn't identify with much in this particular reading. In another experiment, I looked up my daily horoscope. Here's the first result from an online search:

This is not a day for deep thought. You might not even be able to get a grasp on the essentials, so just do your best and try to figure it all out later. Get a friend to help piece it together.

This could apply to anyone and everyone and, if someone is feeling particularly overwhelmed (as people almost always are), they might even feel a special connection to it. Believers in astrology are welcome to continue in their belief, of course, but I'm waiting for some real, testable predictions, as opposed to the usual vague platitudes. When a Tarot card or a horoscope correctly predicts that I'll get a parking ticket Monday night and stub my toe on Friday at 6:22 a.m., I'll be more inclined to listen.

I'd like to end this chapter with a short story on the topic of astrology that I wrote in 2012. It's called "Centaurus":

ETHAN WAS ONLY 12 YEARS OLD WHEN HE PICKED UP HIS FIRST BOOK ON ASTROLOGY. HE WAS FASCINATED BY THE IDEA THAT THERE COULD BE A TRANSCENDENT RELATIONSHIP BETWEEN THE STARS AND EVENTS ON EARTH, CAPABLE OF REVEALING THE INNERMOST SECRETS NECESSARY TO UNDERSTANDING LIFE ITSELF.

HE READ THAT HE WAS A SAGITTARIUS, BORN ON NOVEMBER 25, AND INSTANTLY IDENTIFIED WITH THE SIGN. HE KNEW IT WAS TRUE AS HE READ THE POSITIVE ATTRIBUTES OF THOSE BORN BETWEEN NOV. 22 AND DEC. 21: LUCKY, GREAT LISTENER, AND ENERGETIC. BUT HE ALSO FELT THAT THE NEGATIVE PERSONALITY TRAITS DESCRIBED HIM PERFECTLY: HE WAS EASILY BORED AND OFTEN TOO IMAGINATIVE. AFTER A SHORT PERIOD OF TIME, ETHAN WAS NO LONGER JUST A CASUAL ASTROLOGICAL OBSERVER; HE BELIEVED SO WHOLEHEARTEDLY THAT, AT THE AGE OF 16, HE ADOPTED A PSEUDONYM—CENTAURUS—TO REFLECT HIS TRUE SAGITTARIAN PERSONALITY.

ONE DAY, AT AGE 17, WHEN RECEIVING A PROFESSIONAL READING, THE ASTROLOGER TOLD CENTAURUS THAT, BASED ON THE ALIGNMENT OF THE STARS, HE COULD EXPECT A TRAUMATIC TRUTH TO BE REVEALED IN THE COMING WEEK. CENTAURUS WOULD GET DEVASTATING NEWS THAT WOULD FUNDAMENTALLY RESHAPE HIS LIFE AS HE KNEW IT, ACCORDING TO THE FORTUNE TELLER.

TWO DAYS LATER, IT HAPPENED: CENTAURUS' MOTHER ASKED TO SPEAK WITH HIM PRIVATELY. "ETHAN, YOUR FATHER AND I LOVE YOU MORE THAN ANYTHING—AND I WANT YOU TO KNOW THAT. IT'S TIME YOU KNOW SOMETHING, THOUGH . . . YOU'RE ADOPTED."

CENTAURUS WOULD LATER DISCOVER THAT, NOT ONLY WAS HE ADOPTED, BUT DUE TO A MIX-UP WITH THE SHORT-FORM BIRTH CERTIFICATE, HE AND HIS ADOPTIVE PARENTS HAD BEEN CELEBRATING HIS BIRTHDAY ON THE WRONG DAY. HE WASN'T BORN ON NOV. 25. HE WAS BORN ON NOV. 20. HE WAS A SCORPIO.

"The most cursory look at cold-reading and suggestion tells us that Tarot cards are not evil; psychics do not 'usher in' the Devil or his minions; and even the creepy old Ouija board can be shown to operate via quite everyday, natural, physical forces."

—Derren Brown

NOTES

1. See the discussion in the *Introduction*, especially as relates to the James Randi Educational Foundation.

2. B. R. Forer, "The Fallacy of Personal Validation: A Classroom Demonstration of Gullibility," *Journal of Abnormal and Social Psychology* 44, no. 1 (1949): 118–123.

3. In ancient Rome and elsewhere, for instance, alleged diviners inspected entrails of sacrificed animals in a search for omens. This process is called haruspicy or haruspication.

4. Ashleigh Rainbird, "Miley Cyrus Hires Dog Psychic to Help Her Get over Death of Beloved Pet Floyd," *Mirror Online*, July 22, 2014, www.mirror.co.uk/3am/celebrity-news/miley-cyrus-hires-dog-psychic-3897981.

5. The case is *Cathy Green et al. v. Melissa Bacelar et al.*, case number BC598098, in the Superior Court of the State of California for the County of Los Angeles, Central District.

6. "The Man Behind the Mystery," Banachek Miracles of the Mind, www.banachek.com/about-us/.

7. Suroh got his name from a simple reversal of "Horus," an ancient Egyptian deity associated with the sky, war, hunting, and protection.

8. https://www.facebook.com/SurohTheSeer

9. Suroh the Seer displays a *For entertainment purposes only* notice on all of his websites and banners.

10. While researching for the book and playing Suroh the Seer, I faced the same real moral dilemmas alleged spiritualists face on a daily basis. In one scenario, the participant was so convinced of my powers that she basically begged me to charge her and forced me to come up with excuses not to take payment for services rendered. While the experience as a whole was great, I did not enjoy lying.

11. Last names have been excluded due to privacy concerns.

12. D. Druckman and J. A. Swets, eds. *Enhancing Human Performance: Issues, Theories and Techniques* (Washington, DC: National Academy Press, 1988), 22.

13. Feel free to use my list of questions as a sort of verification questionnaire for so-called psychics. Using these questions and ones like them, you can narrow down exactly what the purported psychic claims to be able to do to ensure you're not duped.

14. Alvarez gave his consent to have our exchange printed in this book and recorded on video for the public. You can find a brief clip of the discussion here: "David G. McAfee Interviews a 'Spirit Psychic,'" YouTube video, uploaded by David G. McAfee, January 5, 2015, www.youtube.com/watch?v=17Mr9LjKrkg.

15. M. Jung-Beeman et al., "Neural Activity When People Solve Verbal Problems with Insight," *PLoS Biology* 2, no. 4 (2004): e97.

16. I didn't press Alvarez on these points because of the nature of the conversation, but it is common for people to cling to quasi-scientific buzzwords when defending their unproven beliefs.

17. Alvarez never directly answered whether it's at least *possible* that he could be mistaken about his abilities. He seemed to only want to stress that he doesn't *believe* he is wrong.

18. I was pleasantly surprised to hear that Alvarez recognized this fact. There are many people who seek out psychics who claim to have answers, and some of them are too emotionally compromised to protect their own interests.

19. This is the power of confirmation bias in action. We seek out the voices of those who already agree with us in order to reinforce our opinions.

20. I found this phrasing interesting because Alvarez "thinks" he has the piece of paper. I find it difficult to believe that he hasn't checked whether he still has it even one time in the years between the Boston Marathon bombings and this interview.

21. It should be noted that, while Alvarez says he is willing to undergo testing, he adds that he wouldn't do so "*where results are demanded.*" Aren't results demanded each time someone pays for a reading? Where does he draw the line?

22. Alvarez seems to contradict his earlier statement here. He originally stated, "*Finding lost people, I have no ability to do.*"

23. This language seems to imply that Alvarez would be fine with using cold reading as long as he says things with which people can connect, but that's exactly how cold reads work. The client interprets meaning in vague statements that could apply to many people.

24. It seems as though Alvarez thinks it's impossible that another psychic has knowledge he doesn't. To me, that is quite telling of his low confidence in (at least others') psychic abilities in general.

25. Alvarez seems to have found a way, in his own mind, to make incorrect predictions the fault of his customers. Yes, this can be "validating," but it doesn't get anyone closer to the truth.

26. I didn't alter my eating or exercise patterns and didn't make any other changes that could interfere with Alvarez's prediction. Although "*digestion issues*" are common and vague, I didn't note anything out of the ordinary within the time period predicted.

27. Angelo Labate et al., "Benign Mesial Temporal Lobe Epilepsy," *Nature Reviews Neurology* 7, no. 4 (2011): 237–240.

28. H. Banister, "Experimentally Induced Olfactory Paramnesias," *British Journal of Psychology* 32 (October 1941): 155–175.

29. "Simple Partial Seizures," Neurology and Neurosurgery, Johns Hopkins University, www.hopkinsmedicine.org/neurology_neurosurgery/centers_clinics/epilepsy/seizures/types/simple-partial-seizures.html.

30. U. Voss U et al. "Induction of Self Awareness in Dreams through Frontal Low Current Stimulation of Gamma Activity," *Nature Neuroscience* 17 (2014): 810–812.

31. Elisa Filevich et al., "Metacognitive Mechanisms Underlying Lucid Dreaming," *Journal of Neuroscience* 35, no. 3 (January 2015): 1082–1088.

32. Erica A. Boschin, Carinne Piekema, and Mark J. Buckley. "Essential Functions of Primate Frontopolar Cortex in Cognition," *Proceedings of the National Academy of Sciences* 112, no. 9 (2015): E1020–E1027.

33. Brian Regal, *Pseudoscience: A Critical Encyclopedia* (Santa Barbara, CA: Greenwood Press, 2009), 29. *"Other than anecdotal eyewitness accounts, there is no evidence of the ability to astral project, the existence of other planes, or of the Akashic Record."*

34. Benjamin Radford, "Astral Projection: Just a Mind Trip," *Live Science*, March 18, 2013, www.livescience.com/27978-astral-projection.html.

35. R. Wiseman and J. Milton, "Experiment One of the SAIC Remote Viewing Program: A Critical Reevaluation," *Journal of Parapsychology* 62, no. 4 (1999): 297–308.

36. Harvey Richman and Courtney Bell, "Paranormal Beliefs Then and Now," *North American Journal of Psychology* 14, no. 1 (2012).

37. "Remote Viewing," UK Ministry of Defence, February 23, 2007 (June 2002, disclosed in 2007). 94.

38. James Randi, "The Matter of Dowsing," *Swift* 2, no. 3/4 (January 1999).

39. Jonathan C. Smith, "Preface," *Pseudoscience and Extraordinary Claims of the Paranormal: A Critical Thinker's Toolkit* (Malden, MA: Wiley-Blackwell, 2010).

40. National Science Foundation, "Science and Engineering Indicators 2014," April 2016, www.nsf.gov/statistics/seind14/index.cfm/chapter-7/c7h.htm.

41. Ulla Koch-Westenholz, *Mesopotamian Astrology: An Introduction to Babylonian and Assyrian Celestial Divination* (Copenhagen: Museum Tusculanum Press, 1995), 11.

42. John A. Paulos, *Innumeracy: Mathematical Illiteracy and Its Consequences* (New York: Hill and Wang, 1988).

43. J. H. Rogers, "Origins of the Ancient Constellations: I. The Mesopotamian Traditions," *Journal of the British Astronomical Association* 108, no.1 (1998): 9–28.

44. If we redrew the constellations today, we could end up with any number of random groupings endowed with meaning from our time period. In two thousand years, historians might ponder the significance of the *"Orion Seacrest"* constellation, for example.

45. James B. Kaler, "Alrescha (Alpha Piscium)," *Stars* (University of Illinois), stars.astro.illinois.edu/sow/alrescha.html.

46. James B. Kaler, "Kullat Nunu (Eta Piscium)," Stars (University of Illinois), stars.astro.illinois.edu/sow/kullatnunu.html.

47. Matt Williams, "Zodiac Signs and Their Dates," *Universe Today*, August 26, 2016, www.universetoday.com/38076/zodiac-signs-and-their-dates/.

48. Amara Graps, "What Is the Speed of the Solar System?" Ask A Solar Physicist FAQs, Stanford SOLAR Center, solar-center.stanford.edu/FAQ/Qsolsysspeed.html.

49. Dr. Sten Odenwald, The Astronomy Cafe, sten.astronomycafe.net/the-astronomy-cafe/.

50. M. G. Bucholtz, *The Lost Science: Esoteric Math and Astrology Techniques for the Market Trader* (iUniverse, 2013).

51. *"Were you born on Aug. 7, for example? Astrologers tell us that is smack-dab in the middle of the sign of Leo, which extends from July 23 to Aug. 22. Thus, one born on this happy day is certainly a classic Leo, correct? Wrong. You are actually born while the sun was in Cancer. Similarly, April 7, which is said to be strong Aries, is actually in Pisces."* —James Randi

52 While astrological claims have never been demonstrated scientifically, some initial-stage studies have found correlations (not causations) between personality traits and the season of a person's birth. X. Gonda et al. "Season of Birth Shows a Significant Impact on the Distribution of Affective Temperaments in a Nonclinical Population," European *Neuropsychopharmacology* 24, 2 (October 2014): S345.

53. Isn't this true of just about everyone?

54. Well, this couldn't be more wrong.

55. What does that even mean?

56. I suppose that's technically true.

57. Pisces characteristics and profile from Tarot.com. Emphasis added.

12

PREDICTIONS, PATTERNS, AND (UNFULFILLED) PROPHECIES

*"What is driving the tendency to discount Joseph Smith's revelations
is not that they seem less reasonable than those of Moses; it is
that the book containing them is so new. When it comes to prophecy,
antiquity breeds authenticity. Events in the distant past, we tend to think,
occurred in sacred, mythic time."*
—Noah Feldman

End-of-world prophecies are, at least in part, extensions of the fear of our own death. Just as we are aware that we will one day die, we know that humans won't be here forever—and we often imagine scenarios in which the earth is destroyed. These predictions aren't rare. In fact, it seems like every year there's another fringe group declaring the end of the world.

In the modern era, we hear about prophecies all the time. If it isn't a prediction from a psychic, it's a vision from a cleric. If it's not a vision from a cleric, it's a dream from a philosopher. And if it's not a dream from a philosopher, it's an ancient text that someone has imbued with new meaning. These alleged depictions of the future are popular because they captivate the imagination and, occasionally, the public at large.

THE (MANY) ENDS OF THE WORLD

In 2014, the *four blood moons* prophecy,[1] based on biblical teachings and promoted by Christian ministers including John Hagee, Mark Biltz, and Irvin Baxter, grabbed national headlines. Baxter, the president of Endtime Ministries who ran with the theory, predicted that "*a major event affecting the Jewish people*" would come to pass between April 15, 2014, and September 28, 2015, when lunar eclipses "*fall on Jewish feast days.*" While Baxter got a significant amount of media attention, and Biltz and Hagee made a lot of money from their best-selling books, *Blood Moons: Decoding the Imminent Heavenly Signs* and *Four Blood Moons: Something Is About to Change*, respectively,[2] the eclipses came and passed without incident. The eBible Fellowship then sought to resurrect the 2015 Armageddon prophecy just days after the final blood moon, claiming the world would be "*annihilated*" on October 7 of that year,[3] but that guess failed, too, as the day passed and the earth remained intact.

Before blood moon fever, many believers bought into a misinterpretation of the famous Mayan calendar that claimed the world would end on December 21, 2012. And prior to the so-called Mayan Apocalypse, there were many similar claims, including those made by the Jehovah's Witnesses, who predicted the end of the world could be in 1975,[4] and by Christian Preacher Harold Camping, who thought that the Rapture would occur on May 21, 2011. Camping thought all the good Christians would be sent to Heaven, leaving the rest of humanity to suffer Hell on Earth. But we are still alive and well and, reminiscent of archaic prophecies of the past, December 21, 2012, and May 21, 2011, featured no Earth-devastating disasters like those anticipated by believers in the Mayan myth and Camping's many followers. Despite the fact that Camping believed (as many do) that the world would end in his lifetime, he died on December 15, 2013.

You may have heard that Camping and his Family Radio Worldwide predicted a similar Armageddon-like event in 1994, and that's true, but these types of prophecies are not unique to Camping or those who promoted the blood moon prophecy. In fact, Tim LaHaye, an evangelical Christian and author of the *Left Behind* series, prophesied along with many others a "global upheaval" on January 1, 2000, but that never happened either.[5] Herbert W. Armstrong, the founder of Worldwide Church of God, also predicted that 1936 would mark "*the end of the Times of the*

Gentiles."[6] Six years later, after his earlier guess went unrealized, Armstrong said Armageddon "*must be at least three or four years away.*"[7] Armstrong amended his dates frequently, later predicting the Rapture in 1982[8] and then "*most certainly during the decade of the 90s.*"[9] Armstrong died in 1986 having seen none of his apocalyptic prophecies fulfilled.

Today every failed Judgment Day prophecy and scientific discovery is another reminder of how unnecessary superstition has become in the modern era, but many evangelical Christians, Muslims, and nonreligious people alike still continue to believe that Armageddon is imminent and cause damage as a result. Prophecies—biblical or not—are vague predictions that have no intrinsic meaning, but that doesn't mean they can't be harmful. I can't count the number of times I've met a believer who said maintenance of the earth is "*completely unnecessary*" because Jesus will return soon to save his followers.

PROPHECIES OF JESUS

These types of End Times prophecies don't solely exist within Christian communities, but they have largely become synonymous with the tradition nonetheless. That's because prophecies have been very popular within Christian sects since the religion's inception. In fact, the first documented (failed) prophecy within the Christian faith was said to have been foretold by Jesus himself, and is represented in the New Testament of the Christian Bible.

Though the would-be Mayan Apocalypse and the May 21, 2011, prophecies did not reach mainstream Christian teachings, the idea of Jesus returning for a large-scale Rapture in the near future is very much a common notion held within modern churches, including Catholic and Protestant sects. Camping and many other Christian leaders simply put a date on the anticipated event. Most followers of the Abrahamic religions believe in some sort of Rapture or End Times prophecy, but when someone says it will happen on a certain day, the idea is often written off by many as ridiculous. It's an interesting phenomenon considering what Jesus had to say about the issue.[10]

Let's take a look at the end of the world prophecies that have their basis in early Christianity. In the New Testament, the Rapture begins in 1 Thessalonians 4:15–17:

. . . we which are alive and remain unto the coming of the Lord shall not prevent them which are asleep. For the Lord himself shall descend from heaven with a shout, with the voice of the archangel, and with the trump of God: and the dead in Christ shall rise first: Then we which are alive and remain shall be caught up together with them in the clouds, to meet the Lord in the air: and so shall we ever be with the Lord.

This Rapture is just one step in a much larger Armageddon-like event, which is outlined in the Book of Revelation and other New Testament works, but when does Jesus say this will occur? On May 21, 2011, as Camping's followers believed? Or in 1995 as David Koresh's followers, the Branch Davidians, would have told you? Actually, Jesus seems to indicate that his return and "Second Coming" would take place within one generation. In Matthew 24:34, Jesus is recorded as saying:

. . . Truly I tell you, this generation will certainly not pass away until all these things have happened..

Many Christian apologists attempt to disregard this as an interpretive error. In other words, they suggest the word "generation" may have been in reference to the generation of the Hebrew people, or some variation of this. Unfortunately for this argument, the Messiah's intentions are clarified in the book of Luke. In Luke 9:26–27, Jesus reportedly says:

Whoever is ashamed of me and my words, the Son of Man will be ashamed of them when he comes in his glory and in the glory of the Father and of the holy angels. Truly I tell you, some who are standing here will not taste death before they see the kingdom of God.[11]

At least from the text, it appears Jesus certainly meant that he would return while some of his first followers were still living—and there is no known resolution for this false prophecy put forth by Jesus. Since these early times of the Christian faith, every generation of believers has felt that the end is near, and it is for this reason that these Armageddon myths continue to spring up year after year. But I often wonder how many Christians are aware of exactly what the Book of Revelation teaches, and how many realize how far-fetched and violent the Second Coming actually is.

The Bible teaches that, in the prophesized Second Coming, Jesus will descend from Heaven on a white horse wearing a robe dipped in blood. The *Prince of Peace* will then wage war and defeat the Anti-Christ (the *beast*) and Satan the Devil in the Battle of Armageddon. According to scripture, a sharp sword will come out of His mouth, so that he may "strike down the nations" and "rule them with an iron scepter." Christians believe that Jesus will cast the devil into the *Abyss* and seal it for a thousand years, and that He will resurrect human bodies from their graves, letting the good live again and condemning the evil. There are dragons, beasts with ten horns and seven heads, angels, and a lamb with seven horns and seven eyes. Christians believe that this event could happen at any time, and many believe it will happen within their own lifetime.[12] Of course, modern believers can choose to interpret these claims as fantasy or however they wish. But it's clear that many early Christians took them as a prophecy to be fulfilled in the future. It should be noted that the authors of the Book of Revelation use the words prophecy, prophesy, prophesying, prophet, and prophets 21 times in various forms throughout the text.

The notion itself is ancient, but prophecies may be more common today than ever before. The good news, however, is that the Rapture predictions from the modern era, including those by Camping, Hagee, Baxter, and others, can now join the growing number of unfulfilled Christian prophecies that began with the one foretold by Jesus Christ in the Bible. These once-popular ideas will be tossed out alongside other end-of-the-world predictions from our past, including those by Heaven's Gate, Charles Manson, Martin Luther, Christopher Columbus, and Pope Innocent III.[13]

From the Christian prophecies outlined above to the all-too-popular 2012 Mayan Calendar misinterpretation, End Times predictions with differing origins have dominated religious discourse throughout the ages. All of these prophecies, however, share one key similarity: to date, none of them have proved to be true, and each predicted Armageddon day has passed by rather uneventfully.

OTHER PROPHECIES IN RELIGIOUS TEXTS

If a holy text aligned with scientific findings, as many believers claim about their books, then we would expect to see discoveries prompted only by a reading. But that's not the case. Instead, we get vague "prophetical" assertions that can't be successfully used to make an accurate and recognizable prediction before an event. That's why the arbitrary prophecies found within all religious texts have been shown to be just as predictive as those of a professional cold reader.

One common example of an alleged biblical prophecy is the so-called mark of the beast,[14] which many modern believers have concluded *must* actually be a reference to government-ordered microchip implants in the right hand or forehead. In order to believe this, however, adherents must completely ignore that the Bible says nothing about microchips and that such a system has never been instituted by any governing body. Just like most alleged prophecies, this mark-of-the-beast idea has been shown to be nothing more than a vague line of text that has been interpreted in numerous ways by people of various times.

In 2013, as President Barack Obama sought congressional approval to attack Syria for its use of chemical weapons, another biblical prophecy resurfaced as seemingly being fulfilled (if only in the minds of believers). The events in Syria were seen by many believers as a sign of the End Times, but I have to be honest in saying their evidence for this connection, a passage from the Bible,[15] isn't impressive or chilling. Here's the quote: "*See, Damascus will no longer be a city but will become a heap of ruins.*" Let's look at the facts: Damascus was first settled in the second millennium BCE, so how many times since then do you think it has been threatened by some sort of military action? If a city in that region didn't see some sort of threat after more than two thousand years, that'd be impressive—not the other way around.

ISLAM AND SCIENTIFIC FOREKNOWLEDGE

A lot of Christian prophecies are rooted in Judaism, which is also the source of Islam and its heavy reliance on predictions and foreknowledge. The Ahmadiyya Muslim Community and many other Muslim apologists suggest their holy book, the Qur'an, foretold everything from fingerprinting to genetic engineering[16] to the speed of light. But it seems as though Allah has cleverly disguised these prophecies in vague pieces of text that could only be interpreted in that way once a discovery has been made. In other words, while many Muslims believe the Qur'an predicted modern communication systems, none will show proof that cell phones and social media websites were believed in and understood hundreds of years ago when the text was written. Instead, they will likely point to Qur'an 81:7, which in some translations reads, *"And when various people are brought together."* Is suggesting at some point in time some group of people will be brought together really a clear "prophecy"? Does it show the authors of the Qur'an had intimate knowledge of future events? My basic reasoning skills tell me no.

These religious predictions are often intentionally vague and therefore difficult to completely debunk, but one common piece of alleged scientific foreknowledge in the Qur'an is particularly interesting because it's blatantly false. A surprising number of Muslims claim that the Qur'an made accurate scientific predictions about *"two seas meeting together"* with a *"barrier which none of them can transgress,"*[17] sometimes in conjunction with a photograph of what looks to be two oceans coming together but refusing to mix. There are common stories that go along with this prophecy, including that French explorer Jacques Cousteau discovered the phenomenon and that it made him accept Islam,[18] but even just a small amount of research shows us that this is merely a myth supporting more myths. Firstly, Cousteau didn't discover the spot where oceans don't mix, because it doesn't exist. And secondly, he never converted to Islam. This is a fact that has been proven and accepted by nearly everyone, including the Cousteau Society, which stated in 1991 that its founder *"has not become a Muslim"* and that the rumor was passed *"without foundation,"* and even certain Muslim groups. Cousteau, who was alive at that time and did not repudiate his foundation's statement, had a Roman Catholic funeral when he died years later.[19]

This piece of alleged Qur'anic prophecy is further called into question by the fact that the false story is often passed along with photos purportedly showing two oceans with different salinity levels that touch but don't mix. The problem with the pictures, taken by Ken Bruland, a professor of ocean sciences at the University of California, Santa Cruz,[20] and photographer Kent Smith,[21] is that they don't depict two oceans meeting at all. According to Bruland, the interesting shot is actually the result of *"glacial rivers"* that carry sediments into the ocean. Experts say this is not a static place *"where oceans meet"* and that, despite appearances, the waters are mixing together all the time.[22]

There is a seemingly never-ending stream of claimed prophecies stemming from the Qur'an, and every year there are more. With each new scientific discovery, apologists for Islam (and other religions) from around the world jump at the chance to say their holy book predicted it hundreds of years ago. When modern astronomers said ancient supernovas were a source of Earth's iron,[23] some Muslims pointed to Qur'an 57:25, which says, *"We sent down iron, wherein is great military might and benefits for the people. . ."* Because the Qur'an states that iron was *"sent down,"* they reason, its writers *must* have been predicting the source of the material in 10-billion-year-old exploding stars. This happened again with the 2016 discovery of gravitational waves,[24] ripples in the curvature of spacetime that were predicted by Albert Einstein.[25] Instead of marveling at the real "prophecy," which was foretold by Einstein through his theory of general relativity, Muslims all over the world pointed to the Qur'an hoping to claim credit. But Qur'an 21:33, the verse most often put forth alongside this claim, doesn't say anything about gravitational radiation or binary star systems. Instead, it says, *"And it is He who created the night and the day and the sun and the moon; all [heavenly bodies] in an orbit are swimming."* Once again, to anyone thinking critically, this verse does not meet the standards of a statement that predicts anything—let alone the direct observance of gravitational waves.

The fact is that none of these scientific discoveries were predicted by the Qur'an or any other holy book—it's always post event rationalization and pattern detection. These are simply findings that, in hindsight, people forced into their religious texts to give the illusion of scientific accuracy. No one has ever read the Qur'an and, through that process, discovered a new scientific theory. It has never provided any new information as far as science is concerned. Furthermore, the Qur'an doesn't describe any novel discoveries with specificity that could actually be helpful, and you can find nearly identical "predictions" in every religion and holy book. For these reasons, vague verses pulled out of context are more like horoscopes than scientific predictions. Believers can make them mean whatever they'd like with a little mental gymnastics.

MAKING A PROPHECY

The beautiful thing about prophecies, the trait that grants them such wide appeal, is that they can be made out of anything or nothing at all. All you need is your imagination and any book, speech, cinema scene, tweet, etc. can be endowed with predictive meaning and world-changing importance. We could take any poorly written teen romance novel, *Twilight* for instance, and, using scientific facts, make it seem as though it is prophetic to anyone who *wants* to believe. That process looks like this:

1. Stephenie Meyer, formerly a receptionist, had little or no knowledge of bats and their biology when she published the first *Twilight* book in 2005.

2. Meyer's book contained vampire characters that sparkled when exposed to sunlight, as opposed to being destroyed by it as traditional vampires would be.

3. Certain types of insect-eating bats, because of their diet heavy in shiny bugs, produce sparkly feces or guano.[26]

4. Therefore, Meyer must have had some form of subconscious knowledge of bat anatomy and habits that was given to her by a god.

The prophecies don't usually stop after one. If *Twilight* predicted sparkly bat guano, what else could its author have foretold? Perhaps the struggle between werewolves and vampires represents contentious elections between liberals and conservatives. Or maybe a child born to the two main characters predicts the coming of a savior figure to the world. When your imagination is the limit, any prophecy can seem reasonable.

I'm not the only one to create my own prophecies using popular books. Dr. Carl H. Fischer, a chief technologist known as Atheist Engineer,[27] compiled a fascinating list of Dr. Seuss works that could be interpreted as prophetic texts. In his post,[28] Fischer shows how *Green Eggs and Ham* could actually have been a prediction about genetically modified foods or about mankind finding the value in molds like penicillin,[29] and that *One Fish Two Fish Red Fish Blue Fish* is really a prophecy for "*evolutionary changes in species and the discovery of the Tiktaalik fossils.*" Fischer lists more than a dozen examples, including prophecies from books like *The Cat in the Hat* and *Oh, the Places You'll Go!*

"*See how it's done? Simply pick a verse and find something plausible that it could be an analogy for after-the-fact,*" Fischer wrote. "*There are enough flowery and non-specific verses in the Bible to satisfy nearly any event.*"

ALLEGED PROPHECIES OF NOSTRADAMUS

There are countless alleged prophecies that people have accepted and promoted throughout human history, but perhaps none are as commonly known or believed as those of French apothecary and astrologer Michel de Nostredame, more commonly known as Nostradamus. Nostradamus is often credited with foreseeing large-scale events, including the September 11, 2001 attacks on the United States, the coming of Hitler, and the sinking of the *Titanic*. But let's look at what Nostradamus the man actually wrote before analyzing the predictive capabilities of Nostradamus the legend.

Claim: Nostradamus predicted that the World Trade Center towers in New York would be attacked and destroyed on September 11, 2001.

What Nostradamus actually wrote: "*Earth-shaking flames from the world's center roar / And make the earth around a 'New City' quiver.*"[30]

What it sounds like: To me it sounds as if Nostradamus was telling a story about a volcano eruption or an earthquake, but nothing indicates special knowledge of a terrorist attack.

Claim: Nostradamus foretold the coming of the atomic bomb.

What Nostradamus actually wrote: "*Near the gates and within two cities / There will be scourges the like of which was never seen, / Famine within plague, people put out by steel, / Crying to the great immortal God for relief.*"[31]

What it sounds like: Nostradamus is clearly writing about some sort of disaster involving two cities, but what do the gates represent? And couldn't these lines just as easily be describing any large-scale fatal event?

Claim: Nostradamus wrote about the assassinations of John F. Kennedy and Robert F. Kennedy hundreds of years before they actually occurred.

What Nostradamus actually wrote: *"The great man will be struck down in the day by a thunderbolt, / An evil deed foretold by the bearer of a petition. / According to the prediction, another falls at night time. / Conflict at Reims, London and a pestilence in Tuscany."*[32]

What it sounds like: This could refer to any great leader, and the "prediction" makes no mention of the second to fall as a relative. The terms are vague enough to fit with anything, but specific enough that we wonder how the assassinations could have caused infectious diseases in Tuscany.

Claim: Nostradamus prophesied the fatal explosion of NASA's *Challenger* space shuttle, which killed seven people in 1986.

What Nostradamus actually wrote: *"Nine will be set aside from the human flock, / Removed from judgment and counsel: / Their fate will be determined on departure / Kappa, Thita, Lambda, dead, banished, astray."*[33]

What it sounds like: The *Challenger* disaster killed seven people, not nine, and although the crash was caused by defective parts from a company called Thiokol, nothing in the prophecy seems to relate to this event at all.

As you can see, Nostradamus wrote his prophecies each in four-line poems often using ambiguous language, so the brief poetic sentences can be interpreted in incredibly varied ways by different readers. His quatrains were ultimately published in a book called *Centuries*, and people all over the world were free to interpret them, using their own preconceived notions as a basis, for more than four hundred years after the author's death. This format has allowed believers to forge their own meanings and to shoehorn current events into short, often nonsensical lines. To make matters worse, due to his popularity, there are thousands of fake Nostradamus prophecies being circulated and many people unquestioningly accept them as legitimate. The key to understanding Nostradamus' popular appeal and reputation as an accurate future-teller lies within his writing style. Benjamin Radford, science writer and author of *Mysterious New Mexico: Miracles, Magic, and*

Monsters in the Land of Enchantment, says Nostradamus was "*clever enough to couch his quatrains in such vague terms that people read whatever they want into them.*" The famous seer "*wrote in Middle French, using vague words, metaphors and obscure, badly dated references,*" according to Radford.

"*Despite his legions of followers, a close analysis of* Nostradamus's *writings reveals that he did not make predictions (statements that come true after you read them) instead he makes post-dictions (statements that appear to come true only after the events happen),*" he wrote for *Live Science*.[34] "*If Nostradamus had truly predicted the September 11 attacks, World War II, or the Challenger shuttle accident, for example, the world should have known about them decades (indeed centuries) before they occurred.*"

OTHER PREDICTIONS

Not all predictions are as old or mysterious as those put forth by Nostradamus. When I said you can make a prophecy out of anything, I meant it. A good example of this is Rick Joyner, the founder and executive director of MorningStar Ministries and Heritage International Ministries, who disclosed a prophecy related to the Super Bowl 50 football championship in 2016. According to Joyner, Bob Jones, an evangelist and founder of Bob Jones University, prophesied in 1988 that "*black panthers are coming to the lumber yard in Charlotte.*" Jones and Joyner initially thought this meant "*some kind of attack was coming,*" but after Charlotte got a National Football League team that built its stadium on an old lumber yard, they "*knew it was a God thing,*" Joyner said.

"*Bob then got more on this, and how they would be prophetic of something that would break out in Charlotte when they won the Super Bowl. If they do win this 50th Super Bowl it will be a sign to us, and the beginning of a great Jubilee,*" Joyner wrote.[35] "*I understand if you did not know Bob and think this is a real stretch, or even crazy, but we witnessed him a number of times tell us who would win either the World Series (which he called 'the world seriousness,' and it was often a remarkable sign of things that would happen in the world,) or other sporting events. Occasionally he would even get scores to games before they were played, which were often signs indicating certain Scriptures etc. that turned out to be prophetic and accurate.*"

The Carolina Panthers ended up losing the game, with the Denver Broncos scoring 24 points to the Panthers' 10, but there was no follow-up from Joyner. He didn't tell us what a loss meant, how common these misses are in prophecies, or why Jones would have had a prediction about his city losing a Super Bowl. He just moved on, like all fortune-tellers must when their guesses have failed, and continued to preach his prophecy-based message.

This failed prediction was just a bad guess, but other alleged prophecies are more like good guesses. For instance, some people say Ralph Epperson, a conspiracy theorist who published a book called *New World Order* in 1990, actually prophesied the coming of a global government controlled by powerful elites. This belief is based on the fact that, in Epperson's book, he describes what the New World Order would look like. He says a number of outlandish things, including that religion and private property ownership will be "*outlawed*," but what most people know about are his notes regarding "the family." Epperson did predict that "*homosexual marriages will be legalized*," which happened in the United States in 2015, so that could be considered a good guess. Within that same paragraph, however, the author suggests that "*parents will not be allowed to raise their children*" and that "*all women will be employed by the state and not allowed to be 'homemakers.'*"[36] Given that none of these other predictions have come to fruition, and only one line of Epperson's New World Order prophecy has even remotely come to pass, I think it's safe to write this off as a lucky accident.

While good and bad fortune and vague terms are factors to consider when analyzing supernatural future-telling, occasionally a seemingly realized prophecy comes down to fraud. In other words, some prophecies appear to have been fulfilled only because they were secretly written after the event they intend to describe. These hindsight "predictions," also called *vaticinium ex eventu* (or prophecy from the event), are intentionally misleading and can be found throughout religious and secular writings all over the world. One of the most popular examples of this is found in the words attributed to Jesus in the Gospels, when he allegedly foretells the destruction of Jerusalem and its temple. Because of the fact that the Gospels were all written after the siege of Jerusalem in 70 CE in which the temple was destroyed, historians consider this prediction to be *vaticinium ex eventu*.[37]

"Have you ever thought what a God would be like who actually ordained and executed the cruelty that is in [the biblical Book of Revelation]? A holocaust of mankind. Yet so many of these Bible-men accept the idea without a second thought."

—C. J. Sansom

NOTES

1. Acts 2:20 and Revelation 6:12.

2. Sarah Bailey, "'Blood Moon' Sets Off Apocalyptic Debate among Some Christians," *Washington Post*, April 15, 2014.

3. Adam Gabbatt, "Christian Group Predicts the World Will Be 'Annihilated' on Wednesday," *Guardian*, October 6, 2015.

4. Richard Singelenberg, "It Separated the Wheat from the Chaff: The 1975 Prophecy and Its Impact among Dutch Jehovah's Witnesses," *Sociological Analysis* 50 (Spring 1989): 23–40.

5. Hanna Rosin, "As Jan. 1 Draws Near, Doomsayers Reconsider," *Washington Post*, December 27, 1999, www.washingtonpost.com/wp-srv/WPcap/1999-12/27/069r-122799-idx.html.

6. Herbert W. Armstrong, "What Is Going to Happen!" *Plain Truth*, June–July 1934.

7. Herbert W. Armstrong, "Democracy Doomed!" *Plain Truth*, April-May 1940.

8. Herbert W. Armstrong, "The World Tomorrow," *Plain Truth*, May 22, 1953.

9. Herbert W. Armstrong, "Brethren & Co-Worker Letters," *Plain Truth*, January 3, 1980.

10. Matthew 24:42: "Therefore keep watch, because you do not know on what day your Lord will come."

11. Another version of this is found in Matthew 16:28: "*Truly I tell you, some who are standing here will not taste death before they see the Son of Man coming in his kingdom.*"

12. Book of Revelation 19: 11–20 and 20: 1–3, 7-15 and John 5:28–29.

13. William P. Lazarus and Mark Sullivan, *Comparative Religion for Dummies* (New York: John Wiley & Sons, 2008), 237.

14. Book of Revelation 13:16–18: "*It also forced all people, great and small, rich and poor, free and slave, to receive a mark on their right hands or on their foreheads, so that they could not buy or sell unless they had the mark, which is the name of the beast or the number of its name. This calls for wisdom. Let the person who has insight calculate the number of the beast, for it is the number of a man. That number is 666.*"

15. Isaiah 17:1

16. Ansar Raza, "Fulfilled Prophecies of the Holy Quran," Al Islam, Ahmadiyya Muslim Community, www.alislam.org/library/articles/prophecies. html.

17. Qur'an 55:19–20

18. Waleed el-Shobaki, "Qur'an's Confirmation of an Amazing Undersea Discovery," TruthPrevailed.wordpress.com, January 7, 2012.

19. Jacques-Yves Cousteau, FindAGrave.com, Memorial no. 9889, June 7, 2000.

20. Ben Anderson, "USGS Researchers Participate in Research Cruise Studying Iron Biogeochemistry in the Gulf of Alaska," US Geological Survey, March 2008.

21. https://www.flickr.com/photos/kentsmith9/4955772693/

22. Ben Anderson, "Mythbusting 'The Place Where Two Oceans Meet' in the Gulf of Alaska," *Alaska Dispatch News*, February 5, 2013.

23. Kate Maguire et al, "PTF10ops—a Subluminous, Normal-Width Light Curve Type Ia Supernova in the Middle of Nowhere," *Monthly Notices of the Royal Astronomical Society* 418, no. 2 (2011): 747–758.

24. B. P. Abbott et al., "Observation of Gravitational Waves from a Binary Black Hole Merger," *Physical Review Letters* 116, no. 6 (2016).

25. Albert Einstein, "Über Gravitationswellen," *Sitzungsberichte der Königlich Preussischen Akademie der Wissenschaften* (Berlin), 1918, 154–167.

26. Scott E. Hygnstrom, Robert M. Timm, and Gary E. Larson, eds. *Prevention and Control of Wildlife Damage*, 2 vols. (University of Nebraska-Lincoln, January 1994)

27. Atheist Engineer, www.atheistengineer.com/.

28. "The 'Prophecies' of Dr. Seuss," Atheist Engineer, June 6, 2015, www.atheistengineer.com/2015/06/the-of-dr-seuss.html.

29. In actuality, *Green Eggs and Ham* was the result of a bet between Seuss and his editor, who challenged him to write a book using fifty words or fewer. Stacy Conradt, "10 Stories behind Dr. Seuss Stories," *CNN*, January 23, 2009, www.cnn.com/2009/LIVING/wayoflife/01/23/mf.seuss.stories.behind/index.html.

30. Peter Lemesurier, *Nostradamus, Bibliomancer: The Man, the Myth, the Truth* (Pompton Plains, NJ: New Page Books, 2010).

31. Edgar Leoni, *Nostradamus and His Prophecies* (Mineola, NY: Dover Publications, 2000).

32. James Kalat, *Introduction to Psychology* (Belmont, CA: Cengage Learning, 2016).

33. Steve Bright, "Nostradamus: A Challenge to Biblical Prophecy?" *Christian Research Journal* 25, no. 2 (2002).

34. Benjamin Radford, "Nostradamus: Predictions of Things Past," *LiveScience*, October 23, 2012, www.livescience.com/24213-nostradamus.html.

35. Rick Joyner, post on Facebook, January 25, 2016, www.facebook.com/RickJoyner.MorningStar/posts/1183456831687132.

36. A. Ralph Epperson, *The New World Order* (Publius Press, 1990).

37. Richard N. Soulen and R. Kendall Soulen, *Handbook of Biblical Criticism*, 3rd ed. (Louisville, KY: Westminster John Knox Press, 2001), 204.

13

AFTERLIVES
AND NEAR-DEATH EXPERIENCES

*"You have two lives. The second one begins
when you realize you only have one."*
—Unknown[1]

As a naturalist, I'm often asked what I believe will happen when I die. But for me, it's not about what I believe; as usual, it's about the evidence. The brain stops working after death. We are no longer alive, and our memories and everything that makes us *us* are no longer available. This is all proven and, if there is something in excess of that, it will have to be shown to exist.[2] Until then, it is common sense to abstain from believing in it.

HUMANS ARE ANIMALS

When approached about my thoughts or opinions on the afterlife by believers, I like to respond by asking, "What do you think happens to a fish or a bird when it dies? Or, for that matter, what happens to a fungus at its death?" It's truly amazing that so many people think humans are somehow divinely separated from other animals, and are therefore deserving of a second, eternal life filled with either pleasure or pain.

If you understand and accept evolution by natural selection, you can see that we are still just animals sharing an ecosystem with other animals—

and we can trace our evolutionary trail back at least 85 million years.[3] *Homo sapiens* is a part of a branch of great apes called the hominin clade, which evolved from our hominid ancestors. In fact, we are the only surviving members of this group, which once included other apes with standing posture, tool use, etc. All of these apes, including our species and the extinct hominine species *Sahelanthropus tchadensis*, as well as all other animals, are members of the *Kingdom Animalia*.

People who don't think humans evolved alongside other animals often argue that we are separate from the rest because we walk upright, or because we have large brains for our size or premature births, and these are all for the most part true. But that doesn't mean we aren't animals. It means we are animals with larger brains, proportionally, than many others—and that, as a result of those large brains and other factors, human babies are born when they are relatively undeveloped. This doesn't make us *superior*, and in many ways this is a disadvantage as our children are brought into this world helpless. As for bipedalism, it's an important part of how humans evolved but it doesn't mean we are special and distinct from other animals. Birds walk on two feet, too, as do some other apes. A number of lizards can even run bipedally—and an ancient lizard-like reptile was likely the first to do so![4]

We have different sets of skills, but humans are not objectively *better* than the other animals, even though so many believe we are somehow spiritually above them. We are animals like any other and we are all made of the same biological materials.[5] We may be more *aware* by our own standards (although there's not yet a way for us to determine this with certainty), but other animals are superior in other ways according to other standards. And many animals, like us, think, feel, change their environments, communicate among themselves, and more.[6] As Southern California attorney Edward Alberola pointed out, *"Those who describe animals as not having any thoughts or feelings come closer to that description than the animals they are trying to describe."*

Humans are inherently inclined to think we are superior to other animals, just as those animals likely see themselves as the center of their worlds. Try to put yourself in the position of an American robin, who could be thinking, "The earth was made for me! If that weren't the case, why would it have all these twigs with which to build my nest?" Despite these skewed perceptions of worth, however, you and I aren't important to the universe, which is indifferent toward animal life in general.[7] Because of our desire to be special or somehow more important than other creatures, many people forget how often our "animal instincts" still guide our daily decisions. From with whom we mate to what we eat and more, the process of evolution by natural selection affects our choices every day just as it does with other creatures. And our wishes and beliefs to be different don't make us so. It was Australian philosopher Peter Singer who drew attention to the fact that humans and many other animals share the most important things in life, including the ability to suffer and feel pain.

"*All the arguments to prove man's superiority cannot shatter this hard fact: in suffering the animals are our equals*," Singer said.[8]

In the end, there's no reason to believe anything special happens to humans after death and any other position is contrary to all available evidence. Think about it: if you accept evolution, but you also believe humans have a "soul" and are therefore subject to a special afterlife beyond what's been proven to exist, then when did we gain that soul? Did *Homo habilis* have a soul? *Homo ergaster*? Do you believe a god or other force spontaneously added a soul once we were officially classified as *Homo sapiens*? Whether the question is of our origin or our destination, I'm more comfortable accepting scientific understandings—as opposed to embracing cultural myths as reality out of familiarity or a desire to feel superior.

AFTERLIVES AS COPING MECHANISMS

Heaven and Hell are the most commonly accepted afterlives, especially in the United States, where polls show about 72 percent of the adult population believes in Heaven and 58 percent in Hell.[9] Contrary to popular belief, however, heavens and hells aren't unique creations of the Abrahamic religions. Both of these concepts have been around for as long as people have had folklore, and they represent our desire for a sense of justice in opposing forces.[10] Versions of these myths that predate Judaism include Aaru (ancient Egyptian), Trayastrimsa (Hindu/Buddhist), and Tartarus (ancient Greek). Heavens and hells make sense to many people because they believe good and bad behaviors should be rewarded and punished, respectively. Despite their popularity and presence in myths from all around the world, however, there is no objective proof either of these planes exist as anything more than literary tools and emotional security blankets.

There is no scientific evidence to reasonably suggest the existence of any afterlife, be it reincarnation, Heaven, Hell, or any other spirit world. These are most likely man-made ideas that arose because we, as members of an intellectually advanced species, are aware of our own impending death. Some people are so fearful of knowing they will die that they cling to illusions—ideas that sound *fair* or just or simply make them feel better in general. In that regard, afterlives are often nothing more than coping mechanisms. We are told that our family members and other loved ones are in Heaven, or that they are ghosts or that they've been reincarnated, for the very same reasons we were told our childhood dog "went away to go live on a farm." It's important to recognize that, while many people believe in various forms of life after death, these concepts have no established place in reality.

The lack of evidence for an afterlife doesn't make me sad because I see that we, like all other animals here on Earth, get one amazing life to live . . . and the fact that it is finite is what makes it special. Not only is this mentality based on facts instead of emotion, but it also encourages us to make the most out of the one life we are guaranteed to have. Mark Twain may have said it best when he said, "Annihilation has no terrors for me, because I have already tried it before I was born—a hundred million years—and I have suffered more in an hour, in this life, than I remember to have suffered in the whole hundred million years put together." I can say that I see death in a similar light as Twain, as I've never feared it, only accepted it as an inevitability—a motivator for accomplishing as much as I can in this life without dreaming up a next.[11]

A popular objection to the commonsense notion that this life is all we get is that, "There must be an afterlife. Our energy can't be created or destroyed!" But this argument is based on a fundamental misunderstanding of "energy." If you talk to any physicist, you'll learn that our energy isn't destroyed at death. Every particle that composes us remains here in this world, the same particles that made up stars billions of years ago; they are just redistributed differently. This energy might disperse into the atmosphere or the earth through cremation or decomposition—but it will always be here.

NEAR-DEATH EXPERIENCES

A lot of people claim to have special knowledge of a particular afterlife that was revealed during a **near-death experience (NDE),** including a neurosurgeon[12] and a six-year-old boy who told his story about meeting angels in *The Boy Who Came Back from Heaven* and later said he made it all up to get "*attention.*"[13] Scientific evidence, however, suggests these events are caused by chemical reactions within the brain and are not real-world occurrences from any external forces.[14] It may surprise you to know that, while they often seem magical when we are experiencing them, NDEs aren't exactly mysterious. By that I mean that, although there *are* differences of opinions among researchers about exactly what parts of the brain are responsible for which types of feelings and hallucinations, these disagreements are scientific—and not theological—in nature.[15] And perhaps most importantly, scientists are looking into and discovering more about NDEs all the time.

One of the scientists uncovering the secrets of NDEs is Dr. Sam Parnia, assistant professor of critical care medicine and director of resuscitation research at Stony Brook Medicine, who led the world's largest medical study on the state of mind and consciousness at the time of death.[16] The international study, which took place over the course of four years, analyzed 2,060 cardiac arrest cases and concluded that there are at least seven types of memories that patients retained related to their own death. Those recollections were categorized as fear, animals/plants, a bright light, violence/persecution, déjà vu, family, and recalling events after recovery from cardiac arrest. Parnia stated that death, contrary to popular belief, "*is not a specific moment but a potentially reversible process that occurs after any severe illness or accident causes the heart, lungs and brain to cease functioning.*"

"*If attempts are made to reverse this process, it is referred to as 'cardiac arrest'; however, if these attempts do not succeed it is called 'death,'*" Parnia wrote in a news release published by Stony Brook. "*In this study we wanted to go beyond the emotionally charged yet poorly defined term of NDEs to explore objectively what happens when we die.*"

Researchers from the University of Maribor in Slovenia have also looked into NDEs. In one study,[17] the scientists investigated whether or not different levels of carbon dioxide play a role in the mystical experiences reported by a relatively high percentage of cardiac arrest survivors.[18]

They looked at 52 heart attack patients and determined that higher concentrations of CO2 *"proved significant"* and that higher serum levels of potassium *"might be important in the provoking of NDEs."*

"As these associations have not been reported before, our study adds new and important information to the field of NDE phenomena," the authors of the study wrote in the conclusion. *"As quality of life of NDE patients might be affected, NDEs warrant further study. Likewise, more rigorous measures to establish good acid-base equilibrium should be adopted in resuscitation guidelines."*

Not all brain specialists agree with the conclusions of the Slovenia study. For example, neuropsychiatrist Dr. Peter Fenwick, a senior lecturer at King's College, London, has rejected the idea that CO2 plays a role in NDEs.

"The one difficulty in arguing that CO2 is the cause is that in cardiac arrests, everybody has high CO2 but only 10 percent have NDEs," Fenwick told *National Geographic*,[19] adding that heart attack patients might not have the brain power necessary for vivid experiences. *"[T]here is no coherent cerebral activity which could support consciousness, let alone an experience with the clarity of an NDE."*

While some researchers have suggested NDEs are dissociative defense mechanisms that occur in times of extreme danger, conflicting studies have put forth explanations based on reduced supplies of oxygen to the brain, endorphins, and abnormal brain activity in the temporal lobes.[20] Still other near-death researchers disagree about the very nature of the experiences themselves. For example, researchers at the Phase Research Center (formerly known as OOBE Research Center) in Los Angeles, which purports to study and help people control out-of-body experiences, lucid dreams, and astral projections, claim they can *"deliberately reproduce"* NDEs. They say their 2012 NDE-simulating experiment,[21] in which 20 volunteers in no danger of dying were able to experience flying through a tunnel and other events associated with near-death memories, *"casts doubt on many earlier theories"* on the origin of these events. Michael Raduga, founder and head of the Phase Research Center, says REM sleep *"may indeed help explain at least a portion of near-death experiences."*

"This is vouched for by the ability to artificially reproduce the near-death experience using techniques for achieving out-of-body experience, itself only being possible during REM sleep," Raduga wrote in the conclusion of the

study. *"In terms of sensation, experiences thus achieved differ in no way from spontaneous near-death ones at clinical death, and specifically—flights through a tunnel towards the light."*

Despite there not being a scientific consensus on the specific origins of NDEs, the fact that this phenomenon can be studied, and even recreated in a laboratory setting by administering ketamine and through other tactics, shows us that it is likely a completely natural occurrence—as opposed to a paranormal or divine one. Dr. Caroline Watt, a senior lecturer in psychology at the University of Edinburgh and a founding member of the school's Koestler Parapsychology Unit, is one of many experts who has criticized supernatural assertions made by NDE researchers, including Parnia's claim that 2 percent of patients who experienced the phenomenon were capable of "seeing" and "hearing" certain events while they were unconscious.

"Basically the objectively verifiable test of awareness was hidden images on shelves. The one 'verifiable period of conscious awareness' that Parnia was able to report did not relate to this objective test," Watt told Sharon Hill of JREF.[22] *"Rather, it was a patient giving a supposedly accurate report of events during his resuscitation. This included hearing an Automated External Defibrillator machine. But it is possible that he had previous experience of such machines, for instance from watching medical dramas on TV. So was he recalling something from a period of unconsciousness, or was he possibly reconstructing a plausible sequence of events based on memory and prior life experience?"*

Watt is also one of the authors of a paper titled, "There Is Nothing Paranormal about Near-Death Experiences: How Neuroscience Can Explain Seeing Bright Lights, Meeting the Dead, or Being Convinced You Are One of Them."[23] In that paper, Watt and neuroscientist Dean Mobbs say the scientific evidence suggests that all aspects of NDEs *"have a neurophysiological or psychological basis."*

"[T]he vivid pleasure frequently experienced in near-death experiences may be the result of fear-elicited opioid release, while the life review and REM components of the near-death experience could be attributed to the action of the locus coeruleus-noradrenaline system," the authors wrote. *"Out-of-body experiences and feelings of disconnection with the physical body could arise because of a breakdown in multisensory processes, and the bright lights and tunneling could be the result of a peripheral to fovea breakdown of the visual system through oxygen deprivation. A priori expectations, where the individual makes sense of the situation by believing they will experience the archetypal*

near-death experience package, may also play a crucial role."

While there are a number of disagreements between scientists on the issues surrounding NDEs, they all agree on two things: (1) the experiences are relatively common, with somewhere between 9 and 18 percent of the population having reported them,[2425] and (2) the content of near-death memories changes based on the patient's culture.

CULTURAL IMPLICATIONS OF NEAR-DEATH EXPERIENCES

There are a number of believers who think their and others' near-death or out-of-body experiences (OOBEs) are proof of an afterlife, but even the most imaginative reports of the various afterlives don't seem much like "life" to me. NDE memories usually consist of vague colors and feelings, and when there are specifics, we don't ever see anything truly groundbreaking—it's often just the same recited lines from the movies. The problem here is obvious: during what are more appropriately called near-death *hallucinations*, people tend to see what they expect to see—what's culturally familiar. In other words, during NDEs, a Christian is more likely to see Jesus and angels while a Hindu will probably see *Yama*, the god of death, and his messengers, called *yamadoots*.

Satwant Pasricha, the head of the Department of Clinical Psychology at National Institute of Mental Health and Neurosciences (NIMHANS) in Bangalore, India, specializes in analyzing NDE reports throughout the country. In one study,[26] Pasricha found that patients who report NDEs might "*go through some common experiences irrespective of their cultural background.*" The specific details of the memories, however, varied greatly depending on belief. One of his subjects, a 60-year-old woman named Javanamma, reported being "*dragged up*" by four yamadoots.

"*I saw one door, and went inside. I saw my mother and father there. I also saw the Yama who was fat and had books in front of him. The Yama started beating the yamadoots for having taken me there instead of another person,*" Javanamma recounted during her interview with the researchers. "*I was asked by my parents and the Yama to be sent back. I was scared to be there because there were so many people, and I was happy to be back so I could see my children.*"

In yet another similar case, Pasricha and his team interviewed Gowramma, a 22-year-old woman who fell unconscious for approximately

10 minutes. She reported having an OOBE in which she could see her body lying down below.

"*I was taken up by some messengers in a jeep to Yamapatna (the place where Yama, the god of the dead, lives). He had a listing of names in the books,*" Gowramma told the scientists. "*Yama looked into the books and told the messengers, 'Send her back; she still has not completed her time.'*"

Others researching NDEs from a phenomenological perspective have similarly discovered notable differences and commonalities between non-Western experiences and those reported by Americans and Europeans. In one cross-cultural analysis,[27] Mahendra Perera, a consultant psychiatrist and senior fellow of psychiatry at the University of Melbourne, Australia, and others concluded that "*although there are common themes, there are also reported differences in NDEs.*"

"*The variability across cultures is most likely to be due to our interpretation and verbalizing of such esoteric events through the filters of language, cultural experiences, religion, education and their influence on our belief systems either shedding influence as an individual variable or more often perhaps by their rich interplay between these factors,*" the authors of the study wrote.

Modern scientific inquiries help us better understand the nature of NDEs, but we must also recognize that these types of near-death reports go back thousands of years. For instance, in the Myth of Er, the legend that concludes Plato's *The Republic*, a man who died in battle is revived and recounts his experiences. He did not see Jesus or Yama, however; instead, he saw "*a shaft of light stretching from above straight through earth and heaven, like a pillar, closely resembling a rainbow, only brighter and clearer,*" among other things.[28] This mythological tale is considered by some experts to be "*the oldest known direct account of an NDE,*"[29] while the oldest verified medical report of such an experience can be traced back to a French military physician in 1740. The doctor, Pierre-Jean du Monchaux, wrote about a patient who was unconscious for a long period of time before waking up and reporting that he saw "*such a pure and extreme light that he thought he was in Heaven.*"

"*He remembered this sensation very well, and affirmed that never of all his life had he had a nicer moment,*" Monchaux wrote, according to Dr. Phillippe Charlier, an archeologist who discovered the account in an old medical text.[30] "*Other individuals of various ages and sexes reported a very similar sensation in the same circumstances.*"

Even during a time in which relying on religious conclusions to everyday questions was commonplace, Monchaux reportedly compared the case to similar incidents involving drowning, hypothermia, and hanging, and proposed a physio-pathological explanation.

"In all these examples, the cause of the pleasant sensation seems to be the same. The effects of the bonds, cold, pressure of surrounding water, depression due to an important phlebotomy, exclude quite entirely the cutaneous veins or leave a very little quantity of blood. What happens then?" he wrote. *"All the blood and humors flow abundantly and quietly in the internal vessels, especially the brain vessels, protected from any external compression. And it is precisely this blood effusion that excites all these vivid and strong sensations."*[31]

The comparisons between NDEs across cultures and time periods show us that brain chemistry, expectations, and beliefs play a huge role in what we see during these experiences, and that the scientific answers—not religious ones—are likely correct. After all, the Christian God probably wouldn't give visions of Yama to dying Hindus and a Hindu deity wouldn't reveal an image of Jesus to Christians whose hearts have stopped. The most likely explanation for commonalities and distinctions in cross-culture NDEs is that there are key similarities triggered by a dying brain, as well as important differences that rely on the patient's own interpretations and preconceived notions.

WHEN KARMA SMACKS YOU DOWN

Karma and reincarnation were created by people, just as heavens and hells were, out of our own knowledge of impending doom and desire to control others' actions. And I don't believe in them for the same reason I don't believe in any unsubstantiated and faith-based concepts: there's simply no hard evidence. Although I'm threatened with Hell more often in my line of work, my first karma warning was pretty entertaining, as well. I was about 15 years old and a friend's mom was lecturing me. *"Have you heard of karmasmack?"* she asked. After a confused silence, she finished. *"It's when karma smacks you down!"*

The woman who threatened me with *karmasmack* was operating under a misunderstanding of the belief system itself. Karma, the supernatural notion in which good works are said to result in favorable outcomes in the next life, is not just some vague "reap what you sow" concept; it's a complicated Buddhist and Hindu belief that integrates with reincarnation. Karma originated in ancient India and is associated with Hinduism, Jainism, Buddhism, and Sikhism. It is best to examine karma within the confines of reincarnation (or Samsara), so it is not thoroughly understood to many people in Western cultures, including self-professed believers.[32] In the United States and elsewhere, many believers have transformed "karma" to arbitrarily describe positive and negative forces *in this life* thought to be generated by good and bad actions, respectively. That misunderstanding of karma has been perpetuated by common usage of the term[33] and the media.[34]

In the transformed *New Age* meaning of karma, believers often claim that rewards and retribution are administered by "the Universe" during this life. This idea is demonstrably false. The fact is that good and bad people don't always get what they deserve, and to suggest otherwise is to ignore mountains of evidence to the contrary. You'd have to ignore every serial killer who has gotten away with his or her crimes, escaping all punishment in every sense of the word, and every child who dies a painful death before having the chance to harm anyone. Of course, when presented with these challenges to New Age karma, believers will regularly disregard them without further consideration, claiming (conveniently) that the cosmic balance of justice can't be measured, quantified, or proven.

Closely linked to New Age karma is the **law of attraction** movement. The so-called "law" of attraction, also known as *The Secret*, is based upon no scientific principles. *The Secret* is a popular self-help book that teaches measurably false ideas, including that *positive thinking* itself (without further action) can create life-changing results, like increased wealth, health, and happiness. The hypothesis essentially states that thinking specific thoughts can cause those thoughts to come to fruition in the form of various material items. The falsely named law of attraction takes advantage of our human urge to believe in something greater, along with our pattern recognition capabilities and tendency toward confirmation bias, to convince believers that their "vision board" is bringing things into their life. While it's great to maintain a positive attitude and thinking about goals may help keep them in mind and therefore could make achieving them easier, *The Secret* is essentially wishful thinking dressed up in New Age clothing.[35]

There's no doubt that some ideas taught in *The Secret* can at times affect a person's behavior in a positive way, but that's not always the case. In fact, announcing goals and intentions, a key component of the belief system, has actually been shown to compromise a person's performance more often than not. According to one study by New York University psychologist Peter Gollwitzer and others, *"people's taking notice of one's identity-relevant intentions apparently engenders a premature sense of completeness regarding the identity goal."*[36] The idea of *The Secret* is also dangerous because our actions (and not our thoughts) are truly responsible for most of our own outcomes, and forgetting that can cause people to waste time and energy on fruitless endeavors when they could be working hard to improve their circumstances. Most importantly, regardless of whether believing in *The Secret* helps someone focus more or less on achieving goals, there's no evidence to suggest that the universe "rewards" any form of thinking with concrete changes. In the majority of cases, much like with prayer and other petitionary superstitions, any "results" from *The Secret* are interpreted based on the believers' expectations. The fact is that no amount of praying, wishing, or vision-boarding will change your future. Whether you're analyzing the possibility of New Age karma, *The Secret*, or anything else, confirmation bias can be a powerful force, so as always I recommend following the objective, scientific evidence—and not mere anecdotes.

When compared to *The Secret*, traditional karma is much more complex. As Michael Shermer explains, in Buddhism, the most fundamental unit of matter is prana, *"a vital energy indistinguishable from consciousness."*

"So matter, energy, and consciousness are the same. Since not only sentience, but the origins of life, consciousness, and morality are inadequately explained by science, it is useful to employ the notion of karma. Here I am afraid the Dalai Lama proffers the same empty explanations as the creationists and Intelligent Design theorists in what we call the 'God of the Gaps,' Shermer wrote.[37] *"Wherever there is a gap in scientific explanation—the origins of life, sentience, consciousness, morality—this is where God, or karma, intervened. But what happens to God/karma when science fills in the gap? Are you going to abandon God/karma from your worldview?"*

Religious karma is not only more complicated than the New Age version, it's also more harmful. For instance, a literal application of karma means that believers could witness a young child experiencing something terrible and, instead of helping, they may assume the victim deserves it based on something he or she did in an unknown "past life." Karma is a completely unfalsifiable idea that is incredibly susceptible to dangerous assumptions and intentional fraud because it relies on information from reincarnation, which itself has never been shown to exist. Reincarnation posits that a soul begins a new life in a new body after biological death and, like most supernatural concepts, it is a byproduct of humanity's wishful thinking. We are aware of our own mortality and the mortality of our loved ones and, as a result, we seek ways to live on—even if it's in another form. We make up stories that are passed down from generation to generation, but that can't be verified or proven. This is a common thread that ties together heavens, hells, reincarnation, ghosts, spirits, and more.

REBIRTH AND REINCARNATION

A number of people from various time periods and cultures, including North American Indians,[38] ancient Greeks,[39] and more, have professed a belief in reincarnation—and that's not surprising. In fact, I understand why the *idea* of reincarnation, or rebirth, is popular. As a metaphor, it's poetic, comforting, and "*can prove useful in grappling with our lives,*" according to author Derek Beres.

"*Rites of passage and overcoming personal trauma are great examples of how one can be rebirthed,*" he wrote for *Big Think*,[40] adding that there is no scientific evidence to suggest reincarnation is a real phenomenon. "*When treated as a 'science,' reincarnation is a relic of our primitive past that we cannot seem to evolve beyond. Still, our spiritual traditions cling to this archaic idea by pretending a discipline ill-suited for such topics provides 'proof' of transmigration.*"

The most common "evidence" put forth for reincarnation is people, especially young children, who say they are able to recount their so-called past lives. There are numerous examples of well-publicized stories with this theme, including Luke Ruehlman, a five-year-old Caucasian boy whose parents say he used to be an African-American woman named Pamela Robinson,[41] and Ryan Hammons, a young boy from Oklahoma whose mother claims he was a movie extra named Marty Martyn.[42] But none have produced evidence for anything beyond vivid imaginations in children and the fact that their families can use Google. While admittedly imaginative, these kids have never shown any data definitively pointing to reincarnation as a fact, and their anecdotes should not be confused for scientific evidence. That's not to say, however, that it would be impossible to prove reincarnation was real. I only mean to suggest that proof would come through scientific research, and not the retelling of vague stories.

Ignoring for a moment that the numbers of humans, and life forms in general, have been in a constant state of flux for millions of years, let's consider the possibility that one death is equal to one birth, with "souls" flowing in between. How would we show this to be true? In order to present the past life "memories" as evidence, one would need to study the subjects in a controlled, scientific environment—a relatively easy task. The researcher would then have to verify information that couldn't possibly have come from any other source. If a child was said to be able to speak in a language that he or she has never encountered, for instance, the scientist would be required to validate the claim and investigate possible natural explanations to rule them out entirely. Those studying subjects with alleged recollections of past lives would be forced to find empirical data that both showed that the stories were true (i.e., the information was not discovered through other methods) and demonstrated how rebirth works in the real world before they could proclaim the phenomenon is the result of human "spirits" being passed into new bodies. In short, simply noting that there is a child who has a memory of some perceived (yet vague) previous life, or a birthmark similar to one of a deceased person, is not good enough.

Many scientists have tried to prove the reincarnation hypothesis, including University of Virginia psychiatry professor Jim B. Tucker, whose work is based partly on cases accumulated by his predecessor Ian Stevenson.[43] These researchers have uncovered some interesting and unexplained cases of children with perceived knowledge of the past that wouldn't be easily obtained, but they have fallen short of proving the existence of reincarnation. Still, serious scientific inquiries into the matter have been hailed by skeptics. Carl Sagan, for instance, referred to childhood past-life memories in *The Demon-Haunted World* as one of three claims in the ESP field that *"deserve serious study."*[44] Sam Harris, the neuroscientist and author who thoroughly debunked the NDE claims of neurosurgeon Eben Alexander,[45] also referred to Stevenson's work in his book, *End of Faith*. In a footnote, Harris states that there *"may even be some credible evidence for reincarnation."* So, what did Stevenson, Tucker, and others discover? Not much. They have raised some interesting questions, but there are several problems with their research and they haven't demonstrated the validity of past lives. According to Jonathan Edelmann, an assistant professor of religion at the University of Florida, and William Bernet, a professor of psychiatry at Vanderbilt Kennedy Center, there are *"a number of weaknesses with the current methodology used by parapsychologists to study reincarnation claims."*

"Considering that many reincarnation cases occur in countries in which belief in reincarnation is part of the cultural matrix, the possibility of interpreting otherwise normal information in light of reincarnation is very strong," Edelmann and Bernet wrote in *Setting Criteria for Ideal Reincarnation Research,* a paper in which they outline a *"rigorous and large-scale reincarnation experiment"* that would ideally settle the debate.[46]

"In most cases, the child was not interviewed so as to exclude the possibility of familial and/or interviewer suggestion, nor in such a way that allows other researchers to observe the interview itself," the authors wrote. *"Generally, the child was present at the time his statements were validated at the designated household, thus introducing the possibility that suggestion occurred."*

The most telling piece of the past life puzzle of all, I think, is that Stevenson, who collected more than 2,500 reincarnation experience stories, failed to convince himself of his own claims. Prior to his death, Stevenson declined to answer whether he believed in reincarnation, stating instead that he and his colleagues have given *"some support to a belief in reincarnation."*

"Before the modern investigations a belief in reincarnation had to rest on the basis of faith, usually inculcated by the scriptures or oral teachings of a traditional religion. Now, one may, if one wishes, believe in reincarnation on the basis of evidence," Stevenson wrote.[47] *"However, the evidence is not flawless and it certainly does not compel such a belief. Even the best of it is open to alternative interpretations, and one can only censure those who say there is no evidence whatever."*

The scientific consensus is important, but nonscientists who believe in reincarnation can also collect data in hopes of confirming or dismissing their own ideas and I encourage them to do so. If you believe psychics can uncover past lives, for instance, I recommend you perform a simple test by locating two independent mediums who you think can do it and then challenging them, separately, to describe the life the subject lived during a specific time period. Once you check their stories against one another, you'll have your answer. Needless to say, no so-called rebirth memory has ever held up under serious scientific scrutiny, and most are the result of human imagination, memory and confirmation biases, and/or outright fraud.

The bottom line is that there's no objective or scientific reason to believe that people are reincarnated, just as no such evidence exists for karma, gods, psychics, good and bad luck, etc. Karma and reincarnation are interesting ideas in certain contexts, but there isn't compelling evidence supporting them and they are, at their cores, a lot like other punishment/reward systems established by other faiths. For example, a Christian who believes in Original Sin might think people deserve negative outcomes because of their ancestors' actions, while, if you believe in karma/reincarnation, you may accept that people deserve horrible things in this life because of their behavior in "*past lives.*" In each case, basing actions on an afterlife that can't be proven allows some otherwise rational people to act without considering earthly consequences. Beres says reincarnation, while an "*attractive idea,*" can become a dangerous and distracting belief when it alters a person's perception of this world—the only one we know exists.

"*That we only get one pass on this giant Ferris wheel can be cause for depression. Yet time and again, when exploring the numerous modalities of rebirth, from the law of karma to the hope of a better world beyond this one, we stumble into one glaring recurrence: By entertaining such philosophies, we inevitably waste valuable time wishing things here were different,*" Beres wrote. "*Instead of changing our circumstances (or our attitude towards existence), we project our attention to some future destination.*"

DRUGS AND OTHER ALTERED STATES

Everyone knows there are some drugs that can make you hallucinate, such as *psilocybin* and *lysergic acid diethylamide* (LSD),[48] but a few substances go further by actually simulating NDEs and OOBEs, thereby contributing to the widespread belief in reincarnation, Heaven, Hell, and other afterlives. The anesthetic *ketamine*, for instance, has reportedly been used to recreate typical near-death memories in a laboratory setting by Dr. Karl L. R. Jansen, a member of the Royal College of Psychiatrists. In his 1996 study,[49] Jansen concluded that the reproduction or induction of NDEs by ketamine "*is not simply an interesting coincidence.*"

"*Ketamine administered by intravenous injection is capable of reproducing all of the features of the NDE which have been commonly described,*" Jansen wrote in the paper. "*Ketamine reproduced travel through a tunnel, emergence into the light, and a 'telepathic' exchange with an entity which could be described as 'God.'*"

The psychedelic compound **N,N-Dimethyltryptamine** (**DMT**) also produces effects that imitate NDEs and other-worldly visions, but, unlike ketamine, DMT is regularly mistaken for an *actual* link to "the spirit world." Some scientists say DMT acts as a neurotransmitter,[50] and others believe it is produced in the pineal gland and is released during trauma,[51] which causes NDE phenomena. But the chemical combination has, to date, only been discovered in the pineal glands of rats,[52] and not in those of humans, leaving that hypothesis unconfirmed. The pineal gland itself, often referred to as an "inner third eye" by some groups and cultures,[53] has been linked to pseudoscience and spirituality for many years. This tradition perhaps began with René Descartes, who referred to the melatonin-producing endocrine gland as the "*principal seat of the soul and the place in which all our thoughts are formed.*"[54] The idea of the pineal gland as a necessary component of being human—a housing for the human spirit—has been put forth by Descartes and countless others, but is demonstrably false because some people are born without a pineal gland as the result of a mutation in the PAX6 gene.[55]

DMT was first synthesized in 1931,[56] but it has been used since at least the sixteenth century by indigenous cultures of Amazonian Peru through the consumption of **ayahuasca,** an allegedly spiritual brew made from leaves of plants that contain DMT and monoamine oxidase–inhibiting (MAO-inhibiting) harmala alkaloids.[57] Ayahuasca is known to cause spiritual revelations, feelings of connection to alternate dimensions, and even hallucinations involving interactions with extradimensional beings or gods. Ayahuasca is similar in many ways to a drink called *umm nyolokh*, which is created by the Humr people of Sudan from giraffe liver and marrow that stores the DMT from the plants they eat and can cause users to see nonexistent giraffes.[58] When people ingest these hallucinogens, they understand that they're hallucinating, right? Wrong. It's commonly believed by the Humr people that umm nyolokh causes one to see the ghosts of dead giraffes, and people all over the world think ayahuasca and DMT genuinely provide a connection to another world or an afterlife.

I've had more than a few people tell me that I'll understand the realities of spiritualism, the soul, and the afterlife if I try certain mind-altering substances, including and especially DMT. My initial reaction to this claim was, "When we take hallucinogens, we hallucinate; that's how it works." After all, we know hallucinogens prey on our "happy receptors" in the brain and create a sensory overload that is well understood by the scientific community,[59] so drug-induced hallucinations of supernatural beings can't possibly serve as proof of the existence of said beings. But knowing those facts isn't enough for many people who continue to insist that I would believe in a transcendent "spirit realm" if I experienced the visions often associated with DMT. Although I was confident in my ability to discern drug-induced supernatural experiences and emotions from what's real, I still wanted to learn more, and I wouldn't have felt comfortable writing about it without experiencing it for myself. I decided to take part in an *Amazonian mind medicine* (aka Ayahuasca) spiritual ceremony and report my findings.

A friend pointed me toward an organization that specializes in these ceremonies, Instituto Superior De Estudios Holisticos Namaste, and I reached out to its founder, an Aztec/Mayan tribe member and mental health professional named Leticia. She gave me permission to record our session for research purposes and we started planning the upcoming trip. My journey began on April 26, but it really started a week earlier when I was asked to abstain from meat, sex, drugs, and alcohol in preparation for the trip. After a 10-hour drive, we arrived at the mountain. Upon arrival, the local healing group requested our cell phones and car keys, which we got back at the end of the trip. They were extremely friendly and spoke Spanish almost exclusively. We didn't even have time to set up our tent when the group began to gather for what I would call a prayer circle. We held hands ("The right hand gives and the left hand receives") and shared what we were thankful for. There were dozens of participants in the circle, including people with Native American heritage and tourists from all around the world. Some people thanked god(s), others thanked their loved ones, but the vast majority of practitioners and fellow participants thanked "Mother Earth."

As per the group's instructions, I hadn't eaten within 24 hours of my arrival on the mountain. Even after the prayer go-round, however, it still wasn't time for lunch. Instead, we walked around the forest hugging trees to feel more connected to the earth. After that exercise, the men and the women took turns in a *temazcalli*, a small sweat lodge powered by rocks left in a fire at the center. The women went first, and then it was time for the men to sit in the super-heated makeshift room, chanting in a circle in almost complete darkness. I spent an hour in the "house of heat" before they opened the enormous tarp enclosing us . . . only to add additional rocks to the scorched stack in the middle of the room. It was too dark to see anything, and every breath felt like I was breathing in flames, so I kept my head down and focused on my breathing. Another hour went by and, finally, it was over. A volunteer hosed us off with cold mountain water and gave me the first piece of food I had in days—a small and dirty slice of orange—which I enjoyed immensely.

After returning to the tent for a brief baby wipe bath to minimize the mud and sweat, we were quickly called down to the ceremony grounds. We were asked to bring from our tents our sleeping bags, blankets, jackets, and anything else we might need during the journey. All the participants sat down around an enormous white circle with torches and a number of symbols purporting to represent other dimensions, the bond between man and woman, and other natural and supernatural notions. The spirit guide and her assistants then proceeded to tell us about all the things that would come, as well as about other important lessons. We were taught about the different dimensions, the history of the drink, and even what we should do if a hallucination tries to hurt us.

Everyone seemed to portray a sense of comradery during the ceremony—there were no fights or disagreements—but one assistant did become visibly upset while discussing a human sacrifice ritual that the history books say his ancestors participated in many years ago. Despite the fact that it is well known that the Aztecs often extracted hearts from people in a ritual honoring the sun,[60] this young man was convinced that his people would never do that. He said the "heart" that was sacrificed was a symbolic one, and not a life-sustaining organ. After he told a few revisionist stories of his ancestors, the assistant instructed us to gather our warm clothes and blankets and meet around a large fire that was off to the side. We were each given a cigarette with dark tobacco to help prepare our bodies for taking the drug, and helpers got cups of ayahuasca tea ready for us.

It wasn't long until people started receiving their drinks. Each person got a small cup filled with ayahuasca and drank it in one gulp. I got my serving before most others, and I was warned as I put it to my lips that I may experience some vomiting. That part of the experience I can confirm.

Despite having no food in my stomach for more than a day, I threw up the dark liquid less than 15 minutes after drinking it. After everyone drank their tea, we all lay down and the drums and chanting began. This time no words were chanted—only noises. It was freezing cold and incredibly uncomfortable, but after a short period of time I could hear other people beginning to enjoy themselves. There was laughing, screaming, and crying, and it seemed like most people there were having some sort of otherworldly adventure. I still felt no different and, not wanting to miss my opportunity, I asked for another helping. Leticia gave me the drink with a cautious look and I drank it quickly. After a couple of hours, and a few trips to the bushes to vomit, I still felt no effects. I decided to sleep until the morning.

The next day, I decided to interview the other participants to learn about their experiences. Most people reported seeing visions similar to those we were told to expect. One participant, David H., told me he encountered a "*dark spirit*" that he was able to conquer. He said he felt much better about facing his real-life concerns after the experience. Some said they saw and connected with gods or aliens, and still others claimed to have met the spirits of animals that guided them to answers to questions they had been subconsciously worrying about. Nobody gave a lot of specific details, often indicating that there weren't words to describe what they had seen, but the similarities between the stories revealed that groupthink or suggestion may have been a factor in the content (but not necessarily the origin) of the visions.

The trip wasn't a total loss, but I didn't have the transcendent spiritual experience I was seeking. I likely needed a more direct source of DMT, which is listed as a Schedule I drug in the United States despite the fact that it has been shown to have no long-term adverse effects[61] and is even considered by many to be a beneficial form of therapy.[62]

I ultimately obtained 150mg of DMT from a friend who is experienced and familiar with hallucinogens and tried it on my own. I did 50mg at a time, through a vaporizer and a glass pipe, but still felt no effects. I have no doubt that the effects are felt by others, but perhaps this experience just isn't for me.

To get a more complete picture of the NDEs, drug-induced visions, and the possibility of afterlives, I sat down with Michael Shermer, a science writer and the editor in chief of *Skeptic* magazine, to ask him some questions. Here is our interview:

McAfee: Based on what we know today about death and about how the brain works, would you say any type of "afterlife" is highly unlikely? Why or why not? (This includes heavens and hells, but also "spirits," reincarnation-based systems, and other vague spiritual claims.)

Shermer: There is no evidence whatsoever of an afterlife of any kind. To the contrary, all of the evidence points to the conclusion that when our physical body and brain dies, our mind, consciousness, and "soul" (the pattern of information that makes up our "self") dies with it.

McAfee: Do you think a person who doesn't have any sort of afterlife belief as a coping mechanism is more likely to fear death than a believer?

Shermer: No, I do not. To the contrary, every religious person I have encountered who has lost a loved one, or who is himself or herself dying, feels just as bad about it as any nonbelieving person I know. And studies show that religious people mourn just as much as nonreligious people do when losing a loved one.

McAfee: You went to Laurentian University in Sudbury, Canada, and used the so-called God Helmet in Dr. Michael Persinger's lab. You said you felt that someone was in the room with you and that you had a "mild out-of-body experience." Did this trip convince you that electromagnetic stimulation of the brain is the key to understanding many (or most) paranormal experiences?

Shermer: No, but I do think Dr. Persinger's research is interesting because it is searching for natural causes of apparently supernatural phenomena. And, of course, people who have such experiences do not have modified motorcycle helmets strapped to their heads delivering electromagnetic stimuli to their temporal lobes. The causes of such experiences are numerous and vary across circumstances and environments, which I document in detail in my book *The Believing Brain*, and Oliver Sacks documents in individual case studies in his many books, especially *Hallucinations*.

McAfee: A number of scientists claim to have "debunked" Dr. Persinger's results in the "God Helmet" experiment. Have you looked into those attempts to duplicate the original results? What did you think of them?

Shermer: I am largely in agreement with the critics of Dr. Persinger that his controls are not tight enough and that some of his results may be due to expectation effects and experimenter bias.

McAfee: Have you personally researched other ways to induce out-of-body or spiritual experiences, such as with DMT, psilocybin mushrooms, or other psychedelics? What would you say to someone who suggests these drugs' effects are evidence of "something beyond"?

Shermer: No, I have not, but Oliver Sacks has, and he tells of his drug-induced trips in his autobiographical book *On the Move*, as has Sam Harris in his book *Waking Up*. I did a television debate with Eben Alexander, the author of *Proof of Heaven*, about his claim that when he was in an induced coma during a medical emergency that caused his brain to swell that he went to Heaven where he saw vivid colors and sounds. I told him that his "*trip*," to my ears, sounds indistinguishable from drug-induced trips by Oliver Sacks and Sam Harris. The fact is the brain can create vivid hallucinations under widely varying stimuli and conditions, and the fact that someone's personal trip feels so real to them only tells us how powerful these experiences are.

McAfee: What do you think is the number one reason afterlife-based myths persist? Is it, for instance, because of our fear and knowledge of impending death? Or do you think it's more because many afterlife-based claims simply can't be tested?

Shermer: The inability to test such claims only reinforces them to believers, but the origin has to do with the fact that we cannot imagine being dead. Try it. Try picturing yourself dead. You can't do it. Oh, you'll say something like "*I see myself lying on the hospital bed / casket with my eyes closed and people standing around crying*," but "*you*" are still in the scene doing the observing. Being dead would be no different from general anesthesia where you are given an injection and it's lights out. We imagine death is something like this but the lights come back on and we are wherever we are (Heaven, for instance), but imagine that the lights go out and never come back on. More dramatically, imagine what you were before you were born. You can't do it. It's nonsensical. Same as death.

McAfee: Since humans don't tend to resurrect, is there such a thing as an "actual-death experience" that can be tested under controlled conditions? For the purposes of our discussion, are patients considered "near death" when they enter cardiac arrest?

Shermer: There's a reason they're called "*near-death*" experiences. The patients are not dead. They're near death. Big difference. An actual-death experience is when someone just dies. It happens millions of times a year—cumulatively more than 100 billion people have lived and died in the past 50,000 years—and not one of them has come back to tell us what it was like on the other side.

McAfee: What do you think about the NDE claims made by patients who were under general anesthesia at the time of the purported visions? Could these experiences persist when the patient has no measurable neuronal activity?

Shermer: Yes, the fact that brain wave activity was not recorded doesn't mean anything. There may be lots of brain activity that goes unrecorded. So what? Our recording devices are not perfect, nor do they record absolutely everything.

McAfee: How do you explain the similarities in near-death experiences across cultures? Does a scientific understanding account for this?

Shermer: How do you explain the differences in NDEs across cultures? Our brains are all built on the same basic design so of course your occipital lobe lights up when you see something just as mine does because our visual cortex is located there. If there is a real Heaven, why does it vary so much across cultures in NDEs? The prudent answer is that Heaven is all in the mind.

McAfee: Do you think top scientists understand how near-death experiences work quite well? Or is there still a lot of research to be done on the topic?

Shermer: We know a lot more than we used to (again, see *The Believing Brain*), but we do not have a cogent theory of consciousness yet so until we do there is much speculating going on.

McAfee: Is there anything else you'd like to add?

Shermer: Live each day like it was the last, or at least the second to last . . .

> *"Assure a man that he has a soul and then frighten him*
> *with old wives' tales as to what is to become of him afterward,*
> *and you have hooked a fish, a mental slave."*
>
> —*Theodore Dreiser*

NOTES

1.   Often attributed to Confucius or Tom Hiddleston.

2.   Michael Shermer, "What Happens to Consciousness When We Die," *Scientific American*, July 1, 2012, www.scientificamerican.com/article/what-happens-to-consciousness-when-we-die/.

3.   Peter Tyson, "Meet Your Ancestors," *NOVA scienceNOW*, July 1, 2008.

4.   David S. Berman et al., "Early Permian Bipedal Reptile," *Science* 290, no. 5493 (2000): 969–972.

5.   When I say that humans are also animals, some people think I'm advocating for veganism, but that's not necessarily the case: animals eat other animals every day. I'm not saying it's "*acceptable*" for us to do so, because I'm not making a moral judgment, but it is important to point out that, evolutionarily and historically speaking, human beings are omnivores. For specific examples, look no further than our digestive tract, which is different from those we see in strict herbivores, and our enzymes that have also evolved to digest meat.

6.   Melissa Hogenboom, "Humans Are Nowhere Near as Special as We Like to Think," *BBC Earth*, July 3, 2015, www.bbc.com/earth/story/20150706-humans-are-not-unique-or-special.

7.   "*The life of man is of no greater importance to the universe than that of an oyster.*" —David Hume

8.   "*Never believe that animals suffer less than humans. Pain is the same for them that it is for us. Even worse, because they cannot help themselves.*" —Dr. Louis J. Camuti

9. "2014 Religious Landscape Study," Pew Research Center, November 3, 2015, www.pewresearch.org/fact-tank/2015/11/10/most-americans-believe-in-heaven-and-hell/.

10. Alan Bernstein, "Heaven and Hell," in *New Dictionary of the History of Ideas*, ed. Maryanne Cline Horowitz (New York: Charles Scribner's Sons, 2005).

11. *"Life is but a momentary glimpse of the wonder of this astonishing universe, and it is sad to see so many dreaming it away on spiritual fantasy."* —Carl Sagan

12. Eben Alexander, "Proof of Heaven: A Doctor's Experience with the Afterlife," *Newsweek*, October 8, 2012, www.newsweek.com/proof-heaven-doctors-experience-afterlife-65327.

13. Bill Chappell, "Boy Says He Didn't Go to Heaven; Publisher Says It Will Pull Book," *NPR*, January 15, 2015, www.npr.org/sections/thetwo-way/2015/01/15/377589757/boy-says-he-didn-t-go-to-heaven-publisher-says-it-will-pull-book.

14. *"Because the everyday occurrence is of stimuli coming from the outside, when a part of the brain abnormally generates these illusions, another part of the brain interprets them as external events. Hence, the abnormal is thought to be the paranormal."* —Michael Shermer

15. *"Any time scientists disagree, it's because we have insufficient data. Then we can agree on what kind of data to get; we get the data; and the data solves the problem. Either I'm right or you're right or we're both wrong. And we move on. That kind of conflict resolution does not exist in politics or religion."* —Neil deGrasse Tyson

16. Sam Parnia et al., "AWARE—AWAreness during REsuscitation—A Prospective Study," *Resuscitation* 85, no. 12 (December 2014): 1799–1805.

17. Zalika Klemenc-Ketis et al., "The Effect of Carbon Dioxide on Near-Death Experiences in Out-of-Hospital Cardiac Arrest Survivors: A Prospective Observational Study," *Critical Care* 14, no. 2 (2010).

18. The authors of the study suggest between 11 and 23 percent of cardiac arrest survivors report NDEs.

19. James Owen, "Near-Death Experiences Explained?" *National Geographic*, April 10, 2010, news.nationalgeographic.com/news/2010/04/100408-near-death-experiences-blood-carbon-dioxide/.

20. Chris French, "Near-Death Experiences in Cardiac Arrest Survivors," *Progress in Brain Research* 150 (2005): 351–367.

21. Michael Raduga, "REM sleep: A Cause of Near-Death Experiences," Phase Research Center, 2012, research.obe4u.com/nde-simulating-experiment/.

22. Sharon Hill, "No, This Study Is Not Evidence for 'Life after Death,'" James Randi Educational Foundation, October 8, 2015, web.randi.org/swift/no-this-study-is-not-evidence-for-life-after-death.

23. Dean Mobbs and Caroline Watt. "There is nothing paranormal about near-death experiences: how neuroscience can explain seeing bright lights, meeting the dead, or being convinced you are one of them." Trends in cognitive sciences, 15.10 (2011): 447-449.

24. Bruce Greyson, "The Incidence of Near-Death Experiences," *Medicine Psychiatry* 1 (1998): 92–99.

25. G. Gallup and W. Proctor, *Adventures in Immortality: A Look Beyond the Threshold of Death* (New York: McGraw Hill, 1982), 198–200. "Have you, yourself, ever been on the verge of death or had a 'close call' which involved any unusual experience at that time?" Nationally 15 percent responded "yes."

26. Satwant Pasricha, "A Systematic Survey of Near-Death Experiences in South India." Journal of Scientific Exploration. Vol. 7, No. 2 (Summer 1993): 161-171.

27. John Belanti et al., "Phenomenology of Near-Death Experiences: A Cross-Cultural Perspective," *Transcultural Psychiatry* 45, no. 1 (March 2008): 121–133.

28. Plato, "The Myth of Er," *The Republic* (New York: Penguin Classics, 1955), 361–362.

29. Marinus van der Sluijs, "Three Ancient Reports of Near-Death Experiences: Bremmer Revisited," *Journal of Near-Death Studies* 27, no. 4 (Summer 2009).

30. Philippe Charlier, "Oldest Medical Description of a Near Death Experience (NDE), France, 18th Century," *Resuscitation* 9, no. 85 (2014): e155.

31. This hypothesis directly contradicts modern research that suggests a *lack* of blood to the brain may play a role in NDEs, but it is important to recognize this effort to reach a plausible scientific answer.

32. Buddhism itself is a commonly misunderstood or misinterpreted religious tradition. The American media's portrayal of Buddhism is one way to account for incongruities between how the tradition is understood and how it is actually practiced, but there are many others. Read more at David G. McAfee, "Buddhisms: Lived and Portrayed Traditions," The Skeptical Writings of David G. McAfee, December 1, 2010, davidgmcafee.wordpress.com/2010/12/01/buddhisms-lived-and-portrayed-traditions/.

33. You know what I mean if you've ever heard someone say, "*Karma's a bitch!*"

34. If you get your education on karmic principles from TV shows like *My Name Is Earl*, you are looking in the wrong place.

35. It should be noted that James Arthur Ray, one of the narrators of the movie version of *The Secret*, was found guilty of negligent homicide after three people died at one of his New Age retreats. Dan Harris and Lauren Effron, "James Ray Found Guilty of Negligent Homicide in Arizona Sweat Lodge Case," *ABC News*, June 22, 2011, abcnews.go.com/US/james-ray-found-guilty-negligent-homicide-arizona-sweat/story?id=13908037.

36. Peter M. Gollwitzer et al., "When Intentions Go Public Does Social Reality Widen the Intention-Behavior Gap?" *Psychological Science* 20, no. 5 (2009): 612–618.

37. Michael Shermer, "Science Without Borders," *New York Sun*, September 14, 2005, www.nysun.com/arts/science-without-borders/19969/

38. Warren Jefferson, *Reincarnation Beliefs of North American Indians: Soul Journey, Metamorphosis, and Near Death Experience* (Summertown, TN: Native Voices Books, 2009).

39. Charles H. Kahn, *Pythagoras and the Pythagoreans* (Indianapolis, IN: Hackett Publishing, 2001).

40. Derek Beres, "The Science of Reincarnation?" Big Think, December 4, 2012, bigthink.com/21st-century-spirituality/the-science-of-reincarnation.

41. Andy Campbell, "Boy, 5, Claims He Lived Past Life as Woman Who Died in Chicago Fire," *Huffington Post*, February 19, 2015, www.huffingtonpost.com/2015/02/20/boy-reincarnated-woman-chicago-fire_n_6715128.html.

42. J. B. Tucker, *Return to Life: Extraordinary Cases of Children Who Remember Past Lives* (New York: St. Martin's Press, 2013).

43. Ian Stevenson, *Twenty Cases Suggestive of Reincarnation* (Charlottesville, VA: University of Virginia Press, 1980).

44. Carl Sagan, *The Demon- Haunted World*, New York: Random House, 1996), 285. ISBN 978-0-394-53512-8.

45. Sam Harris, "This Must Be Heaven," Sam Harris Blog, October 12, 2012, www.samharris.org/blog/item/this-must-be-heaven.

46. Jonathan Edelmann and William Bernet, "Setting Criteria for Ideal Reincarnation Research," *Journal of Consciousness Studies* 14, no. 12 (2007): 92.

47. Ian Stevenson, "Some of My Journeys in Medicine" (Flora Levy Lecture in the Humanities, University of Southwestern Louisiana, Lafayette, LA, 1989), med.virginia.edu/perceptual-studies/wp-content/uploads/sites/267/2015/11/some-of-my-journeys-in-medicine.pdf.

48. Other substances like alcohol and cannabis—and even deep meditation or a lack of sleep—can make people see things that aren't really there, too.

49. K. L. R. Jansen, "Using Ketamine to Induce the Near-Death Experience: Mechanism of Action and Therapeutic Potential," in *Yearbook for Ethnomedicine and the Study of Consciousness* (Jahrbuch furr Ethnomedizin und Bewubtseinsforschung), ed. Christian Rätsch and John Baker (Berlin: VWB Verlag, 1996).

50. J. V. Wallach, "Endogenous Hallucinogens as Ligands of the Trace Amine Receptors: A Possible Role in Sensory Perception," *Medical Hypotheses* 72, no. 1 (2009): 91–94.

51. Rick J. Strassman, *DMT: The Spirit Molecule: A Doctor's Revolutionary Research into the Biology of Near-Death and Mystical Experiences* (Rochester, VT: Park Street, 2001).

52. S. A. Barker et al., "LC/MS/MS Analysis of the Endogenous Dimethyltryptamine Hallucinogens, Their Precursors, and Major Metabolites in Rat Pineal Gland Microdialysate," Biomedical Chromatography 27, no. 12 (July 2013): 1690–1700.

53. Richard M. Eakin, "A Third Eye: A Century-Old Zoological Enigma Yields Its Secrets to Electron-Microscopist and Neurophysiologist," *American Scientist* 58, no. 1 (1970): 73–79.

54. Gert-Jan Lokhorst, "Descartes and the Pineal Gland," in *The Stanford Encyclopedia of Philosophy*, ed. Edward N. Zalta (Summer 2016 edition), plato.stanford.edu/entries/pineal-gland/.

55. Tejal N. Mitchell et al., "Polymicrogyria and Absence of Pineal Gland Due to PAX6 Mutation," *Annals of Neurology* 53, no. 5 (2003): 658–663.

56. R. H. F. Manske, "A Synthesis of the Methyltryptamines and Some Derivatives," *Canadian Journal of Research* 5 no. 5 (1931): 592–600.

57. José Carlos Bouso et al., "Personality, Psychopathology, Life Attitudes and Neuropsychological Performance among Ritual Users of Ayahuasca: A Longitudinal Study," *PLoS One* 7, no. 8 (2012): e42421.

58. Ian Cunnison, "Giraffe Hunting among the Humr Tribe," *Sudan Notes and Records* 39 (1958).

59. F. X. Vollenweider, "Brain Mechanisms of Hallucinogens and Entactogens," *Dialogues in Clinical Neuroscience* 3, no. 4 (2001): 265–279.

60. David Carrasco, *City of Sacrifice: The Aztec Empire and the Role of Violence in Civilization* (Boston, MA: Beacon Press, 2000).

61. José Carlos Bouso et al., "Personality, Psychopathology, Life Attitudes and Neuropsychological Performance among Ritual Users of Ayahuasca: A Longitudinal Study," *PLoS One* 7, no. 8 (2012): e42421.

62. Daniel I. Brierley and Colin Davidson, "Developments in Harmine Pharmacology—Implications for Ayahuasca Use and Drug-Dependence Treatment," Progress in Neuro-psychopharmacology and Biological Psychiatry 39, no. 2 (2012): 263–272.

14

ALIEN INTERVENTION

"Our best telescopes have shown us that there are basically an unlimited number of planets in the universe. To think that Earth is the only one where life could have developed is just self-importance. But to think that intelligent life has traveled all the way here and is sneaking around observing us is also just self-importance."

—Chris Hadfield, Canadian astronaut

Many people, religious and nonreligious alike, look for answers in alien intervention. This is partly because some humans maintain a religious urge to believe in *some* governing or controlling force, but there are a number of factors that come into play, including the fact that alien life itself is entirely possible and—I would argue—probable. Dr. Frank Drake would agree. His famous Drake equation, written in 1961, used data on average star formation and planet-to-star ratios to estimate that there are between 1,000 and 100,000 intelligent alien civilizations in the *Milky Way galaxy* alone.[1] That number varies depending on the calculations and many scientists have their own guesses, but it's certainly possible that alien life exists elsewhere—and we are actively searching for it. In fact, Ellen Stofan, chief scientist for NASA, said during a 2015 panel discussion that we will likely discover "*strong indications*" of extraterrestrial life within 10 years and "*definite evidence*" within 20 or 30 years.[2]

The possibility (and arguable probability) of the existence of extraterrestrial civilizations can lead some people on a slippery slope of reasoning and incorrect conclusions. Those people think, "Alien beings must exist, and they could be infinitely more advanced technologically, so why wouldn't they intervene in earthly affairs?" There are many reasonable answers to that question, but the primary flaw in this line of thinking is its reliance on numerous assumptions. Firstly, we don't know intelligent aliens exist yet. We suspect it, and it would make sense, but we have yet to *prove* they are out there despite our best efforts. There are some pieces of evidence that could point in the direction of intelligent alien life, such as the *Wow! Signal*, a strong, 72-second radio signal detected once in 1977,[3] but even that could potentially have emanated from a pair of comets that were in the right area of the sky at that time.[4] This lack of real proof is often referred to as *Fermi's paradox*, named after physicist Enrico Fermi, which describes the apparent contradiction between the estimates regarding high numbers of communicative ETs, provided by Drake and others, and our lack of hard evidence pointing to their existence.[5] Robert H. Gray, author of *The Elusive Wow: Searching for Extraterrestrial Intelligence*, has criticized Fermi's paradox, calling it a "*myth*" that has "*inhibited the search for E.T.*"

"[T]he suggestion that we should not look for intelligent life elsewhere *because we don't see aliens here is simply silly*," wrote Gray, who has searched for radio signals from other worlds at observatories including the Very Large Array.[6] "*Our searches typically 'see' a spot on the sky no bigger than the Moon at any moment, which is only a tiny fraction of the sky. If we want to find something interesting in our era, we might need to look harder.*"

The second assumption often made by those who posit the existence of alien visitors to Earth is that these so far undiscovered aliens are advanced enough to reach us and have a desire to do so. Because we haven't discovered alien life, we can't make claims about its technological development or intentions. A lot of people (especially those who are heavily influenced by fictional accounts) have this vision of extraterrestrials as incredibly advanced super-beings capable of traversing the cosmos with ease, but we can't even say what materials make up their bodies or what they breathe, let alone what stages of tool development they've gone through or what types of machines they can build.

Because we don't know with certainty that extraterrestrial life exists, attributing events on earth—such as ancient buildings, crop circles, UFOs, etc.—to aliens is putting the cart before the horse. Personally, I think it's likely that life does exist elsewhere in the universe, but I'm skeptical toward believers' claims that extraterrestrials have visited humans on Earth—either now or in the distant past—because I haven't seen hard evidence suggesting that's the case. If credible data surfaces showing that aliens have been to Earth, I'd believe it. But until then, I'll continue to treat those extraordinary claims in the same way as I would those made by Bigfoot believers and Christians who claim to have been visited by Jesus.

ANCIENT ALIENS

Ancient Aliens, a documentary-style television series propagating the ancient alien hypothesis previously proposed by Erich von Däniken and others, recently repopularized the self-centered notion that all (or at least a vast majority) of the miracles in ancient times, usually recorded in the Bible or in archaic Greek and Egyptian texts, were actual events that should be attributed to alien visitors. The show's creators not only take a number of ancient cultures' religious and mythological tales at face value, but also attempt to "explain" those occurrences using ET overseers—as opposed to gods or, the most likely explanation, human ingenuity and imagination. Ancient alien hypothesizers often focus on our ancestors' stories and structures, which can seem mysterious to us, but ignore the fact that people continue to write about and experience similar things today. Many of these believers, for instance, ignore alleged miracles present in the *Book of Mormon*, the tales of L. Ron Hubbard in *Dianetics*, and even the alleged divine visions of cult-leader David Koresh. Where does one draw the line regarding which stories do and do not require the intervention of unproven extraterrestrial or divine beings? The fact is we don't need gods or aliens to explain the origins of religions, and there are plenty of modern examples that prove this beyond a reasonable doubt.

Many people have suggested that psychotropic plants and drugs played a role in the development of many religions, and, while that's entirely possible,[7] it's also unnecessary. Humans are and always have been imaginative, creative, and intelligent. We know how religions arose in the past and can see how they do today. In fact, through historical and archaeological analyses, researchers can actually witness how religion itself evolved from simple sun-worship systems to multifaceted anthropomorphized god-based hierarchies over time. This knowledge we have as a society makes it completely unnecessary and counterproductive to invent mysteries that require alien intervention, but that doesn't stop some ancient alien believers from making arguments based on ignorance. For example, many hypothesizers argue that numerous civilizations wouldn't have worshiped sky-dwelling rulers if they didn't really exist in some form, in this case as flesh-and-blood creatures. However, this is a known misconception to anyone who has studied religions and their origins. Not only are there ancient sea gods, earth gods, underworld gods, etc., but many gods came from the sky because our ancestors looked there for their answers, just as we do today. Water, warmth, mystery, and more are all contained in the sky and they always were, so it's natural that any mythology would hold it in such high esteem.

One doesn't need to believe Jesus walked on water to understand the origin of Christianity or believe Muhammad ascended to Heaven on a winged steed to understand how Islam began. Taking ancient rumors as mistranslated facts is intellectually dishonest. If we believed everything people who lived thousands of years ago said about developments in their lifetimes and about other ancient people, this would be a very different world. We might think flying, fire-breathing dragons existed and that Atlantis was a historical landmark, or we may believe, as Aristotle argued, that the heart—and not the brain—was the center of sensation and movement.[8] When considering these assertions, we have to look at plausibility, historical precedence, independent verification, and more; a claim simply isn't enough.

ALIEN OF THE GAPS

The ancient alien hypothesis, much like a lot of spiritual and religious conclusions, is based on conjecture and gaps in knowledge. Believers identify occurrences for which they don't have (or accept) a satisfactory explanation and, instead of attributing the unknown events to gods or other supernatural forces, they suggest a different type of extraterrestrial life form must have been responsible. The difference between the "God" answer and the ancient alien answer is that aliens are natural and arise biologically, which means they are more likely to exist, but their presence also wouldn't answer any questions about the origins of life or matter itself. The ancient alien idea just pushes the biggest mysteries back even further.

Believers who accept the notion of ancient aliens often think humans needed help to evolve and to get where we are today, but that, somehow, our alien overlords did not. The questions remains: if we were created by aliens, who created them?

More specifically, the ancient alien idea is similar to the religiously motivated *intelligent design* (ID) movement, especially when it is applied to the construction of pyramids and other ancient structures. In each case, believers analyze a final product—either an archaic monument or the earth itself—and then make up an answer as to its origins. Ancient alien hypothesizers and ID believers alike will often ignore any mistakes or flaws in the creation of the product and then leap to the conclusion that an unknown yet supremely powerful force must have created something so "perfect." In the same way that ID proponents might consider the earth's features a clear signature of divine force(s), ancient alien believers may suggest strange cave paintings and other ancient artworks depicting alienesque creatures point to ET visitation. While creationists discard the natural processes that shaped our planet and the solar system itself, those who subscribe to the ancient alien hypothesis ignore that humans are creative storytellers. We know from historical records that art has always been around and we know from surrealist artists that not all drawings of humans look exactly the way humans look. There were representations of unicorns and dragons and countless other mythical beasts across a variety of cultures, as well, but that doesn't mean that the creatures were real; it just means people were people.

Michael Shermer explains that the ancient alien hypothesis itself is *"grounded in a logical fallacy called argumentum ad ingorantiam, or 'argument from ignorance.'"* The illogical reasoning, he says, concludes that a lack of a satisfactory explanation for the origins of the Nazca lines of Peru, the Easter Island statutes, the Egyptian pyramids, and more means aliens from outer space must have built them.

"Ancient aliens arguments from ignorance resemble intelligent design 'God of the gaps' arguments: wherever a gap in scientific knowledge exists, there is evidence of divine design. In this way, ancient aliens serve as small 'g' gods of the archaeological gaps, with the same shortcoming as the gods of the evolutionary gaps—the holes are already filled or soon will be, and then whence goes your theory?" Shermer wrote for *Scientific American.*[9] *"In science, for a new theory to be accepted, it is not enough to identify only the gaps in the prevailing theory*

(negative evidence). Proponents must provide positive evidence in favor of their new theory. And as skeptics like to say, before you say something is out of this world, first make sure that it is not in this world."

The ancient alien idea is harmful not only because it is a false belief, but also because it takes appreciation for our ancestors' hard work and redirects it toward imagined, unseen, and unknowable beings—in much the same way modern religious believers' wonder toward the natural world is often surrendered to god(s). Our ancestors were creative, intelligent, and resourceful people who were capable of amazing feats without extraterrestrial or divine intervention. So, while an ancient alien believer might point to complex pyramids and cross-culture similarities between large structures as proof of ET intervention, to me it shows that our ancient relatives were industrious, talented, and able to independently figure out the best ways to stack rocks. As Gene Roddenberry, the creator of the original *Star Trek* series, has said, *"Ancient astronauts didn't build the pyramids. Human beings built the pyramids, because they're clever and they work hard."*

WHERE'S THE EVIDENCE?

While it may be possible, as ancient alien hypothesizers suggest, that an alien life form came to earth to mine gold,[10] help our ancestors to build pyramids, or otherwise substantially change the course of human history, I just don't see it as very probable. Those aliens would have had to intentionally erase all evidence of their existence, just as a deity would. And while many believers have faith that the aliens would be capable of such a feat, you can't make a successful case for their existence by basing all the "evidence" on the fact that the evidence isn't there. "Aliens/gods would be too smart to leave evidence!" and, "**The Government** hid the evidence!" are not acceptable answers, either. If you follow that line of thinking, you may as well believe in trolls who steal your socks at night. After all, sometimes your socks are missing, and trolls would certainly know better than to reveal themselves and jeopardize their mission. There are a lot of explanations as to how our ancestors accomplished many of the feats that some claim to be impossible, and most of those explanations don't involve unproven interstellar travel and are therefore better alternatives. Even if one of these ancient methods is completely unknown to us scientifically, I'm fairly certain I'm capable of *making up* something more likely than hyper-intelligent aliens who came here to command humans to do manual labor before leaving without a trace of their ever having been here.

I want to be clear in stating that I'm not opposed to the ancient alien hypothesis; I'm just against unsubstantiated claims and pseudoscience in general. If intelligent alien beings were discovered, and scientists confirmed that these aliens were indeed responsible for various events throughout our history, I would be excited to spread the word and tell the world. I would write essays and books about the amazing new discovery and I would happily admit to having been wrong all those years for doubting it. It would truly be an incredible find. All that said, I hope I'd get the chance to ask these exceptionally advanced beings about their motives for traveling such vast distances just to help our ancestors use blocks in a more efficient manner.

Ancient alien intervention and ancestry should be handled, like most far-fetched and unsubstantiated claims, with Occam's razor. If something is confusing to you, you should investigate it and look at all possibilities, but don't simply conclude that unverifiable and unseen forces must be responsible. Think about what makes the most sense. What's the simplest solution? Does your conclusion require numerous assumptions about beings that have never been shown to exist? If so, it may be time to rethink your position.

MODERN ALIEN SIGHTINGS AND UFOS

It's important to note that not all alien beliefs are of the ancient variety. From alleged government conspiracies in Roswell, New Mexico, to crop circles and ever-convincing stories from farmers who say they've been probed, modern alien visitation is another commonly held (yet equally unsubstantiated) belief. Surveys suggest up to 77 percent of American adults believe there are signs that aliens could have been to earth[11] and about 45 percent think extraterrestrials have actually visited our planet.[12] Former Democratic presidential candidate Hillary Clinton has even been quoted as saying she thinks we "*may have been*" already visited by aliens, but she added that "*we don't know for sure.*"[13] Additionally, according to Colorado-based Mutual UFO Network (MUFON), one of the largest and oldest UFO investigation organizations, more than 6,000 people in the

United States reported sightings of unidentified flying objects (UFOs) in 2011 alone. A number of other well-known people, including American politician Dennis Kucinich,[14] have also reported UFO sightings. While Kucinich stopped short of saying he believed in alien visitation, only noting mysterious lights in the sky, many alleged UFO witnesses insist on identifying the objects they see as necessarily out-of-this world—despite the "unidentified" qualifier. Neil deGrasse Tyson, in his book *Space Chronicles: Facing the Ultimate Frontier*, cautions people to remember what the "*U*" in "*UFO*" stands for.

"You see lights flashing in the sky. You've never seen anything like this before and don't understand what it is. You say, 'It's a UFO!' The 'U' stands for 'unidentified,'" Tyson wrote. *"But then you say, 'I don't know what it is; it must be aliens from outer space, visiting from another planet.' The issue here is that if you don't know what something is, your interpretation of it should stop immediately. You don't then say it must be X or Y or Z. That's argument from ignorance."*

Tyson is referring to "*UFO*" as it is commonly used, but that isn't the only definition. The U.S. Air Force, which coined the term in 1952, first stated that a UFO was *"any airborne object which by performance, aerodynamic characteristics, or unusual features, does not conform to any presently known aircraft or missile type, or which cannot be positively identified as a familiar object."*[15] Because of this definition, UFOs were defined as such only after remaining unidentified following an investigation by experts. That limited definition has largely been forgotten as colloquial use of the term has evolved, however, and many people even started using other descriptors, such as unidentified aerial phenomenon (UAP), to disassociate strange objects in the sky from extraterrestrial assumptions.[16]

One thing we should all be able to agree on is that UFO doesn't necessarily mean "alien." If someone sees something unidentified, I accept that. What I'm not willing to do, however, is make the enormous leap of faith it would take to classify that alleged sighting as an example of extraterrestrial visitation. Those who insist they've been abducted or otherwise contacted by extraterrestrials will often provide photos and videos of "unidentified flying objects," and then in the next breath attempt to identify them as vehicles from another planet—effectively making them IFOs. But they are called "*unidentified*" for a reason, and there is usually a natural (and terrestrial) explanation readily available for each of these events. UFO sightings in no way prove alien visitation, and to make that assumption is to adopt the argument from ignorance in a manner akin to the "alien of the gaps" discussed above. Knowing that weather balloons, drones, and Chinese (sky) lanterns exist, and that the military tests new aircraft all the time, it's hard to imagine how people can see mysterious lights or objects in the sky and assume aliens must be the source. In addition to those just named, many UFOs can be explained by atmospheric phenomena, light aberrations, mass hallucinations, swamp gas, hoaxes, and even *earthquake lights*—rare glowing lights sometimes seen prior to seismic events.[17]

Sightings of UFOs or, more commonly, UFLs—unidentified flying lights—are common for many reasons, including the fact that some people simply don't have the research skills or background information required to identify certain terrestrial craft. Perspective is also important; many people have reported seeing an alien-seeming ship only to later see it at another angle and discover it was something as simple as an airplane or helicopter. And sometimes lights in the sky are just that—lights, in the sky, produced from an earthly source, either as an unintended consequence of normal activity or as a deliberate hoax. These are, of course, not the only rational explanations for UFO sightings, but these answers are almost always more probable than superintelligent alien beings traveling throughout the galaxy just to give a few humans and their neighbors a personal light show. For these reasons and many others, the blurry pictures you've seen don't prove aliens exist. Photos of lights in the sky are proof of aliens just like pieces of toast that seem to resemble Jesus are proof that Christianity is the one True religion. If you think you see an alien spacecraft, however, I would still recommend trying to capture it the best way you can. The only thing less impressive than photos are unsupported anecdotes. While images of lights in the sky don't prove aliens exist, stories about lights in the sky don't prove anything at all.

Alien visitation belief isn't all about lights in the sky—there are also those who claim to have been abducted by aliens. The authors of one poll estimated that nearly four million Americans may have been abducted by ETs,[18] and other researchers have claimed that between 5.5 and 6 percent of the population have reported having similar experiences.[19] I don't think all these people are lying, nor do I believe they were picked up by a sky lantern or swamp gas, but I do think these claimants are mistaken about what they've experienced. In fact, I compare these abduction stories to those of religious visions, which are often quite similar. People say gods or angels visit them as they sleep, or cause a "sign" to appear in the sky, in the same way other believers might claim to have been visited by extraterrestrials. But in each case, there is an explanation, usually involving general confusion, sleep paralysis, abuse of hallucinogens, mental disorder, or fraud.

To get a more complete picture regarding the belief in modern alien visitation, I sought out Robert Sheaffer,[20] one of the leading skeptical UFO investigators and a founding member of the UFO subcommittee of the well-known Committee for Skeptical Inquiry (formerly CSICOP). He's also the author of *Bad UFOs* and a founding director and past chairman of the Bay Area Skeptics, a skeptics group in the San Francisco Bay Area.

McAfee: A huge number of people claim to see UFOs each year, and some of those objects are said to defy natural laws as we understand them. Do you think all these people are simply mistaken? What would you tell them about their purported experiences?

Sheaffer: The great majority of the public cannot identify Venus and Jupiter, or bright stars, or a satellite passing overhead. So when a person having no familiarity with astronomy reports seeing something unknown to them, there is no reason to think that anything unusual is happening. As for objects alleged to defy natural laws, that is a very strong indication that the reported sighting is inaccurate. It has been said many times, "Extraordinary claims require extraordinary proof," and in the absence of extraordinary proof—multiple independent and consistent observers, with photos and videos, and even radar and other technological detections—you don't have anything. "Extraordinary claims with little or no proof" is just not going to cut it.

McAfee: Do you think there is any good evidence for alien visitation on earth? What would you say is the most compelling piece?

Sheaffer: No, there is no "good evidence" at all. Nothing is "compelling." There are a few cases we can't wrap up completely, usually because of incomplete information, or because of claims containing elements that simply can't be true. I suppose you could say that they are "solved" as insufficient or inconsistent information. We invariably end up with less "evidence" than one would expect if such dramatic reports were in

fact real. There are no hidden nuggets of solid cases, just a lot of claims without solid foundation.

McAfee: UFOs have been seemingly constant throughout history, with tales of unidentified objects going back thousands of years. Do you think it's possible there is an undiscovered natural phenomenon at the root of many of these?

Sheaffer: It's not true that UFOs have been "seemingly constant" throughout history, although some authors have "jazzed up" reports in ancient chronicles to make them seem to support that conclusion. The best-known book promoting "ancient UFOs" is *Wonders in the Sky* (2009) by Jacques Vallee and Chris Aubeck, which looks into over 500 cases of what are supposed to be sightings of unidentified objects in the sky from centuries past. However, careful investigation by researchers Jason Colavito and Martin Kottmeyer show that their descriptions of many of these cases are based on bad translations, secondhand sources, etc. (Look up "Colavito Blunders in the Sky".) Most of these cases are based on very little information. Combine that with the religious, astrological, and supernatural interpretations contained in these reports, and there is very little objective substance on which to base any claims.

While the possibility of some unknown natural phenomenon cannot be ruled out, I consider it to be extremely unlikely. One thing to remember is that centuries ago, practically anything unusual that happened was given a religious, astrological, or supernatural explanation. Phenomena that we are familiar with today—brilliant meteors and meteor showers, comets, aurorae, etc.—were interpreted in terms of religious events, or as portents of some great calamity. Thus the descriptions we are given may not seem to describe any known phenomenon because their descriptions are colored in terms of the common beliefs of the time.

McAfee: You are a professional skeptic who debunks UFO claims, but do you believe in alien life? If you think it might exist, do you think it could be intelligent and could one day visit us?

Sheaffer: Here we are touching on what I call the prime UFO fallacy: whenever I say to a group of people that I do not believe in alien visitations, almost invariably somebody will object, "What makes you so sure that we are the only intelligent civilization in the universe?" I reply that I never said that, but in their minds this is what they think they have heard. This is the same as asserting: If aliens exist somewhere in the universe, then they must be here now. When stated so directly, it is easy to see how absurd it is. But the prime UFO fallacy is very widely held.

"Believe" is the wrong word to use in talking about alien life. Our universe is unimaginably vast, much more vast than the human mind can comprehend. We know that there are something like a hundred billion stars in our galaxy alone, and at least that many galaxies in the observable universe. That's a whole lot of solar systems, and based on what we now know we can conclude that many, if not most, of them have planets—some of which are probably similar to Earth. We know that life was able to evolve here on Earth, given a few billion years. So it would be absurd to conclude that this could not happen elsewhere.

However, most people have simply no idea of the size of the universe, or of the insane amounts of energy required for accelerating (and decelerating) space ships to near light speed. See chapter 8 of my book *Bad UFOs* for a full discussion of this. It would be just as difficult for ETs in some distant solar system to reach us as it would for us to reach them. So no, I do not expect to see any visitors from deep space just suddenly appearing in our vicinity.

McAfee: What do you think of sleep paralysis as it relates to alien abduction claims? Do you think this natural medical condition could explain a large number of those alleged experiences?

Sheaffer: Beyond any doubt, sleep paralysis plays a role in UFO abduction belief. The Harvard psychologist Susan A. Clancy shows this in her book *Abducted: How People Come to Believe They Were Kidnapped by Aliens*. Throughout history, people have been interpreting dreams and nightmares as experiences from some "other realm" of existence—angels, demons, witches, whatever. Today, that "other realm" is interpreted by many people as experiences involving UFOs and aliens.

McAfee: Is there anything else you'd like to add?

Sheaffer: The late British Fortean skeptic Hillary Evans wrote, "It is safe to say that no anomalous phenomenon has generated so rich an anomaly-cluster as the flying saucer." In addition to simple UFO sightings, we have the men in black, UFO crashes, military and intelligence conspiracies, NASA conspiracies, alien abductions, crop circles, alien autopsies, alien-human hybrids, cattle mutilations, etc., and the list just continues to grow. Neither Bigfoot nor Nessie, nor ghosts or angels, come even close.

During the mid- and late twentieth century, our culture became steeped in science fiction. Stories of rocket ships and space travel were commonplace. You can find stories of abductions by space aliens very much like contemporary accounts in the Buck Rogers comics as early as 1930. Then at the close of World War II, we not only had Cold War concerns about possible advanced weaponry developed in secret by either the United States or Soviet Union, and rockets began to actually travel into space. It is no wonder that in an environment such as that, people were prone to misperceive ordinary objects seen in unusual circumstances as alien spacecraft coming to earth to keep watch over our use of nuclear weapons—or perhaps even to conquer us!

McAfee: If aliens did visit Earth, do you think the world governments would try to hide that information from everyone else? Why or why not?

Sheaffer: If aliens actually did visit Earth, I don't see how it would be possible for any government to hide that fact. Their interstellar craft would have to be much bigger than the small asteroids that astronomers routinely detect. When their craft approached Earth, they would be easily visible to the naked eye. Diligent amateur satellite watchers would detect them very quickly, and would compute their orbit. News of these sightings would quickly saturate the Internet. People would be talking about nothing else. The notion of some government (let alone many governments) hiding secrets about alien encounters is too absurd to take seriously.

THE TRUTH IS OUT THERE

Conspiracy theories involving government cover-ups are incredibly popular (see chapter 15), and concealment of alien life on earth is one of the most commonly seen representations of that. Millions of people believe in alien visitation, and about 30 percent of the American population believes that the government has deliberately covered it up.[21] In other countries that number is significantly lower, with only about 17 percent of people in the U.K. professing a belief in alien cover-ups,[22] but these beliefs span the globe and have persisted over time. The alien cover-up narrative, which has been bolstered in recent years through fictional media representations found in movies like the *Men in Black* franchise and television series such as *The X-Files*, got its start in 1947 after a UFO allegedly crashed in Roswell, New Mexico. That incident was initially reported as a fallen weather balloon, but the government later revealed that a downed U.S. Air Force surveillance balloon, dubbed Project MOGUL, was the source.[23] Speculation about an alien crash landing at the Roswell site has continued, despite a countless number of fruitless probes into the event and dozens of previously classified documents being made public. The event has been called *"the world's most famous, most exhaustively investigated, and most thoroughly debunked UFO claim."*[24]

Alien cover-up beliefs vary from believer to believer, with some suggesting aliens actively work with a number of government agencies around the world and others portraying a more passive relationship. Many believers claim ETs allow people to reverse engineer their technology, which they say explains our rapid advancement (that is actually explained by our ability to communicate and build upon new ideas), and still others have even more complex theories, including that President Dwight Eisenhower actually met with a group of aliens to sign the so-called *Greada Treaty* in 1954. There isn't any real evidence for this assertion, and it is based solely on stories put forth by a few individuals and the fact that the president went to a dentist appointment for a few hours, yet people continue to believe it.[25] And for those who do insist that the government is hiding alien contact from the citizens of the world, I would only ask what possible reason the extraterrestrials would have for agreeing to such a deal with mere humans. In order to even reach us from the nearest habitable planet, these incomprehensibly intelligent creatures would have to be so far advanced, that any treaty with us would be like the world governments of Earth agreeing with dung beetles not to destroy or disrupt them.

If there is no treaty, and aliens (or time travelers, as some suggest) are actually visiting Earth for strictly observational purposes without leaving a shred of evidence, then the governments of the world would likely be oblivious to it, not complicit in it. I think this idea is most succinctly demonstrated by Stephen Hawking, former Lucasian Professor of Mathematics at the University of Cambridge and author of *A Brief History of Time*, who said, "*If the government is covering up knowledge of aliens, they are doing a better job of it than they do at anything else.*" Frankly, it's more likely that governments are lying about their own new technologies than about alien life forms traveling from light years away only to hover in our atmosphere and be spotted by random people in arbitrary locations—without leaving any solid proof.

EVIDENCE PUT FORTH

Regardless of a lack of hard evidence, many alien believers still insist that aliens have landed on Earth and that the world governments are engaged in a massive global conspiracy to hide it. Personally, however, I tend to side with Dr. Hawking on this issue in part because I've never seen anything that indicates our political institutions are capable of such an enormous cover-up—and the same goes for the notion that the attacks on September 11, 2001, were executed by the U.S. government and that an ultrapowerful *Illuminati* controls everything, including the economy. These might be fun or intriguing ideas, but, practically speaking, any cover up at that level of complexity is likely to be exposed by one of the many people involved. Thom Tran, a stand-up comedian and former noncommissioned officer (NCO) in the U.S. Army, jokes about the notion that military personnel would be capable of keeping a large-scale secret such as the existence of aliens.

"*My problem with the X-Files show is the alleged military involvement in alien cover-ups. There's always a black-ops team hiding or killing aliens,*" Tran said. "*You want me to believe that there's a group of soldiers that knows there are aliens and didn't tell anyone? We couldn't keep the Seal who shot Bin Laden from opening his mouth and you think a bunch of privates know there are aliens and kept it a secret? As an NCO I couldn't keep my Joes from telling their stripper girlfriends the grid coordinates of our next op and you want me to believe they can keep their mouths shut about aliens?"*

In an attempt to overcome the absence of physical proof for alien visitation, many believers point to Dr. Steven Greer's *The Disclosure Project*, which seeks to *"fully disclose the facts about UFOs, extraterrestrial intelligence, and classified advanced energy and propulsion systems."*[26] Unfortunately for those who cling to them, these *"research projects"* are common in pseudoscience and don't often provide anything more than testimonies and misinterpreted or forged documents. *The Bigfoot Disclosure Project*, which is dedicated to revealing government knowledge of the *"Bigfoot phenomena,"* is another prime example of this tactic used to gain legitimacy among people who value scientific findings. That project includes a number of stories and papers that purportedly show a connection between government agencies, citizen witnesses, and Bigfoot.[27] Needless to say, none of this data has even been independently verified or published in peer-reviewed scientific journals.

The argument becomes particularly murky when those who insist there's a government cover-up of alien life on earth use the personal opinion of a government official as evidence. They say, *"The corrupt government is covering up alien visitation. We can't trust anything they say!"* And then go on to declare that, because a few representatives of that same corrupt government *believe* (still without presenting solid evidence) in visiting aliens, they must necessarily be real. One common example of this self-contradicting appeal to authority involves Paul Hellyer, a former Canadian minister of defense, who has suggested that aliens visit earth and in fact live on U.S. Air Force property.[28] It's important to note that, when a politician or elected representative endorses alien visitation as Hellyer has, it's no different to me than when any other citizen does so. It is possible that the move is motivated by a real belief, but the official's testimony isn't authoritative merely because the person is or was employed by some government or another. People who work for the government believe in all sorts of crazy things, just as other people do. And in the case of Hellyer, he specifically stated that he came to his conclusions after watching a UFO special on ABC and reading a book about the subject—not because he had discovered top-secret government documents that he could then reveal. Unless the person has hard evidence of alien visitation, which Hellyer and others have failed to present, then I'm simply not interested.

Because of this lack of empirical evidence, the alien visitation myth, like many other similar supernatural or paranormal claims, hinges almost exclusively on personal sightings and anecdotes. In order to bolster their claims, many alien believers will blend appeals to experience and authority, insisting that pilots and high-ranking government officials' opinions on the matter are somehow more definitive than the scientific consensus. Personally, however, I trust astrophysicists over pilots on the issue of extraterrestrial life. Pilots can only say they saw something that they didn't recognize. That doesn't mean it's an alien life form—it doesn't even mean anything, really. It could be the result of a visual illusion, a hallucination caused by high altitude, a military craft from the pilot's own country or another nation, a unique lighting effect, or any number of things. So, until there is physical evidence, I think it's safe to assume aliens haven't been flying alongside pilots in our atmosphere at any point. Steve Lundquist, a former pilot and retired U.S. Air Force officer who served for 20 years, has a TS/SCI (Top Secret/Sensitive Compartmentalized Information) clearance and speaks to skeptic groups about how even the most credible expert witnesses can make simple mistakes. He discusses a mission during which he and others flew from Egypt to Saudi Arabia and saw "*an aircraft about 45 miles ahead*" that "*never showed up on the radar at all.*" It turns out, however, that what they were seeing was actually the planet Venus.

"*So, why would someone who has such an extensive data-set of information and knowledge at his disposal make such a classic mistake? To put it bluntly, it's because our brains suck!*" Lundquist said, adding that the crew realized their mistake and avoided the embarrassment of filling out a surface-to-air fire report. "*The cautionary tale here is not that you should throw out all eyewitness reports of everything. Just take it with a grain of salt, and of course question the conclusions that the eyewitness made based on what they saw.*"

VISITATION VS. EXISTENCE

For the sake of clarity, I should state again that I simply haven't seen any compelling evidence for the claim that extraterrestrials have *visited Earth*. But saying the data isn't there to suggest aliens come to our planet is not the same as saying that Earth is the only planet that harbors life. While I don't *believe in* intelligent aliens, I do accept that it is statistically probable that life exists elsewhere and will accept it is a reality once it is discovered. In other words, while I consider it likely that aliens exist, I see nothing to be gained by *believing in* them by default based on my or anyone else's opinion. I need facts.

Our own existence is evidence that life can arise, so life elsewhere is certainly a possibility, but we don't know enough about our origins to pinpoint any specific details about how common it is in the universe. I personally think—and I'm sure many would agree—that it's likely that life in some form exists elsewhere, but speculation and estimates regarding probability do not equal proof of aliens. And if we don't have solid evidence showing the existence of extraterrestrial life forms in general, we certainly can't prove there are beings that would have the ability and desire to come to Earth. It's one thing to form an opinion that extraterrestrials probably exist, but it's quite another to insist without hard evidence that those aliens are not only capable of interstellar travel, but also that they choose to regularly visit a commonplace planet for the purpose of unseen observation . . . only to then be spotted by thousands of random people.

While it is a person's right to believe as they see fit, that doesn't make all beliefs right and it doesn't change the expectation of evidence for any particular claim. As such, unsupported and unlikely scenarios, including massive, worldwide extraterrestrial cover-ups and ancient astronaut theories, should be classified as nothing more than speculation, imagination, and gullibility, until proven otherwise. In fact, the alien visitation theory in general is entirely based on conjecture and anecdotal tales. Without hard evidence, believers conclude not only that highly advanced extraterrestrials exist, but also that they've developed technology that allows them to defy physics and that they have an active interest in observing us. The alien enthusiasts then proceed to suggest that, even though these aliens have technology we can't comprehend, people see them all the time in our skies. It really makes me wonder, if advanced aliens visit Earth with the goal of hidden observation, then why are their craft so frequently seen with bright, flashing lights?

"Imagine if the dinosaurs had tried picturing the rulers of their planet 100 million years hence. They'd undoubtedly envision these creatures as . . . dinosaurs! Conceiving of aliens as polished versions of ourselves is appealing, but unconvincing."

—Seth Shostak

NOTES

1. "The Drake Equation." SETI Institute, www.seti.org/drakeequation.

2. Krishnadev Calamur, "'Definite Evidence' of Alien Life within 20–30 Years, NASA Chief Scientist Says," *NPR*, April 8, 2015, www.npr.org/sections/thetwo-way/2015/04/08/398322381/definite-evidence-of-alien-life-within-20-30-years-nasa-chief-scientist-says.

3. John Kraus, "We Wait and Wonder," *Cosmic Search* 1, no. 3 (1979): 31.

4. Antonio Paris and Evan Davies, "Hydrogen Clouds from Comets 266/P Christensen and P/2008 Y2 (Gibbs) Are Candidates for the Source of the 1977 "WOW" Signal," Washington Academy of Sciences, 2015, planetary-science.org/wp-content/uploads/2016/01/Paris_Davies-H-I-Line-Signal.pdf.

5. Eric M. Jones, "Where Is Everybody? An Account of Fermi's Question," Los Alamos National Laboratory, March 1, 1985, www.osti.gov/scitech/servlets/purl/5746675/.

6. Robert H. Gray, "The Fermi Paradox Is Not Fermi's, and It Is Not a Paradox," *Scientific American*, Guest Blog, January 29, 2016, blogs.scientificamerican.com/guest-blog/the-fermi-paradox-is-not-fermi-s-and-it-is-not-a-paradox/.

7. R. Doblin, "Pahnke's Good Friday Experiment: A Long-Term Follow-up and Methodological Critique," *Journal of Transpersonal Psychology* 23, no. 1 (1991): 1–25.

8. Charles G. Gross, "Aristotle on the Brain," *Neuroscientist* 1, no. 4 (1995): 245–250.

9. Michael Shermer, "How Beliefs in Extraterrestrials and Intelligent Design Are Similar," *Scientific American*, July 1, 2013, www.scientificamerican.com/article/how-beliefs-extraterrestrials-and-intelligent-design-are-similar/.

10. Author Zecharia Sitchin proposed that aliens called Anunnaki came to Earth to mine gold—a claim that has been repeated by the *Ancient Aliens* producers and many others. To me, this idea demonstrates an inflated sense of self-importance. Gold is only valuable because we say it is, so to assume beings from other solar systems have a similar desire for that particular chemical element reveals an earth-centered view of the universe.

11. Alon Harish, "UFOs Exist, Say 36 Percent in National Geographic Survey," *ABC News*, June 27, 2012, abcnews.go.com/Technology/ufos-exist-americans-national-geographic-survey/story?id=16661311.

12. "Americans Pass Judgment on the Plausibility UFO's, Extraterrestrial Visits and Life Itself," Ipsos, June 29, 2015, www.ipsosna.com/news-polls/pressrelease.aspx?id=6902.

13. Daymond Steer, "Clinton Promises to Investigate UFOs," *Conway Daily Sun*, December 30, 2015, www.conwaydailysun.com/newsx/local-news/123978-clinton-promises-to-investigate-ufos.

14. Jean Dubail, "Kucinich at Debate: 'I Did' See a UFO," *Cleveland Plain Dealer*, October 31, 2007, blog.cleveland.com/openers/2007/10/kucinich_at_debate_i_did_see_a.html.

15. United States Department of the Air Force, "Unidentified Flying Objects Reporting," Air Force Regulation 200-2, August 12, 1954, available at www.cufon.org/cufon/afr200-2.htm.

16. United States Air Force Declassification Office, "Unidentified Flying Objects," www.secretsdeclassified.af.mil/Home/Top-Flight-Documents/Unidentified-Flying-Objects.

17. Michael A. Persinger, "Transient Geophysical Bases for Ostensible Ufo-related Phenomena and Associated Verbal Behavior?" *Perceptual and Motor Skills* 43, no. 1 (1976): 215–221.

18. Budd Hopkins, David M. Jacobs, and Ron Westrum, *Unusual Personal Experiences: An analysis of the Data from Three National Surveys Conducted by the Roper Organization* (Las Vegas, NV: Bigelow Holding Corporation, 1992).

19. David M. Jacobs, *Secret Life: First-Hand Accounts of UFO Abductions* (New York: Simon & Schuster, 1992).

20. In the past, Sheaffer has been skeptical of climate change claims, calling it "*a godsend to politicians who want a bigger government, and greater government control over the economy.*" He chose not to discuss this topic in the interview.

21. Will Dahlgreen, "You Are Not Alone: Most People Believe That Aliens Exist," YouGov, September 28, 2015, today.yougov.com/news/2015/09/28/you-are-not-alone-most-people-believe-aliens-exist/.

22. Will Dahlgreen, "You Are Not Alone: Most People Believe That Aliens Exist," YouGov, September 24, 2015, yougov.co.uk/news/2015/09/24/you-are-not-alone-most-people-believe-aliens-exist/>.

23. Richard Weaver, "Report of Air Force Research Regarding the 'Roswell Incident,'" with Memorandum for the. Secretary of the Air Force, July 27, 1994, media.defense.gov/2010/Dec/01/2001329893/-1/-1/0/roswell-2.pdf.

24. B. "Duke" Gildenberg, "A Roswell Requiem," *Skeptic* 10, no. 1 (2003).

25. Michael Salla, "Eisenhower's 1954 Meeting with Extraterrestrials: The Fiftieth Anniversary of First Contact?" Exopolitics, February 12, 2004, exopolitics. org/Study-Paper-8.htm.

26. S. M. Greer and T. C. Loder III, "Disclosure Project Briefing Document," Disclosure Project, 2001, www.disclosureproject.org.

27. "The Bigfoot Disclosure Project," North America Bigfoot Search, www. nabigfootsearch.com/Bigfootdisclosureproject.html.

28. Arjun Varma, "Aliens Are Living among Us, Declares Former High Ranking Politician Who Wants US to Reveal UFO Secrets," *International Business Times*, April 23, 2015, www.ibtimes.co.uk/aliens-are-living-among-us-declares-former-high-ranking-politician-who-wants-us-reveal-ufo-secrets-1497976.

15

THE BOY WHO CRIED CONSPIRACY

"I'm constantly annoyed that people are distracted by false conspiracies such as 9/11, when all around we provide evidence of real conspiracies, for war or mass financial fraud."
—Julian Assange, WikiLeaks Founder[1]

My position on conspiracies is often misrepresented, so let me be clear: I *know* government officials and executives at large companies—like all people—lie. I just follow evidence to determine when they are lying and to what extent. I'm an activist against corruption, but only when it's real, because fighting imagined conspiracies is harmful when there are so many real problems. Once you realize that every **9/11** "Truther" and "**chemtrail**" enthusiast could be working to solve world hunger, or protesting verified and unjust corporate influence on legislation, the sad reality is more apparent than ever: many people choose to ignore real problems in favor of fighting against nonexistent ones.

I write about false conspiracy claims for the same reasons I write about any sort of faulty belief or superstition: because I'm skeptical of extraordinary assertions that aren't backed up by facts and because unsubstantiated ideas that arise from lapses in critical thinking can cause real harm in the world. By perpetuating unsupported and far-fetched conspiracy theories based solely on government or corporate distrust and conjecture, so-called conspiracy theorists are effectively crying wolf, drawing attention away from legitimate journalists and researchers who are attempting to uncover real corruption. There are devastating and legitimate problems on this planet, so it hurts to see people wasting their time on conspiracy guesses with no supporting evidence. When a person accuses George W. Bush of planning and executing 9/11 in a diabolical scheme involving millions of people, for instance, he or she distracts from the very real and very unethical way his administration capitalized on those attacks to achieve its own goals.[2]

In addition to encouraging people to ignore real issues, unproven conspiracy theories can cause damage by altering the mindset and behavior of some believers. One example of this is the case surrounding James F. Tracy, the Florida Atlantic University professor and conspiracy theorist who was fired from his tenured position at the college after he allegedly harassed the parents of a six-year-old boy who was killed during the mass shooting at Sandy Hook Elementary School in 2012. After Tracy's termination, the young boy's father, Lenny Pozner, received *"several death threats"* from theorists who believed the massacre was *"an elaborate hoax designed to increase support for gun control."*[3] Another case of harm by conspiracy involves the city of Calgary, Alberta, which removed all fluoride from its drinking water largely based on false claims that it was unsafe at low levels.[4] Years after the city council's decision, dentists and dental hygienists reported seeing a dramatic rise in child tooth decay.[5] It's undeniable that an unlimited number of imagination-based schemes are conjured up in the minds of those who see only in black and white terms, and they can cause people to act—and vote—irrationally. If a person believes that world leaders are actually reptilian shape-shifters, for instance, he or she isn't likely to make good choices when it comes to installing those officials.

PROVEN CONSPIRACIES ARE NOT CONSPIRACY THEORIES

Unlawful government conspiracies have been carried out in the past and they will continue to occur, but the existence of verified crimes is irrelevant to the veracity of the unfounded, global conspiracy *theories* that millions of people continue to believe without question. In other words, the fact that there are some documented conspiracies can never be used as evidence for the validity of current alternative theories. Watergate, for instance, is a well-known and proven conspiracy in which the Richard Nixon administration tried to cover-up its involvement in a break-in at the Democratic National

Committee headquarters. But does this prove that the moon landings were staged or that the government is poisoning us with chem-trails? Absolutely not.

Operation Northwoods, a proposed false-flag operation in the early 1960s to justify a U.S. invasion of Cuba, is another planned scheme that was later publicly revealed, and one that alternative theorists often cite as evidence that modern-day government conspiracies are taking place all around us. The problem with this line of thinking isn't just that Operation Northwoods was actually rejected by the John F. Kennedy administration, or that the plan involved simulated attacks that didn't necessarily threaten the lives of American citizens, or that none of the people involved in that plot are in positions of power today. The real issue is that this conduct, while deplorable, lends no credence to the fringe conspiracy theories, in *completely different political administrations and eras*, that don't have hard evidence to turn them into more than mere guesses. If the authorities were investigating a murder that occurred last year, and they found a 50-year-old journal in your grandfather's house linking him to a potential killing when he was much younger, should you be indicted for the current crime due to your relation to him?

Criminal acts among government officials are everyday events, which is why I find it interesting (and ultimately harmful) that people make up and propagate unfounded conspiracies based on nothing but conjecture and *government of the gaps* arguments. In fact, that so many conspiracies have been proven in the past should show how difficult it really is to keep an enormous, worldwide secret while leaving absolutely zero evidence of any illicit conduct. It is for this reason—and the fact that "conspiracy" is such an ambiguous term—that I prefer to call those who perpetuate these unproven narratives "alternative theorists." *Alternative theorists* are often not looking for justice, but instead they are seeking a new reality. Others have started referring to the alternative theories themselves as "conspiracy hypotheses" because, unfortunately, there are people in the world who think "9/11 was an inside job!" is the same type of (scientific) *theory* as evolution by natural selection.

These speculative claims not only distract from efforts to pinpoint real corruption, but also dull critical thinking skills and sow doubt and confusion where it's unnecessary. Historically, proven conspiracies haven't involved hoaxes as enormous as the moon landings or massive government plots to kill thousands of American citizens for seemingly no reason, but that doesn't mean that these things couldn't be true. What it does mean is that it would be prudent to follow the evidence instead of simply accepting any antigovernment narrative, as many alternative theorists do. Verified conspiracies are generally uncovered through the work of police, journalists, independent investigators, and the media, and not by YouTube personalities pushing their own unsubstantiated alternative scenarios without hard evidence or credible sources. These conspiracy theories are often portrayed in alternative media outlets as facts despite the existence of incontrovertible evidence demonstrating the contrary, so it's important to remember that you shouldn't get all your information from a single source—whether it's a so-called holy book or a conspiracy theory website.

DON'T BELIEVE EVERYTHING YOU READ

Information is more readily accessible than ever in this generation, with billions of books available at the click of a mouse. That makes this the age of information for anyone fortunate enough to have Internet access, but it also means we are in the age of *mis*information. People have access to science textbooks and the world's most notable literature, but they can just as easily choose to visit an unreliable website created earlier that morning by someone with no understanding of the topic at hand, or a purported news source with an ulterior motive or hidden agenda. More access to more information can equal more knowledge, but it can also contribute to the propagation of nonsense. Alternative theories are no exception. They often spread online like wildfire, largely because they tap into our subconscious fears and desires. The virality of these narratives is compounded by the fact that sensationalized stories, regardless of veracity, are often given more weight in the media due to their entertainment value—a result of the fact that even legitimate news publications have started counting "clicks" and altering their output accordingly. The popularity of these elaborate modern myths, along with increasing availability of false data online, leads some people with conspiratorial tendencies to accept theories with little or no real evidence. David Dunning, a professor of psychology at Cornell University and one of the first to study and observe the **Dunning–Kruger effect**—a cognitive bias that compels unskilled individuals to be unaware of their inadequacies and perceive themselves as much more well-equipped than they actually are—says the Internet offers some people benefits. Others, he said, will *"be misled into a false sense of expertise."*[6]

"My worry is not that we are losing the ability to make up our own minds, but that it's becoming too easy to do so. We should consult with others much more than we imagine," Dunning said. *"Other people may be imperfect as well, but often their opinions go a long way toward correcting our own imperfections, as our own imperfect expertise helps to correct their errors."*

So, how widespread are these beliefs? In April 2013, Public Policy Polling released a study of American voters that found 28 percent of those surveyed believed in a *"secretive power elite with a globalist agenda conspiring to eventually rule the world through an authoritarian government, or New World Order."*[7] The same survey also reported that 21 percent of American voters believe an alien craft crashed at Roswell in 1947, that 4 percent said they believe shape-shifting reptilian creatures control our world by taking on human form and gaining power, and that 22 percent of Republican respondents think that President Barack Obama is the "Anti-Christ." You may think some of these ideas are jokes, but many people take them seriously. David Icke, a conspiracy theorist who believes in the shape-shifting lizard people who manipulate our societies, even has a YouTube channel on which he posts videos of famous people licking their lips while talking, claiming that to be "reptilian" behavior. Not only do many people believe the information disseminated through these videos, but they also completely ignore the fact that most reptiles don't lick their lips, or even have lips. Many do, however, use their tongues to pick up and analyze scents, something human anatomy cannot accomplish.

Far-fetched and unfalsifiable conspiracy theories are spread in a number of ways, including through misleading online documentaries and articles that are designed to be convincing to those unfamiliar with the underlying facts. I've seen more conspiracy documentaries than I can remember, including the popular *Loose Change, Zeitgeist, Explosive Evidence* movies, and many more. They can certainly be convincing to some, but it's not difficult to create similar false narratives. In fact, it's been shown time and time again that people can make up any remotely plausible conspiracy theory, produce an accompanying misinformation documentary, and convince a significant portion of the population of something false. This happened with an Animal Planet mockumentary on the evidence for "mermaids" in 2013.[8]

To test this hypothesis on a relatively small scale, I disseminated via social media a series of graphics featuring false information and *"fine print"* with warnings like, *"These statements have not been evaluated by the Food and Drug Administration or any other regulatory agency or scientific organization. In fact, I made them up. Please remember to check your sources, especially when information validates your preexisting opinion."* Despite the fact that the fine print cautioned readers not to take the information seriously because it was merely an exercise in critical thinking, and regardless of how outlandish my claims were, each graphic was spread far and wide, with a number of them being shared hundreds of thousands of times and popping up on well-known conspiracy sites. My first image in this series included a photograph of a *Hydnellum pecki*, an inedible mushroom sometimes called the *"bleeding tooth fungus,"* and stated that it was actually a photo of Monsanto's *Roundup Ready* pomegranate with seeds that melt if not eaten within two weeks. Another graphic simply stated that orange juice pulp *"increases brain matter and I.Q."* and that genetically modified orange juice removes said pulp.[9] By playing on people's preconceived ideas and emotional reactions, I was able to convince them of some pretty far-fetched things.

If you do have a conspiratorial mindset that has fostered a belief in one or more unproven alternative theories, I recommend a new approach to look at the issues more rationally. Go back to the sources that convinced you, or more likely that supported your preconceived notions, and look at them again with a more skeptical eye. Ask more questions, be more critical, and you might find that you've been misled. As is always the case when searching for what's true, the next step is to seek more objective sources, avoiding unknown blogs and consistently unreliable alternative/fake news agencies. There are millions of websites and so-called news outlets that provide false or misleading information, but a few of the most commonly cited yet unreliable sources of information include: *Natural News, Collective Evolution, World Truth TV, Secrets of the Fed, InfoWars, Examiner, Underground Health, Real Farmacy, World Truth, The Blaze, Why Don't You Try This, PrisonPlanet, Mercola, Daily Mail, ConservaPedia, Holy Books, Zeitgeist, Above Top Secret, Before It's News, Answers in Genesis, Discovery Institute, World Net Daily, Daily Caller, The Rush Limbaugh Show, The Alex Jones Show*, and more. Other outlets, such as FOX News, MSNBC, *Daily Kos, Addicting Info, Huffington Post*, etc., provide more reliable information but with the guidance of a specific political agenda.

Whether you're consulting the above-mentioned unreliable or biased organizations or any other sources for information, it's always best to seek out the underlying scientific studies or references and gather your data from there. While some news outlets provide consistently more credible information than others, I don't trust any sources as absolute fact. Instead, I review a wide variety of sites and look at the citations and details.

WHY DO PEOPLE BELIEVE?

If the world is filled with poorly researched claims and false information, then why do people believe in these far-fetched hypotheses at all? It's partly because they *want* to believe them. These elaborate modern myths are similar to other unfounded beliefs in that they rely heavily on *confirmation bias*, which allows the believer to selectively filter facts to suit his or her established beliefs, and *inductive reasoning* (as opposed to *deductive reasoning*), which fosters broad generalizations being made from specific observations. These two factors allow the believer to make false conclusions based on general premises and reinforce those beliefs by only viewing material that already supports them, such as information from conspiracy-based websites. In one scientific study looking into conspiracy theory belief itself, researchers found that conspiracists primarily interacted with conspiracy-based pages and links and had a *"lower trust in other information sources."* The study, which sampled 1.2 million people online, also found that the theories *"find on the internet a natural medium for their diffusion."*

"[U]nsubstantiated claims reverberate for a timespan comparable to the one of more verified information and . . . usual consumers of conspiracy theories are more prone to interact with them," the authors of the study wrote in its conclusion.[10] *"Narratives grounded on conspiracy theories tend to reduce the complexity of reality and are able to contain the uncertainty they generate."*

If the urge to believe in one particular narrative is driving someone, and not a desire to uncover the truth, that person's standard for evidence is lowered when it comes to that topic. They might take the words of every self-proclaimed "whistleblower" at face value without any further information, and then disregard personal testimonies from government officials who deny the accusations. The believer may at times need only a rumor to form a belief, or they may base their claims on nothing more than the fact that "Classified" files exist. If it's secret, they reason, it must be an incriminating government conspiracy. But confidential doesn't mean "cover-up," and there are a number of seemingly benign reasons for documents to be categorized as "Classified."

Quassim Cassam, a professor of philosophy at the University of Warwick in Coventry, England, says people often think conspiratorially not because of the information they've absorbed, but because of their intellectual character traits. Cassam, who acknowledges his position is controversial, uses a fictional theorist named Oliver to show how gullibility, closed-mindedness, and other intellectual vices play a role in conspiracy theory belief.

"*Those who know him well say that he is easily duped, and you have independent evidence that he is careless in his thinking, with little understanding of the difference between genuine evidence and unsubstantiated speculation,*" Cassam wrote.[11] "*Suddenly it all begins to make sense, but only because the focus has shifted from Oliver's reasons to his character. You can now see his views about 9/11 in the context of his intellectual conduct generally, and this opens up the possibility of a different and deeper explanation of his belief than the one he gives: he thinks that 9/11 was an inside job because he is gullible in a certain way. He has what social psychologists call a 'conspiracy mentality.'*"

STATISM AND NATIONALISM

It's important to remember that there's a difference between being skeptical of massive, unproven alternative theories and simply clinging to a mainstream account because you trust the government. In other words, discounting far-fetched and unsubstantiated conspiracy claims is not the same as embracing "the official story." For many alternative theorists, however, these issues are black and white: you either believe every crazy notion they put forth or you're a "*government-worshiping statist.*" It's true that I am skeptical of the massive unproven conspiracy theories that I see peddled daily, but I am in no way a *statist*. Like blind faith, blind allegiance to a state has caused a substantial amount of harm, historically and in modern times, and extreme forms of nationalism, like jingoism and state (often American) exceptionalism, often hold believers hostage in the same way religions and other false beliefs do. I address this in my first published book, *Disproving Christianity*:

But religion, theism, and spirituality aren't the only mind-altering constructions within humanity that have spawned dangerous ideas; nationalism, for example, has a similar effect on people. It is the 'blind faith' that these institutions often create in individuals and groups that has caused many of the world's largest violent disputes.[12]

The state is a "sacred cow" for many people, but I personally think I lack whatever gives us a propensity to feel extreme unsupported patriotism, school spirit, and similar mindsets. Even as a young kid in school, I remember conscientiously objecting to rallies and noticing the attendees' tendency toward groupthink. Much like the late, great George Carlin, I could never understand ethnic or national pride, either.[13]

"Because to me pride should be reserved for something you achieve or attain on your own, not something that happens by accident of birth. Being Irish isn't a skill, it's a fuckin' genetic accident," the stand-up comedian said. *"You wouldn't say, 'I'm proud to be 5'11". I'm proud to have a predisposition for colon cancer.' So why the fuck would you be proud to be Irish, or proud to be Italian, or American or anything?"*

I agree with Carlin, but this issue is not about ethnic pride or about whether or not government officials have their constituents' best interests in mind—those are often just distractions thrown out by alternative theorists hoping to discount skeptics' opinions or requests for evidence. What is this all about, then? It's about following the evidence regardless of expectations and speculated motives. So, while I acknowledge that elected officials (like all people) do lie to their constituents and that no country is perfect, I also realize that doesn't automatically make "the government" guilty of causing every major disaster through a series of nefarious plots. We still need evidence to prove those things to be true. Once all the data is put forth, a person applying critical thinking skills can generally separate substantiated corruption from outlandish ideas completely lacking evidentiary support.

MALICE OR STUPIDITY?

I dislike corrupt politicians and inefficient governments as much as the next rational guy, but being greedy and inept doesn't necessarily make a politician, or anyone, culpable for every far-reaching alternative scheme someone posts online. I've seen evidence that politicians can lie, but I haven't seen data showing they can work together in the way most massive conspiracy theories would require. In fact, aside from the lack of empirical evidence to support them, the main reason I doubt most far-fetched conspiracy theories is not that I trust politicians, but that I don't think they are competent enough to pull off the intricate worldwide plots of which they're accused. Most of such allegations rely on hundreds of thousands of cooperating government officials working harmoniously with one another without any leaks or mistakes—a situation that's highly unlikely to say the least.

A study from Oxford University seems to support my position that it would be difficult to keep large-scale conspiracies under wraps.[14] Dr. David Robert Grimes, a physicist and cancer researcher at Oxford, used the number of people involved in a particular plot and other factors to create an equation that debunks the idea of massive, long-lasting conspiracies that pervade society for many years. He found that, even with parameter estimates favorable to conspiratorial leanings, the conspiracies "*tend rapidly towards collapse.*"

"*Even if there was a concerted effort, the sheer number of people required for the sheer scale of hypothetical scientific deceptions would inextricably undermine these nascent conspiracies. For a conspiracy of even only a few thousand actors, intrinsic failure would arise within decades,*" Grimes wrote in the peer-reviewed study, adding that, for hundreds of thousands, failure would be assured in less than five years.

"*It's also important to note that this analysis deals solely with intrinsic failure, or the odds of a conspiracy being exposed intentionally or accidentally by actors involved—extrinsic analysis by non-participants would also increase the odds of detection, rendering such Byzantine cover-ups far more likely to fail.*"

When contemplating the possibility of far-reaching government conspiracies that cause disastrous effects, I like to employ *Hanlon's razor*, a philosophical principle that helps us to rule out unlikely explanations for phenomena. The razor, possibly named for Robert J. Hanlon, states that one should "*Never attribute to malice that which is adequately explained by stupidity.*"

GOVERNMENTS ARE PEOPLE

Those who perpetuate unfounded conspiracy theories have a tendency to morph "the government" into a singular, all-powerful entity that must either love or hate everyone, but this mentality ignores that all governments are made up of individuals with their own intentions, motives, flaws, and agendas. Governments are composed of people, and people are prone to deception, greed, and other bad things, but that doesn't mean one can always assume the government is at fault and blame the lack of evidence on the unproven conspiracy itself.

A lot of believers go as far as to claim that governments are covering up lifesaving cures or even actively poisoning their people, but, assuming leaders are as greedy and capable as many alternative theorists believe, killing off the population means killing their profits. According to that worldview, who are "they" supposed to market to? Who would they brainwash and control? That's not to mention that people who work for the government, and their families, are susceptible to the same problems as us. They can't poison the food or water supply without endangering their family, or at least people who they love and hold dearly. Similarly, high-ranking officials and corporate executives likely aren't hiding "the cure" for cancer,[15] if for no other reason than doing so would risk their lives and the lives of those they care about.[16] Furthermore, if American pharmaceutical companies are involved in a scheme to conceal cancer remedies, as some theorists have suggested, how would they halt research from the rest of the world's scientists? Why couldn't someone else just *rediscover* the cure? Steven P. Novella, a clinical neurologist and assistant professor at Yale University School of Medicine, says the idea that they would all be in on a massive conspiracy to hide the greatest cure known to mankind is *"beyond absurd."*

"For those who think the profit motive is sufficient explanation, not all of the people and institutions named are for profit," Novella wrote for *Science-Based Medicine*.[17] *"And what about countries with socialized medicine who could dramatically reduce their health care costs if a cancer cure were found? Is Canada, the UK, all of the European Union, in fact, in on the conspiracy to protect American cancer treatment profits? It's as if hidden cure conspiracy theorists forget that there are other countries in the world."*

The same logic that disposes of the hidden cure and mass-poisoning myths can be applied to the belief that the government is hiding the existence of poisonous "chem-trails," supposedly caused by top-secret fuel additives and spraying mechanisms attached to passenger jets.[18] These lines that often follow planes are commonly (and scientifically) known as *contrails* or condensation trails, but a large number of alternative theorists think they are part of a government conspiracy to kill citizens, make them sick, or control the weather, or that they are used for some other sinister yet undisclosed purpose. The most common piece of "evidence" presented by believers for chem-trails is the (often only perceived) fact that more and more contrails are being seen in the skies over time. They often recall the past, when the sky was "clear," and then compare that (perhaps flawed) memory to what they see today. The best explanation for an increase in visible contrails, which have existed since planes could fly at a high altitude, could be heightened air traffic or newer engine designs, but it's probably not a *"government conspiracy to poison us all."* If the chemicals in a contrail five miles in the air are dangerous to you on the ground, they are a risk to people just about anywhere, so unless you see high-ranking officials wearing gas masks when outside or avoiding the open air entirely, you can conclude those same people probably aren't endangering themselves and loved ones out of nothing more than loyalty to their respective governments.

The common alternative narrative is that contrails quickly dissipate in the sky, while chem-trails—with their potentially fatal (yet often vague) chemical additions—remain in the sky for hours on end. However, this position is based entirely on a misunderstanding of the science behind vapor trails, which can disappear quickly or be persistent and long lasting depending on the circumstances. For those who do believe in chem-trails, imagine that contrails are clouds, because that's exactly what they are. They are composed of frozen water vapor, so the higher up they are, or the colder the air is in that particular part of the sky, the longer they stay. They're just man-made clouds, so they behave the same way as clouds found in nature. Furthermore, if chem-trails existed, it would be relatively easy to test the vapor and report (scientifically, with peer review) the specific poisons that are present, yet this hasn't happened. People have presented evidence of certain elements in rainwater or dust and proclaimed it proof that chem-trails exist, but they have never identified contrails as the source. In fact, one of the only serious studies on the topic, published by J. Marvin Herndon,[19] was retracted after the journal's editors and other scientists discovered a number of errors and *"crucial concerns."* Dr. Paul B. Tchounwou from

Jackson State University disclosed a mistake made in the reported value for average leachate concentration of aluminum that "*invalidates the conclusions of the article.*" He also uncovered flaws in data collection in general.

"*The chemical compositions obtained for rainwater and HEPA air filter dust are only compared to chemical compositions obtained for coal-fly-ash leaching experiments. The author did not attempt to compare his results to chemical compositions of other potential sources,*" Tchounwou wrote in the retraction article.[20] "*Thus, at this stage, the work is preliminary since it is not clear what the source of these chemicals is.*"

Tchounwou further noted that he and Dr. Franck Vazquez, chief scientific officer of Multidisciplinary Digital Publishing Institute, thought the language of the initial paper was "*not sufficiently scientifically objective for a research article.*"

Let me be clear: being skeptical of the chem-trail conspiracy theory is not the same as denying that some forms of weather control are possible. *Geoengineering*, while it remains on a small scale for now, is a real science that involves complicated and possibly dangerous procedures. However, there isn't a single link between these efforts to control our environment and the long, thin contrails you see in the sky every day. There is no contrail/chem-trail distinction because there are no "chem-trails." That's not a system that has ever been shown to be used for chemical delivery in geoengineering attempts, nor would it be a very efficient one. In other words, yes, there are some efforts to control our climate. However, they are not linked to airplanes or contrails or visible white streaks in the sky.

To drive this point home, and reiterate that governments are composed of human beings like you and me, I wrote this brief summary:

THE GOVERNMENT DOESN'T LOVE YOU.
THE GOVERNMENT DOESN'T WANT TO KILL YOU.
IT DOESN'T WANT TO TAKE YOUR GUNS OR POISON YOUR FAMILY.
THE GOVERNMENT DOESN'T HAVE FEELINGS OR INTENTIONS.
GOVERNMENTS ARE JUST GROUPS OF PEOPLE, HIRED TO REPRESENT US.
IF YOU DON'T LIKE YOUR GOVERNMENT, WORK TO CHANGE IT.

CONSPIRACY THEORY CHALLENGE

If corruption exists, I want it uncovered; I just don't want false allegations born of ignorance to get in the way of real investigations. Even though there are a huge number of false claims hurled daily, I do believe in justice, and I think that any politicians guilty of conspiracy should be held liable for their actions. That's why I encourage those who believe a particular conspiracy theory to do everything possible to prove it and make sure the responsible parties face consequences. If you really believe an alternative narrative to be true, you should work as hard as you can to establish the facts and expose that truth. Once you've gathered enough data and you think you have the evidence required to prove, for example, that the George W. Bush administration planned the attacks of 9/11, that vaccines cause autism, or that chem-trails exist, then you should hire a lawyer and take your case to an international court. You should show the judge(s) all of your scientifically valid evidence and expose the government for what it is. Even without the legal system, however, you can use your evidence to get independent journalists to join your cause and help you show the citizens of your country that their government perpetuated what could potentially be one of the largest conspiracies of all time. If the evidence is truly compelling, any responsible person who discovers it would do everything in his or her power to prove it to the world.

Unfortunately, most believers don't take me up on my *conspiracy theory challenge*. Instead, acting out of a deep mistrust for government, alternative theorists are more likely to simply perpetuate misleading and debunked YouTube videos and documentaries produced by other conspiracy-minded "experts" with whom they agree. Many theorists will even insist that it's impossible to bring a country like the United States to justice for any alleged misdeeds, ignoring the numerous times in which international courts have ruled against America and other nations. If the corruption is indeed that deep, however, so much so that courts completely independent of the United States are a part of the conspiracy, that's even more of a reason to show American citizens what their government officials are up to. A few good journalists could make their careers if they could prove even one of the many far-reaching conspiracies already believed in by many, even if the scientific facts and disclosures are only accepted by the so-called court of public opinion.

When asked to provide empirical evidence required to prove their claims beyond a reasonable doubt, those who perpetuate false conspiracy claims often resort to the assertion that the ultra-competent politicians responsible have simply eliminated all evidence. But *no evidence* does not equal *evidence*, and it never will. You can't claim that gods, aliens, or the government hid every piece of proof supporting your claims. When you do, it always sounds the same:

> "GOD IS SO GREAT THAT HE HID ALL THE EVIDENCE FOR HIS EXISTENCE. HE WANTED US TO HAVE FAITH!"

> "OUR ANCIENT ALIEN OVERLORDS WOULD BE TOO SMART AND ADVANCED TO HAVE LEFT EVIDENCE OF THEIR TIME ON EARTH!"

> "THE GOVERNMENT IS SO POWERFUL AND CORRUPT THAT IT HID ALL THE EVIDENCE FOR MY FAR-FETCHED AND UNSUBSTANTIATED CONSPIRACY CLAIM!"

No matter the topic of discussion, "someone stole the evidence" cannot be used as evidence of anything in and of itself. You shouldn't base your beliefs on speculation, or information that may be uncovered in the future, or documents you think have been hidden, because there are just too many assumptions involved. And if you have to start with assumptions and not facts to form your arguments, that is the first clue that you might be emotionally involved and need to take a step back and reevaluate. As Isaac Asimov said, "*Your assumptions are your windows on the world. Scrub them off every once in a while, or the light won't come in.*"

GOVERNMENT AS A GOD

The pro–conspiracy theory arguments are often focused on the notion that the conspirators are capable of covering up anything—including all documents and possible loose ends regarding the government-sanctioned murder of thousands of citizens. In this way, false conspiracy theories are similar to religious beliefs. Those who put forth these unproven alternative series of events have an enormous amount of *faith* in the government's ability to plan, execute, and cover up enormous terrorist acts across the globe (yet they underestimate incredibly motivated religious fanatics with time to plot). To me, this shows how people crave conspiracies for the same reason they crave gods. They want a higher power to be responsible; they want to live in a world in which someone is there, pulling the strings.[21] To some, the only thing scarier than a world run by the Illuminati or a god is the reality: a world run by no one in particular.

Where believers see a secret and powerful force capable of anything, I see flawed individuals. I see how our governmental bodies behave and what they're capable of. I see that our representatives lie, cheat, and steal, just like anyone else, and that they're often caught for doing just that. What I don't see is evidence to support the conclusion that nearly every single politician is somehow part of (or capable of being part of) enormous cover-ups that would span across the globe and political party divides, and throughout successive administrations. Most alternative theorists themselves would likely claim to have little confidence in elected officials' abilities to govern, or even pass simple legislation, but they somehow find it easier to believe they're capable of masterminding and executing massive, conspiratorial plots to the detriment of all citizens. Their belief in the government as an all-powerful deity is just too strong to be upset by mere facts and voting records.

In the same way a religious fundamentalist might call scientific discoveries that challenge his or her beliefs the work of the devil, dogmatic alternative theorists often discount all opposition as part of the grand conspiracy itself. This black and white mentality is clearly flawed because it's not fair or logical to assume that anyone who disagrees on specific, far-fetched, and unproven claims is necessarily a part of the cover-up, or that they are embracing government authority for some monetary benefit. Yet, as someone who speaks out against unsubstantiated claims of all sorts, I've been accused of being a part of more conspiracies than I can count. David Aaronovitch, a British journalist and author of *Voodoo Histories: The Role of Conspiracy Theory in Shaping Modern History*, describes the hypocrisy of this mindset in general.

"*It goes without saying, doesn't it, that any of us who argue against the conspiracy theories are part of the conspiracy?*" he said. "*It's interesting that, for conspiracy theorists, it's quite often the case that they cannot accept the sincerity of others. Their own sincerity is not in doubt; the sincerity of others is a huge problem.*"

For the record, I'm not a member of the Illuminati, I'm not in the pocket of Big Pharma, and I haven't been paid off by the government. I just haven't seen empirical evidence to back up many ultra-complex conspiracy claims I encounter in daily life. If anything, I'm a shill for "Big Evidence." That's my only real agenda.

THE ILLUMINATI

There is no more god-like force in alternative theory lore than *The Illuminati*, a mysterious and powerful cabal that is thought by many to control the world. Studying the history of the defunct secret society, while perhaps not as impressive as the myth that is alive today, shows us a much more realistic story. The Bavarian Illuminati, which was founded by a German law professor,[22] was only around for about 10 years.[23] The group wanted to emphasize the importance of secularism and reason and, when its members came to power, influence public policy to reflect their values. The Illuminati in Bavaria didn't fully realize its goals, and was outlawed and ultimately disbanded, but its legend lives on today.

In modern times, the Illuminati refers to an unknown and essentially all-powerful group that counts nearly every major world leader among its ranks. Believers say the Illuminati quietly controls everything, from elections to the music industry, and that its members, allegedly including everyone from world leaders like President Barack Obama to singers such as Jay Z and Madonna, often feature the group's symbolism—the most well-known of which is the triangle—in their works. Despite the vast network of conspirators supposedly present within today's Illuminati, there isn't a single piece of evidence for its existence at all. There are zero leaks, recordings, or slipups demonstrating that the group is still active, and believers can only point to its powerful members as the reason for that. They are so incredibly competent, according to theorists, that they can entirely conceal their high-profile operations without any information on them being revealed.

Believers in the Illuminati often point to music videos and award ceremonies in which popular artists seem to be outwardly expressing Illuminati triangles, saying these clips prove there is an imminent New World Order attack coming from the global elite class, but these alternative theorists are only victims of their own mind. More often than not, singers, actors, and politicians aren't surrounding themselves with Illuminati images. Instead, the theorists' pattern-seeking brains pick them out due to their own perception biases. This is the same process behind why you might notice more white cars after buying one for yourself, as well as the reason why some people claim to see the number 23 as a constant in every facet of their lives. The fact is that, like the number 23 and white cars, you can't avoid being near triangles sometimes—it's one of the most fundamental geometric shapes. Furthermore, I've always wondered why a group as powerful as this legendary Illuminati would be so focused on these subtle advertising efforts. Dave Sirus, a writer for *Saturday Night Live*, points out the ridiculous nature of the Illuminati triangle belief in popular culture.

"*The Illuminati is the belief that the most powerful people on Earth are in a conspiracy to leave giant clues that they're part of a conspiracy*," Sirus tweeted.[24]

NUMEROLOGY AND SYNCHRONICITY

The effect responsible for the perceived repetition of triangles by some Illuminati believers is probably not too far off from something you experience in your daily life. Do you feel like you look at the clock more often when it's on a certain number, like 11:11? Many people do. There are a lot of supernatural theories for why people are drawn to these numbers, especially when it comes to 11. Some people say seeing the number will grant you one wish, while others believe it's an angel trying to communicate with you. People who believe in numerology might even think seeing 11 somewhere is especially important, considering it is the first of the so-called Master numbers.[25] We have plenty of paranormal explanations, but what does science say? Why are people drawn to clocks at 11:11? The answer is simple: they aren't. It only seems that way because the number has been given significance in some cultures. In other words, if 11:11 means something to you, you will notice it more. You might look at the clock 30 times in a four-hour period and not even realize you looked at all, but the one time you glance up and it reads "11:11," you register the significance and it sticks out in your mind. This is part of the pattern-recognition skill set for which humans are known, and the phenomenon, despite being linked by many people to numerology and other allegedly supernatural notions or forces, is well known and well studied. The interesting thing is that, for some people, "12:34" is the number they think they see most often. Similarly, someone who was born on December 19 might be "drawn to" clocks when they read 12:19. It's all a matter of perception.

Noticing recurring patterns is common with humans, and it's part of what has made us a successful species, but sometimes we are so good at it that we notice patterns that aren't actually there. This is the case when someone believes the number 11 appears to them more frequently and in a meaningful way, but there are many other examples. The 23 enigma, for instance, describes the belief that most major tragedies and developments in the world are connected to the number 23. The number itself is said to mean any number of things depending on the believer, from good luck to bad luck and everywhere in between, but this act of noticing it over and over again is just another form of selection bias. Author Robert Anton Wilson, who is often credited with popularizing the so-called enigma, has admitted that people can see the clustering illusion effect with anything—not just the number 23. He also said most conspiracy theorists suffer from "varying degrees of paranoia."

"When you start looking for something you tend to find it. This wouldn't be like Simon Newcomb, the great astronomer, who wrote a mathematical proof that heavier than air flight was impossible and published it a day before the Wright brothers took off," Wilson said.[26] *"I'm talking about people who found a pattern in nature and wrote several scientific articles and got it accepted by a large part of the scientific community before it was generally agreed that there was no such pattern, it was all just selective perception."*

Coincidences happen all the time, but many people feel the need to attribute those random chance events to something greater or more meaningful. This happens with numbers like 11 and 23, but these only represent a small subset of potential examples. How many times have you been humming along with an *earworm*, a song or tune stuck in your head, only to have it play on the radio minutes later? Have you ever been talking about your sister just as she called? These events don't mean you are a psychic and, in fact, they don't mean much of anything at all. Statistically, it is likely that, at some point, you would receive a call from your sister while discussing her. Think of all the times you mentioned her name and the phone didn't ring, and think of every song you've had repeating in your head that didn't suddenly start playing. You tend to disregard those misses, while remembering and categorizing the inherently more interesting and unexpected (and therefore notable) hits. This phenomenon of noticing unrelated coincidences and attributing meaning to them is called *synchronicity*, and it was first coined by Swiss psychiatrist Carl Jung. Jung, who used the concept to promote paranormal ideas,[27] may have introduced the notion of inherently meaningful acausal connections, but many others have championed it, as well. As Jonathan C. Smith pointed out, *"Popular paranormalists have made much of coincidences."*

"A present-future coincidence might be seen as a prophecy, an event that correctly follows an omen or prediction. A present-present coincidence might suggest a set of events that are remarkably linked by some paranormal process outside of the world of causality," he wrote. *"The best way to explore what is going on is to contemplate a variety of remarkable coincidences."*

SKEPTICISM VS. DENIALISM

Many alternative theorists claim they are "just asking questions" about the government's stories surrounding particular events, ever remaining doubtful of their claims, and that by doing so they are practicing rigorous skepticism. But the problem isn't with asking questions; it's with the conjecture-based assertions that follow. False conspiracy theories aren't just about questioning authority; they're about making up and perpetuating false versions of events without hard evidence. If you're wondering where to draw the line, here it is: if you don't perpetuate unfalsifiable and conspiratorial claims out of your own ignorance, using the government of the gaps fallacy, then you probably aren't a part of the alternative theory problem. David Aaronovitch explains this quite well:

"As long as conspiracy theorists are confined to raising what they call 'disturbing questions' about the official theory, they're on safe ground," he said. *"But as soon as they get into the business of saying what their theories are clearly, what they think happened, then they have to begin to meet some evidential tests too. And it's at this point that conspiracy theories inevitably falter."*

While it's true that skepticism in a broad sense is based on questioning claims, pure distrust of governmental entities is not synonymous with *scientific* skepticism—and it isn't a methodology that will help you get to real answers. In fact, to me it seems most alternative theorists have the very faith that scientific skepticism makes unnecessary, although they may put it in different places than other believers. I understand not trusting the government blindly, but what I don't get is how people claiming to be skeptics can trust random, poorly designed websites even more. This pseudo-skepticism that allows for belief in grandiose and unfounded conspiracy claims is not about an honest search for reality, but about paranoia, gaps in knowledge, and reaffirming previously held ideas.

Doubt is healthy and important, but if you don't follow up with critical thinking and a real, objective search for evidence, and instead you treat the government parties differently than others, it becomes stubbornness and denial. And *denialism* isn't skepticism. Skepticism, as a process for determining the truth, is about questioning claims and looking at the evidence presented. Once the facts are gathered, a skeptic makes a determination based on those facts, and not based on a prior belief that one party is wrong and engaged in a cover-up. Denialism, on the other hand, is characterized by a refusal to believe something despite the overwhelming evidence that it is true.[28]

Lee McIntyre, a research fellow at the Center for Philosophy and History of Science at Boston University, explains that it's important to distinguish between when we believe or disbelieve because of a high standard for evidence and when we are *"just engaging in a bit of motivated reasoning and letting our opinions take over."*

"When we withhold belief because the evidence does not live up to the standards of science, we are skeptical. When we refuse to believe something, even in the face of what most others would take to be compelling evidence, we are engaging in denial," McIntyre wrote for the *New York Times*.[29] *"In most cases, we do this because at some level it upsets us to think that the theory is true."*

For a good lesson in the differences between skepticism and denial, we need to look no further than the television series *The X-Files*. Federal Bureau of Investigation (FBI) Special Agent Fox Mulder, the character who serves as the believer in the show, is actually a good example of a skeptic. Yes, he *"wants to believe,"* but he doesn't usually do so without good reason. Mulder is curious. He asks questions and he always investigates thoroughly until he finds a reliable source or uncovers a paper trail. He doesn't simply accept extraordinary claims on a whim despite the fact that, in his world, those claims often have merit. He's right, and he proves it time and time again. FBI Special Agent Dr. Dana Scully, on the other hand, who represents the "skeptical" mindset, is actually not a good skeptic at all—she's a denier. Scully, a Catholic, not only embraces her religious faith without applying any skeptical inquiry whatsoever, she also continues to doubt the existence of paranormal beings and high-level conspiracies despite seeing overwhelming evidence showing they are real. She is proven wrong repeatedly, yet she maintains her steadfast denial and reluctance to investigate certain matters. Scully is good at doubting far-fetched assertions, but she isn't a good skeptic because she lacks Mulder's passion and curiosity and because her conclusions are shaped by preconceived notions and not scientific proof.

MOON LANDING "HOAX"

When I think of denialism, moon-landing hoaxers often spring to mind before anything else. This isn't an incredibly popular conspiracy theory, with numerous polls showing only about 6 percent of the U.S. population doubts that we sent people to the moon,[30] but it is intriguing nonetheless. The belief that NASA never executed manned missions to the moon, and that photos and videos from these events were actually staged in a movie studio in 1969, is particularly interesting to me because there is verifiable proof that we have been there. For one, the lunar laser ranging experiment accurately measures the distance between Earth and the moon using lasers on Earth aimed at retroreflectors planted on the moon during the Apollo program.[31] In case that piece of clear, accessible evidence wasn't good enough, in 2015, NASA made more than 10,000 raw, high-resolution moon-landing photos available to the public.[32] That's not to mention that, as former astronaut and second man on the moon Buzz Aldrin has pointed out, the context of the moon landing as part of the Space Race during the Cold War means that a hoax is highly unlikely. That's because *"the Russians would have exposed by now if we didn't land,"* according to Aldrin. The evidence against the alternative theory doesn't end there. As Neil deGrasse Tyson explains, there are all kinds of facts that prove we went to the moon.

"You can look at the Saturn V rocket, which got us to the moon and back, and calculate how much fuel is in there, and watch the thing take off, and ask yourself: where the hell do you think this thing is going?" Tyson asked. *"There's enough fuel to get you to the moon, and stuff left over to come back. It's not just going down to the grocery store—it is a Saturn V rocket."*

So why would some people continue to adhere to an idea that has been definitively debunked? International businesswoman Margaret Heffernan, in her book *Willful Blindness: Why We Ignore the Obvious at Our Peril*, suggests that willful blindness *"doesn't have a single driver, but many."*

"Our blindness grows out of the small, daily decisions that we make, which embed us more snugly inside our affirming thoughts and values," Heffernan wrote.[33] *"And what's most frightening about this process is that as we see less*

and less, we feel more comfort and greater certainty. We think we see more—even as the landscape shrinks."

We know moon-landing hoaxers are wrong, but does this belief cause harm? It did for at least one man. Moon-landing denier Bart Sibrel, who claims all six Apollo moon landings from 1969 to 1972 were staged, approached Apollo 11 crew member Aldrin in 2002 and called him *"a coward, and a liar, and a thief."* Sibrel continued to harass the retired engineer, telling him that he needed to *"repent"* and asking him to swear on the Bible that he went to the moon. Aldrin, who had been lured to the location under false pretenses, finally punched the man in the jaw. Sibrel tried to pursue criminal charges, but the Los Angeles County District Attorney's Office ultimately concluded that Aldrin was provoked and that it was *"unlikely a jury would find Aldrin guilty of a misdemeanor battery charge."*[34]

FLAT EARTH CONSPIRACY

Moon-landing deniers aren't the only alternative theorists who accept their narrative despite verifiable evidence to the contrary. Recently, there has been an uptick in the belief that Earth is actually flat, and not an oblate spheroid as photographic evidence, mathematics, and basic observations have shown. The Flat Earth conspiracy, which posits that NASA scientists, world governments, and any people who can do simple calculations are hiding the truth that Earth is flat, is especially notable because it is a belief that has become increasingly popular in the twenty-first century. It's commonly believed that scientists hundreds of years ago thought Earth was flat and that everyone else accepted it as a fact, but this is actually a popular misconception repeated even in some textbooks.[35] The reality is much more interesting: ancient Greeks knew Earth was (nearly) spherical by measuring shadows, and educated people have understood that fact ever since.[36] Contrary to popular belief, even Christopher Columbus and his crew, often credited with "discovering" the Americas, knew the shape of Earth.

So why do some people believe Earth is flat today, when our ancestors knew better? The answer lies partly within the power of popular culture and the ease with which misinformation spreads in our technological era. The modern Flat Earth belief got its start with an English writer named

Samuel Rowbotham, who published a book called *Earth Not a Globe* in the 1800s and based his theories largely on biblical interpretations.[37] The torch was later passed to Samuel Shenton, who founded the International Flat Earth Society (IFES), but the belief fell in popularity when IFES shut down in 2001 due to the death of its then-president Charles K. Johnson.[38] The society and its core beliefs were resurrected yet again in 2004 as *"a place for free thinkers and the intellectual exchange of ideas."*[39] The modern incarnation of the Flat Earth Society now has a popular website, which includes the world's largest public collection of literature on the topic, but it isn't fully responsible for the increasing adherence to the belief. Instead, the surge came from famous figures, including a recording artist known as B.o.B, who proposed the Flat Earth hypothesis without any scientific backing whatsoever. B.o.B first mentioned his belief in a Flat Earth in January 2016 on Twitter, prompting a discussion with Neil deGrasse Tyson, who attempted to convince the singer that he was wrong. B.o.B then released a song called *"Flatline,"* in which he accused Tyson and NASA of feeding false information to the public in exchange for monetary compensation. Tyson's rapper nephew released a song response, and the astrophysicist himself responded, as well.

"Alright, listen B.o.B once and for all . . . it's a fundamental fact of calculus and non-Euclidean geometry, small sections of large curved surfaces will always look flat to little creatures that crawl upon it," Tyson said on an episode of Comedy Central's *The Nightly Show*, pointing to Isaac Newton's statement that, if he saw further than others, it was only because he stood on the shoulders of giants (his predecessors).[40] *"So that's right, B.o.B, when you stand on the shoulders of those who came before, you might just see far enough to realize the earth isn't fucking flat."*

Tyson added that, in a free society, you can and should be able to think whatever you want.

"If you want to think the earth is flat, go right ahead," he said. *"But if you think the world is flat, and you have influence over others, as would successful rappers, or even presidential candidates, then being wrong becomes being harmful to the health, the wealth, and the security of our citizenry."*

A number of people sided with B.o.B and other famous believers, including model and actress Tila Tequila,[41] even though no one has presented empirical data to prove their claims. These high-profile Flat Earthers continue to push the claim despite the fact that most of them have eyes, and some may even have telescopes, and they are capable of seeing other planetary bodies and their semi-spherical shapes. Do they believe every other object in the sky is rounded except for Earth? Or that the other planets are merely painted on a black tarp in the sky?

The lesson here is that celebrities aren't always right. You shouldn't believe Earth is flat because B.o.B. said so, just like you shouldn't avoid vaccines because of Jenny McCarthy. But that doesn't mean celebrities are always wrong, either. When Leonardo DiCaprio won an Oscar for Best Actor in a Leading Role, he used his acceptance speech to draw attention to the most prominent example of denialism today, and the one that could have the most far-reaching implications: refusal to accept the reality of global climate change.

"*Climate change is real; it is happening right now. It is the most urgent threat facing our entire species, and we need to work collectively together and stop procrastinating,*" DiCaprio said. "*We need to support leaders around the world who do not speak for the big polluters, but who speak for all of humanity, for the indigenous people of the world, for the billions and billions of underprivileged people out there who would be most affected by this.*"

CLIMATE CHANGE

There is clear evidence, including temperature measurements, pollen analyses, cloud cover observations, and unique weather patterns, demonstrating that our climate is in the process of shifting. That fact itself isn't too jarring, considering that Earth has gone through many natural changes over the course of its history, but this time around the data shows that fossil fuels are a major catalyst. In *Cosmos*, Neil deGrasse Tyson explained the differences between "climate" and "weather," as well as how we can actually measure our effects on changing climate patterns.

"*The strongest force driving climate change right now is the increasing CO2 from the burning of fossil fuels, which is trapping more heat from the Sun,*" Tyson said. "*All that additional energy has to go somewhere. Some of it warms the air. Most of it ends up in the oceans. All over the world, the oceans are getting warmer.*"

It's important to note that the idea of anthropogenic global climate change isn't based on Tyson's opinion, nor is it based on the opinions of any person. Its foundation is built on measurable facts and data. There is a clear scientific consensus on the matter, with more than 97 percent of scientists who study the phenomenon agreeing that humans are contributing to it,[42] and most of the people who deny the reality seem to be protecting their vested interests or hoodwinked by those who are. Some corporate executives who rely on less regulated carbon dioxide emissions,[43] for instance, and—through their lobbying efforts—certain policymakers in the United States,[44] have actively attempted to undermine the established science on climate change and sow the seeds of doubt. There has been some pushback in the form of efforts to hold fossil fuel companies accountable for misinformation,[45] but, for many, the scheme is working. People all over the world, including up to 25 percent of Americans,[46] believe climate change is all just part of a plan by "Big Science" to pull the wool over the public's eyes. To what end, however, I'm not sure. It seems the only symptom of accepting our role in this particular climate event would be reduced emissions, more green jobs, and an increasingly stable environment. Regardless of the rampant science denial in this area, the facts remain the same: climate change is real and we are part of the problem. This has been confirmed by every major scientific body that deals with the issue, including the Intergovernmental Panel on Climate Change (IPCC),[47] the National Academy of Sciences,[48] the American Meteorological Society,[49] the American Geophysical Union,[50] and more. Naomi Oreskes, professor of the history of science and director of graduate studies at Harvard University, explains that the idea that there is discord among climate scientists "*is incorrect.*"

"*Many details about climate interactions are not well understood, and there are ample grounds for continued research to provide a better basis for understanding climate dynamics. The question of what to do about climate change is also still open,*" Oreskes wrote in an essay for *Science.*[51] "*But there is a scientific consensus on the reality of anthropogenic climate change. Climate scientists have repeatedly tried to make this clear. It is time for the rest of us to listen.*"

The science denialism and anti-intellectualism present within the anti–climate change movement is not rare or unique. In fact, in many ways, it is similar to what we see in those who strictly oppose life-saving vaccinations. In each case, you have people with conspiratorial and antiscience mentalities working overtime to convince the general public that the vast majority of peer-reviewed, scientific studies are wrong and that scientists themselves are covering up the truth. The doubt surrounding the theory of evolution by natural selection is another example of modern denialism, and there are many more, but the good news for us is that science itself doesn't depend on the beliefs of others.[52] Comedian John Oliver, when commenting on a poll showing that one in four Americans disbelieved in climate change, made this point extremely clear.

"You don't need people's opinion on a fact," Oliver said. *"You might as well have a poll asking, 'Which number is bigger, 15 or 5?' or 'Do owls exist?' or 'Are there hats?"*

Questioning things is great and researching is even better, but settling for a shady hypothesis and rejecting the obvious truth is worse than simply saying, "I don't know." The only way to upset established scientific knowledge is with your own more compelling scientific findings, so if you doubt evolution or climate change or the effectiveness of vaccines, or any other matter on which there is a scientific consensus, I hope you'll do the work to prove you are right instead of spreading misinformation based on fear and ignorance. Healthy inquiry and real investigation is one thing, but making your own outrageous, faith-based assertions is quite another. The fact that a person distrusts scientists or a particular government doesn't mean they are guilty (or even capable) of any alleged crimes, so at some point real evidence has to be put forth.

THE 9/11 "TRUTHER" MOVEMENT

You can find a conspiracy theory surrounding just about anything, including the term "conspiracy theorist" itself, which some have asserted is merely the result of a government conspiracy to stigmatize those who question authority. So it's only natural, in the wake of any large-scale world event or attack, that some conspiracy-minded people will say things "don't add up" and attempt to replace reality with their own opinions. But those opinions are irrelevant when we are dealing with the facts.

One of the most popular alternative theories today is the so-called *9/11 Truther movement.* According to a 2008 world opinion poll,[53] 15 percent of those surveyed said they believed the U.S. government was behind the attacks that targeted the World Trade Center and the Pentagon on September 11, 2001, with 46 percent of respondents saying Al-Qaeda was likely responsible and 25 percent saying they didn't know. Believers in this particular myth are often under the impression that those of us who are skeptical of their claims are merely nationalists who doubt that the Bush administration would ever do such a thing, and some even go as far as to say that the large-scale "inside job" hypothesis hasn't been proven because the subject itself is taboo. For me, however, this is not the case. I'm fully aware that President George W. Bush and his allies could have committed (and perhaps did commit) atrocities while in office, but I simply haven't seen any empirical data showing that they committed this particular one. The subject isn't off-limits for me, either. I welcome open inquiry into any topic and I regularly discuss and entertain 9/11 conspiracy apologists' claims. Each time, however, believers fail to provide a single shred of hard evidence for the inside job theory, the *no-plane theory*, or the myriad of other unsubstantiated, speculation-based narratives put forth.

Because of the popularity of this particular myth, I've compiled a number of questions to help believers critically analyze their ideas. If you *do* believe 9/11 was an inside job, I hope you'll consider asking yourself the following:

1. If you think no plane hit the Pentagon on 9/11, and that it was actually a missile of some kind, then what happened to American Airlines Flight 77, which carried 64 people who disappeared that day? These are people with families and careers and years of documented histories and they were all killed in the plane that was destroyed almost entirely when it careened into the Pentagon wall on September 11. If you doubt this verifiable occurrence, which was witnessed by many people and confirmed by investigators on site, you should be able to present a viable alternative. You should have some evidence for what happened to the plane and its dozens of passengers.

2. It's commonly believed by alternative theorists that the United States attacked its own buildings as a false flag, so that American citizens would rally behind the government in its war against "*terrorism*" abroad. However, if the Bush administration had orchestrated the events of September 11, wouldn't those in charge have blamed Iraqi terrorists to make the invasion that followed more easily justified? The 19 people who reportedly carried out the plot included 15 men from Saudi Arabia, two from the United Arab Emirates, one from Egypt, and one from Lebanon,[54] but zero from Iraq, which is where one of the

wars that followed took place. If you believe the inside job hypothesis, then you must be able to explain this disparity.

3. If the Bush administration planned and executed the attacks on 9/11, then what was the motivation of the hijackers themselves? If these men weren't expecting a reward of virgins and paradise in the afterlife, then why did they agree to become martyrs? A big part of determining guilt is looking for a motive, and with a suicide mission this is even more important. Is the government paying the attackers' families millions of dollars? If so, there should be a paper trail. The fact is that Osama bin Laden, about a year after the events transpired, outlined motives that included religious division and oppression, U.S. support of Israel, the presence of U.S. troops in Saudi Arabia, and more.[55]

4. Alternative theorists often claim there must have been bombs in the World Trade Center towers because their destruction "*looked like*" a controlled demolition. Forgetting for a moment that it's impossible to tell if something was intentionally demolished by merely observing a collapse (especially to the untrained eye), and ignoring that no building that tall has ever been purposefully destroyed using those tactics,[56] and glossing over the fact that no real evidence for this claim has ever been uncovered, why do explosive devices necessarily denote an inside job? Even if the Twin Towers were brought down by bombs within the buildings, couldn't they have been planted by the terrorists—and not by Bush—perhaps as a backup plan?

5. Why did the American government need to kill 2,996 of its own people to go to war? It has shown that it can easily capitalize on opportunities provided by others. Do you doubt that there are extremists, religious and otherwise, in the Middle East and elsewhere who would love to do harm to the United States? Wouldn't it have been easier for the government to wait for an unforeseen attack to take place or to simply not stop one that was already in the works? And even if leaders in the Bush administration wanted to pull off their own false flag, instead of relying on outsiders, why wouldn't the conspirators simply fake an attack and report the deaths of a number of citizens? Surely a group with the power to pull off the alleged 9/11 conspiracy would be able to create the illusion of a catastrophic event similar to some of the

proposals from Operation Northwoods, the planned false flag operation from the 1960s that was never put into action.

6. Finally, and most importantly, is it *possible* that you're wrong? Could you have been misled by conspiracy-minded "*experts*" and documentaries based on conjecture? If this is even within the realm of plausibility, I hope you'll take another (more critical) look at the evidence and your stance on the issue.

My sincere hope is that these questions and other similar queries will help 9/11 Truthers apply the same skepticism to their own beliefs as they do to the official reports. If they are consistent in their analyses, they will see that the alternative explanations, of which there are too many to count, leave far more questions than they answer.[57]

BUILDING 7

"Building 7!" has become a battle cry for alternative theorists who claim there was a government conspiracy to destroy the Twin Towers and other buildings using bombs planted inside them days or weeks before 9/11. These believers in the inside-job notion posit that the planes were flown into the structures just before the detonation of the bombs, which served as the real catalyst for the collapses, or even that the planes were actually holograms that couldn't have done any physical damage.[58] This would explain, according to theorists, why 7 World Trade Center, which was located in the World Trade Center complex near the North Tower, fell when it wasn't directly impacted by a plane. But, if that were the case, and the U.S. government (or anyone else, for that matter) took the time to plant explosive devices and arrange for planes to collide with the Twin Towers containing them, why would they have randomly detonated explosive devices in a third building that didn't receive any damage? Why wouldn't they have arranged for three planes or three holograms? Certainly the shadowy elite capable of such a massive conspiracy would also be able to recognize that a plane didn't hit Building 7, so how did they make such an error? This act itself would undermine the entire point of flying the planes into the other two buildings in the first place, as well as the idea that the government is competent enough to pull off a conspiracy of this magnitude without leaving a trace of verifiable evidence.

Alternative theorists who believe in a government conspiracy surrounding the attacks of September 11 also point to a BBC broadcast from that fateful day as evidence of an inside job. In the report, a news personality seems to describe the collapse of Building 7 before it actually occurs. The foreign reporters are discussing how *the building had been weakened*" and how there were "*fears of possible further collapses around the area,*" but Building 7 appears to still be standing on a screen behind them, proving to some believers that the media outlet was part of the conspiracy. To properly address this piece of "evidence," I want to assume for a moment that the alternative theorists are correct. If the attacks on 9/11 were part of an inside job, and this video proves it, what does that mean? Well, for one, it means the U.S. government—while attempting to carefully carry out the bombings without a single leak or slipup—gave a British news agency and its reporters a script of the events of that day before they actually happened. It would mean that, instead of allowing news outlets to report the collapses as they were witnessed, the conspirators themselves revealed the conspiracy and provided forward-looking information to foreign broadcasters about Building 7's failure. Since that probably didn't happen, because it makes absolutely no sense, why *did* the BBC seem to report the news prior to the collapse of Building 7?

If you were watching the news that day, you might remember that Building 7 received a substantial amount of damage from debris and that nobody was surprised when it fell. The building had been burning for hours and those who were paying attention saw flames pouring out of a majorly affected building and knew it was only a matter of time before it was completely destroyed. The massive fires went largely ignored by the first responders from the Fire Department for the City of New York, primarily because Building 7 was empty and their efforts were focused on rescuing survivors from the Twin Towers. Those who *were* fighting the fires in Building 7 ultimately withdrew their efforts hours before the afternoon collapse. They declared that the building had been fatally damaged, and prepared for it to fall. So, how did BBC reporters describe the collapse before it happened? It's simple: they made a mistake. They acted prematurely based on numerous other news reports that described Building 7's "imminent" collapse. Being in the United Kingdom, they were relying on second- and third-hand accounts for new developments and, due to heightened levels of stress and panic, they made an error. This isn't revolutionary, because news outlets get things wrong all the time, and it isn't an unexplainable prophecy, either.

If you think Building 7 is some sort of smoking gun pointing to a government conspiracy on 9/11, I recommend you take an honest look at the investigators' reports and anything else that details the position of the scientific consensus.[59] Look at peer-reviewed articles on the events of that day,[60] and analyze detailed pieces put out by *Popular Mechanics* and *Structure Magazine*.[61] If you do, and you're intellectually honest in your approach, you'll see that there isn't much mystery left to this horrifying and deadly event in our history.

ARCHITECTS AND ENGINEERS

One of the most common objections from within the Truther movement involves Architects and Engineers for 9/11 Truth (AE911Truth), an organization dedicated to finding architects, engineers, and self-proclaimed demolition experts who dispute the results of the official probe into the attacks of September 11. Alternative theorists often point to this group's petition, which currently has 2,444 signatories from people claiming to be within those fields, and ask, "Could 2,000+ architects and engineers *really* be wrong!?"

The short answer is, "Yes, they could be wrong." Any argument based upon, "[X number of people] can't be wrong!" is itself wrong. The appeal to popularity underestimates human gullibility because billions of people believe all sorts of ridiculous things, and they are very often incorrect. That said, many alternative theorists consider AE911Truth to be definitive proof that the Bush White House planned the events that unfolded on 9/11. The organization seeks a "*new investigation*," but there are few details about exactly what that would entail. Do they want the same government they believe had a role in orchestrating the attacks to reinvestigate? Is there something preventing anyone from running their own, independent investigations (as many have)? This vagueness in the AE911Truth mission is why I encourage those who want a new investigation to start a crowd-funding campaign. If they believe the facts should be analyzed again, they should fund the project, instead of seeking a new government-sanctioned probe that they would likely disregard anyway.

While alternative theorists often hang their hat on the fact that

AE911Truth has almost 2,500 architects, engineers, and students who call for a new investigation into the events of September 11, that number is nowhere near what could be called a consensus in the field. In fact, it is quite the opposite. According to the National Council of Architectural Registration Boards, there are 105,847 architects licensed in the United States.[62] There are also more than 1.5 million engineers in the country, *not* including students. That means for every 765 licensed architects and engineers in America, there is approximately one student or professional who has signed an online petition for a new investigation—that is less than 0.13 percent. A scientific consensus is achieved when there is significant harmony among interpretations of solid evidence, not when an extremely small minority group professes a nonspecific disagreement with "the official story."[63] When asked about the conspiracy theories surrounding the attacks on September 11, Noam Chomsky, an American linguist and political activist known for his criticisms of the U.S. government, alluded to the AE911Truth petition and those who support it.

"You're right that there's a consensus among a miniscule number of architects and engineers, a tiny number, a couple of them are perfectly serious, they are not doing what scientists and engineers do when they think they've discovered something," Chomsky told a 9/11 conspiracy apologist during a lecture in Florida. *"What you do when you think you've discovered something is write articles in scientific journals, give talks at the professional societies, go to the civil engineering department at MIT or Florida or wherever you are, and present your results, then proceed to try to convince the national academies, the professional society of physicists and civil engineers, the departments of the major universities, convince them that you've discovered something."*

The AE911Truth organization is not unlike the Creationists' Dissent from Darwin campaign, which purports to represent more than 800 scientists in the United States and around the world who have signed a statement expressing their skepticism of *Neo-Darwinism*, or evolution by natural selection.[64] According to the Dissent from Darwin website, the group's statement was first drafted in 2001 by the Discovery Institute and can be signed by anyone who holds a Ph.D. in a science or technology field like biology, chemistry, mathematics, engineering, or computer science, or an M.D. if they also serve as a professor of medicine. To illustrate why amassing such a list of a minority group of scientists, engineers, computer scientists, and doctors who doubt a scientific consensus isn't the same as evidence that could actually dispute that consensus, the National Center for Scientific Education created Project Steve, a "tongue-in-cheek" list of scientists with the given name "Steven" who accept evolution as reality. This parody list, which currently has more than 1,350 signatures, shows that scientific findings aren't decided by petitions or minority groups, but by the scientific facts, and its lesson can be equally applied to the premise of the AE911Truth agenda.

In conclusion, while I suppose it is within the realm of possibility that a huge number of U.S. government officials and civilians conspired to kill thousands of American citizens on 9/11, or that they faked the moon landings in the 1960s, I don't think it's likely because I haven't seen hard evidence to support those claims. And if I were convinced, for instance, that the U.S. government executed the domestic attacks on 9/11, as many alternative theorists are, I would do anything in my power to bring the plot to light. I would leave the country and continue my work from a safe distance, and I would relentlessly pursue proof no matter what. Many believers, however, simply aren't willing to take the steps necessary to make a real difference. To me this shows that some alternative theorists, like theists and other believers, often care more about "knowing" something you don't than about the real issue.

> *"The main thing that I learned about conspiracy theory, is that conspiracy theorists believe in a conspiracy because that is more comforting. The truth of the world is that it is actually chaotic. The truth is that it is not The Iluminati, or The Jewish Banking Conspiracy, or the Gray Alien Theory. The truth is far more frightening. Nobody is in control. The world is rudderless ..."*
>
> *—Alan Moore*

NOTES

1. I chose this quote by Assange not because it is definite proof that the attacks on September 11, 2011, weren't orchestrated by the Bush administration or some shadowy elite group, but because Assange—through WikiLeaks—had

access to a trove of leaked information from every corner of the world. The data provides an abundance of evidence for all sorts of governmental misdeeds, but out of the millions of leaked documents and dozens of whistleblowers, nothing points directly to any sort of internal conspiracy surrounding the 9/11 attacks.

2. It should also be noted that, if 9/11 was part of an enormous plot staged by Bush as a means to go to war, there were many easier ways to reach the same end result.

3. Susan Svrluga, "The Father of a Boy Killed at Sandy Hook Gets Death Threats; Some People Say the Shooting Was a Hoax," *Washington Post*, Grade Point Blog, January 13, 2016, www.washingtonpost.com/news/grade-point/wp/2016/01/13/the-father-of-a-boy-killed-at-sandy-hook-gets-death-threats-from-people-who-say-the-shooting-was-a-hoax/.

4. "Calgary Removing Fluoride from Water Supply," *CBC/Radio Canada*, February 8, 2011, www.cbc.ca/news/canada/calgary/calgary-removing-fluoride-from-water-supply-1.1022279.

5. "Dental Decay Rampant in Calgary Children, Pediatric Dentist Says," *CBC/Radio Canada*, December 8, 2014, www.cbc.ca/news/canada/calgary/dental-decay-rampant-in-calgary-children-pediatric-dentist-says-1.2864413.

6. Georgina Kenyon, "The Man Who Studies the Spread of Ignorance," *BBC*, January 6, 2016, www.bbc.com/future/story/20160105-the-man-who-studies-the-spread-of-ignorance.

7. PPP surveyed 1,247 registered American voters between March 27 and March 30, 2013. The margin of error for the overall sample is +/-2.8% and the poll was not paid for or authorized by any campaign or political organization.

8. David Shiffman, "Why Animal Planet's Fake Documentaries About Mermaids Are Dangerous," *Slate*, May 30, 2013, www.slate.com/articles/health_and_science/science/2013/05/mermaids_aren_t_real_animal_planet_s_fake_documentaries_misrepresent_ocean.html.

9. If a person chooses to consume only organic foods because they enjoy them, that's perfectly fine. But false claims about GMOs are false claims nonetheless.

10. Alessandro Bessi et al., "Science vs Conspiracy: Collective Narratives in the Age of Misinformation," *PloS One* 10, no. 2 (2015): e0118093.

11. Quassim Cassam, "The Intellectual Character of Conspiracy Theorists," *Aeon Essays*, March 13, 2015, aeon.co/essays/the-intellectual-character-of-conspiracy-theorists.

12. David G. McAfee, *Disproving Christianity and Other Secular Writings*, 2nd ed., rev. (Dangerous Little Books, 2011).

13. I am proud to be an American in that I value its innovative contributions to the world, but our great nation is not without its flaws. This is my type of patriotism . . . and it is based on the evidence.

14. D. R. Grimes, "On the Viability of Conspiratorial Beliefs," *PLoS One* 11, no. 1 (2016): e0147905.

15. There will likely never be a single "cure" for all types of cancer, so the claim that one exists is already based on a fundamental misunderstanding of the concepts involved.

16. I've heard conspiracy theorists argue, *"No President of the U.S. has had cancer!"* This is simply not true. Many U.S. presidents have had cancer, both in and out of office, including Jimmy Carter and Ronald Reagan.

17. Steven Novella, "The Hidden Cancer Cure*,"* *Science-Based Medicine*, February 23, 2011, www.sciencebasedmedicine.org/the-hidden-cancer-cure/.

18. A number of believers have sent me patent applications as *"proof"* of chem-trails, AIDS cures, etc., but all that really tells me is they don't understand the patent system. People can apply for a patent for just about anything.

19. J. Marvin Herndon, "Evidence of Coal-Fly-Ash Toxic Chemical Geoengineering in the Troposphere: Consequences for Public Health," *International Journal of Environmental Research and Public Health* 12, no. 8 (2015): 9375–9390.

20. Paul B. Tchounwou, "Retraction: Herndon JM Evidence of Coal-Fly-Ash Toxic Chemical Geoengineering in the Troposphere: Consequences for Public Health," *International Journal of Environmental Research and Public Health* 12, no. 9 (2015): 10941–10942.

21. I feel particularly bad for alternative theorists who are also theists; they have two supposedly all-powerful forces that they believe are controlling or ruling over them.

22. Vernon Stauffer, *New England and the Bavarian Illuminati* (New York: Columbia University Press, 1918), chapter 3.

23. "Meet the Man Who Started the Illuminati," *National Geographic*, April 12, 2017, www.nationalgeographic.com/archaeology-and-history/magazine/2016/07-08/profile-adam-weishaupt-illuminati-secret-society/.

24. Dave Sirus (Brick), tweet, May 22, 2014, twitter.com/DaveSirus/status/46955970832435609.

25. Hans Decoz, "Master Number 11 Numerology," Numerology.com, www.numerology.com/numerology-numbers/11-master-number.

26. Robert Anton Wilson, *Robert Anton Wilson Explains Everything*, audio cassette, Sounds True, Inc., 2001.

27. Main Roderick, *Jung on Synchronicity and the Paranormal* (Princeton, NJ: Princeton University Press, 1997), 1.

28. *"There are two ways to be fooled. One is to believe what isn't true; the other is to refuse to believe what is true.* —Søren Kierkegaard

29. Lee McIntyre, "The Price of Denialism," *New York Times*, Opinionator, November 7, 2015, opinionator.blogs.nytimes.com/2015/11/07/the-rules-of-denialism.

30. Frank Newport, "Landing a Man on the Moon: The Public's View," Gallup News Service, July 20, 1999.

31. P. L. Bender et al., "The Lunar Laser Ranging Experiment Accurate Ranges Have Given a Large Improvement in the Lunar Orbit and New Selenophysical Information," *Science* 182, no. 4109 (1973): 229–238.

32. Project Apollo Archive, www.flickr.com/photos/projectapolloarchive/albums.

33. Margaret Heffernan, *Willful Blindness: Why We Ignore the Obvious* (New York: Simon and Schuster, 2011).

34. "Astronaut Avoids Assault Charges," *Los Angeles Times*, July 5, 2002.

35. James W. Loewen, *Lies My Teacher Told Me: Everything Your American History Textbook Got Wrong* (New York: New Press, 2008).

36. Direct adoption of the Greek concept by Islam: F. Jamil Ragep, "Astronomy," in *Encyclopaedia of Islam*, 3rd ed., ed. Kate Fleet et al. (Leiden: Brill, 2010), referenceworks.brillonline.com/entries/encyclopaedia-of-islam-3/astronomy-COM_22652?s.num=179&s.start=160.

37. Robert Schadewald, "Scientific Creationism, Geocentricity, and the Flat Earth," *Skeptical Inquirer* 6 (1981): 2.

38. Cole Hamel, "Flatter than a Pancake," *Scientia Review*, www.scientiareview.org/pdfs/324.pdf.

39. Flat Earth Society, www.tfes.org/.

40. It's worth noting that this quote, while found in a 1676 letter from Newton, can be traced back at least as far as Bernard of Chartres in the twelfth century.

41. Rachel Feltman, "Dear Tila Tequila: Here's Why the Earth Isn't Flat (Even When It Looks Like It Is)," *Washington Post*, January 8, 2016, www.washingtonpost.com/news/speaking-of-science/wp/2016/01/08/dear-tila-tequila-heres-why-the-earth-isnt-flat-even-when-it-looks-like-it-is/.

42. J. Cook et al., "Quantifying the Consensus on Anthropogenic Global Warming in the Scientific Literature," *Environmental Research Letters* 8, no. 2 (June 2013).

43. Sybille van den Hove, Marc Le Menestrel, and Henri-Claude De Bettignies, "The Oil Industry and Climate Change: Strategies and Ethical Dilemmas," *Climate Policy* 2, no. 1 (2002): 3–18.

44. A. C. Revkin and K. Q. Seelye, "Report by EPA Leaves Out Data on Climate Change," *New York Times*, June 19, 2003.

45. Jason Barbose, "Momentum Builds in California to Hold Fossil Fuel Companies Accountable for Climate Science Misinformation," Union of Concerned Scientists, May 16, 2016, blog.ucsusa.org/jason-barbose/fossil-fuel-companies-accountable-climate-science-misinformation.

46. Lydia Saad, "One in Four in US Are Solidly Skeptical of Global Warming," Gallup, April 22, 2014.

47. J. J. McCarthy, ed., *Climate Change 2001: Impacts, Adaptation, and Vulnerability* (Cambridge: Cambridge University Press, 2001).

48. National Academy of Sciences Committee on the Science of Climate Change, *Climate Change Science: An Analysis of Some Key Questions* (Washington, DC: National Academy Press, 2001).

49. American Meteorological Society, "Climate Change Research: Issues for the Atmospheric and Related Sciences," *Bulletin of the American Meteorological Society* 84 (2003): 508–515.

50. American Geophysical Union, *Eos* 84, no 51, 574 (2003).

51. Naomi Oreskes, "The Scientific Consensus on Climate Change," *Science* 306, no. 5702 (2004): 1686–1686.

52. "*The good thing about science is that it's true whether or not you believe in it.*" —Neil deGrasse Tyson

53. "International Poll: No Consensus On Who Was Behind 9/11 World Public Opinion, September 10, 2008.

54. David Johnston, "Two Years Later: 9/11 Tactics; Official Says Qaeda Recruited Saudi Hijackers to Strain Ties," *New York Times*, September 9, 2003.

55. Osama bin Laden, "Full Text: bin Laden's 'Letter to America,'" *Observer* (London), November 24, 2002.

56. "World Records," Controlled Demolition, Inc., www.controlled-demolition.com/world-records.

57. *"If conspiracy theorists applied even a tenth of the scrutiny and demand for evidence they place on the 'official story' upon their own theories, those theories would crumble like a sandcastle under a wave."* —Unknown

58. Glenn Canady, "Smoking Gun Proof Holographic Planes Used on 9/11—Left Wing Disappears Before Plane Hits Building!" Before It's News, March 1, 2015, beforeitsnews.com/alternative/2015/03/smoking-gun-proof-holographic-planes-used-on-911-cockpit-disappears-into-thin-air-after-going-through-building-3115708.html.

59. *Final Report on the Collapse of World Trade Center Building 7, Federal Building and Fire Safety Investigation of the World Trade Center Disaster*, National Institute of Standards and Technology (Washington, DC: U.S. Government Printing Office, November 2008).

60. A. S. Usmani, "How Did the WTC Towers Collapse: A New Theory," *Fire Safety Journal* 38, no. 6 (2003): 501–533.

61. Ramon Gilsanz and Willa Ng, "Single Point of Failure: How the Loss of One Column May Have Led to the Collapse of WTC 7," *Structure Magazine*, November 2007, 42–45.

62. "NCARB's 2013 Survey of Registered Architects," National Council of Architectural Registration Boards, December 30, 2013, www.ncarb.org/News-and-Events/News/2013/12_2013ArchitectsSurvey.aspx.

63. I should note that, while you're not necessarily wrong just because the vast majority of the best scientists in a field disagree with you, unless you have evidence to prove them wrong, it's a good indicator that you should reexamine your position.

64. "Homepage," Dissent From Darwin, www.dissentfromdarwin.org/.

16

FAITH HEALING
AND "ALTERNATIVE" MEDICINE

"It is unethical and potentially dangerous for licensed health professionals
to naively and uncritically accept paranormal treatments. Yet I have seen
physicians and therapists embrace the mystery energies of qi, the curative
power of prayer, and the healing magic of shamans—and pride themselves for
their openness to alternative cultures, and sensitivity to non-Western wisdom."

—Jonathan C. Smith

At some point in time, in order to achieve our full potential, humans as a collective will have to acknowledge that prayer and other faith-based "healing" techniques are nothing more than false hopes dressed as miracles. Unfortunately for us, however, today many people still rely on them . . . and we have the death certificates to prove it.

The follies of faith are represented by more than just holy wars and deadly attacks inspired or justified (often only in part) by religion. Every day, people around the world are harmed by myths and superstitions not only through allegedly "divine" acts of violence, but also by a lack of medical attention due to misplaced confidence in prayer or other unsubstantiated rituals posing as treatments. Falling prey to the snake-oil salesmen of our time, unsuspecting patients by the millions become victims of false hope and, more importantly, false remedies. The bottom line: friends don't let friends rely on any form of placebo-based faith healing when they require real medical treatment. If you keep someone from seeing a medical professional in favor of prayer or homeopathy or any other so-called alternative medicine, you aren't "doing it the natural way" or "leaving it in God's hands." You're causing real harm and putting lives at risk.

Seth Andrews, author of *Deconverted: A Journey from Religion to Reason* and other titles, points out that prayer "*can give comfort in times of medical crisis,*" but cautions people not to rely on it.

"*It can also be a cop-out . . . an excuse for people to do absolutely nothing substantial and yet declare they have moved mountains,*" he wrote. "*As science-based medicine fights in the trenches to win the battles against malady and misfortune, the vacuous appeals to magic bellow from the fringe, and the faithful stand ready at every victory to claim that their specific god should get the credit.*"

WHAT IS FAITH HEALING?

When you hear "*faith healing,*" you likely think of a religious televangelist who carefully chooses subjects and manipulates viewers into thinking they've been healed. You probably think of someone like Benny Hinn, who claims to have healed blindness, deafness, cancer, AIDS, and more at his *Miracle Crusades,*[1] yet was admitted to a conventional hospital for his own ailments when he suffered from heart problems.[2] Or perhaps Christian minister Rod Parsley comes to mind. He also advocates miraculous faith healing practices but decided to seek help from medical doctors in the form of radiation treatments when he was diagnosed with throat cancer.[3] When you hear "*faith healer,*" you probably think of people who heavily exaggerate for religious effect—people like those charismatic pastor John Richard Wimber spoke out against.

"*I also visited several healing meetings ... and became angry with what appeared to be the manipulation of people for the material gains of the faith healer ... Dressing like sideshow barkers,*" Wimber wrote.[4] "*Pushing people over and calling it the power of God. And money—they were always asking for more, leading people to believe that if they gave they would be healed.*"

People like Hinn, Parsley, and other conventional faith healers do a huge amount of harm, but the fact is that there are a lot of so-called alternative treatments out there that—just like traditional faith healing—

are not really medicine at all. I'll be referring to these practices, which have no proven health benefits and are often performed for a fee and at the expense of real medical services, collectively as "faith healing." To me, faith healing is defined as any attempt to improve one's health through a means that has not been scientifically proven—and therefore requires blind faith. Today there are probably too many of these "alternative medicine" practices to list, and many people rely on them, but, as Australian actor Josh Thomas has said, "*you can't really put the word alternative before medicine.*"

"*You can put the word alternative before ideas, you can have alternative fashion, you can have alternative music, but you can't have alternative facts,*"[5] Thomas said on a 2015 episode of *Please Like Me*. "*Putting alternative before medicine, that's like pointing at a dog and saying that's my alternative cat. It's still not a cat.*"

Does the fact that there are so many forms of fraudulent healing (too many to cover in this chapter, to be sure) show it has merit? No—all it reveals is that people are regularly deceived based on wishful thinking. But the fact that there are millions of false cures and faulty healing processes does lead to an interesting phenomenon: True Believers in one form of faith healing might outwardly reject others as nonsense, while remaining ignorant of the fact that they all have exactly the same amount of scientific backing—zero. For instance, I've met people who spent years studying and teaching the "science" of crystal healing yet think homeopathy and religious faith healings are "preposterous." I've also met a great number of religious believers who pray for good health all the time, but would never consider trying something like acupuncture. It's important to acknowledge that these various methods of faith healing, while they may be different in origin, method, and levels of cultural acceptance, are the same when it comes to their lack of established effectiveness.

The fact that faith healing isn't reliable doesn't seem to bother many practitioners, from homeopaths to Christian Scientists, who often (conveniently) claim that their methods simply take belief, time, and patience to work. But anyone considering this argument should keep in mind that any ailment cured with faith healing and time could equally be cured absent the magic. Your common cold, anxiety, headaches, etc. will all likely go away with nothing more than the passage of time, rendering faith healing useless or redundant in these cases. However, if you can show that homeopathy or an equivalent practice cured you of a terminal illness, or any significant and verifiable disease for that matter, then the scientific community will be more than interested in your findings.

THE PRAYERCEBO EFFECT

Relying solely on intercessory prayer (divine petition)[6] to better your health is like taking your sluggish car into the automotive shop for a tune-up, only to have the mechanic pop the hood for an hour and do absolutely nothing. You might leave the shop happier, believing the mechanic had done his or her job, and you may even notice small things that seem like improvements. Maybe you feel as though the car accelerates more quickly or the brakes seem to be functioning better. But, just as is the case with prayer and positive thoughts, any purported results likely stem from the customer's (or patient's) own mind. I call this the *prayercebo effect*: a positive effect, produced by a request to a god, that can't be attributed to a god and must therefore be a result of the belief itself. The prayercebo effect is obviously modeled after the *placebo effect*, which was pioneered by French psychologist Émile Coué and others in the 1800s and continues to be studied and utilized in modern medicine today.

Given what we know about medical placebos and spiritual or religious prayercebos, we can conclude that, whether a patient is exposed to prayer, Reiki, homeopathy, therapeutic touch, or any other faith-based "healing," the person in need of medical help is actually the active ingredient in his or her own "treatment." This means that the patient—and not the so-called healer—is the ultimate cause of any beneficial changes experienced due to psychological factors, willful deception, or coincidence. Faith-based systems that utilize the placebo effect also include Ch'i, prana, and other mystical and unmeasurable energies that have never been shown to exist in observable scientific settings. Considering the enormous number of tests involving these mysterious powers, the most likely explanation for the lack of positive data that has been published on them is that the ideas are simply made up, much like the strikingly similar *Force* of *Star Wars* fame, with the obvious difference being that the *Force* was shown to be a real and demonstrable power within the fictional universe created by George Lucas. In reality, however, these so-called cosmic energies and forces only "work" because people believe in them—it's the placebo effect in action. This phenomenon is responsible for any and all positive changes resulting from faith-based nontreatments because they, by definition, lack any real substance capable of providing legitimate relief.

Some say that faith healers and other frauds who utilize the (well-documented) placebo effect and keep people from seeking real medical care are still benefitting those they serve—after all, if someone is feeling better, that's good, right? But people who make this argument often don't acknowledge or realize that the placebo effect is already regularly utilized by "mainstream" physicians when appropriate, to make people feel healthier without expensive procedures or dangerous medications. If a small feeling of improvement is all that is needed, then—in some instances—that may be the best action. The problem begins, however, when the placebo effect is mistaken for a "cure" or used instead of necessary medical advice. There is no need for entire multibillion-dollar industries to be built around false cures, especially when those who sell them often discourage patients from seeking legitimate therapies and spread misinformation about modern medicine, because the placebo effect is already being put to use. In fact, I think one of the best aspects of the placebo effect is that, according to recent research,[7] it can sometimes work even when you know it's a placebo[8]—rendering the deception component of homeopathy and other woo-based faith-healing methods completely unnecessary.

In addition to generally "feeling better" due to the placebo effect, some believers purport to experience overwhelming emotions, tingling sensations, and other positive feelings when being prayed for or touched by so-called healers. But what they are experiencing has been shown time and time again to be the result of their own internal emotions and hormones—and not an external force or deity. Psychologically, we tend to feel comforted by touch,[9] especially in times of extreme stress. In fact, the feeling can be comparable to what some music fans report at their favorite concerts, or even what you might experience when you see a loved one for the first time after an extended absence. These feelings might be caused by a number of different feel-good chemicals in the brain, including *dopamine, oxytocin, serotonin,* and *endorphins.* In other words, it's simple brain chemistry—and not religion or pseudoscientific miracle cures—that is responsible for the euphoria you might get during group prayer or a one-on-one session with a faith healer of any kind.

A REAL-LIFE HORROR STORY

You might not always think of demons and possessions when the topic of alternative medicine arises, but so-called exorcists are a form of faith healer because they utilize many of the same deceptive tactics to achieve their results. In fact, you might say exorcisms were among the earliest faith-healing methods. Long before Christianity arose, the practice was linked to Hinduism through the *Atharva Veda*,[10] one of that religion's four holy books, but today most people associate exorcisms with the Catholic Church—and for good reason. The Jesus of the Bible was said to have performed at least seven major exorcisms, including on a blind and mute man[11] and other people who couldn't see[12] or speak.[13] Presumably, because the New Testament writers didn't understand the genetic and environmental factors that can cause these problems, they attributed them to demonic possessions that Jesus could then cure. In the modern era, however, we have more information on these subjects and you won't find too many thinking people who believe blind people are possessed by evil spirits. That's a good thing, but it needs to go even further . . . we need to realize that no illnesses are caused by demons so that we can focus on real medicine and not fantasy.

Today exorcisms are well known thanks to horror movies, but the reality is actually much more terrifying because real people can be seriously injured, killed,[14] or convinced that a life-threatening ailment from which they still suffer has been eliminated. Demons have never been shown to exist, so, in most cases, "exorcisms" are performed on those suffering from hysteria, Tourette's syndrome, epilepsy, schizophrenia, trichotillomania, or dissociative identity disorder, and even occasionally on presidential candidates, such as Senator Ted Cruz as he campaigned in New Hampshire,[15] and not on people who have been hijacked by the devil. In addition to those common ailments, anti-NMDA (N-methyl D-aspartate) receptor antibody encephalitis, a form of encephalitis categorized and named in 2007, can cause agitation, paranoia, psychosis, violence, seizures, and bizarre movements—all symptoms that mimic what some believers might think of as demonic possession.[1617] To make matters worse, those conducting exorcism ceremonies often create the illusion that they actually work by utilizing the placebo effect, groupthink, and the *power of suggestion* (i.e. *hypnotism*). Not only are people with legitimate illnesses not getting the real treatments they need, they and their families are also regularly led to believe good health is only a few "the power of Christ compels you!" chants away when the issue is likely much more complex.

Exorcisms were more popular in the past, but they still occur today. In fact, the ritual continues to be a formal part of the Roman Catholic Church, which defines exorcism as what happens *"when the Church asks publicly and authoritatively in the name of Jesus Christ that a person or object be protected against the power of the Evil One and withdrawn from his dominion."*[18] Recent polling suggests that about 51 percent of U.S. adults believe a person can be possessed by the devil or some other spirit,[19] and 46 percent believe in the power of exorcism, despite the fact that these things have never been shown to exist in any verifiable way. There are some believers in demonic possession who will claim that natural sicknesses have been ruled out, or that the allegedly possessed individual performed feats of superhuman strength, had adverse reactions to certain *"holy"* objects, or levitated, but these are nothing more than unsupported claims. In most cases, people who make these assertions have seen one too many fictional films dealing with the topic. Certain aspects of the typical movie-style possession, like negative reactions to any object, could be psychological or a result of faking. But there isn't any evidence to suggest human levitation could occur unaided under any circumstances, so if they can prove this has happened they could change the way we view science (and the world in general).

FAITH HEALING IN MY LIFE

Believers in some form of faith healing or another will accuse me of being closed-minded on the subject, but that couldn't be further from the truth. I've been interested in so-called faith healers and their work for as long as I can remember, and I've personally tried crystal healing, acupuncture, and a number of similar "alternative medicines" in an attempt to deal with my own issues, as well as performed independent investigations on countless other supernatural and pseudoscientific healing claims. However, unfortunately for us and the scientific and medical communities at large, none of these miracle cures have ever been shown to accomplish anything beyond the power of the placebo effect.

Don't get me wrong. There is certainly a time and place to utilize placebos. When I was very young, for example, if I got a scrape or a burn, my older sister would have me close my eyes so that she could apply "magic medicine." There was no real treatment—it was just spit or water—but I usually felt better as a result of the placebo effect and that's all I really needed at that time. This process is no different (although admittedly it was much cheaper and less harmful) than the tactics used by faith healers who continue to fool millions of adults each and every day.

My interest in faith-based "medicine" began early. When I was about 10 years old, a friend of my family told me that I could cure my cold through crystal healing and gave me a book on the subject. I was fascinated by the book and the prospect of magical rocks that could make me feel better. I followed all the instructions diligently and repeated the process multiple times per day for more than a week, but I realized my symptoms subsided at about the same rate as they did without the "treatment." I did the same thing each time I felt ill and ultimately concluded that the system wasn't working. I remember being upset that someone would lie to me about this so-called miracle cure, until I realized she believed it herself. I now know that crystals are functionally identical to all other placebo-based "medications," and not just to me, but also to every scientist who has rigorously tested them and to every peer-reviewed, scientifically valid study. If new research suggests otherwise someday, I'll reconsider my position. But the anecdotal "It worked for me!" claims will never suffice, especially because placebo "works" just as well.

ACUPUNCTURE

I didn't stop experimenting with faith-healing methods after my experience with the crystals. As an adult, I also submitted myself to a number of other so-called alternative pain management systems that were wholly unsupported by scientific data. First I tried acupuncture and, while I thoroughly enjoyed the relaxation, sounds, smells, etc., it didn't help to cure my chronic neck pain from which I had been suffering for years.[20] For those who don't know, acupuncture is defined as *the method of treatment based on influencing the body by inserting needles in the specific points of human body, called acupoints.*[21] Acupuncture, derived from ancient Chinese Medicine, is very popular throughout Asia and the United States, and has even been applied to veterinarian medicine,[22] but it remains problematic because the process relies on acupoints and even the flow of a mysterious energy called "qi," neither of which have ever been shown to exist. This poses a significant challenge to acupuncturists, according to Steven P. Novella, who says *"carefully controlled scientific studies consistently show that it does not matter where you stick the needles or even if you insert needles."*[23]

"To further support this conclusion, the perceived effectiveness of acupuncture does not depend on the degree of training or experience of the acupuncturist (so whatever they are learning has no effect), but only upon how warm and nice they are to the patient," Novella wrote for *Science-Based Medicine*.[24] *"In short, acupuncture is an elaborate placebo."*

Am I saying that acupuncture can't be relaxing or calming, or that it can't provide some positive effects? No, of course not. In fact, I'm stating the opposite: acupuncture is so often relaxing and calming, it so regularly causes positive effects, that those feelings are mistaken for cures. Through scientific inquiry, we should be able to look at and explain these good outcomes associated with acupuncture. If the needles aren't unblocking built-up qi energy flowing through our bodies, then what is happening? There are a lot of potential contributors. In addition to the placebo effect from the expected cure, the discomfort from the needles could distract a person from other points of pain, or perhaps endorphins released by the pins trigger a general sense of euphoria. But these benefits aren't long-term solutions, and they should be recognized for what they are: momentary positive feelings.

People all over the world think acupuncture is more effective than placebo, and many believers suggest it can cure just about anything from hot flashes[25] to AIDS,[26] but absolutely nobody presents peer-reviewed scientific data proving these claims because it simply doesn't exist. There are hundreds of controlled, scientifically valid studies on acupuncture, each showing the practice to be no more effective than placebo.[27] There are some smaller studies showing results that barely surpass the placebo effect, but in these cases a thorough look at the researchers' processes will often reveal some sort of pro-acupuncture bias. The phenomenon of *cultural bias* is why Chinese studies on Chinese acupuncture are more likely to report positive results than studies from the United States,[28] but there are other research and publication biases, too. That's part of why studies with support from pharmaceutical companies sometimes report more positive results (i.e., the drug worked) than those funded by the government.[29]

If you believe acupuncture is a "cure" for anything—that it is more than a relaxing and peaceful experience often used to distract from pain—then you should be able to describe the process by which it works. If you ignore the scientific explanations for its benefits, which are supported by the lack of peer-reviewed studies pointing to acupuncture alone as more effective than placebos, then you always have the answer given by acupuncturists themselves: the needles correct imbalances in a mystical energy, called qi, which flows through undetected channels in our bodies, referred to as "meridians." That's not to say you can't still frequent acupuncturists if you enjoy the experience, but you should treat your real medical problems with real medicine. If you are intellectually honest about the facts and about your reasoning, the knowledge that acupuncture relies on placebo won't necessarily affect your future experiences.

It's important to note that, even if I had seen results with the crystals or acupuncture, my personal experience would never be considered scientifically verifiable evidence proving their efficacy. My experience with crystals and the continuance of my chronic muscle pain after receiving **chiropractic** and acupuncture treatments are no more proof of those methods' inefficacy than believers' tales of positive experiences are proof that they work.

WHEN THERE'S A FORK IN THE ROAD, DON'T TAKE THE HOMEOPATH

Homeopathy is one of the most prevalent faith-healing mechanisms in the world today. While it may be a popular trend at the moment, it is not *new* by any stretch of the imagination. In November 2009, British surgical oncologist Michael Baum and Edzard Ernst, an academic physician and researcher, called fellow doctors' attention to how long homeopathy has been around without its claims being verified by scientific evidence. In their article, published in the *American Journal of Medicine*, they also referred to homeopathy as "*among the worst examples of faith-based medicine.*"

> *Homeopathic principles are bold conjectures. There has been no spectacular corroboration of any of its founding principles ... After more than 200 years, we are still waiting for homeopathy 'heretics' to be proved right, during which time the advances in our understanding of disease, progress in therapeutics and surgery, and prolongation of the length and quality of life by so-called allopaths have been breathtaking.*[30]

Homeopathy is the idea that, contrary to all evidence, remedies can be prepared by repeatedly diluting a substance until almost no "active ingredients" are remaining. The problem with this notion isn't just that it is unreliable and false, and that it has been debunked by every person who has intentionally "*overdosed*" on homeopathic pills,[31] but that people die all the time from easily curable diseases because they are treated by homeopaths who often instruct the patient to disregard modern medicine.[32] I'm not the only one who sees homeopathy as an issue. In fact, the BBC reported in November 2015 that government officials in the United Kingdom were "*considering whether homeopathy should be put on a blacklist of treatments.*"[33] And the National Health Service itself says there "*is no good-quality evidence that homeopathy is effective as a treatment for any health condition.*" There is a similar sentiment from the medical community in Australia, where the Royal Australian College of General Practitioners (RACGP) asked pharmacists not to sell products based on homeopathy, which "*has no effect beyond that of placebo as treatment for various clinical conditions.*"[34]

"*Homeopathic products are sometimes considered harmless as they are generally administered at a high dilution. Some may not even contain a single molecule of the original source material,*" RACGP officials wrote in their position statement, pointing to issues associated with treatment avoidance and lack of product regulation. "*However, there are a number of risks associated with the use of homeopathy.*"

When a pharmaceutical company in the United States tries to gain approval by the U.S. Food and Drug Administration (FDA) for a new drug, the corporation is required to conduct enough scientific testing to establish that it has medicinal value above that of the placebo effect. Unlike real medical treatments and pain medications, however, homeopathic substances aren't regulated by the FDA (or many other similar agencies around the world) and manufacturers aren't generally held responsible when they are shown not to work or to have unadvertised negative side effects. Homeopathic medicines don't have (or need) this regulation because they have no healing or damaging properties, but unfortunately that doesn't stop manufacturers and sellers from misrepresenting their products' efficacy to everyday consumers who are duped out of their money and well-being. This lack of regulation in the enormous market of "alternative medicine" has caused numerous lawsuits,[35] and some groups, such as the

Center for Inquiry (CFI), have even asked the FDA to label homeopathic substances as untested and unproven. Consumers spend $3 billion per year on highly diluted pills and elixirs with very little or no active ingredients, but many aren't aware that these so-called medicines aren't evaluated by the government, according to CFI.

"When people get sick or hurt, they are confronted with countless products that claim to be able to make them better," said Ronald A. Lindsay, then-president and CEO of CFI, in a statement on August 20, 2015. *"They cannot be blamed for not distinguishing between effective remedies and pseudoscience from the 1700s if both products share the same store shelves, and there is no labeling on homeopathic drugs to indicate they are given a pass by the FDA. Clear labeling on homeopathic products, that catches consumers' attention and informs them that the FDA does not evaluate these products for safety or effectiveness, is an easy way to ensure that people looking to treat their illnesses are not fooled into thinking that homeopathic drugs are real medicine."*

Although unrecognized "natural" remedies aren't always regulated, there has been significant research to determine whether or not they work. In November 2015, for instance, Australia's Department of Health published a report finding that 17 *"natural therapies"* are simply not effective and therefore don't deserve a rebate on private health insurance. The study, conducted by Chief Medical Officer Professor Chris Baggoley, revealed that there were some health benefits to massage therapy, yoga, tai chi, and others, but that, *"Overall, there was not reliable, high-quality evidence available to allow assessment of the clinical effectiveness of any of the natural therapies for any health condition."* The therapies investigated by the Australian government included aromatherapy, Ayurveda, homeopathy, naturopathy, reflexology, and more.[36]

Prior to gaining support (and therefore regulation) from health authorities, proponents would have to satisfactorily show that homeopathy cured a specific ailment. Before that's even remotely possible, believers would first need to demonstrate—scientifically—that the dilution methods practiced by the vast majority of homeopathic manufacturers are capable of curing anyone of anything. Unfortunately for believers, because there is little, if any, of the so-called active ingredients left in the final products, the results have been shown in study after study to be the same as the placebo effect.[37][38] Until that healing power is proven, to claim a homeopathic healing would be to assume a positive outcome was caused by the so-called treatment itself—and that's not necessarily the case. This is the *post hoc, ergo propter hoc* logical fallacy, and also the foundation of superstition, prayer, witchcraft, and more.

To be clear: I'm not saying natural remedies can't ever work and that only pharmacies can dispense viable medicine, but all remedies must be shown to actually have healing properties before they can be considered beneficial. I've noticed a lot of people say "homeopathic" when they mean "natural," but these are not synonyms. There's a difference between placebos, like homeopathy pills, and proven natural healing agents, such as *aspirin* (as acetylsalicylic acid) derived from the bark of a willow tree. As Jonathan C. Smith explains, "alternative medicine" has become a catchall category that combines paranormal approaches with basic nutritional supplements, exercise, and relaxation.

"*A patient may experience benefit from a relatively benign approach involving vitamins or exercise and conclude that alternative medicine has value*," Smith wrote. "*He or she may then feel comfortable exploring more risky borderline paranormal and paranormal alternative treatments. Knowing what's paranormal, and what's not, can help us navigate this medical minefield.*"

Because "faith healing" and "natural remedy" are such vague terms, applying to dozens of systems spanning the history of humanity, it is important to nail down some definitions and address the major practices individually.

CHIROPRACTIC CONFUSION

Chiropractic is an alternative medicine that exists in many incarnations, including some that posit spinal joint dysfunction as a major contributor to nonmusculoskeletal diseases. The process was founded by nineteenth-century "magnetic healer" and salesman Daniel David (D. D.) Palmer, who said spine manipulation could cure deafness and just about anything else,[39] but it has been altered and revised and remains widely practiced today. The problem with chiropractic, in fact, is that it is *too* widely practiced, with Centers for Medicare & Medicaid Services data showing that the Medicare program paid $496 million for chiropractic treatments in the United States in 2012.[40]

Instead of being used as a last-ditch effort to remove back pain in adults, chiropractic services are being offered for all kinds of ailments and to just about anyone—including young children—often with disastrous results. Some believers insist against all evidence, for example, that chiropractic care can cure a number of non-spine-related ailments in kids, including infant colic.[41] These claims are made more troublesome by the fact that young people are often seriously injured when chiropractic "adjustments" go wrong.[42] In one case study, for instance, a six-year-old boy suffered stroke-like symptoms brought on by neck trauma from a visit to a chiropractor.[43] In another unfortunate case, a 30-year-old man died after suffering from a stroke in the chiropractor's office.[44] There have been numerous other deaths linked to chiropractic manipulations, leading some researchers to conclude that *"the risks of this treatment by far outweigh its benefit."*[45]

Some modern chiropractors rightfully attempt to distance themselves from the system's origins as a cure-all process founded by a woo healer, and from Palmer's "Innate Intelligence" theory on the organizing properties of living things. Chiropractic historian Joseph C. Keating Jr., for instance, said chiropractors *"stick out like a sore thumb"* among professionals who claim their practices are based on science due to their *"unrelenting commitment to vitalism."*

"So long as we propound the 'One cause, one cure' rhetoric of Innate, we should expect to be met with ridicule from the wider health science community," he said.[46] *"Chiropractors can't have it both ways. Our theories cannot be both dogmatically held vitalistic constructs and be scientific at the same time."*

Even with modern revisions and fewer mystical practices, chiropractic medicine is no more effective than other manipulative therapies—such as physical therapy and massage—and it's sometimes much less safe. Chiropractic can be a safe complementary technique when it is practiced carefully and in an extremely limited manner, but it becomes pseudoscience when its proponents claim that disorders of the neuromusculoskeletal system greatly affect general health.

MISCELLANEOUS FAITH-HEALING PRACTICES

While chiropractic and acupuncture receive a strangely high level of acceptance, even among mainstream medical practitioners, they aren't the only faith-healing systems on which people rely. Some other practices with smaller followings, such as *therapeutic touch* (TT), enjoy a position that affords them even less public scrutiny. TT, also known as healing touch therapy, teaches that every person has an energy field and that its practitioners are able to heal because they are somehow able to be sensitive to it. It is yet another form of mysticism/placebo healing that has been debunked at almost every stage of scientific inquiry. One study published in the *Journal of the American Medical Association* found that practitioners of therapeutic touch couldn't detect the presence or absence of a hand (or its "energy field") placed a few inches above theirs when their vision was obstructed.[47] In interpreting those results, Simon Singh and Edzard Ernst concluded in their 2008 book *Trick or Treatment* that "*the energy field was probably nothing more than a figment in the imaginations of the healers.*" The American Cancer Society has also weighed in on TT, saying, "*Available scientific evidence does not support any claims that therapeutic touch can cure cancer or other diseases.*" This is simply another addition to the pantheon of modern woo beliefs that so many people subscribe to, often out of gullibility and/or wishful thinking.

Certain faith-healing practices are stranger than others. Some people believe, for instance, that the key to good health lies in "quantum entanglement." Perhaps taking advantage of the fact that quantum mechanics is often misrepresented and misunderstood, proponents of quantum entanglement healing say your quantum information energy (QI) gets intertwined with other QI and causes big problems that can be fixed for a fee.[48] Still others believe a special type of "slapping" therapy can cure everything from diabetes to breast cancer. Hongchi Xiao, a self-proclaimed healer in China, charges $1,800 for a week-long alternative medicine workshop that includes slapping, fasting, and stretching. This system, which often leaves patients with several lasting bruises, reportedly led to the death of a seven-year-old diabetic boy from Australia in 2015.[49]

Whether you're researching traditional faith healing, chakra alignment, Reiki, or the restorative power of *cupping*, which utilizes suction cups on the skin,[50] it's important to know about alternative "cures" because unsubstantiated and false medicinal claims can be dangerous. Regardless of which faith-based practice a person chooses, if it hasn't been proven to have healing properties, they run the risk of significant harm if not used in conjunction with established, demonstrably effective medical care. In the United States, this problem is compounded by the fact that nearly every state has a law that, to some extent, keeps parents from being held responsible for medically neglecting their children—as long as they have some religious or spiritual justification. This is supposed to promote religious freedom, but states like Idaho,[51] Arkansas, and West Virginia have broad exemption laws that allow parents to effectively murder their children without legal consequences.[52]

Some say more children die in Idaho due to faith-based religious neglect than in any other state.[53] The Gem State drew national attention in 2016 when it was revealed that five children died unnecessarily due to religious-based medical neglect three years earlier. Since then, some legislators have tried to repeal the state's deadly faith-healing statute, which allows parents to choose prayer over medical care without consequence, but they have so far been unsuccessful. Canyon County Sheriff Kieran Donahue, who is himself a Catholic, has announced his intentions to change the law. He formed an investigative unit at his sheriff's department to probe the death of every child connected to the Followers of Christ, a small Christian sect that, much like Christian Scientists, champions faith-healing and opposes modern medicine. Some people who grew up in the church say it was "violently abusive both physically and mentally," and others defend the group, but either way one thing is clear: if there is even a single preventable death as a result of this "religious freedom" statute, and there have been many, then the law should be changed. These are children who can't protect themselves, or choose for themselves, and we are allowing them to die because their parents don't believe in medicine. This is something that *needs* to change.

Robert W. Tuttle, who serves as the David R. and Sherry Kirschner Berz Research Professor of Law and Religion at The George Washington University Law School, says most states *"have much narrower exemptions for faith healing."*

"These narrower laws provide an exemption only in cases in which the child is not seriously harmed," Tuttle told Pew Research Center's Forum on Religion & Public Life.[54] *"Moreover, even when exemptions protect parents from criminal prosecution, they still allow courts to impose other penalties, such as ordering that the child receive medical care or removing the child from the parents' custody."*

CHURCH OF CHRIST, SCIENTIST

While many people believe in faith healing, one group has made a successful religion out of the idea. Members of the *Church of Christ, Scientist*, a sect of Christianity founded by Mary Baker Eddy in 1879, claim that their religion's practitioners can heal wounds in an instant with nothing more than the power of prayer. The church's website includes healing accounts by people around the globe who say they've been cured of cancer, infertility, depression, drug addiction, and even unemployment. Many believers, misleadingly referred to as "Christian Scientists," use their healing system as their first choice over legitimate medical treatments, including drugs and life-saving surgeries. They believe in following what they regard as the example of Jesus, bringing the real or ideal man more clearly into thought and consequently into human experience. Christian Scientists believe that Jesus was "the Wayshower," in perfect resonance with the Christ Consciousness, a proof by example of the divine method of healing sin, sickness, and death. According to the Christian Science belief, there are no limits to the type of medical conditions that can be healed through prayer—and that includes healing of physical wounds and even resurrections.

After researching this Christian denomination's "spiritual healings," I took a trip to the Tenth Church of Christ, Scientist, in Los Angeles to see for myself. I sat down with a Christian Science Reading Room attendant, who chose to remain anonymous.[5556]

McAfee: Do you think it's possible that some of what you call "healing" is actually explained by your own mind, perhaps through simple distraction methods or the placebo effect? How do you know it's different from a natural process?

Attendant: We distinguish between the brain and God because of the clarity with which God communicates.

McAfee: Have you ever seen any healings for yourself, first hand, of a physical ailment? For example, have you witnessed spontaneous limb regeneration of an amputee, or the resurrection of a corpse?

Attendant: I do know—I didn't actually see it as it happened, but my mother's friend was a Christian Science practitioner and her sister passed away and was resurrected by the sister. I saw the sister afterward but I wasn't there to see the actual situation.

McAfee: And are there reports of similar resurrections that you hear from other believers?

Attendant: Oh yeah.

McAfee: My hesitation is the fact that, if there were resurrections happening, people might be more aware of it. It would be in the media; it would be recognized by scientists. I figure every doctor, if they know that they could resurrect somebody, they would do that and they would become Christian Science practitioners. They would no longer be medical professionals but church employees.

Attendant: You would think so. Several things to that effect. One is, it's not an everyday occurrence, so it's not like it's happening all the time. Two, we, Christian Scientists, tend to be very quiet and private about things and so, when you're working through a physical problem, you tend not to make it terribly well known. We have 125 years of written healings written in books in the Reading Room, but we don't tend to put them out there so people don't pick up on them.

McAfee: But isn't that what the religion wants to do, is put itself out there to try to get people to see that they can do this? You don't want to keep it all to yourselves, do you? If I were a Christian Science practitioner and I were capable of bringing people back to life, I would be at hospitals, resurrecting people right there. I wouldn't be just charging when people call up, I would be doing it to help my fellow man. There's never been a record of anything like that. It seems like that would be something that is really prevalent.

Attendant: You're right, and I don't even really know why it's not so prevalent. Although practitioners are going to hospitals. In fact, you've reminded me of when I was teaching in the mountains. One of our students, in the middle of the night, ran the car into a tree and wasn't supposed to live—through the night even. And his parents were off in Europe, so they weren't even around to help. He was in the hospital, and this was years and years ago so I don't remember all the details, but he was in the hospital for easily a month or two and his parents came home fairly quickly and they were Christian Scientists and there was care going on all the time. They worked it all through. For one thing

he lived through the night, then there was all this surgery, then he wasn't supposed to walk, then he wasn't supposed to do this, that, and the other thing. All of those were met, ultimately. That kind of thing actually does happen. Again, we don't stand on the corner hollering and screaming about it. Practitioners are in the practice of Christian Science full time, so that is how they live. They deserve to be paid like doctors or anyone else.

McAfee: If you personally lost a finger, your thumb fell off today, and you knew for a fact that there was a Christian Science practitioner one mile away that you could see and there was also an emergency room a mile away where they could reattach your thumb, which one would you go to?

Attendant: That's a very good question and I'm not quite sure. I would have to be in the situation to know for sure. My first thought would be my own prayer, dealing with it right away. Fear sometimes gets in the way of prayer and takes over your thinking, and so the fear would be what would lead me one way or the other, probably. Unless I was really feeling confident that, yes, this is a healing happening, and then I would probably call the practitioner first. And then see if I was feeling like this isn't working and I needed something more immediate, then I'd potentially go to the emergency hospital.

> *"The exposé of fraud and error in science is made almost exclusively by science. But the exposure of fraud and error in faith-healing is almost never done by other faith-healers."*
>
> *—Carl Sagan*

NOTES

1. "Hinn's Healings?...," Let Us Reason Ministries, www.apologeticsindex.org/h04.html.

2. Sarah Bailey, "Televangelist Benny Hinn Has Been Admitted to the Hospital for Heart Trouble," *Washington Post*, March 25, 2015.

3. Jennifer LeClaire, "Battling Throat Cancer, Rod Parsley Shares the Battle Against His Mind," *Charisma News*, October 21, 2015, www.charismanews.com/us/52753-battling-throat-cancer-rod-parsley-shares-the-battle-against-his-mind.

4. John Wimber and Kevin Springer, *Power Healing* (New York: Harper Collins, 1991).

5. The phrase "alternative facts" would later be coined by President Trump's representative Kellyanne Conway in her defense of a false statement made by the White House regarding inauguration attendance.

6. There are many different forms of "*prayer*," including some that resemble deep thought or even meditation. For the sake of this chapter, however, we will be discussing petitionary prayer through which the believer seeks real changes in the physical world via a request to a deity.

7. T. J. Kaptchuk et al., "Placebos without Deception: A Randomized Controlled Trial in Irritable Bowel Syndrome," *PLoS One* 5, no. 12(2010): e15591.

8. Steve Stewart-Williams and John Podd, "The Placebo Effect: Dissolving the Expectancy versus Conditioning Debate," *Psychological Bulletin* 130, no. 2 (March 2004): 324–340.

9. Alberto Gallace and Charles Spence, "The Science of Interpersonal Touch: An Overview," *Neuroscience & Biobehavioral Reviews* 34, no. 2 (2010): 246–259.

10. Usha Srivastava, *Encyclopaedia of Indian Medicines* (Pinnacle Technology, 2011), 5–6.

11. Matthew 12:22–32, 3:20–30; Luke 11:14–23.

12. Matthew 9:32–34.

13. Matthew 9:27–31.

14. Faith Karimi and Joe Sutton, "Police: Maryland Mom Kills 2 of Her Children during Attempted Exorcism," *CNN*, January 19, 2014.

15. "Exorcists to Ted Cruz: 'Leave Your Power-Hungry Demonic Soul!'" AOL.com, February 9, 2016, www.aol.com/article/2016/02/09/exorcists-to-ted-cruz-leave-your-power-hungry-demonic-soul/21310147/.

16. Guillaume Sébire, "In Search of Lost Time from 'Demonic Possession' to anti–N-methyl-D-aspartate Receptor Encephalitis," *Annals of Neurology* 67, no. 1 (2010): 141–142.

17. Josep Dalmau et al., "Clinical Experience and Laboratory Investigations in Patients with Anti-NMDAR Encephalitis," Lancet Neurology 10, no. 1 (2011): 63–74.

18. Catechism of the Catholic Church, paragraph 1673.

19. Katie Jagel, " Poll Results: Exorcism," YouGov, September 17, 2013.

20. I have since been diagnosed with *cervicocranial syndrome* and I'm undergoing regular treatment.

21. Bartosz Chmielnicki, "Acupuncture—Definition," Evidence Based Acupuncture, www.evidencebasedacupuncture.org/acupuncture/acupuncture-definition/.

22. Brian Palmer, "If Your Veterinarian Offers Acupuncture, Find a Different Vet," *Slate*, May 5, 2014, www.slate.com/articles/health_and_science/science/2014/05/alternative_medicine_for_pets_veterinarians_should_not_perform_acupuncture.html.

23. David Colquhoun and Steven P. Novella, "Acupuncture Is Theatrical Placebo," *Anesthesia & Analgesia* 116, no. 6 (2013): 1360–1363.

24. Steven Novella, "An Industry of Worthless Acupuncture Studies," *Science-Based Medicine*, August 26, 2015, www.sciencebasedmedicine.org/an-industry-of-worthless-acupuncture-studies/.

25. Jun J. Mao et al. "Electroacupuncture versus Gabapentin for Hot Flashes among Breast Cancer Survivors: A Randomized Placebo-Controlled Trial," *Journal of Clinical Oncology* (2015): JCO-2015.

26. Eleanor Webber, "Acupuncture and HIV: The 'New' Weapon in the Fight Against HIV/AIDS," *Acufinder Magazine*, Summer 2007.

27. Ting Bao et al., "Patient-Reported Outcomes in Women with Breast Cancer Enrolled in a Dual-Center, Double-Blind, Randomized Controlled Trial Assessing the Effect of Acupuncture in Reducing Aromatase Inhibitor-Induced Musculoskeletal Symptoms," *Cancer* 120, no. 3 (2014): 381–389.

28. R. Barker Bausell, *Snake Oil Science: The Truth about Complementary and Alternative Medicine* (Oxford: Oxford University Press, 2007).

29. Ben Goldacre, "Trial sans Error: How Pharma-Funded Research Cherry-Picks Positive Results [Excerpt]," *Scientific American* 13 (2013).

30. M. Baum and E. Ernst, "Should We Maintain an Open Mind about Homeopathy?" *American Journal of Medicine* 122, no. 11 (November 2009): 973–974.

31. "'Overdose' Protest against Homeopathy," *BBC News*. January 30, 2010.

32. "More Details Arise on Parents Charged with Homicide in Child's Death," *Rocket-Courier*, June 11, 2015, www.rocket-courier.com/node/141065#. VX111HD3aK0.

33. James Gallagher, "Homeopathy 'Could Be Blacklisted,'" *BBC News*, November 13, 2015, www.bbc.com/news/health-34744858.

34. "Position Statement: Homeopathy," Royal Australian College of General Practitioners, May 2015. www.racgp.org.au/download/Documents/Policies/Health%20systems/PPI-PositionStatement-Homeopathy-v1.pdf.

35. One case is *Kim Allen et al. v. Hyland's Inc. et al.*, case number 2:12-cv-01150, in the U.S. District Court for the Central District of California.

36. Chris Baggoley, *Review of the Australian Government Rebate on Natural Therapies for Private Health Insurance* (Canberra: Australian Government Department of Health, 2015), www.health.gov.au/internet/main/publishing.nsf/Content/phi-natural-therapies

37. Edzard Ernst, "A Systematic Review of Systematic Reviews of Homeopathy," *British Journal of Clinical Pharmacology* 54, no. 6 (2002): 577–582.

38. Klaus Linde et al., "Impact of Study Quality on Outcome in Placebo-Controlled Trials of Homeopathy," *Journal of Clinical Epidemiology* 52, no. 7 (1999): 631–636.

39. Daniel Redwood and Carl S. Cleveland III, *Fundamentals of Chiropractic* (St. Louis, MO: Mosby, 2003).

40. "Historic Release of Data Gives Consumers Unprecedented Transparency on the Medical Services Physicians Provide and How Much They Are Paid," press release, Centers for Medicare & Medicaid Services (Baltimore, MD), April 9, 2014.

41. Clay Jones, "Chiropractic Vs. Conventional: Dueling Perspectives on Infant Colic," *Science-Based Medicine*, September 13, 2013, www.sciencebasedmedicine.org/chiropractic-vs-conventional-dueling-perspectives-on-infant-colic/.

42. S. Vohra et al., "Adverse Events Associated with Pediatric Spinal Manipulation: A Systematic Review," *Pediatrics* 119, no. 1 (2007): e275–e283.

43. Stephen R. Deputy, "Arm Weakness in a Child Following Chiropractor Manipulation of the Neck," Seminars in Pediatric Neurology 21, no. 2 (June 2014): 124–126.

44. Meg Alexander, "30-Year-Old Dies after Visit to the Chiropractor," *KFOR*, November 4, 2014, kfor.com/2014/11/03/30-year-old-dies-after-visit-to-the-chiropractor/.

45. E. Ernst, "Deaths after Chiropractic: A Review of Published Cases," *International Journal of Clinical Practice* 64, no. 8 (2010): 1162–1165.

46. Paul Benedetti and Wayne MacPhail, *Spin Doctors: The Chiropractic Industry under Examination* (Toronto: Dundurn, 2003).

47. Linda Rosa et al., "A Close Look at Therapeutic Touch," JAMA 279, no. 13 (1998): 1005–1010.

48. Danica Collins, "Heal with Quantum Entanglement," *Underground Health Reporter*, undergroundhealthreporter.com/heal-with-quantum-entanglement/.

49. "Diabetic Boy, 7, Dies after 'Slap Therapy'" *Yahoo7 News*, May 1, 2015, au.news.yahoo.com/a/27503140/diabetic-boy-7-dies-after-slap-therapy.

50. Helen Manber and Matthew Kanzler, "Consequences of Cupping," *New England Journal of Medicine* 335, no. 17 (1996): 1281–1281.

51. Scott Logan, "Otter Calls for Legislative Review of Faith-Healing Law," *KBOI*, February 11, 2016, kboi2.com/news/local/otter-calls-for-legislative-review-of-faith-healing-law.

52. It should be noted that the natural progression of unchecked religious exemptions to criminal laws tends toward abuse and confusion. In April 2017, for instance, an appeals court ruled against an inmate who argued his twenty-seven-year sentence on drug charges should be reversed because it was his *religious duty* to sell heroin. The judges rejected his argument not because it was ludicrous, but because Anderson was "distributing heroin to others for non-religious uses."

53. "Child Faith-Deaths in Idaho," Child Abuse in Idaho: Deadly & Legal, idahochildren.org/articles/worst-in-nation/.

54. Joseph Liu, "Faith Healing and the Law," Pew Research Center, August 31, 2009, www.pewforum.org/2009/08/31/faith-healing-and-the-law/.

55. "David G. McAfee Interviews an Attendant at a Christian Science Reading Room," YouTube video, uploaded by David G. McAfee, September 15, 2012, www.youtube.com/watch?v=_dg-GC26aQg.

56. I noticed that the attendant had a so-called "*lazy eye*," also known as amblyopia, a lifelong condition. When asked why she hadn't sought a spiritual healing for the impairment, she replied that it "*wasn't a priority*."

17

CULT CRISIS

"Among other things Jonestown was an example of a definition well known to sociologists of religion: a cult is a religion with no political power."
—Thomas Wolfe

You hear a lot about individual cults in the media, like when a member of the Grail Movement is accused of skinning her son and feeding him to relatives,[1] or when the leader of the Fundamentalist Church of Jesus Christ of Latter-Day Saints (FLDS) is sentenced to life in prison for sexually assaulting a 12-year-old,[2] but how much do you really know about cults themselves? Did you know that every single religion that exists now or has existed at any time in human history began as a cult? In fact, there is no real difference between the two, except for that a religion is more widely accepted. This shouldn't scare you. Sure, there are some dangerous and destructive cults,[3] but, just like with religions, there are others that are not deadly or even harmful to others in any way.

A lot of people don't believe that all religions begin as cults, but it's not up for debate. Historians can trace various faiths back to their original roots when they had only a handful of supporters and were seen as evil or strange by outsiders. Take Christianity, for instance, the world's most popular religion.[4] What we know today as the Christian religion began as a small sect of Second Temple Judaism in the middle of the first century. There were several Jewish sects around this time, including the Christians,

Pharisees, Sadducees, and Zealots.[5] Members of the Christian sect were persecuted early on, as is the case with most minor religious groups and cults within a culture engulfed by a larger tradition, and eventually Christianity became a distinct religion of its own. Historian Shaye J. D. Cohen, the Littauer Professor of Hebrew Literature and Philosophy in the Department of Near Eastern Languages and Civilizations at Harvard University, says Early Christianity *"ceased to be a Jewish sect when it ceased to observe Jewish practices"* such as circumcision.[6]

Religions arising without divine intervention or communication may seem like a complicated process, but nothing makes it easier to understand than the existence of cargo cults. These "cults" are actually just local religious traditions that tend to spring up under certain stressful conditions, including in areas where colonizing groups interact with native people. Cargo cults believe in assistance from ancestral spirits and they often have charismatic leaders, but these groups are most well known for their belief that an abundance of food and supplies—or cargo—will appear if certain rituals are performed. Some cargo cults imitate soldiers and create mock airplanes, airports, or radios out of local materials like straw and wood as a means of attracting supply drops. People belonging to one particular cargo cult, dubbed the Prince Philip Movement,[7] even believe that Prince Philip, Duke of Edinburgh, the husband of Queen Elizabeth II, is a divine being. This phenomenon, perhaps above all else, demonstrates how easily cults (and eventually religions) can arise without any help from gods.

LESSER-KNOWN CULTS

Christianity is the most popular religion and we understand a lot about its roots as a Jewish cult. We also know a lot about Jim Jones and his devastatingly fatal Jonestown settlement where more than 900 people died,[8] as well as some other modern cults, such as the FLDS, which has been under public scrutiny for many years. Popular media covered when FLDS leader Warren Jeffs was placed on the FBI's Ten Most Wanted List,[9] when he was arrested,[10] and even when the cult's new leaders pleaded not guilty to allegations of food stamp fraud.[11] If you were around in the 1990s, you probably also remember hearing about the Heaven's Gate group, which became infamous when its founder convinced almost 40 people to commit mass suicide while wearing black-and-white Nike sneakers.[12] The members of that group believed they were extraterrestrials who needed to kill themselves to reach an alien spacecraft. We can see that news agencies do enjoy covering some cult stories, but what you may not know is that most minor religious factions (and their activities) fly well under the radar. According to a review by the International Cultic Studies Association, there are approximately 5,000 cults with about 2 million adherents in the United States alone,[13] but we rarely hear about many of them.

Lesser-known groups include Lafayette Morehouse, a decades-old commune in California that has been called a "*sex cult*,"[14] the Brownsville Assembly of God, which hosted annual "revival" services attended by more than 2.5 million people,[15] and Gloriavale Christian Community, a small group in New Zealand whose members are often referred to as "*Cooperites*" after their founder Neville Cooper, who was sentenced to jail in 1995 on sex abuse charges.[16] There's also the Sterling Institute of Relationship, a for-profit counseling business that New York–based psychotherapist and deprogramming expert Kathryn May unequivocally calls a cult.[17]

"*Any therapy that promotes itself as the answer but won't tell you what they actually do is suspect. It's mind control and mind control is always dangerous. Getting out from under such group-supported thinking is a long, hard process,*" she said. "*It means the person getting out has to face the fact that they've been living a fantasy, and nobody wants to know that they've been duped. Sterling presents himself as the good father these men and women are convinced they never had. And he preys on people's wish to find quick fixes for everything. He attracts people who are vulnerable.*"

While some may say these small groups are unworthy of mention, it should be noted that every religion began as a cult—a small group of people with similar religious ideals, usually characterized by devotion directed toward a particular figure or object. It is only after time passes and belief becomes more commonplace that a cult obtains special standing as a "religion."

TWO BY TWOS

One of the most interesting low-key cults, in my opinion, is known as the *Two by Twos*. This group, which gets its name based on its practice of sending out preachers in twos, in accordance with the Bible,[18] was founded in Ireland by a man named William Irvine in the late nineteenth century.[19]

Members of the Two by Two community often call it "*The Truth*" or "*The Way*," but there are a number of other monikers, as well, including "*Cooneyites*," a pejorative term derived from the name of one-time coleader Edward Cooney. The Two by Twos, which used its missionary methods to spread all around the world, is different from most other cults or religious groups in that it has no statement of belief other than the Bible itself. Not much is known about this particular community,[20] but some of its rules, including the 1903 requirement for members to give up their worldly possessions and commit themselves to celibacy and obedience, have been controversial. I was able to talk to Kenton Mills, a 34-year-old former member from Canada, who said the church members (or "*friends*") in his old group live normal lives, "*except most don't have a TV.*" The ministers, or "*workers*," he said, must still give up their possessions.

"*They literally have everything in a suitcase,*" Mills told me in an e-mail interview, adding that the group claims to be "*the modern continuation of the original ministry of Jesus.*"

"*I was taught as a child that this ministry is a continuation of the Jesus's original preachings and we are just living the modern-day version,*" Mills said. He left the church seven or eight years ago after being "*disciplined*" for having a child out of wedlock.

"*Even though the mother was my fiancé; it still was a big deal to them,*" Mills wrote.

He also said he had doubts since he was young, and he rebelled due to the "*boring*" nature of the services themselves.

"*I was kept in line though through indoctrination and the fear of a literal hell. The fear of hell coupled with childhood brainwashing are powerful tools. I can attest to that,*" Mills told me. "*As I got older the fear of hell constantly weighed on me and eventually led to me to 'profess' at the age of 16 and then be baptized when I was about 21. These are requirements to be able to avoid hell and be eligible for heaven.*"

Mills explained that he only stuck with the church because of his family and the "*real fear of hell.*"

"*Thinking back on it now brings feelings of anger and outrage that an organization would see the fear of hell tactic as a blessing,*" he said during the interview.

THE POWER OF INDOCTRINATION

If you weren't raised in a cult, or by extremely religious individuals in general, you probably aren't aware of just how powerful the process of indoctrination can be. You might ridicule people who *"drink the Kool-Aid"* of a specific person or group,[21] but you likely don't understand the psychology behind their adherence. Are they gullible? Dumb? Guided by their emotions? Possibly, but not necessarily.

Cults rely heavily on indoctrination, and sometimes on multiple generations of children being exposed to the same brainwashing techniques. Adolescents are often thought of as the most valuable members in cults because they will (more often than not) believe what they are taught growing up and help spread that message. This is an anthropological observation that can be confirmed by a basic review of ancient and modern religions and cults, and it was known to at least one author of the Hebrew Scriptures, who wrote, *"Start children off on the way they should go, and even when they are old they will not turn from it."*[22]

When a religious parent teaches only his or her religious tradition, the child will usually grow up believing in it. In fact, you can teach your children to worship a head of lettuce and—provided there's the right amount of fear instilled in those who doubt it—the belief will likely persist until it's exposed to the scrutiny of skepticism. After all, what reason would the child have to doubt his or her parents, especially in the face of devastating consequences? In the kid's mind, why would the family lie?

I like to use the hypothetical Lettuce Cult as an example of the power of indoctrination. Imagine a like-minded man and woman with three children, two daughters and a son, whom they teach all about the Lettuce God that was shredded for their sins. They tell their kids that Lettuce deserves worship and praise, and that it was responsible for life itself, all while cautioning them against doubt. "The Lettuce does not like to be questioned! You owe everything to it," the parents tell their children, adding that those who are skeptical simply "hate the Head of Lettuce."

Everything revolves around Lettuce for the family. They won't eat it for dinner, but they do begin every meal with a thankful incantation, often involving the phrase, "Lettuce pray." They might even get upset and protest when they see people on TV mistreating their leafy deity. This belief doesn't just persist, but it thrives over time. The children might be homeschooled, or perhaps they are taught that everyone else at school is completely wrong about their beliefs, as is the case in many heavily religious families. Either way, the Lettuce belief lives on because their community, in this case a small and trusted family, strongly advocates it.

The parents might use established religious concepts to give credence to their fringe beliefs and ensure their children retain them. They might say, for instance, that Christianity got everything right except for when its early scribes omitted that Jesus was actually a head of lettuce. "The devil has caused all other Christian denominations to make this huge error, even blaspheming by declaring that a cracker can be our lord's body, but do not be deceived!" the parents might say. "For if you are, you will be boiled for eternity."

Under the right conditions, the Lettuce Cult could theoretically grow and become a full-fledged religion. After a number of years, over the course of which numerous other families may join the first group's community (or compound), the beliefs that once seemed ridiculous and laughable could be accepted by dozens, or even hundreds. Perhaps one day, after a disagreement with the Lettuce Cult leadership, a couple of families could split off to create their own group, one that properly interprets romaine lettuce—and not iceberg—as the divine creator. Welcome to the first Lettuce-based Holy War, which sparks hundreds of years of disputes over scriptural interpretations and housing and land rights. Thousands of years later, when all of the original context is forgotten and the majority of the country worships Lettuce as a result of aggressive missionary work, we may even see the first Lettuce-worshiping President of the United States. *Kale to the chief!*

WESTBORO BAPTIST CULT

One of the most prominent groups that is classified as a cult is **Westboro Baptist Church (WBC),** a Kansas-based fringe religious group founded by Pastor Fred Waldron Phelps Sr., who died of natural causes at age 84 on March 14, 2014.[23] WBC has become synonymous with extreme Christian fundamentalism—especially as it relates to the group's attitude toward homosexuals.[24] The church purports to represent primitive Baptist and Calvinist principles, and its members travel throughout the United States (and sometimes elsewhere) picketing funerals of soldiers, well-

WESTBORO BAPTIST CHURCH HEADQUARTERS IN TOPEKA, KANSAS.
PHOTO TAKEN DURING MY TRIP THERE IN 2015.

known members of the LGBTQ community, and anything else likely to gain media attention. They have held more than 50,000 protests in more than 915 cities, according to their website.[25]

WBC members, some of whom have been barred from entering Canada[26] and the United Kingdom,[27] often preach against the "God loves us all!" mentality that some cultural or liberal Christians have adopted, instead choosing to highlight the many times in the Bible in which God expressed his *"divine hate."* Due to their unorthodox beliefs and the actions that result from them, the WBC has been labeled as an anti-LGBT hate group—one of just five hate groups in Kansas—by the Southern Poverty Law Center.[28] Here are just a few of the church's frequently cited biblical passages about hatred from God:

- Leviticus 20:23: *"And ye shall not walk in the manners of the nation, which I cast out before you: for they committed all these things, and **therefore I abhorred them**."*

- Deuteronomy 32:19: "*And when the LORD saw it, **he abhorred them**, because of the provoking of his sons, and of his daughters.*"

- Psalm 5:5: "*The foolish shall not stand in thy sight: **thou hatest all workers of iniquity**.*"

- Romans 9:13: "*As it is written, Jacob have I loved, but **Esau have I hated**.*"[29]

On January 12, 2014, a few months after *Fast and Furious* movie franchise star Paul Walker died in a fatal car accident,[30] members of WBC made stops throughout Los Angeles picketing various "Whorehouses," "Dog Kennels," and "Child Rapists," also known as liberal Protestant and Catholic churches. The group ultimately made their way to the Golden Globe Awards in Beverly Hills, where they protested those who will "*try and preach Paul Walker into Heaven.*" During the WBC's exhibition, I met up with lifetime member Isaac Hockenbarger, who was 19 at the time of the interview, to ask a few questions about cults, faith, and science.[31]

McAfee: Would you consider the Westboro Baptist Church a cult in any way?

Isaac Hockenbarger: I don't care what you want to call us. If we're a cult, well then our charismatic empathic leader is Christ.

McAfee: So, you don't have a problem with the technical term "cult"?

Isaac Hockenbarger: I don't care what you call us because, quite frankly, what Christ said was "*If you love me, the world is going to hate you.*" How awful a thing is it to call someone a cult? It's pretty bad. The world hates us.

McAfee: I for one don't hate WBC or any other church. And there's a factual definition that determines whether or not it's a cult, but I argue that any major religion is just a larger version of that.

Isaac Hockenbarger: The brainwash of "God loves everyone" is sad. It's spelled out so many times in so many different ways across the Bible.

McAfee: Does the WBC accept outsiders as new members?

Isaac Hockenbarger: Absolutely, it happens on occasion. But it's going to come out if you don't actually believe. You have to prove you believe it; it's called the fruits—the fruits of their work. You've got to show that you believe, not just say it.

McAfee: Do you think that your sect of Christianity is more biblically literate than the majority of other denominations?

Isaac Hockenbarger: I don't think you can call yourself a Christian without being biblically literate, and it's an everyday thing. It's constant learning. The most fundamental law of logic is that if there is but a single counterexample to your theory, you are wrong. As it is written, "*Jacob have I loved, but Esau have I hated*." We can't just change definitions of words because we don't like them. Hated means hated, but we aren't talking about human hate. We are talking about a fixed determination to punish those who don't follow his commandments.

McAfee: I agree that the Judeo-Christian god is portrayed in most of the Bible as hating homosexuals, or whatever your version of hating is, but you're working under the presupposition that Christianity is true and that all that exists. You're really just working with ancient texts like everybody else.

Isaac Hockenbarger: We could work under the presupposition of atheism being true, and what then?

McAfee: Since there's no evidence to support the existence of any deities or supernatural entities of any kind, not believing should be the default position.

Isaac Hockenbarger: We can all think that we're the smartest people in the world and "*Stephen Hawking it up*" and what would it gain us?

McAfee: Intelligence, intellect, and education. By pursuing scientific advancement, we can understand the world how it actually it is.

Isaac Hockenbarger: If you're right, so what. If I'm right, you're screwed. That's the simplistic version.

MEMBERS OF THE WESTBORO BAPTIST CHURCH PICKETING THE GOLDEN GLOBES IN LOS ANGELES.
PHOTO TAKEN IN 2014.

McAfee: That's called Pascal's Wager, and it's long been debunked. But the typical wager there would be that you lost nothing. You guys have kind of lost your whole lives, following this really extreme sect.

Isaac Hockenbarger: What would you have gained?

McAfee: Living an evidence-based life is great. You don't just listen to whatever your family tells you, or your culture, or anything. You just look at facts.

Isaac Hockenbarger: You keep acting like you don't want to offend me by saying cult, but you tell me I listen to my family. No, I don't.

McAfee: Just like any Christian, you were born into a family and you listen to them. It's still indoctrination if it's a small cult or a big religion. You teach your children something and you don't allow anything else other than that.

Isaac Hockenbarger: That's a lie. We live absolutely normal lives.

McAfee: Are you encouraged to question your actual faith and interact with people who have left the church?

Isaac Hockenbarger: Absolutely, people leave all the time. Most of my family doesn't belong to the church anymore.

McAfee: And you have nothing against them for that?

Isaac Hockenbarger: No, absolutely not. But I'm not "buddy buddy" with them.

McAfee: Why not? They're still your family. Have you been taught not to be "buddy buddy" with them?

Isaac Hockenbarger: Because it's simple. They went their way; I'm going my way. It's in the Scriptures.

McAfee: But what if you look at the Scripture from another religion? Why is your religion's Scripture the "right" one?

Isaac Hockenbarger: It's what you choose to believe, just like you can choose to believe in the Big Bang, or whatever.

After speaking with Isaac, I learned more about his and others' experiences at Westboro Baptist Church through his older brother and former WBC member Michael Hockenbarger. Michael, 25 years old at the time of our e-mail discussion, graciously agreed to share his perspective on the WBC's true motives and intentions.

McAfee: What is your relationship to Isaac? When was the last time you spoke to him?

Michael Hockenbarger: Isaac is my brother, the youngest of seven. I am number five. It has been a little over eight years now since I have seen him or spoken to him.

McAfee: When and under what circumstances did you leave the cult? Do you consider yourself religious now?

Michael Hockenbarger: I was forcibly thrown out in October 2005. It wasn't my choice, and I didn't want to leave. They had excommunicated my father earlier that year, so I was sent to live with him. School was not pleasant. Isaiah [another WBC member] and his friend constantly ridiculed, humiliated, and assaulted me, but I was too afraid to confront them or talk to teachers. That was my only semester at Topeka West High School.

Strangely enough, it is their emphasis on education that led me to doubt in the first place a few months after being kicked out. The research into ancient religion led me to a revelation of sorts. It is all the same. All of it. Hindu, Zoroastrian, Christian, Wicca, it doesn't matter. It is an outdated, primordial attempt at explaining the world around us, and exerting control over the masses.

My parents still believe in all the same bigotry that the cult does. Many of us who left found other churches and religions, or fell off somewhere in the apathetic department. I'm the only outright atheist I know of (aside from Nate).[32] The idea of continuing to believe in a deity that would allow its adherents to torture each other the way they do is appalling to me. Add that to the fact that zero evidence has ever actually been presented for sky wizards, and you get an atheist.

McAfee: Isaac told me that, while he is not "buddy buddy" with friends and family who left the cult, he is still allowed to interact with them regularly. To your knowledge, is that accurate?

Michael Hockenbarger: Should Isaac even look at us, he would be thrown out. Same with Jennifer, Charles, and Katherine (my other cultist siblings). They say to the outside world that they can, but it is a bald-faced lie. Should he do so, he would face the exact same ostracism, torment, and eventual excommunication that the rest of us did. Paul (from the Bible) says that those without faith are a poison to the church, to be cast out and shunned. (Matthew 18:15–20, 1 Corinthians 5:1–12, 2 Corinthians 6:14, 2 Thessalonians 3:6, Ephesians 5:11, and many more).

McAfee: Did you hold a protest sign for the Westboro Baptist Church? What can you tell me about that experience?

Michael Hockenbarger: Of course. It is expected of the children to attend the pickets. I've been to several places around the country, including a time when I was on the front cover of a Pennsylvania newspaper. Most of the time, it was pretty boring, to be completely honest. The most that happens is some moron will flip them the bird. That being said, there were more than a few instances where I have been in legitimate fear for my life on the picket line. People throw things, pop their cars over the curb and swerve at us, initiate brawls, and shoot at them. Once, a guy stopped in the middle of traffic at 17th and Gage [in Topeka, Kansas] to accost me (15 at the time) for my sign "*Thank god for 9/11.*" He hit me, knocked me over, and tried to take the sign from my possession. This isn't one of those little hand-held signs you are used to. This is a big billboard type with support trusses that is nearly six feet tall. It wasn't pleasant being tangled in that mess with a guy 100 lbs. and a foot bigger than me. Another time, when leaving a gay pride parade in Chicago, a woman chased us down despite police paddy wagon transport, and threatened James [Hockenbarger] with a switchblade. At the time, he claimed an angel barred her path. Now, I'm sure she just didn't have the courage to tangle with us.

I enjoyed the antagonistic debates and arguments in those days. I still do, and from time to time play devil's advocate to argue the points from their perspective. I don't believe in sky fairies, but enjoy debate, and have had the dogma drilled into me my whole life. As Big Josh once said, "*You can take the Phelps out of the compound, but you can't take the compound out of the Phelps.*"

McAfee: What is the real goal of WBC? Do they want to convert others, or to publicly humiliate homosexuals?

Michael Hockenbarger: This cult has but one purpose. The purpose isn't conversion, or anything like it. That purpose is merely gaining attention for their message. The reason they use the terms and strategies they do is purely for the shock factor, purely to convince you, and other authoritative figures and media outlets, to talk about them. They truly don't care if you call them a cult. By talking about them at all, you have given them all they could ever want. The only way to mitigate the damage they do, not only to me, my parents, and my friends, but also to the public, homosexuals, atheists, and everyone else is NOT give them attention!

McAfee: The WBC has a strong emphasis on illuminating what they call the "sin" of homosexuality, but the Bible itself deals with homosexuality in only a relatively small number of passages. Do you have any insight into why the cult is so focused on it?

Michael Hockenbarger: It has to do with the "*zeitgeist*," or the spirit of the times. Our country has had sweeping advances in the administration of homosexual rights recently, so that is the issue they glommed on to, and the issue the media covers the most. They preach against adultery, fornication, Catholicism, and just about anything else you can think of. This is just the issue that garners the most attention.

McAfee: Would you say WBC members are well versed on the Bible?

Michael Hockenbarger: We spent a great deal of time studying theology, not just the Bible, when I was young. I've read apocrypha, sutras, the Dao De Jing, the Qur'an, Torah, Talmud, etc. We were required to be well versed in Martin Luther, Joseph Caryl, John Gill. We did comparative translation analysis on individual Greek, Hebrew, and Aramaic words to understand the source material. I don't come from a group of inbred hillbillies, like most "*experts*" say. Highly intelligent and well-read are much more accurate phrases. As teenagers, we were required to memorize and recite on demand large passages of the Bible, especially segments that came up on the picket line, like the ones Isaac rattled off to you.

Are they well versed? This is subjective to me. Personally, yes, I believe they are more biblically literate than most modern seminary students by the age of 10. I know I out-quoted and debated priests and preachers at that age. Many liberal Christians would point out some verses they appear to disregard, but they know these passages, and can fully explain them. You know as well as I do that there are thousands of contradictions in that amalgam of rhetoric and fables known as the Bible.

McAfee: Do you think the WBC practices a warped extremist form of fringe Christianity, or do you think it teaches strict adherence to the Bible?

Michael Hockenbarger: They are Christians. They preach what Jesus preached. He chased people with whips, threw people out of the temple, cursed fig trees, flipped some tables, and caused all kinds of hell without breaking too many laws. He didn't kill anyone, he never condoned rape, and he defined marriage in the Christian sense. They are the ugly truth of Christianity, not extremists. When they start razing cities and killing every man, woman, child, and livestock beast, we can talk about extremism. They have an opinion, and they state it, the same as you or me, or the most vocal homosexual advocate.

McAfee: Do they really believe what they preach?

Michael Hockenbarger: Without a doubt. They also believe they are always right, and nobody else has anything of value to say. How could someone preach such vitriol without believing every word? Anyone who doesn't tends to leave. The children are harder to understand. We have been taught that the Bible is the infallible word of God since before the age of reason. We didn't know anything else. The children there have no alternative system, because they were never exposed to them in earnest. We look at other holy books and disregard them as lies and propaganda. In some ways, these people are no different than the psychotic Muslims who blow themselves up to garner attention. Yet they don't commit acts of violence. Is what they say wrong and offensive? Yes. Do we have a right to stop them? No. They are doing no actual harm to anyone outside the cult.

McAfee: Would you say WBC members are dumb or generally uninformed, as they are often portrayed?

Michael Hockenbarger: Nurses, attorneys, computer engineers. These people aren't stupid. They know they don't follow conventional logic. They know what they do infuriates people. Gramps learned from his time in the Civil Rights Movement. They know every means of spreading their message. People like you and the news are the easiest and most effective. They won't stop. Their message is pretty clear. "*We are right, you are wrong, and we are going to mock you for eternity while you are in Hell.*" No matter how sociopathic that sounds, they firmly believe they are correct, and that they are doing exactly what Jesus commanded them to do. 2 Timothy 3–4 is a great example of what they feel their duty is.[33]

McAfee: Do you think the WBC shows what religious fundamentalism can do when taken to extremes? Do you see a difference between commonplace religious indoctrination and what the WBC practices?

Michael Hockenbarger: I don't see a difference. "*Commonplace*" Christians send checks, cash, money orders, and letters of support to the church all the time. "*Commonplace Christians*" just don't have the cojones to stand on the street corner and say it. Jack Wu, a recent addition to the cult, ran for school board solely on the platform that he was from the cult and wanted to instill biblical values in the school. He got nearly a third of the votes, as I recall. These beliefs are far from isolated. This is what Christianity looks like, all over. Most just try to cloak it in deceptive words.

Are they a little more extreme than others? Only in the way they deal with one another. I know of few other cults that actively attack and vilify one another for any perceived flaw. Jehovah's Witnesses and more fundamentalist Mormons are the only others I can think of that do anything similar. My experience hasn't been all that different than boys thrown out of the Fundamentalist Church of Latter-Day Saints compounds because they were competition for teenage girls. They will seemingly at random choose a person, then attack them relentlessly. Secluding them, mocking them, harassing them. In my case, they forced me to ridiculous amounts of manual labor. It went beyond the usual eight or so hours a day to new heights.

McAfee: Do you think the WBC plays a role in showing Christians the dangerous nature of their religion, or do you think most people simply write them off as "not True Christians"?

Michael Hockenbarger: As reprehensible as what they say is, it is the beliefs passed down for nearly two millennia in that faith. That is what Christianity looks like, whether some Christians want it to be or not.

Every time a Christian votes against gay marriage, they are showing their colors. The exact same colors as the WBC. The truly dangerous Christians are the sneaky *"God loves everyone"* Christians. At least you know where my family stands. I have no idea how anyone can get love out of that cesspool of hate and vitriol of a book. They are liars, plain and simple. I don't see talking as dangerous. *"My book says gay people are gross"* or head chopping? Which is actually dangerous? They don't burn people at the stake, many other Christians still do. They don't kill people for being accused of fornication, other Christians still do. These people are mild compared to some Christians.

McAfee: What do you think your family members still with WBC say about you now?

Michael Hockenbarger: I don't have to guess. I know what they say. Nothing they have to say about me is nice, despite all I did for them when I was there. The children are taught to hate those who leave, and more so for those they throw out. There is no forgiveness.

McAfee: Is there anything you'd like to add?

Michael Hockenbarger: I'm serious when I say that there is only one method to deal with people like them. They will never engage in violence, so they cannot do harm you don't do to yourself. Like any bully, ignoring them is the only answer. Dragging them to court is a waste of time and money, because they will win and spread their message. Talking to them affirms their goal. Counterpicketing provides them entertainment and spreads their message through the coverage of the counterprotest. The only way to mitigate them is for everyone to ignore them. Don't honk. Don't flip them off. Don't write an article about them. Don't give them the time of day. Ignore them.

In order to get a more complete picture of the WBC cult, I reached out to one of the most well-known former members: speaker, author, and LGBT rights activist Nathan "Nate" Phelps. Like Michael Hockenbarger, Nate is an atheist—and perhaps the only other WBC escapee who publicly holds that position. I asked Nate via e-mail to put the first two interviews into perspective so that we can have a more accurate look into the WBC and its beginnings.

McAfee: In your mind, what's the difference between a "cult" and a "religion"? What is Westboro Baptist Church to you?

Nate Phelps: Definitions talk about a charismatic leader, isolation, Us vs. Them, etc. as the descriptors of a cult. That doesn't make sense to me because you see these same variables in groups called religions or even political groups. There is also a general inclination to label any group that has odd ideas as a cult. But, let's face it, every major religious organization in the world makes claims far more bizarre than what we hear from marginalized groups like WBC. I tend to see the differences narrowed down to the size and community acceptance of the group. With that in mind, WBC would be a cult.

McAfee: Your father, Fred Phelps, died in March 2014 and was reportedly excommunicated from the church prior to that in August 2013. Are you aware of the circumstances surrounding that intrachurch conflict?

Nate Phelps: Unfortunately, most of what I know is hearsay. One niece was still there during the creation of the eight-member board of elders that apparently makes the decisions now. She indicated that there was a conflict between them and my father that ended with him being removed from his position and the building. One story was that he was kicked out for treating other members bad. I literally laughed out loud when I heard that. If that were the criteria he never would have started WBC. Another story was that he was beginning to show signs of softening his beliefs, which is a death knell at WBC.

McAfee: You escaped the WBC on your eighteenth birthday, but how long did it take before you gave up the doctrine of Calvinism? And before you became an atheist?

Nate Phelps: It was a long journey. I avoided religion for about five years after I left. I eventually returned when my children were born because I wanted them to feel included. I immersed myself in an evangelical-free church for the next 10 years or so. It was very difficult

to accept the kinder, gentler version of Christianity because we had learned from day one that accepting a lighter version of the Bible was a sign of weakness and hypocrisy. I ended up in counseling on two different occasions. One of those times was with a counselor who had a theology degree as well. Between that period and my own efforts to make sense of it all, I began to move away from the notion of a real supernatural being. There were a handful of events that took place in the 1990s, through 2005, that brought me to the point of atheism.

McAfee: Did you ever hold a sign for WBC, or did the picketing activism come after your departure?

Nate Phelps: I left in 1976. Their campaign began in 1991. But the elements of their campaign were going on in a variety of venues throughout our childhood. Condemning people for their lack of faith, creating enmity with members of the community, stirring up media attention . . . all of these activities were always present in one form or another in our lives.

McAfee: As a member of WBC as a child, were you expected to learn about other religions? How were other worldviews portrayed or taught?

Nate Phelps: Our primary source of information about other religions and philosophies came from our father on Sundays. He was meticulous in picking out each belief system, explaining why it was in opposition to the one Truth, then attacking the leader(s) of that system personally. School education about other religions was sparse in my experience growing up in the '60s and '70s, but what we did hear we readily dismissed because of our "*knowledge*" from church.

McAfee: What role does the WBC believe their media attention serves?

Nate Phelps: This gets interesting. First some groundwork. My father spoke lovingly and longingly about the two men in the Bible who never died (Enoch & Elijah). When I was there his teaching moved closer and closer to the idea that death is a judgment from god. He also spent a lot of time "*predicting*" the return of Christ. His studies, and his knowledge of the passages that say no man knows the timing of the return, led him to a conclusion that Christ would return somewhere around the year 2000, give or take 13 years. One final piece: in my father's studies and teachings, he identified a number of specific precursors to the return of Christ. A few of those are: that all men on earth must hear the Truth, and that 144,000 Jews need to be converted.

So you put all this together with the fervent knowledge that the WBC is the only place on Earth where the truth exists, and you have a perfect set of ingredients for them to conclude that they are intimately involved in paving the way for Christ's return. For those who have followed them closely, several years back they turned their focus on Jews. They picketed synagogues, Jewish centers, and funerals of Jews. Their stated intent was to put God's truth to their lips to help facilitate the salvation of the 144,000.

Now to finally answer your original question: They are constantly looking for more and better ways to reach large audiences. Their goal is to finally reach that magic tipping point where the final person on Earth hears, and therefore receives, God's judgment and wrath. In their world, this will cause a celestial lever to be pulled that releases the Kracken . . . er . . . Christ.

McAfee: Why do you think you were able to see past the indoctrination and the fear of escaping when so many others haven't been able to do so?

Nate Phelps: I hate this question. I don't know for sure. I only know that I grew up in a terribly violent home. I know that much of that violence, specifically including the verbal, was directed at me. I know that I believed my father's message about me. I recall specifically as a teenager walking through the mental process of calculating how long I would have to the year 2000 and feeling a sense of urgency to leave that place of pain and live my life to the fullest until I had to face God's wrath and judgment at the age of 42. I also know that I harbored a lot of questions about how we could be so special and be so cruel at the same time. I wondered about how someone like Elton John could bring so much good into the world but the only thing that mattered to God was that he had sex with the wrong people.

I know I spent years searching for the kinder, gentler God that appeared in the zeitgeist of the '70s and '80s. I know that I never got satisfactory answers to the questions I had about everything religious. I also know it's possible that my conclusions are colored by my experiences. That's not to say I think I'm wrong, just that my conclusions are colored. I know that I did a tremendous amount of work studying this question. I know that I had a strong, strong bias toward finding God. I believed that there would come a time that I would hear the right sequence of words from the right person and it would all fall in place.

But the biggest thing I know is that, in spite of the limitations my father's words placed in my mind, I developed a rich system of belief that argued for a natural view of the world. A big part of me just "*knew*" that these magical explanations were too complex and unknowable as religion tried to explain the universe. When my father argued that God caused tornados, I constantly asked the question in my own mind: why can't it just be that cold air meets hot air and creates tornados?

In 2004, when I read Michael Shermer's *The Science of Good & Evil*, everything fell into place. The sense of relief I felt as I read this book was profound. Finally, someone out there arguing for my view of the world.

McAfee: Are you in regular contact with any other escapees of WBC? I imagine you all have extremely interesting stories and perspectives.

Nate Phelps: My older brother Mark and I worked for 25 years together. My younger sister Dortha left several years after us. Both Mark and I maintain a relationship with her as well. I also keep in touch with several of the score of nieces and nephews who have left.

McAfee: Do you see a difference between commonplace religious indoctrination and what the WBC practices?

Nate Phelps: The only difference is the content.

McAfee: Does the WBC play a role in showing Christians the dangerous nature of their religion, or do you think most people simply write WBC off as not "True" Christians?

Nate Phelps: It depends on where you are on that continuum. WBC is definitely polarizing. No one gets to sit on the fence in this debate. I have to say I get just as offended with the "*that's not my god*" argument as I do with the hateful rhetoric of my family. Just recently I posted a horrific video that gave us a window into the moment a young gay man was cut off from his family who "*didn't want the neighbors to think they condoned his 'choice.'*" The resulting comments included a number of "*that's not my god*" arguments. In response I wrote this: "*A number of you have posted on here that this isn't real Christianity. I believe a more accurate statement is 'I'm not an historical Christian.'*" Of course this is real Christianity. These people didn't make this up. The Bible speaks in a number of places on the subject of same-sex sex. Further, the position of the Christian Church in modern history has opposed it. To dismiss this as aberrant is simply not accurate.

That said, it is true that many Christians have embraced a more contemporary idea of Christianity that quietly ignores these passages in favor of equality on this matter. A big part of this kinder, gentler Christian is to argue that God doesn't hate, that Jesus' message was about love and acceptance. Again, this is NOT an historical position of the Church.

You may see this as splitting hairs, but I see it as a huge, huge issue. As long as people continue to say that this kind of hateful conduct is not real Christianity, we can continue to downplay the importance that religion plays in creating these hateful ideas that do oh-so-much harm. It is, and was, Christian preachers who put forth the idea that gay is evil. Full stop.

If you want to separate yourself from this behavior, it is necessary to separate yourself from the label of Christian. If you have embraced the new, loving Christ, call it something else ... be a Jesusite.

McAfee: Is WBC growing? Have you seen evidence to suggest that they're inspiring other churches to undertake similar fundamentalist activism?

Nate Phelps: No and no. Just the opposite. I know the membership of the church has shrunk by 50 percent or better, by their own admission. As for inspiration . . . there are always extreme viewpoints. It's hard to say that there are more because of them. Well, let's just say, I don't perceive it.

McAfee: The WBC has a strong emphasis on illuminating what they call the "sin" of homosexuality, but the Bible itself deals with homosexuality in only a small number of passages. Do you have any insight into why the church is so focused on it?

Nate Phelps: I've heard that argument before. Maybe it's because of what I learned growing up, but I don't really think that's a good argument. The Bible is supposed to be the inspired, inerrant word of a divine creator. If he just says it once, that's plenty of attention on a subject from the standpoint of a believer.

I have no experience to speculate on why my father sees the reality of homosexuality as evil other than what he has always asserted. A passage in Romans 1, from his interpretation, treats homosexuality as a uniquely evil sin that God "*turns you over to.*" To Fred, this implied that it was a sin you couldn't turn back from so obviously God really, really, really doesn't like it.

But bear in mind that just as much as they focus on it, America and the world was already focusing on it. In the broader sense, if the WBC has decided to become a harkening angel to God's judgment of the world, what better "*sin*" to focus on in this time. If he had been born 50 years earlier, I'm satisfied that their signs would read "*God Hates Niggers*" as the black community struggled for their own justice and equality.

McAfee: Just as common cultural Christians write off negative and violent passages in the Old Testament, it seems as though the WBC is forced to ignore the positive and loving aspects of the New Testament. Would you say that's an accurate assessment?

Nate Phelps: No. They believe all the passages expressing God's love are written for the believer. Just like the humorous game of adding "*in bed*" to the end of your Chinese fortune, they add "*for or of believers*" where they see mention of God's love. "*The world*" in John 3:16 is the world of believers.

McAfee: With the rise of support for same-sex marriage in the United States, do you think WBC will be further marginalized by the general public?

Nate Phelps: How could they be more marginalized? I think the more important outcome of this battle will be the further marginalization of religion in general. Once again the archaic ideas of an impossible idea are demonstrably wrong. Once again "*absolute Truth*" isn't.

McAfee: What do you think your family members still with WBC say about you now?

Nate Phelps: I was interviewed by a reporter when I was in Clayton, Missouri, to give a talk for a GSA [Gay-Straight Alliance] club. He had recently spent a few weeks with the church ahead of writing an extensive piece on them. It was a pointed interview. I had the real sense that he had heard a lot about me from them and wanted to challenge me and my version. He ended the interview by saying "*you know . . . your family . . . they really, really hate you.*" I admit it was very difficult to hear. I sat stunned for a few moments then I told him, "*They don't have the right to say that anymore. They ostracized and shunned me 35 years ago, they don't get to keep playing that emotional card.*"

McAfee: Is there anything else you'd like to add?

Nate Phelps: For me my public speaking efforts have stopped being about the WBC and focus primarily on changing the mindset of North America. There are millions of people here who suffer daily, hourly, because of nonsensical ideas. America loves their Constitution as long as it supports their bias. Well, that's not how it works. That document, more than anything else, protects the minorities from the wolven (okay, I made that word up) ferocity of a prejudiced majority. It is past time that we all understand that we have NO right to even debate the withholding of equal rights to all. It is past time that we all understand that that secular document trumps any holy book we contrive.

Black, white, gay, straight, foreign, domestic, Christian, Muslim, male, female, and transgender people become just people in the sanctuary of the Constitution and the heart of the Humanist.

EXPOSING SCIENTOLOGY

For an example of a modern cult that has been relatively successful in terms of growth, look no further than **Scientology**, a registered religion that has made a practice of seeking out and converting celebrities with money, connections, and notoriety in order to gain legitimacy in the public eye. The most prominent Scientologist is Tom Cruise,[34] of *Top Gun* and *Mission: Impossible* fame, but the church's list also includes *Saturday Night Fever* star John Travolta, *Mad Men* actress Elisabeth Moss, and many, many more.[35] High-level Scientologists and Hollywood elite alike were shocked when Leah Remini, who was raised in Scientology[36] and is known best for her role as Carrie in *The King of Queens*, announced her departure from the church. She cited a number of reasons for her decision, including confrontations with Cruise, and ultimately published her memoir, *Troublemaker: Surviving Hollywood and Scientology*, on November 3, 2015. In the book, Remini says she was "*a big fan*" of Cruise until she got to know him.[37]

"*I'm sure many people could say the same thing about me or any other celebrity. But this is different; most actors are not in charge of your faith,*" the actress wrote. "*I don't doubt that Tom is in Scientology because he believes in it, but to me he has simply been given too much power by his church.*"

I had heard a lot about Scientology through popular media, but, due to the investigative nature of my writing, I decided to take a closer look at the cult, its practices, and how it actually works. As part of my investigation into Scientology, I took part in a number of so-called intelligence quotient (IQ) and stress tests at the local Church of Scientology headquarters in Los Angeles—I did everything but purchase their $50 book. I immediately gained a sense for what Scientology is in practice: untrained counselors using unapproved methods to "cure" diseases that can be treated medically or aren't even really there. The cult mentality was also immediately apparent during the group's testing procedures. The church's preliminary personality questionnaire, for instance, included questions like, "*Do you prefer to take a passive role in any club or organization to which you belong?*" and, "*Would you give up easily on a given course if it were causing you a considerable amount of inconvenience?*" One question that I found particularly interesting, and was perhaps included by the cult's leaders as a "red flag" of sorts, asked, "*Are you logical and scientific in your thinking?*"

After the group's *Oxford Capacity Analysis* test, which is deceivingly named and is in no way affiliated with the University of Oxford, I was told that I have an "*IQ*" of 138 but that I am depressed and therefore in need of their services. Despite my numerous written and verbal indications that I was happy and living a fulfilling life, the Scientology representative said I'm *"too intelligent for my own good"* and that I will *"continue to be unhappy,"* even if I don't notice it, unless I do as they say. I was immediately instructed to sign up for counseling courses that could, in time, yield results and even increase my IQ. After the testing and precounseling, I sought to speak to someone who was more familiar with Scientology and its history.

Jamie DeWolf is a slam poet, stand-up comedian, and filmmaker from Oakland, California—but he's also the great grandson of someone he calls *"one of the greatest con men of the last century."*

Lafayette Ronald Hubbard—better known as L. Ron Hubbard—was the founder of Scientology and DeWolf's great grandfather on his mother's side. In 1953, Hubbard incorporated the Church of Scientology after failing to pass off his teachings as a legitimate self-help system and to protect his people from allegations that they were practicing medicine without licenses.[38] Famous for its proscriptions against modern psychiatry, fierce litigation efforts, and science fiction–based belief system, Scientology has continued to thrive for years without Hubbard at the helm.

DeWolf said that, although Scientology teaches some very farfetched ideas, it's not far from what so-called legitimate religions teach. Scientologists believe that Xenu, the dictator of the *"Galactic Confederacy,"* brought billions of his people to earth in a DC-8-like spacecraft 75 million years ago.

"Everyone has to give Christianity its respectful distance, but when it comes to Scientology, people are more than happy to mock it out loud and laugh in its face—claiming their beliefs are ridiculous," DeWolf said. *"Christians believe in a magic apple and a talking snake and a boat with every organism on the planet floated around for 40 days . . . who is more ridiculous?"*

In a performance filmed for NPR's *Snap Judgment* in 2011, DeWolf told the previously unheard story of L. Ron Hubbard, from the point of view of someone who was written out of his biography. After seeing the powerful video,[39] in which DeWolf says Hubbard went from *"pennies to prophet,"* I asked him to tell me more about his great grandfather and the Church of Scientology. DeWolf, who sports a Scientology symbol tattoo on his right arm, sat down with me to discuss his own religious upbringing, his encounters with the Church of Scientology's secret police force, and more. Here's an edited transcript of our discussion:

McAfee: Although L. Ron Hubbard was your great grandfather, you weren't raised a Scientologist. Instead, you were brought up to be a Baptist Christian. Do you feel like religion was forced on you as a child?

Jamie DeWolf: Absolutely. I think that religion is forced on most people. If you're a child and you're not given a choice in the matter—and you're basically just told this is how the world works, it isn't voluntary. It was definitely forced upon me . . . I grew up with the anti-Christ as my boogeyman and I thought Armageddon would end the world. Christianity is an apocalyptic cult—it literally ends with death and destruction. The same death and destruction that David Koresh believed in, the same death and destruction that what they would deem a *"crazy psychotic cult"* would believe in. There is no real happy ending to the Bible—in Armageddon, the whole world becomes the devil's fuck-toy and, after that, God comes down with a flaming sword out of his mouth and slays all his foes. Particularly as a young kid, this stuff absolutely terrified me—I thought it was going to happen at any moment and they constantly remind you that it can happen at any moment. I went to a Bible study camp where they told us that the Rapture was going to happen on Saturday. I had to go the whole week calculating and wrestling with the idea that I was going to be dead—that my entire life was basically over.

McAfee: You've been openly critical of many religions. How would you define your own religious beliefs?

Jamie DeWolf: My great grandfather was a cult leader and I grew up Baptist Christian . . . let's just say that I have a healthy dose of skepticism toward any kind of theology that someone's going to hand me on a plate. These days, I think I'm going to start believing in the Greek gods again—Zeus and Hades and all those old-school gods. Somebody has to be making those waves, there must be a man living in the ocean! Why not, you know? They have a better backstory. Plus, in Christianity they've removed all female power whatsoever. Even just the fact that you have a holy trinity that is a father, a son, and a ghost—that's not a ménage à trois, that's a NAMBLA [North American Man/Boy Love Association] pamphlet. People don't think about the idea that they've removed any female presence. I find that to be fundamentally insulting and it's used as a tool to instinctively encourage a misogynistic and patriarchal culture. They actually teach that Eve actually precipitated the fall of man—I think that's reprehensible.

McAfee: The San Francisco Chronicle reported that in 2001 that your mother and girlfriend were visited by Scientology agents who asked about your comments on Scientology in your poetry. What did the agents want? Have you had any further interactions with them?

Jamie DeWolf: Yes, I did a performance about him in the year 2000. It was at a very early incarnation of *Tourettes Without Regrets* and I did a long piece about the beliefs of Scientology. It was recorded and someone put it up on www.mp3.com and it went to the top of the spoken word chart as a download. Within two or three days, Scientologists were at my house. My brother actually answered the door first and they gave him a cover story, saying that they were working with me on a performance. But my brother was confused because he was a part of a lot of my shows. My mother came to the door and she identified them right away—she said she could sense there was something off about the whole situation. She asked them what show it was and the name of the venue—they didn't have any answers. They finally asked whether or not she knew that I was claiming to be the great grandson of L. Ron Hubbard. She said, "*Of course, he is. And you're talking to his granddaughter right now.*" I've had no direct contact with them since then, but I'm sure they've kept tabs on me—I know how they operate.

McAfee: I recently visited an L. Ron Hubbard Life Exhibition Museum in Hollywood. The exhibit portrays Hubbard as a military hero, a world traveler, and a scholar. How accurate are those representations? Why aren't your family members mentioned?

Jamie DeWolf: I've actually been there three times and I've always gone in secret, sometimes in minor disguise. I've been taken on the tour and it's absolutely amazing that they believe it—it's the most ridiculous and absurd narrative possible. It shows him as a little red-haired boy being a blood brother to Indians and then walking with a staff over the Himalayan mountains and studying at the feet of wise men and being a dogfighter pilot and a submarine commander and a nuclear physicist and on and on and on. Of course, if this were true, this would be—as they claim—the greatest human being that has ever walked the planet. Ever since he was at a young age, he was always bloating his sense of self-importance. He loved to tell stories—obviously that's how he made his living in the early day. He was a prolific writer with a huge imagination. I think he wrote himself into being this heroic archetype and was able to convince this entire army that he created that he was the man that he always wanted to be—that he was an amazing war hero instead of being relieved of command, that he was machine-gunned twice in the back, and so on. He was a science fiction writer who ended up writing what he claimed to be a science; it's like Stephen King attempting to convince you that werewolves are real and that he was in a fight with a vampire last weekend. He certainly was audacious and he certainly traveled a lot, but I'd say that 99 percent of that is at least outright exaggeration. It's ridiculous the staggering amount of lies that he's been able to pack into that narrative.

McAfee: I've never been to Clearwater, Florida, the headquarters of the Church of Scientology Corporation. What is it like there?

Jamie DeWolf: It is cult Disneyland—it's absolutely, jaw-droppingly frightening. It's a sleepy little town that they completely devoured in the seventies. It was basically the first town where L. Ron landed when he was tired of being on a ship and running from different governments. When they landed, they consumed the town . . . moved right in. When you go there now, they've completely made the city succumb to their will. They own the majority of the real estate in the downtown area, they have their own bus line, they have little cult clones walking around in pseudo-military uniforms, they have more than 300 security cameras, and if you're a critic and you walk into a liquor store, they won't sell you anything. They bought their way into Mecca.

McAfee: One of the attributes that makes Scientology so dangerous is that it portrays itself as a science. Why do you think people are sucked into a religion that fundamentally clashes with scientific findings?

Jamie DeWolf: I think it's actually more dangerous that it calls itself a religion, because if it's a science you can ask for case studies and evidence, which is what the psychiatric community did when *Dianetics* first came out. That's why the loathing for psychiatry is so built-in to the DNA of Scientology that it's even carried forth by Tom Cruise and Kirstie Alley and a lot of the outspoken celebrity members. The psychiatric community was about to bankrupt L. Ron Hubbard because he was making fraudulent claims. That was how he turned it into a new religion almost overnight—so that it protected them; and it has protected them ever since.

McAfee: You once said, "Even amongst cults, they're a singular breed," referring to Scientology. What do you think separates Scientology from similar cults or religions?

Jamie DeWolf: I don't know of any other cult that has its own secret police force. I don't know of any cult that has such a history of brutal litigation, stalking, surveillance, and break-ins. There is no other cult that has infiltrated the IRS, CIA, FBI, and State Department. I can't think of another cult that completely takes every last cent that you have, that will give you loans and figure out the mortgage and deed on your house—they literally look at you like meat with assets. There's never been a cult like this.

After the interview, I reached out to DeWolf to see if he had any further interactions with the church or its representatives since our talk. While he said he hadn't, DeWolf did announce in May 2014 that he had discovered—and authenticated—writings he attributed to his grandfather, L. Ron Hubbard Jr., the son of the founder of Scientology. DeWolf read passages from the unpublished manuscript aloud in Clearwater, Florida, the city that houses Scientology's headquarters.

"*I'm the son of God. I mislead you slightly. I'm the son of the man who creates gods. Again, I mislead you slightly. I'm a son of the man who created and founded Dianetics and Scientology, which creates gods,*" DeWolf read. "*I'm a son of L. Ron Hubbard. This book is my dying declaration. My last will and testament. My father will order my death.*"

Ronald Edward DeWolf, who was born Lafayette Ronald Hubbard Jr. and was also called "*Nibs*" Hubbard, died of diabetes complications in 1991.

"Here's an easy way to figure out if you're in a cult:
If you're wondering whether you're in a cult, the answer is yes."

—*Stephen Colbert*

NOTES

1. John Bingham, "Cannibal Relatives Ate Boy Alive," *Telegraph*, June 20, 2008, www.telegraph.co.uk/news/worldnews/europe/czechrepublic/2162250/ Cannibal-relatives-ate-boy-alive.html.

2. Jim Kyle, "Polygamist Leader Warren Jeffs Sentenced to Life in Prison," *CNN*, August 10, 2011, www.cnn.com/2011/CRIME/08/09/texas.polygamist. jeffs/.

3. "Michael Ryan, Man Convicted in 1985 Cult Killings, Dies in Nebraska Prison," *CBS News*, May 25, 2015, .cbsnews.com/news/michael-ryan-man-convicted-in-1985-cult-killings-dies-in-nebraska-prison/.

4. "The Global Religious Landscape," Pew Research Center, December 18, 2012, www.pewforum.org/2012/12/18/global-religious-landscape-exec/.

5. Frederick Fyvie Bruce, *New Testament History* (Galilee Trade, 1971).

6. Shaye J. D. Cohen, *From the Maccabees to the Mishna*, Library of Early Christianity, ed. Wayne Meeks. (Philadelphia, PA: Westminster Press, 1987).

7. Paul Chapman, "Why a Tribe in Vanuatu Believes Their God Prince Philip Is Set to Visit," *Telegraph*, April 25, 2015, www.telegraph.co.uk/news/ worldnews/australiaandthepacific/vanuatu/11563091/Why-a-tribe-in-Vanuatu-believes-their-god-Prince-Philip-is-set-to-visit.html.

8. David Chidester, *Salvation and Suicide: An Interpretation of Jim Jones, the Peoples Temple, and Jonestown* (Bloomington, IN: Indiana University Press, 1991).

9. "FBI Announces New Top Tenner," FBI, May 6, 2006, www.fbi.gov/ news/stories/2006/may/jeffs050606.

10. Kirk Johnson, "Leader of Polygamist Mormon Sect Is Arrested in Nevada," *New York Times*, August 30, 2006, query.nytimes.com/gst/fullpage.ht ml?res=9B05E4D8113EF933A0575BC0A9609C8B63.

11. "Polygamous Church Leaders Indicted Over Allegations of Food Stamp Fraud," *NPR*, February 24, 2016, www.npr.org/sections/thetwo-way/2016/02/24/467958518/polygamous-church-leaders-indicted-over-allegations-of-food-stamp-fraud.

12. B. Drummond Ayres, Jr., "Families Learning of 39 Cultists Who Died Willingly," *New York Times*, March 28, 1997, www.nytimes.com/1997/03/29/us/families-learning-of-39-cultists-who-died-willingly.html.

13. Edward A. Lottick, "Prevalence of Cults: A Review of Empirical Research in the USA," paper presented at the International Cultic Studies Association, Universidad Autonoma de Madrid, July 14, 2005, www.culteducation.com/brainwashing45.html

14. Nellie Bowles, "Nicole Daedone's Mission of Orgasmic Meditation," *San Francisco Chronicle*, January 12, 2011, www.sfgate.com/style/article/Nicole-Daedone-s-mission-of-orgasmic-meditation-2368554.php.

15. Margaret M. Poloma and John C. Green, *The Assemblies of God: Godly Love and the Revitalization of American Pentecostalism* (New York: NYU Press, 2010).

16. Kurt Bayer, "Gloriavale Religious Commune: Hard Road Out of Commune," *New Zealand Herald*, March 13, 2015, www.nzherald.co.nz/nz/news/article.cfm?c_id=1&objectid=11416412.

17. Paul Smart, "The Sterling Men of Woodstock: A Series (Part III)–The Psychology of Cults and Secret Societies," Woodstock Times, August 15, 2002, www.culteducation.com/group/1261-sterling-institute-of-relationship/10328-the-sterling-men-of-woodstock-a-series-part-iii.html

18. Mark 6:7

19. George D. Chryssides, *The A to Z of New Religious Movements* (Lanham, MD: Scarecrow Press, 2006).

20. Arnold Parr and Christine Wilson, "Leaving the Cooneyites: Analysis of the Leaving Process for Long-term Members of a Sect," *Australian Religion Studies Review* 11, no. 1 (1998).

21. This figure of speech derives from the Jonestown deaths, where many of Jim Jones' followers were forced or manipulated into drinking a powdered beverage mixed with cyanide.

22. Proverbs 22:6

23. Daniel Burke, "Westboro Church Founder Fred Phelps Dies," *CNN*, March 25, 2014, www.cnn.com/2014/03/20/us/westboro-church-founder-dead/.

24. In the end, instead of shouting "God hates fags," the Westboro Baptist Church may as well be holding signs that say, "Santa hates poor kids." It's the same thing because, while each statement may be (arguably) accurate, neither is relevant to society as a whole.

25. "Home Page," Westboro Baptist Church, www.godhatesfags.com.

26. "Church Members Enter Canada, Aiming to Picket Bus Victim's Funeral," *CBC/Radio Canada*, August 8, 2008, www.cbc.ca/news/canada/manitoba/church-members-enter-canada-aiming-to-picket-bus-victim-s-funeral-1.703285.

27. "Anti-Gay Preachers Banned from UK," *BBC News*, February 19, 2009, bbc.co.uk/2/hi/uk_news/england/hampshire/7898972.stm.

28. "Groups," Southern Poverty Law Center, www.splcenter.org/fighting-hate/extremist-files/groups.

29. "Bible Verses about the Hatred of God," Westboro Baptist Church, www.godhatesfags.com/bible/God-hates.html.

30. Ed Payne and Tiffany Ap, "Paul Walker Death: Actor's Fatal Accident His Own Fault, Porsche Says," *CNN*, November 17, 2015, www.cnn.com/2015/11/17/entertainment/paul-walker-death-lawsuit/.

31. "David G. McAfee interviews a member of Westboro Baptist Church," YouTube video, uploaded by David G. McAfee, January 12, 2014, www.youtube.com/watch?v=Cc6KQUYRlOE.

32. He is referring here to Nathan "Nate" Phelps, who will be featured later in this chapter.

33. 2 Timothy 3–4: "*But mark this: There will be terrible times in the last days. People will be lovers of themselves, lovers of money, boastful, proud, abusive, disobedient to their parents, ungrateful, unholy, without love, unforgiving, slanderous, without self-control, brutal, not lovers of the good, treacherous, rash, conceited, lovers of pleasure rather than lovers of God.*"

34. Claire Hoffman and Kim Christensen, *Los Angeles Times*, December 18, 2005, www.latimes.com/news/la-fi-scientology18dec18-story.html.

35. "Famous Scientologists," *Los Angeles Times*, n.d., www.latimes.com/entertainment/gossip/la-et-famous-scientologists-pictures-photogallery.html.

36. Daniel Sieberg, "Leah Remini: Working Hard as a Queen among Kings," *CNN*, April 20, 2001, edition.cnn.com/2001/CAREER/jobenvy/04/20/leah/.

37. Leah Remini and Rebecca Paley, *Troublemaker: Surviving Hollywood and Scientology* (New York: Ballantine Books, 2015).

38. Stephen Kent, "The Creation of 'Religious' Scientology," *Religious Studies and Theology* 18, no. 2 (1999): 97.

39. "Jamie DeWolf: The God or The Man," *Snap Judgment* podcast, March 5, 2016, snapjudgment.org/jamie-dewolf-god-or-man.

CONCLUSION: MY CRYSTAL BALL

"That's how you get to the truth, folks. Open inquiry, honest investigation, and acceptance of the line of evidence no matter where it leads."
—Phil Plait

If you've made it this far, you've probably had a belief or two challenged by this book. For those of you who did, you should know that my intention wasn't to make you feel dumb, nor has my writing ever been motivated by hate. My goal is to encourage everyone to think critically and to be skeptical. I want to help people dispose of their false beliefs and rethink the ideas with which they may have been indoctrinated as children. At very least, I want to further popularize the scientific method, spur discussion on important ideas, and make individuals think about things they would otherwise ignore, such as potential inaccuracies within their religious texts or belief systems in general. Although it may seem like it at times because of the stagnancy of religious texts and the "unconfirmed" nature of other supernatural assertions, promoting scientific skepticism isn't the same as mocking anyone's beliefs; it's about a search for the facts.

I don't want to ridicule those who believe differently, and I definitely don't want to take away anyone's rights. I write about rational, scientific inquiry because I want to help demystify the world. My goal is to help everyone question the things around them, especially those they once took for granted as being true, and never end the search for evidence. I want every person to at least have the chance to rid themselves of false beliefs, and I'm not exempt from this. I'm on my own lifelong journey to shed flawed ideas (and much more). In fact, I think part of my interest in studying religious traditions and other supernatural concepts stems from my own innate and lifelong tendency toward irrational, ritualistic thoughts and behaviors.[1] I have been able to use this experience as a tool to better understand the nature of illogical beliefs.

I've never been one to preach hate. If I "preach" anything, it's logical thinking. How many people can honestly say they disagree with that? My decision to look for the truth in everything is a personal one, but I try to promote evidence-reliant thinking for all—partly because I have a vested interest in others' behavior. I recognize that, if you think better, you are more likely to act better. I would argue that, by looking at the historical harms of false beliefs and bad thinking in general, we can conclude that scientific skepticism is actually a prudent way to ensure human progress and therefore a necessary endeavor.

Holding a false belief doesn't make you dumb or worthy of ridicule; it just makes you wrong. And being wrong isn't always a bad thing. Being unable to admit it and alter that perspective, however, is bad. We may not like the feeling we get when we are wrong, but when we are, it's best to be grateful that we've learned something and move on. What makes this process difficult for many in their daily lives is the fact that, when ideas turn to beliefs, people tend to shut themselves off to the possibility that they could be wrong. So, when you begin a discussion with, "I have no doubt ..." it's possible that you've already committed the first error.

OUR BLIND SPOTS

I consider myself a naturally skeptical person, but I—like everyone else in the world—have accepted things as true without sufficient evidence. We all have rational blind spots. Even some of the biggest world governments have spent millions of dollars on so-called remote viewing, psychic warfare, and dowsing rods to search for oil, water, and bombs. No individual or global power is immune from the appeal of superstition, but that doesn't change the fact that none of these supernatural forces have evidence to support them that is both verifiable and scientifically valid.

I don't think having false beliefs makes you a bad person. The fact is that we've all been gullible at some moment in our lives—we've all been wrong before. To me, it's what you do next, once you've discovered you're wrong, that's most important. Do you seize the opportunity to educate yourself further, or do you reject the new information out of hand? If you used to hold a belief you now see is false, whether it's a religion or just a widespread urban legend, do you now feel stupid for having been duped? Or do you see that time as more of a learning experience? Maybe both? My recommendation is that, when you feel dumb about a belief you hold or once held, don't run from it; embrace it. That feeling should call attention to new knowledge you can acquire.

No matter how long you have been a skeptic, it is possible for irrational beliefs and behaviors, including those you held dear in the past, to influence your thoughts. You might be convinced of a new false idea by a source you find reliable, or perhaps an old superstition will rear its head in the form of an urge to pray or read a horoscope. This stuff happens because that's how we are wired. It's just a part of life—part of our evolutionary development. But it's also exciting because, when it does occur, we get to see first-hand how powerful the human brain actually is. We not only get to observe how the mind is able to create patterns, emotions, hallucinations, and more without any external force whatsoever, but we also get the opportunity to correct our faulty thinking in a meaningful way. With enough practice, we often have the ability to "logic away" our unsubstantiated ideas with nothing more than the power of critical thinking.

Because our subconscious brains have the ability to find patterns in meaningless data, understanding reality is easier when we challenge ourselves with questions. If you think you have evidence for any supernatural force or unsubstantiated idea, for instance, you might think, "Is coincidence more likely?" Usually, it is, and that's a more logical answer. It may further help to ask yourself what separates your story from those of millions of others. Does yours have some sort of physical or otherwise verifiable evidence? Do you have any way to determine the validity of your supernatural experience using the scientific method? Because until you do, it's still just a story.

Asking ourselves questions is hugely beneficial, but what if you want to challenge someone else's claim without conducting extensive scientific studies? We can get closer to the truth regarding others' ideas by giving momentary credence to even the most ridiculous of notions, and following the logical thought process to debunk them. Imagine a colleague arrives 10 minutes late to work and says, *"You'll never believe what happened to me this morning! I was driving down the road, minding my own business, and a bunch of office furniture fell out of the delivery truck in front of me. Chairs were bouncing off my windshield and, because I swerved to avoid the falling items,*

I ended up hitting an embankment! Sorry I'm late, everyone." You could (and probably would) take your coworker's word for it, but if you wanted to dig deeper, just assume everything is true and compare the expected results with reality. If chairs were bouncing off the windshield, there would likely be some scratches on the glass or the hood of the car. Are there? Likewise, hitting an embankment could cause some damage. What do you observe? With this type of an accident, what else would you expect to see? There is probably a police report, there may be photos taken afterward, or there may even be something on the local news! All you have to do is use your reasoning skills to make conclusions based on the claims at hand and then see how the real results measure up.

THE "OPPOSITION"

Unfortunately for me, speaking out about false claims—especially those (like the ones put forth by religions) that are entirely unsubstantiated yet wildly popular in the United States and around the world—hasn't always been well received. It's interesting (to say the least) being an activist when it comes to such controversial topics because I get to learn new things about people and their beliefs every day, but also because I get a significant amount of hate mail. And when I get those angry messages, the sender often has a special false belief, a sacred cow they haven't discovered yet and are currently dealing with. The most exciting part for me is that, sometimes, I get to be part of their journey to facts. I also do my best to entertain each piece of these potentially constructive criticisms as if they are well intended and possibly accurate. It can get tiresome considering each and every insult as if it were grounded in fact, but it's worth it to be able to occasionally improve my behavior or change my ideas when I find it's necessary to do so. As German astronomer and mathematician Johannes Kepler said, "*I much prefer the sharpest criticism of a single intelligent [hu]man to the thoughtless approval of the masses.*"

Those who do oppose me on a personal level should note that their concerns probably aren't related to my core message: people should analyze their beliefs carefully and hold no idea above criticism. Contrary to what some suggest, I don't want everyone in the world to believe the same things as me; that would be pretty boring! If people think clearly and look for evidence supporting their own beliefs, then that's good enough for me. I hope even my most dedicated critics can see that I have good intentions. Even if you disagree with me, I hope you can understand that I truly want to promote evidence-based thinking above all else, and that it is a good thing. If you think I'm wrong about a particular subject, perhaps your sacred cow or my own, it doesn't change the fact that scientific skepticism in general is the best way to determine what's real. I have a lot of people who disagree with me daily on everything from religion to reptilian overlords, but I see it as a good thing because the people who don't share my views are those from whom I can learn the most.

Some people disagree with my work merely because I don't accept their stories as facts. In some cases, it seems as though the believers—in religions, ghosts, unfounded conspiracy theories, or anything—think everyone should all be as easily convinced as they are, and they get upset because scientific skeptics aren't. It's perfectly fine that they are persuaded by an ancient text or by a man saying things on a video, but not all of us believe everything we were raised to—or everything that sounds pleasing to us. If there is real scientific evidence and/or legitimate documents and a paper trail that proves a point, that's what I'm interested in.

OUTGROWING THE SUPERNATURAL

It's the Bible, in 1 Corinthians 13:11, that says, "*When I was a child, I talked like a child, I thought like a child, I reasoned like a child. When I became a man, I put the ways of childhood behind me.*" I would say this is not only a piece of valuable advice that the Bible has to offer (although the idea itself is likely much older), but it's also one that can be applied to religion, the supernatural, and bad thinking in general.[2]

As a child, people likely told you all sorts of untruths to make you feel better or make difficult explanations easier. As we grow and learn, we discard these "answers" in favor of what's real—but many people hold on to the falsehoods as adults, often utilizing them as a sort of security blanket and occasionally causing real damage. This harm is what I fight against. However, just as a skeptic need not give up the sense of awe often associated with spirituality, it's not required—or advisable—to crush the curiosity inherent in children by not exposing them to "false" ideas and ancient traditions. In fact, I see the rituals surrounding holidays and other cultural superstitions and fables as especially good introductions to larger myths. I think it is possible to teach kids about the Tooth Fairy and Santa and other childhood "white lies" by casting them as games instead of truths. I would do what I could to instill a sense of wonderment and excitement around the cultural celebrations while making it clear that they aren't really magical; after all, children are great at using their imaginations. Greek mathematician and philosopher Hypatia of Alexandria once said that to teach superstitions as truth is "*a most terrible thing.*"

"*Fables should be taught as fables, myths as myths, and miracles as poetic fancies. To teach superstitions as truths is a most terrible thing,*" she wrote. "*The child mind accepts and believes them, and only through great pain and perhaps tragedy can he be in after years relieved of them. In fact, men will fight for a superstition quite as quickly as for a living truth, often more so, since a superstition is so intangible you cannot get at it to refute it, but truth is a point of view, and so is changeable.*"

WHAT WOULD THE WORLD BE LIKE?

A lot of people ask me why I'm so desperate to show that supernatural forces don't exist, but I think this question itself is a result of the asker's biases. In fact, there are a lot of things I hope I'm wrong about. I personally would *love* for some paranormal entity to be discovered (and, consequently, measured and defined) in a groundbreaking study. At very least, the verified existence of gods or ghosts or psychics or any form of "afterlife" would change the way we look at science and give us something entirely novel to study. At most, if the discovery was properly utilized, it could change the world as we know it. Jonathan C. Smith argues that undeniable proof of a single superstition or phenomenon that can't possibly be explained scientifically means "*that the worldview of science has a defect.*"

"*This in turn could require a new physics, a new astronomy, and perhaps even a new appreciation of the ultimate mysteries of the universe,*" he wrote. "*Yes, if your rabbit's foot worked, really worked, everything could change.*"

As you can see, I really *do* want these supernatural ideas to be true. The problem is that my hopes can't be used in place of evidence, and I must therefore separate my desires from my beliefs. No matter how much we want something to be true, our feelings won't change the facts. And the facts are what I use to decide what's real and what's not. As Carl Sagan said, "*I don't want to believe. I want to know.*"

We've spent a lot of time showing why supernatural and divine forces probably aren't real, so now it's time to turn the tables. Let's peer into our crystal ball and see what the world would look like if supernatural claims were verifiable and supported by evidence. Here's a story I wrote about a typical day in that world, one in which many superstitious, religious, and paranormal claims are true:

MY CRYSTAL BALL

THE DARK-HAIRED LADY'S VOICE WAS LIKE A GLASS OF WARM MILK, AND I COULD FEEL MYSELF DRIFTING OFF TO SLEEP. I TRIED TO FIGHT IT. I HAD TO STAY AWAKE TO SEE WHAT THIS PSYCHIC SAID I HAD IN STORE, BUT HER HYPNOTIZING TONES, SOFT MUSIC, AND CANDLE-LIT ROOM MADE THIS A DIFFICULT TASK. I DISTRACTED MYSELF BY PLAYING WITH THE CORNER OF A TABLECLOTH, THE SHINY SILVER FABRIC ON WHICH HER CRYSTAL BALL SAT CLOUDY AND OMINOUS. THE SEER'S HANDS MOVED FROM THE TABLE TO THE CRYSTAL, HER FINGERS BRUSHING IT GENTLY AS THEY GLIDED BY. THE CLOUDS IN THE BALL BEGAN TO SHIFT ALMOST IMMEDIATELY, LIKE A STRONG WIND WAS BLOWING THEM AWAY AND REVEALING A CLEAR BLUE SKY. AT THIS POINT, I WAS NO LONGER STRUGGLING TO KEEP MY EYES OPEN. I WAS WIDE AWAKE AND LOOKING FOR THE TRICK. DID SHE HAVE A HIDDEN BUTTON BENEATH THE CLOTH? WAS THIS A SPECIAL CRYSTAL BALL WITH AN INTERNAL PROJECTOR? YOU PROBABLY WON'T BELIEVE WHAT I EXPERIENCED NEXT, AS THE CLOUDS WERE SWEPT AWAY AND THE VISION BECAME CLEAR, BUT I'LL TELL YOU ANYWAY. I WAS TRANSPORTED INTO ANOTHER WORLD, ONE INSIDE THE CRYSTAL BALL, AND EVERYTHING BECAME SO . . . REAL.

I WOKE UP IN MY BED, WITH NO MEMORY OF HOW I GOT THERE. THERE WAS NO PSYCHIC LIGHTING HER CANDLES ONE BY ONE, NO CRYSTAL BALL, AND NO SILVER CLOTH. MY EYES WERE OPEN FOR FEWER THAN FIVE SECONDS WHEN I HEARD A YELL THAT WAS UNLIKE ANYTHING I'D EVER HEARD BEFORE. I JUMPED OUT OF BED AND GRABBED THE NEAREST THING TO ME, MY ALARM CLOCK, AND THROW IT AT A MAN RUSHING INTO MY ROOM AT TOP SPEED WHILE SCREAMING. MY THROW WAS PERFECT, BUT OF NO USE, BECAUSE THIS WASN'T A MAN AT ALL. THE CLOCK WENT DIRECTLY THROUGH THE CREATURE'S STOMACH AND CONTINUED THROUGH THE OPEN BEDROOM DOOR AND DOWN THE STAIRS, BUT THE ANGRY BEAST WASN'T DETERRED. HE WAS LESS THAN 10 FEET FROM ME WHEN, OUT OF NOWHERE, HE STOPPED

IN HIS TRACKS. HE DIDN'T CHOOSE TO STOP, THOUGH; HE WAS STOPPED BY SOME SORT OF BARRIER. IT WAS LIKE WATCHING A BIRD FLYING DIRECTLY INTO A CLEAR GLASS WINDOW. STUNNED, THE SPECTER STUMBLED AROUND FOR A MOMENT UNTIL A FAMILIAR-LOOKING MAN WEARING SOME HIGH-TECH GEAR STEPPED INTO THE DOORWAY. HE PLACED A LITTLE ELECTRONIC DEVICE ON THE GROUND, AND THE TERRIFYING YET TRANSPARENT MAN WAS QUICKLY SUCKED INSIDE OF IT. THE THREAT WAS GONE, BUT I WAS STILL TREMBLING AS I ASKED MY SAVIOR, "WHAT IS GOING ON?"

"MY NAME IS ZEKE BALDWIN, AND I'VE BEEN TRACKIN' THIS GHOST FOR ALMOST TWO WEEKS. I DIDN'T WANT TO WAKE YOU, SO I JUST SET MY SALT TRAP THERE AND WAITED FOR HIM TO COME RUNNIN' THROUGH THAT DOOR," THE MAN SAID, POINTING DOWN AT THE PREVIOUSLY UNSEEN LINE OF SALT ON THE FLOOR. "MY APOLOGIES FOR DISRUPTIN' YOUR SLEEP, BUT HE WAS A NASTY ONE AND WE HAD TO GET HIM."

"YOU . . . MEAN TO TELL ME THAT SALT STOPPED THAT THING?" I STUTTERED. "WAIT. AREN'T YOU THAT GHOST HUNTER GUY FROM THE REALITY TV SHOW?"

"TV SHOW? NO, SIR! NOTHING GLAMOROUS ABOUT MY REALITY. I WORK FOR SPIRIT CELL," BALDWIN SAID, NOTICING THE BEWILDERED LOOK ON MY FACE. "YOU NEVER HEARD OF SPIRIT CELL? WE ARE NUMBER FIVE ON THE FORTUNE 500 AND WE ARE GROWING MORE EVERY DAY! I'M THEIR TOP CATCHER."

I FELT LIKE I WAS IN A BAD DREAM, BUT I HAD ENOUGH COMPOSURE TO ASK THE MAN FOR MORE DETAILS. AFTER A FEW SECONDS OF SILENCE, I SAID, "WHAT EXACTLY DO YOU CATCH? WHAT WAS THAT? WHAT ARE YOU GOING TO DO WITH IT?"

"THIS WAS A CATEGORY FOUR GHOST, MY FRIEND. STRONG ONES LIKE THIS AREN'T SO COMMON, WHICH IS WHY I HAD TO TRACK HIM TO YOUR HOUSE," BALDWIN EXPLAINED, ADJUSTING HIS UTILITY BELT. "WE CATCH 'EM IN THESE POWER BOXES AND THE ENERGY FROM THEIR ATTEMPTS TO ESCAPE POWER, WELL, JUST ABOUT EVERYTHING. WHAT DO YOU THINK RUNS THAT ALARM CLOCK YOU THREW OUT THE DOOR?"

I STILL FELT AS THOUGH THIS HAD TO BE A DREAM, BUT I STARTED TO PUT THE PIECES TOGETHER NONETHELESS. I WAS IN A WORLD IN WHICH GHOSTS WERE REAL, AND GHOST HUNTERS WEREN'T TV SHOW GIMMICKS. IN FACT, THIS ONE WAS EMPLOYED BY A MULTIBILLION-DOLLAR COMPANY THAT HARNESSES AND SELLS ENERGY FROM APPARITIONS. I THANKED THE MAN

FOR HIS HELP, AND HE EXITED THE ROOM, GHOST IN HAND.

"I'LL BE BACK NEXT TIME ONE OF THESE PUPPIES DECIDES TO CALL THIS PLACE HOME! YOU ALL SEE THEM AS A MENACE, BUT THIS HERE IS GOLD," BALDWIN SAID AS HE WALKED OUT THE DOOR.

I THOUGHT THE WORST WAS OVER, SO I PUT ON SOME CLOTHES, GRABBED MY KEYS AND WALLET, AND WENT TO THE BATHROOM TO BRUSH MY TEETH. TO MY SURPRISE, THERE WERE GOVERNMENT-ISSUED WARNINGS ON MY MIRROR. ONE READ, "DO NOT REPEAT 'BLOODY MARY,' 'CANDY MAN,' OR ANYTHING SIMILAR WHILE USING THIS DEVICE. SIDE EFFECTS CAN BE FATAL."

CONFUSED, I SAID ALOUD TO THE EMPTY ROOM, "WHY CAN'T I SAY BLOODY MARY? I MEAN AFTER THE MORNING I HAD I COULD USE A BLOODY MARY!" I LAUGHED TO MYSELF WHILE I BRUSHED MY TEETH AND RINSED IN THE SINK. "HA, BLOODY MARY," I SCOFFED AS I TURNED TO LEAVE THE BATHROOM. I DIDN'T GET FAR, THOUGH. BEFORE I COULD EXIT, I HEARD A LOUD SHATTER AND A SCREECH THAT SOUNDED LIKE A MILLION NAILS ON A MILLION CHALKBOARDS. I GRABBED MY EARS AND TURNED AROUND TO SEE A HORRIFYING, GHOSTLY WOMAN COVERED IN BLOOD AND EMERGING FROM THE NOW-BROKEN MIRROR. I IMMEDIATELY SPRINTED OUT OF THE BATHROOM, OUT OF THE BEDROOM, DOWN THE STAIRS, AND STOPPED ZEKE'S TRUCK AS HE WAS PULLING OUT OF THE DRIVEWAY.

"HELP! THERE'S ANOTHER!" I SCREAMED AS I POUNDED ON HIS WINDOW. THE CATCHER CALMLY GOT OUT OF THE TRUCK AND SAID, "I'LL TAKE CARE OF THIS. YOU JUST GET OUT OF HERE."

I GOT IN MY OWN CAR AND TURNED THE KEY, BUT NOTHING HAPPENED. WELL, NOTHING EXCEPT AN ERROR MESSAGE ON THE DIGITAL DISPLAY. IT READ: "YOU DID NOT CHECK ROUTE. YOU MUST CHECK ROUTE USING AN APPROVED METHOD." I GLANCED AROUND MY CAR AND SAW A BIG BLACK EIGHT BALL RESTING ON A STAND THAT SIMPLY SAID, "SHAKE ME." I HAD NO IDEA WHAT WAS GOING ON, BUT IT REMINDED ME OF MY CHILDHOOD GAMES, SO I SHOOK THE BALL AND CHECKED ITS RESPONSE. IT SAID, "YOU ARE LIKELY TO ENCOUNTER DANGER." THE CAR'S DISPLAY LIT UP AGAIN, THIS TIME SAYING, "CAR CANNOT START DUE TO FORESEEN DANGERS. PLEASE TRY AGAIN LATER."

I STARTED TO LEAVE THE CAR WHEN I FELT IT RISING OFF THE GROUND, SLOWLY. I HESITATED A MOMENT, UNABLE TO IMAGINE WHY MY CAR WOULD BE LEVITATING, AND ROLLED OUT WHEN IT WAS ABOUT THREE FEET HIGH. I LOOKED UP TO SEE A HUGE METALLIC FLYING SAUCER WITH MESMERIZING

LIGHTS. THE CRAFT'S RED TRACTOR BEAM WAS LOCKED ON MY BLUE SEDAN, MAKING IT APPEAR PURPLE AS IT ROSE ABOVE THE GROUND. THE CAR WAS BARELY MOVING AT FIRST, BUT, AFTER ABOUT 10 SECONDS, THE SHIP SUCKED IT UP IN ALMOST AN INSTANT AND DISAPPEARED JUST AS QUICKLY. I HAD NO VEHICLE, NO HOUSE, AND NO IDEA WHAT WAS HAPPENING. JUST AS I STARTED TO WONDER IF MY CAR HAD ALIEN ABDUCTION INSURANCE, I LOOKED UP TO SEE AN ENORMOUS GORILLA EATING BERRIES FROM A BUSH 100 FEET AWAY. IT MUST HAVE HEARD MY GASP BECAUSE IT TURNED TO FACE ME INSTANTLY. THE GORILLA STARTED BARRELING TOWARD ME, BUT NOT ON FOUR LEGS. IT WAS RUNNING LIKE A PERSON. THIS GORILLA WAS A SASQUATCH AND HE WAS NOT HAPPY THAT I INTERRUPTED HIS MEAL. I RAN AS FAST AS I COULD IN THE OTHER DIRECTION, DODGING MAGICAL PIXIES AND JUMPING OVER A DEAD ANIMAL IN THE ROAD THAT MAY HAVE BEEN A CHUPACABRA. I FOUND MYSELF AT THE END OF THE ROAD, GASPING AND TERRIFIED, WHEN I LOOKED BACK TO SEE BIGFOOT HAD GIVEN UP HIS PURSUIT. I WASN'T ALONE, HOWEVER. I SAW SOMETHING FALLING—NO, FLYING—DOWN FROM THE SKY. I WAS TOO TIRED TO RUN AGAIN, SO I STAYED, AND IN A MATTER OF MOMENTS IT WAS CLEAR THAT THE OBJECT WAS A PERSON . . . A WOMAN ON A BROOMSTICK. THE WITCH LANDED GRACEFULLY AND POINTED AT ME, BUT I WASN'T STICKING AROUND FOR MORE. I SPRINTED BACK TOWARD HOME, KEEPING IN MIND THE ANGRY BIPEDAL APE WHO WAS RECENTLY IN THE AREA. I ALMOST REACHED THE SIDEWALK IN FRONT OF MY HOUSE WHEN I SAW THE STREET HAD BEEN SPLIT OPEN FROM END TO END AND THERE WAS FIRE POURING OUT. ASSUMING THERE WAS SOME SORT OF AN EARTHQUAKE, I GOT A RUNNING START AND LEAPED OVER THE HOLE IN THE EARTH. I WAS IN THE AIR, ALMOST TO THE OTHER SIDE, WHEN I FELT SOMETHING GRAB MY ANKLE. I FELL FACE FIRST ON THE PAVEMENT, BUT I WAS BEING DRAGGED INTO THE CREVICE BY WHAT LOOKED LIKE A DEMON OR DEVIL. I KICKED THE CREATURE'S HAND WITH ALL MY MIGHT, LOOSENING ITS GRIP AND ALLOWING ME TO ESCAPE. I SCOOTED BACKWARD A FEW FEET BEFORE I TURNED TO SEE ZEKE, WHO WAS WALKING OUT OF MY HOUSE SMILING AND HOLDING A SMOKY POWER BOX, WHICH I CORRECTLY ASSUMED CONTAINED MY OLD FRIEND BLOODY MARY.

"I GOT HER! SHE WAS A TOUGH ONE, BUT I GOT HER. I HAVEN'T SEEN ONE OF THOSE IN A WHI . . . WHAT HAPPENED TO YOU? IS THAT A PORTAL TO HELL BACK THERE, BOY?" ZEKE ASKED. "YOU LOOK LIKE YOU'VE HAD A STRING OF BAD LUCK. DID YOU SEE A BLACK CAT, OR SOMETHIN'?"

"I HAVE NO IDEA WHAT'S GOING ON! THERE WAS A UFO AND A BIGFOOT AND A WITCH! I CAN'T DRIVE MY CAR AND I DON'T KNOW WHAT TO DO," I SAID DESPERATELY BEFORE CATCHING MY BREATH AND TAKING A MOMENT TO THINK. "WELL . . . I DID BREAK A MIRROR THIS MORNING, THE ONE WITH BLOODY MARY."

"OH, THAT'S IT! I GOT JUST THE THING. COME HERE," ZEKE SAID, PULLING A CLOVER FROM HIS VEST POCKET. "THIS HERE IS A FOUR-LEAF CLOVER AND, AS LONG AS YOU HANG ON TO IT, IT WILL BALANCE OUT THE BAD LUCK FROM YOUR MIRROR BREAK. YOU REALLY OUGHT TO BE MORE CAREFUL."

I TOOK THE CLOVER AND PUT IT IN MY PANTS POCKET, WHICH GAVE ME AN INSTANT SENSE OF RELIEF. ZEKE ALSO GAVE ME A RABBIT'S FOOT, A GOOD LUCK PENNY, A BOTTLE OF HOLY WATER, AND SOME OTHER ITEMS FOR WHICH HE SAID SPIRIT CELL WOULD BILL ME. I COULD FEEL THEM WORKING ALREADY. THE FIERY HOLE IN THE GROUND CLOSED UP, THE WITCH AND UPRIGHT APE WERE NOWHERE IN SIGHT, AND I COULD FINALLY RELAX. ZEKE WAS JUST PULLING AWAY WHEN ANOTHER CAR, WELL, A LIMOUSINE, ARRIVED AT MY HOUSE. A WOMAN STEPPED OUT, AND THERE SHE WAS: THE PSYCHIC, THE DARK-HAIRED LADY FROM THE SHOP.

"PLEASE LET ME OUT OF THIS PLACE!" I SCREAMED TO HER. "WHATEVER POINT YOU ARE TRYING TO MAKE, YOU'VE MADE IT. I DON'T HAVE DOUBTS ANYMORE. YOU'RE A REAL PSYCHIC!"

SHE JUST LOOKED AT ME AND SAID, "SIR? SIR, CAN YOU HEAR ME? WAKE UP. I HAVE OTHER CLIENTS, YOU KNOW, PEOPLE WHO TAKE ME AND MY WORK SERIOUSLY."

I JERKED AWAKE TO SEE I WAS STILL IN THE PSYCHIC'S STORE, THE CRYSTAL BALL WAS STILL CLOUDY, AND THE CANDLES WERE PARTIALLY MELTED.

"YOU MISSED MOST OF YOUR READING, BUT IT'S OK. I CAN SUMMARIZE," SHE SAID AS HER NOSTRILS FLARED. "YOU'RE GOING TO HAVE SOME GOOD LUCK AND SOME BAD LUCK, YOUR DEAD FAMILY MEMBERS ARE SAFE AND THEY MISS YOU, AND YOU SHOULD LOOK OUT FOR THE NUMBERS 4 AND 13."

"*OH*," SHE ADDED, "AND THAT'LL BE $350."

* * *

Now that we've seen what it would be like if supernatural claims had merit, let's see if we can look at a different parallel universe. Can you imagine a world in which every person was willing and able to question and analyze his or her most foundational beliefs, even and especially those they've been taught since childhood, without hesitation or cognitive dissonance? Let's create that world.

NOTES

1. I have been diagnosed with obsessive-compulsive disorder, which for me is characterized by a number of daily rituals that I think I must perform in order to "feel like myself" or to avoid (often self-imposed) consequences. These seemingly irrational thoughts are something I must face daily, which may contribute to my desire for truth.

2. Although I'm sure there will be those who suggest otherwise, I am in no way claiming to be an expert in all of the practices and traditions discussed throughout this book. In fact, the truth is closer to the opposite: I wrote *No Sacred Cows* because I consider myself a student who only wants to learn more about a variety of subjects.

INDEX

ABOUT THE AUTHOR

David G. McAfee is author of *Atheist Answers: Rational Responses to Religious Questions, Mom, Dad, I'm an Atheist: The Guide to Coming Out as a Nonbeliever,* and *Disproving Christianity and Other Secular Writings*. He is also coauthor of two books for children, *The Belief Book* and *The Book of Gods*. He holds a degree in religious studies from the University of California–Santa Barbara and lives in Southern California.